Eaten Alive at a Chainsaw Massacre:
The Films of Tobe Hooper

ALSO BY JOHN KENNETH MUIR
AND FROM McFARLAND

The Encyclopedia of Superheroes on Film and Television, 2d ed. (2008)

Horror Films of the 1980s (2007)

Horror Films of the 1970s (2002; paperback 2008)

An Analytical Guide to Television's One Step Beyond, 1959–1961 (2001; paperback 2006)

Terror Television: American Series, 1970–1999 (2001; paperback 2008)

The Films of John Carpenter (2000; paperback 2005)

A History and Critical Analysis of Blake's 7, *the 1978–1981 British Television Space Adventure* (2000; paperback 2006)

An Analytical Guide to Television's Battlestar Galactica (1999; paperback 2005)

A Critical History of Doctor Who *on Television* (1999; paperback 2008)

Wes Craven: The Art of Horror (1998; paperback 2004)

Exploring Space: 1999*: An Episode Guide and Complete History of the Mid–1970s Science Fiction Television Series* (1997; paperback 2005)

Eaten Alive at a Chainsaw Massacre

The Films of Tobe Hooper

JOHN KENNETH MUIR

McFarland & Company, Inc., Publishers
Jefferson, North Carolina, and London

The present work is a reprint of the illustrated case bound edition of Eaten Alive at a Chainsaw Massacre: The Films of Tobe Hooper, *first published in 2002 by McFarland.*

LIBRARY OF CONGRESS CATALOGUING-IN-PUBLICATION DATA

Muir, John Kenneth, 1969–
    Eaten alive at a chainsaw massacre : the films of Tobe Hooper / by John Kenneth Muir.
       p.   cm.
    Includes bibliographical references and index.

    ISBN 978-0-7864-4461-8
    softcover : 50# alkaline paper

    1. Hooper, Tobe, 1943–   I. Title.
PN1998.3H686M85   2009
791.43'0233'092—dc21   2002008206

British Library cataloguing data are available

©2002 John Kenneth Muir. All rights reserved

No part of this book may be reproduced or transmitted in any form or by any means, electronic or mechanical, including photocopying or recording, or by any information storage and retrieval system, without permission in writing from the publisher.

Manufactured in the United States of America

McFarland & Company, Inc., Publishers
  Box 611, Jefferson, North Carolina 28640
    www.mcfarlandpub.com

To Frank "Doc" Leftwich, a horror connoisseur,
a helluva guy and a lifelong fan of Mr. Barlow

Contents

Introduction   1

Part I: A History and Overview of Tobe Hooper's Career   9

Part II: The Feature Films of Tobe Hooper   49
    1. *The Texas Chain Saw Massacre* (1974)   49
    2. *Eaten Alive* (1976)   68
    3. *The Funhouse* (1981)   74
    4. *Poltergeist* (1982)   82
    5. *Lifeforce* (1985)   93
    6. *Invaders from Mars* (1986)   103
    7. *The Texas Chainsaw Massacre Part 2* (1986)   112
    8. *Spontaneous Combustion* (1989)   120
    9. *Tobe Hooper's Night Terrors* (1993)   124
    10. *The Mangler* (1995)   128
    11. *Crocodile* (2000)   135

Part III: Television Movies and Miniseries   141
    1. *Salem's Lot* (1979)   141
    2. *I'm Dangerous Tonight* (1990)   149
    3. *John Carpenter Presents Body Bags* (1993)   153
    4. *The Apartment Complex* (1999)   157

Part IV: Genre Television Series   163
    1. *Amazing Stories*: "Miss Stardust" (1987)   163
    2. *Freddy's Nightmares*: "No More Mr. Nice Guy" (1988)   164
    3. *Tales from the Crypt*: "Dead Wait" (1991)   167

4. *Nowhere Man*: "Absolute Zero" and "Turnabout" (1995)   168
5. *Dark Skies*: "The Awakening" (1996)   170
6. *Perversions of Science*: "Panic" (1997)   172
7. *The Others*: "Souls on Board" (2000)   173
8. *Night Visions*: "Cargo" (2001)   174

Part V: Conclusion   177

Appendix A: Recurring Characters, Imagery and Themes   179
Appendix B: Mr. Homage   183
Appendix C: Ranking the Feature-Length and Television Films   185
Notes   187
Bibliography   191
Index   195

Introduction

Nearly thirty years after its premiere, director Tobe Hooper's (1943–) breakthrough feature film, *The Texas Chain Saw Massacre* (1974), remains a blessing and a curse for the larger-than-life Texas-born filmmaker, at least so far as his career in Hollywood is concerned. A blessing because, despite its notorious title, the film remains a smash hit with critics and horror film audiences; a classic of its kind, even. A curse because its reputation hounds Hooper wherever he goes and limits the opportunities open to him as a working filmmaker in the youth-centric entertainment industry of the new millennium. Like fellow baby boomer genre directors Wes Craven and John Carpenter, Tobe Hooper is renowned first and foremost as a "horror movie" director and much of his cinematic work has been limited to that genre despite his considerable gifts with comedic and action-oriented material. Hooper so expertly (and so viscerally...) directed the Grand Guignol tale of a bizarre rural psychopath named Leatherface that the buzz (of both the chainsaw and the notorious film) has proven inescapable. Even detours to music videos (for Billy Idol and the Cars) and dramatic television (CBS's *The Equalizer*) have proved unsuccessful in changing that. The saw, it seems, really *is* family.

Unlike his horror film compatriot Wes Craven, director Tobe Hooper has not overseen any mainstream box office hits (such as *Scream* [1996] and its 1997 and 1999 follow-ups) in some twenty years. And, unlike that genre-bending *auteur* John Carpenter, he isn't famous for any ongoing movie franchises outside of the popular (and seemingly endless) *The Texas Chain Saw Massacre* series. While Carpenter has consistently held audience attention with classics like *The Thing* (1982) and *Halloween* (1978), he has simultaneously directed big-budget sequels such as *Escape from L.A.* (1996) and shepherded notable independent releases such as *Vampires* (1998) and *Ghosts of Mars* (2001). These new releases inevitably carry attention back to Carpenter's previous body of work at the same time they earn him new fans. By contrast, Tobe Hooper's last theatrical release was 1995's *The Mangler*, a largely forgettable adaptation of a minor Stephen King short story. His genre work since then has been relegated mostly to television and direct-to-video features and many of those are low profile at best.

And yet, among the knowledgeable about such things, Tobe Hooper remains solidly ensconced as one of the "big five" horror maestros of the late 20th century. Along with Craven, Carpenter, George Romero and David Cronenberg, Hooper is among the most skilled of all genre directors toiling in Hollywood, able to tap into audience fears and adrenaline rhythms with seemingly boundless energy, directorial ingenuity and even a richly ironic sense of humor. There is something inherently dangerous and liberating about the works of this artist and even the weakest of his films breaks barriers, heightens the viewer's blood pressure, and seems to plug into a no-holds-barred sense of escalating insanity. Wes Craven (whose debut feature, *The Last House on the Left* [1972] featured a chainsaw murder two years before *Chain Saw* [1974]) has publicly acknowledged Hooper's finely hewn "sense of danger," especially in regard to the director's most famous film:

> When I first saw this [*The Texas Chain Saw Massacre*], I remember thinking, whoever made this must have been a Mansonite crazoid. A filmmaker like Tobe Hooper can convince you you're really at risk in a theater—that's quite an attainment [1].

Still, Hooper is probably the least acknowledged and sparsely praised of the five aforementioned horror film directors, for reasons that concern politics, Hollywood power games, luck, and coincidence more than his unique skills as a filmmaker.

Firstly, there's the seemingly undying *Poltergeist* controversy. In 1981–82, as the popular supernatural film was being shot in Los Angeles, rumors flew fast and loose through Hollywood that *Poltergeist*'s überproducer Steven Spielberg—*not the credited director, Tobe Hooper*—was actually responsible for the direction of the film. The industry press enthusiastically ran with this story in reviews of the movie and innumerable behind-the-scenes reports, and to a very significant extent Hooper's reputation has never been able to live down the gossip. When one considers that *Poltergeist* remains the highest-grossing film with Hooper's name attached to it, one begins to sense the level of damage this assertion has wreaked on his career. Oddly, "ownership" of *Poltergeist* shouldn't be *that* important in any discussion of Hooper's merits as a filmmaker (outside box office considerations) when one remembers that other films in his canon (especially *The Texas Chain Saw Massacre* and, oddly, *Invaders from Mars* [1986]) received as favorable critical notices.

In the intervening 20 years since the *Poltergeist* controversy erupted, moviegoers have seen two decades of films produced by Steven Spielberg, but directed by other talents, and the debate has been largely settled. Nearly every time this creative behind-the-scenes arrangement has occurred, the same old talk about Spielberg's input and importance in the creative process is bandied about. John Landis directed a segment of *The Twilight Zone: The Movie* (1983) and allegedly did not see eye-to-eye with producer Spielberg during its making or in its aftermath, following the accident that claimed the life of actor Vic Morrow. Director Joe Dante stood at the sharp end of some negative press regarding the level of violence in his Spielberg-produced *Gremlins* (1984) and just recently, Joe Johnston was the victim of the same phenomenon regarding his direction of the much-troubled third installment of the *Jurassic Park* franchise (in 2001). Given the details of these later partnerships, perhaps Tobe Hooper merely had the misfortune of being the *first* director to collaborate with producer Spielberg, the towering king of Hollywood. Importantly, he did so during an era when Spielberg was being adored and even worshipped by fans and critics alike for such contemporary blockbusters as *Raiders of the Lost Ark* (1981) and *E.T.* (1982). Critics wanted *Poltergeist* to be a Spielberg picture too. The film was easier to parse that way and Tobe Hooper's presence in the director's chair got in the way of a very basic desire to credit "one man" with two consecutive acts of film genius (*E.T.* and *Poltergeist*).

Hooper's second career roadblock is likely *The Texas Chain Saw Massacre* itself, a film that for all of its incredible values, remains a lightning rod for controversy. There are those who have seen it, love it and appreciate it, and then there are those who will *never* see it, simply because of its unsavory-sounding title. A non-hardcore horror fan visiting the video store may be inclined to

Introduction 3

Have chainsaw will travel. Leatherface (Gunnar Hansen) leaves the family homestead in Tobe Hooper's breakthrough horror hit, *The Texas Chain Saw Massacre* (1974).

rent a film called *Halloween*, *Scream*, or even *A Nightmare on Elm Street* rather than the brutal, exploitative sounding *The Texas Chain Saw Massacre*. So, even though *Chain Saw* is a superior example of the horror genre, its very name is off-putting, even threatening, to the casual movie fan. It doesn't help that the film was banned in Great Britain for more than a dozen years and that many who haven't seen the film judge it merely by its savage title.

Thirdly, many of Hooper's films were overlooked or seriously misinterpreted during their original theatrical runs in the late 1980s. Alas, this is simply an occupational hazard for the intrepid horror film director in contemporary, conservative America. Mainstream critics are loath to take genre pictures seriously and horror is the lowest of the low, a dark-horse genre that, to many reviewers, is barely more legitimate than pornography. Critics ignored *The Funhouse* (1981), a widely underrated Hooper gem and savagely attacked *Lifeforce* (1985), though it, like John Carpenter's *The Thing*, has attained the status of "classic" more than a decade after its release. And Tobe Hooper's *Salem's Lot* (1978), one of the best Stephen King adaptations yet filmed, is routinely ignored for the simple reason that it aired on television—and if there's anything lower than horror films, it's horror TV.

As for *The Texas Chainsaw Massacre 2* (1986) and *Invaders from Mars*, both films earned widespread critical praise for their stylized forays into political satire, but were simply too remote and *avante garde* to earn widespread acceptance among mainstream audiences of the era. In the late 1980s, all moviegoers were demanding of the genre were a few dead teenagers (in the *Friday the 13th* films) and inventive, special effects-oriented death scenes (witness the later *Nightmare on Elm Street* movies). Hooper's

Chainsaw sequel took the high road instead, poking fun at yuppies, mocking the new American fascination with the Vietnam War (courtesy of Oliver Stone's *Platoon*) and even tweaking the role of traditional heroes (with Dennis Hopper's Texas Ranger, Lefty, proving every bit as deranged as his quarry, Leatherface). Hooper's equally subversive remake of a 1950s science-fiction standard, *Invaders from Mars*, artfully and humorously connected two conservative decades: the '50s and the '80s. Both of these projects bucked the trend of empty-headed horror entertainment in the late '80s, but as a consequence of their wit and unique subtext were ignored or disliked by audiences.

By any standard, *The Texas Chain Saw Massacre*, *The Funhouse*, *Poltergeist*, *Lifeforce*, *Invaders from Mars* and *The Texas Chainsaw Massacre 2* are an interesting bunch of genre films; some better than others. But the fact remains that audiences, critics and Hooper have only been *sympatico* on two occasions: *The Texas Chain Saw Massacre* and *Poltergeist*. Hooper bashers can write off either of these winners as (a) lurid exploitation, or (b) sponsored by the immaculate perfection that is Steven Spielberg.

Other films in Hooper's oeuvre are, frankly, problematic. He left the set of *Eaten Alive* (1976) before the film was finished because of a dispute with the producers, yet the final feature bears his name despite the early departure. Cannon Films went bankrupt before *Night Terrors* (1993) could be released theatrically and it went straight to video. To cut costs, *The Mangler* was filmed in South Africa with a foreign crew and so it seems to be just a bit "off" from American film standards.

And if ever a director were trapped in a "damned if you do, damned if you don't" scenario, it is Tobe Hooper. He has been criticized for returning to the world of chainsaws for the unrated *Texas Chainsaw Massacre Part 2* and then reviled for *not* returning to the world of chainsaws for follow-up sequels *Leatherface* (1990) and *Texas Chainsaw Massacre: The Next Generation* (1995). At times, the director must wonder exactly what the world expects of him.

Considering the ups and downs of Hooper's film career, a reader might rightly ask why this artist is worthy of a book length study. The answer becomes plain when Hooper's curriculum vitae is viewed in a larger context. This is a man who, virtually without resources, masterminded one of the most terrifying, ingenious and revolutionary horror films ever made, *The Texas Chain Saw Massacre*. Love it or hate it, the film is absurd, horrific, tense, terrifying, over the top and beyond the pale. On the strength of this virtuoso debut, Hooper went to Hollywood—and was subsequently denied final cut on *every* motion picture with his name on it for more than a decade.

That's an object lesson for future directors, isn't it? Especially now that so many independent directors of the 1990s like Kevin Smith, Ed Burns, Paul Thomas Anderson, Spike Jonze and their ilk are also becoming "big" studio players. Tobe Hooper made that perilous transition long before this "next generation" and thus his journey is one worth studying. Stated in broad strokes, Hooper was on the cutting edge of film boundaries in the '70s, then a big-budget mainstream, A-list studio director in the '80s. Finally, in the '90s, he was cast out from the very establishment that had so knowingly blunted his edge, and returned to the realm of low budget horror (*Crocodile* [2000]).

Yet today, with admirable focus and determination, Hooper has remained a hard-worker in the realm of TV and TV movies, directing episodes of *Tales from the Crypt*, *Dark Skies*, *The Others* and *Nowhere Man*. For a boy who grew up devouring Bill Gaines' ghoulish EC Comics, this result is a not so much a retreat from stardom as it is a voyage home. Indeed, much of Hooper's work before his genre television phase already demonstrated his nostalgic love for short-form, comic horrors. It is not difficult to discern that Hooper's films (including *Invaders from Mars, Spontaneous Combustion* [1989] and *The Mangler*) reflect the era (the late '40s and 1950s) of his youth in mood, setting and art design. Or that other films knowingly reference his love for the horror entertainment of that bygone era (*Salem's Lot, The Funhouse, Invaders from Mars,* and *Lifeforce*). Hooper may be "missing in action" from big-budget filmmaking, or suffering a "slide" (2), as some reviewers have asserted over the last few years, but his most recent efforts *(The Apartment Complex* [1999], and *Crocodile* [2000]) are refreshingly modest and straight forward—the very kind of films that would have pleased fans of Roger Corman or Jack Arnold in earlier decades. And, as at least one critic has written, "like him or not, Hooper became a major force in the development of horror movies in the seventies" (3).

Wes Craven is the consummate philosopher, exposing social and political hypocrisies and addressing them in the horror film. John Carpenter is the *auteur*, the stylist, the technician with the consistent *modus operandi*. By contrast, Hooper's work is notable for two competing (and often conflicting) instincts. On one hand, he is maestro of the *homage*, the purposeful gazing back at the history of horror films that he grew up with and adored. On the other hand, there is his zeal and willingness to leap outside the barriers of traditional film narrative to take audiences on ever more wild rides. In fact, Hooper's films might adequately be described as post-modern because they inevitably rocket beyond traditional conventions of structural framework, climax and resolution and head, kamikaze-like, into a plane of insanity. Though his movies begin with familiar settings (the 1950s, suburbia, the road movie), these trappings quickly become secondary, even moot. As L.M. Kit Carson, author of *Paris, Texas* and *The Texas Chainsaw Massacre Part 2*, wrote so pointedly:

> De Palma and ... Romero had only recently corkscrewed fresh blood into the horror genre ... but they were sophisto guys who'd kept the "it's-only-a-movie" deal with the audience. Hooper was a new deal—simply this; *no deal.* Hooper was a scare-director who was methodically unsafe, who the audience (you) finally just couldn't trust.... He'd go too far, then go farther ... and go farther again, and kick it again ... then get in an extra kick, then it's over ... then one more kick.... No deal, friend [4].

In the course of Hooper's best films, rationality, realism, situational logic and other cornerstones of traditional film storytelling go right out the window. Perhaps that is the reason why many critics don't appreciate his work: he is purely and simply championing the *surreal* in film, the excesses (and strange beauties) of unpredictability. That's why *Poltergeist*, at least to this author's eyes, is without a doubt a Hooper film. The film's "logical" plot ends when a diminutive psychic (played by Zelda Rubinstein) cleanses the haunted suburban house of evil and the little Freeling child (Carol Anne) is rescued by her adoring parents. But *Poltergeist* doesn't close when this plot resolves and the spirits find the light of the afterlife. *Not even close.* It goes "farther" when the evil spirits reveal (for the first time) sexual stirrings towards Mrs. Freeling (JoBeth Williams); it "goes farther" when the children are threatened by an organic, plant-like maw leading to Hell (previously in the film, the spirits were embodied by glowing white lights and delicate wisps of energy); then it "goes farther again," as rotting corpses burst out of the ground, willy-nilly. This is a Hooper coda pure and a simple, a climax beyond a climax beyond a climax, an acceleration of pace and fear that goes far beyond the bounds of the logical or realistic and straight into the surreal. A study of Spielberg's pantheon would find few parallels to this unusual, post-narrative crescendo.

Webster's Dictionary defines surrealism as a "form of art in which the fantasies of the subconscious are presented in images without formal order or relation." That phrase perfectly captures the texture of many Hooper films, from *Invaders from Mars* (itself a dream), and *The Texas Chain Saw Massacre* (with its many irrational, nightmare qualities), to *Lifeforce* (in part, a sexual fantasy) and even *Poltergeist*. In each and every one of these films, "the formal order" (the traditional order of conventional film narrative) is shattered in favor of a new one; an order of accelerating, escalating, irrational terror and often uneasy laughs.

Andre Breton, who wrote *Manifestoes of Surrealism*, also determined that surrealism was the literary recapitulation of a dream/nightmare state and therefore in defiance of what most people consider conventional logic. Specifically:

> [Surrealism] proposes to express—verbally, by means of the written word, or in any other manner—the actual functioning of thought. Dictated by thought in the absence of any control exercised by reason, exempt from any aesthetic or moral concern.... Surrealism is based on the belief in the superior reality of certain forms of previously neglected associations, in the omnipotence of dreams, in the disinterested play of thought. It tends to ruin ... all other ... mechanisms and to substitute itself for them in solving all the principal problems of life [5].

In light of this definition, *Invaders from Mars* is surely surreal: a dream that substitutes a boy's mental phantasm for conventional reality. *The Texas Chain Saw Massacre* is surreal because it feels like an unending, irrational nightmare. *Poltergeist* is surreal too because its gonzo climax replaces the up-until-then tightly structured narrative with a nonsensical, but intense coda that, as author Peter Nicholls notes, "features the earth itself literally vomiting up corpses in a *grand guignol* episode that has nothing to do with the rather remote, but touching sequences involving the little girl trapped in another dimension" (6). Consider also that one of Hooper's works, *Night Terrors*, actually focuses on the Marquis De Sade, a figure widely recognized as an early contributor of surrealistic literature.

This steadfast dedication to the surreal dominates many Hooper projects and appropriately, many of his movies might even be viewed as extensions of the most recognized and celebrated literary work of surrealism in the English language: Lewis Carroll's *Alice in Wonderland*. Consider that lengthy dinner-table sequences in *The Texas Chain Saw Massacre* and its sequel represent a sort of "tea party," a gathering of diverse characters (like the Mad Hatter and his guests, or Leatherface and his clan). In both works, these diners seem to abide by twisted rules of etiquette and a different definition of "normal" than most folks. And, in both cases, a female who is outside the "bizarre" world is forced to participate in the social gathering. Consider also that in many of Hooper's films, the terror commences when a character (usually a female like Alice) falls down a hole (or portal) into another, often subterranean, world (*Invaders from Mars*, *Poltergeist*, *The Texas Chainsaw Massacre 2*). Even in *The Apartment Complex* (1999), Hooper's heroine is named "Alice." Significantly, she lives in the aptly named "Wonder View Apartments." Alice in Wonder View?

This perspective of Hooper as a devotee of surrealism, coupled with his ongoing "nostalgic" homage for the film delights of his youth, reveals the consistency and depth of artistry in his quarter-century long career in film. If Craven will be remembered as horror's Pirandello, bound and determined to construct and de-construct postmodern, reflexive realities, and Carpenter is its Howard Hawks, a good old-fashioned entertainer with a consistent bag of tricks, then Tobe Hooper is no less than terror's Lewis Carroll. Ruthlessly deploying the tenets of surrealism, this director has led audiences on ever-more-harrowing journeys into the subconscious mind and the hearts of human darkness. It's a trip that the more literal minded have not always been willing to take, but if one is willing to be swept away by the method in this director's madness, the dedicated viewer might find that Tobe Hooper, like the malevolent entities of *Poltergeist*, knows "what scares you."

Part I
A History and Overview of Tobe Hooper's Career

Born in Austin, Texas, on January 25, 1943 (though various sources indicate 1942, 1945, and 1946), future cult director Tobe Hooper arrived in our midst just before the beginning of the baby boom that introduced a generation of American fantasy filmmakers, including John Carpenter, John Landis, George Lucas and Steven Spielberg, to the world. As if to set the stage for her son's choice of professions, Hooper's expectant mother (who worked with her husband in the hotel business) went into labor with Tobe while watching a movie at the State Theater in Austin. As Hooper is prone to state it, he was "breastfed" (1) by the movies, though today the director prefers a diet of Cuban cigars.

Years later, Hooper would report that both of his parents were avid movie fans and that their fascination with film was transferred to him almost upon birth. This process of movie "indoctrination" was aided in no small part by the family's selection of living quarters during Tobe's earliest days: a hotel near the Texas Capitol surrounded on all sides by movie houses: the Capitol, the Paramount, the Queen and the State (2). Of his early and pervasive love of movies, Hooper revealed the following to interviewer Michael Ventura:

> I started watching movies at a very early age—like 3…. My memories from childhood are mostly memories of movies rather than my own life because I spent a lot of time in a movie theatre. My dad had a hotel, and he had a movie theatre in San Angelo, Texas, so I stayed in the movie theatre when they went out to dinner…. It wasn't until San Francisco in the '60s that I realized that life wasn't a movie [3].

As Hooper absorbed everything he saw unfolding on the silver screens of local theaters, developing an early and complete understanding of film grammar, he simultaneously fostered a love of magic, a trait shared many years later with the young protagonist, Mark Petrie (Lance Kerwin), of Hooper's TV movie *Salem's Lot* (1978). By age eight, Hooper was working as a "paid, professional magician" (4). And, like colleagues George Romero, Stephen King and John Carpenter, young Hooper stumbled on another source of inspiration in the mass media of the 1950s: *comic books*, particularly the EC (Educational Comics) horror comic books of William Gaines such as *Tales from the Crypt, The Haunt of Fear, Shock Suspen-Stories, Weird Science* and *Vault of Horror*.

Many historians and social critics have compared these protean genre comics to horror films, as both media seek to terrorize their intended audiences through unusual and gripping visualizations. It's an apt comparison and many *Tales from the Crypt* comics could be easily read today as storyboards for Carpenter, Romero or even Hooper horror films of the 1970s, '80s and '90s.

Perhaps more importantly, *Tales from the Crypt* and its graphic comic ilk offered a rather complete narrative circle, a form of entertainment wrapped in a compact, easily digestible passage. Each horrific comic offered witty humor through the presence of a wicked host figure (like the Crypt Keeper, the Old Witch and the Vault Keeper), and these ghouls would frequently crack wise about the horrible, violent situations depicted in the magazine's pages. This juxtaposition of humor and fear was an important element of the comics and later in Hooper's films as well. Also, there was a high moral content to most of the comic stories, with the bad characters often receiving "cosmic justice" or a terrible "comeuppance" for their transgressions against an established ethical code. Conventional logic was often overturned in these adventures so as to allow for the possibility of the supernatural and the comic books vividly reflected the feel of their era, the early to mid 1950s. As Digby Diehl writes significantly of that time in *Tales from the Crypt: The Complete Archives*:

> Horror comics of the 1950s appealed to teens and young adults ... trying to cope with the aftermath of ... Nazi death camps and the explosion of the atomic bombs at Hiroshima and Nagasaki.... Fifties kids came of age ... during an era punctuated by outbursts of national paranoia. School duck-and-cover drills nourished the fear that at any moment a nuclear attack could send us into shelters to live on Ritz crackers for years.... It was difficult for adolescents to deal with these deep seated fears ... rational or otherwise [5].

One obvious way to deal with such fears was to see them released, acknowledged, and thereby dealt with, in comic book form. It's called *catharsis*, and that's what EC was all about: singling out societal fears and reflecting them back, sometimes in absurd fashion, at readers. Surviving a ghoulish and hair-raising EC comic was like running a gauntlet of a fashion, a test of one's survival skills. If a kid could manage to keep turning those pages, even in the face of the grotesque and the terrible, then the fears of day-to-day life, from McCarthyism to the Cold War, were survivable too.

Likewise in the 1970s. The dreads of that epoch would be similarly pinpointed and thereby made palatable in films such as *The Texas Chain Saw Massacre,* a project that boasted more than a passing resemblance to the EC comics of the 1950s. Like the movies he adored as a child, *Tales from the Crypt* and its comic brethren thus represent key critical components of Tobe Hooper's directorial psyche. Their leaps of logic, not to mention horrific imagery, came to inform many of his decisions as a director. In 1986, Hooper acknowledged the importance of EC comics to his generation of filmmakers and to his own films:

> ... EC comic books were ... these ghoulish little tales ... illustrated by ... terrific artists. They were absolutely frightening, unbelievably gruesome ... I started reading these comics when I was about seven. I loved them. They were not in any way based on logic. To enjoy them, you had to accept that there is a Bogey Man.... Since I started reading these comics when I was young and impressionable, their overall feeling stayed with me ... they were probably the ... most important influence on *The Texas Chain Saw Massacre* [6].

Indeed, these remarks by Hooper reveal a double insight into his work. He notes that by his perception the EC comics were not based in "any way" on "logic" and one can see in many instances that the same criticism (or compliment) might be paid his body of film work. Secondly, Hooper's recollection that the comics were "absolutely frightening" and "unbelievably gruesome" are reminiscent of the reviews for many of Hooper's films, from *The Texas Chain Saw Massacre* and *Poltergeist* right up to 1995's *The Mangler.* Like Romero and Carpenter, Hooper transmuted the power and strengths of

EC comics into another venue: *film*. The only difference between these artists remains in how they interpreted the EC ethos in their work. Romero picked up on much of the literal, physical EC trappings, producing films about the dead literally returned to life (a common trope of the comics). Carpenter's take on EC was wittier and more technically stylized, grooving on the ghoulish humor and far-out scenarios of the comic books (as *John Carpenter's Body Bags* [1993] so dramatically attests). For Hooper, the lack of logic, or the "super real" (the origin of the world "surreal"), and the piling up of gruesome, frightening incidents, were to become paramount features in his work.

By age ten, Hooper the magician, comic book aficionado and movie fan was already a practicing filmmaker, shooting short, silent films with an 8-mm camera (including an adaptation of *Frankenstein!* [7]) and casting friends in starring roles. But Hooper's teenage years were difficult for a variety of reasons. His father and mother had split up, their marriage failed, and Hooper's father died of a long-term illness when Hooper was still a young man. Hooper himself faced some illnesses in his teenage years and spent time in a hospital following a car accident in 1960. After recovering, he attended the University of Texas (in the film department) and actively began to pursue his dream of becoming a professional filmmaker. As had often been the case, he was inspired to pursue his dream by images he had witnessed on a silver screen:

> I saw at the State Theater a long time ago a short subject called "Skater Dater" by Noel Black. It was this silent basically no-dialogue short subject that was nominated for an Academy Award. It looked like it cost next to nothing. But it got a lot of press. So that made me think: You can do it. I think that was probably my first glimpse that things could be done different ... outside the Hollywood system [8].

Since Hooper had already been directing short films, one on 16 mm (called *The Abyss*) no less, it seemed natural that his career could develop along the same path. For a time he was employed by an insurance company, shooting short "documentaries" that encouraged unsuspecting, would-be clients to purchase life insurance before some terrible disaster befell their family. Then, impressed with the twenty-year-old Hooper's cinematic abilities, the president of the company offered to finance a short film entitled *The Heisters* (1963). The winner of several awards in Australian and California film festivals, this ten minute production mixed violence and humor, later a staple of Hooper's professional career, and led to other assignments.

While directing nearly five dozen commercials for a company called Film House, Hooper helmed a documentary entitled *The Peter, Paul and Mary Special* that was aired on several PBS stations across the United States (9). In the same span of years, he also directed a documentary about the preservation of architectural landmarks, called *Down Friday Street,* which won an award at the New York Film and TV Festival (10).

Then in 1969 came Hooper's first—and mostly forgotten—feature film, entitled *Eggshells*. This was Hooper's first "big" budget production, costing some $100,000. It was a 90-minute fantasy and social commentary concerning a group of hippies sharing a commune house where something strange, "a crypto-embryonic-hyper-electric" (11) and perhaps malevolent entity, was dwelling in the basement. *Eggshells* nabbed the gold medal at the Atlanta Film Festival (12), but the art film made nary a ripple on the national stage despite the accolades won by Hooper for its stylish, experimental atmosphere. His big break, his ticket to Hollywood, was not to come for another four years.

The Texas Box Office Massacre

With *Eggshells* a financial failure (but critical success), and film work drying up in Texas, Tobe Hooper faced the early 1970s (and his thirtieth birthday) without the specter of a hit that could catapult him to Tinsel Town. Although he was a local hero of sorts, regarded as "the only true professional filmmaker in Austin in 1973" (13), he still knew his best work was ahead. As the now famous tale has been repeated many times, Hooper's inspiration for his runaway hit *The Texas Chain Saw Massacre* came during a Christmas time visit to Montgomery Ward's hardware department, where he was promptly trapped in a mob of unruly holiday shoppers. Hooper's eye (and mind) drifted to a wall of chainsaws for sale and then to a wicked exit strategy from his predicament. He was left with the powerful notion that a chainsaw would make a deadly—*and highly cinematic*—weapon. From that ingenious spark, Hooper collaborated with Texan illustrator/writer Kim Henkel on a script for a feature-length horror film that would focus on the chainsaw as one of its primary props. Known first as *Head Cheese*, then *Leatherface* (the name of the movie's lead psycho-killer), the movie didn't become known as *The Texas Chainsaw Massacre* until filming was complete.

Though rambunctious holiday shoppers were the ostensible inspiration for the chainsaw story, the macabre antagonists of *The Texas Chain Saw Massacre*, a family of lunatic cannibals preying on unwitting travelers, originated from another source. In fact, Leatherface's clan came from the self-same source as Alfred Hitchcock's 1960 masterpiece *Psycho*: the life and crimes of mid-west serial killer Ed Gein. Tobe Hooper has reported many times that as a child he visited relatives in Wisconsin and heard stories of real-life psycho Gein and was terrified by them. Those memories became key to the grisly events in the screenplay of *Chain Saw*, at least in a way. On the DVD audio commentary of *The Texas Chain Saw Massacre*, Hooper recalls being aware of Gein's crimes and of being influenced by them, but not knowing the maniac's name until after *Chain Saw* was made. Like *Hansel and Gretel* or a fairy tale, the story of Gein was merely a tale that adults frightened children with in Wisconsin and Hooper remembered his exposure to these "urban legends."

Born in 1906, the real Ed Gein was raised by an overbearing, religious mother and an alcoholic, abusive father. He lived a difficult life on a large farm in rural Plainfield, Wisconsin. After his older brother, Henry, died in mysterious circumstances, Ed lived alone with his mother until she also passed away. The death of Augusta Gein was apparently the catalyst that set off this bizarre criminal's famous reign of terror. In no time, he transformed the family farmhouse (also the location of terror in *The Texas Chain Saw Massacre*) into a bizarre headquarters where grave robbing, murder, transexualism and cannibalism were the freaky order of the day. He made masks from the skin of his human victims and built furniture made of human bones (both elements of Leatherface's pad, as well). He pretended to be his own mother (which no doubt was the inspiration for Norman Bates) and gleefully went about his grotesque business until finally arrested for murder in December of 1957. The policeman searched Gein's barn and discovered (among other atrocities) a decapitated body hung on a meat hook (another startling image that *The Texas Chain Saw Massacre* would modify). Gein's crime spree became national news as 1958 arrived and the insane Gein spent the rest of his life in mental health facilities until his death in 1984. Besides *Chain Saw* and *Psycho*, other films that have "cannibalized" the Gein story include 1973's William Girdler film *Three on a Meathook*,

1974's *Deranged*, and Jonathan Demme's 1991 Academy Award winner, *Silence of the Lambs*.

Though writer Kim Henkel and Tobe Hooper's collaboration on *The Texas Chain Saw Massacre* related to a crime spree of the 1950s, it also aggressively reflected the aura of the early 1970s film movement. The so-called "new freedom" in the cinema that gave rise to violent features like Stanley Kubrick's *A Clockwork Orange* (1971), Sam Peckinpah's *Straw Dogs* (1971), John Boorman's *Deliverance* (1972) and even Wes Craven's *The Last House on the Left* (1972), also permitted the Texas filmmakers to carry the intensity of their drama further than many other horror films had yet dared.

The Texas Chain Saw Massacre also reflected the growing "malaise" of the 1970s. The energy crisis was upon the nation and, significantly, the terror in *The Texas Chain Saw Massacre* began when a van of teenagers ran out of gasoline in the middle of nowhere and were unable to procure more fuel. Forced to kill time in a dark, isolated corner of rural Texas (read: Vietnam), they ran into Leatherface's primitive but powerful clan (the Viet Cong?). At the September 2000 Directors Guild Directors Retreat at the UCLA Conference Center at Lake Arrowhead, Hooper explained some of the zeitgeist of his most powerful film and its age:

> We had run out of gas in the country, there were lines to get gasoline so that's where the [characters] running out of gas comes from. And a lot of people had been put out of jobs so that's where [the unemployed slaughterhouse workers] comes from ... a physician also told me about when he was a pre-med student and a friend of his skinned a cadaver's face, cured it and wore it as a mask to a Halloween party. So that's where Leatherface comes from [14].

Other reviewers have also read very deep 1970s insights into the film. The "white" farmhouse—a mockery of American suburbia—has often been viewed as a metaphor for Richard Nixon's White House: a corrupt, twisted version of the American ideal. The many bones and skeletons inside Leatherface's house are outnumbered by the skeletons of Nixon's Vietnam War, and so forth. Even the notion that four peaceful "groovy" teenagers could meet (or meat?) such a gruesome fate in America, a step beyond *Easy Rider*'s gloomy, Southerner-baiting finale, was a comment on the sudden end of the hippie era. Though *The Texas Chain Saw Massacre* has been interpreted to mean a dozen (sometimes conflicting) things, Hooper knew only that he wanted to make a film to reflect the times:

> There was death on television constantly from the news. It was in the papers ... it was all around us. We were finding that what the leaders told us was not necessarily the complete truth.... There were filmmakers who wanted to say something and really they only had one arena that they could say it in and have it ... be seen.... I liked the genre because it was one that I could feel an emotion in [15].

Despite crafting a script that would modify a "real" incident (the Gein case) and reflect the vicissitudes of 1970s social issues, Tobe Hooper and Kim Henkel still had a major, *practical* problem: raising the money to produce the film. Much has been written about this financial situation, but suffice it to say that the financing of *The Texas Chain Saw Massacre* was so convoluted an enterprise that it makes the year 2000 presidential election recount in Florida look orderly and consistent. In brief, Kim Henkel and Tobe Hooper formed a company called Vortex, which raised part of the money for the film. In lieu of paying the actors all of their salaries up front, Vortex offered them percentage points of the film's gross, based on Vortex's take and to be paid once receipts came in. But Vortex (and the Film Commission of Austin) were not alone in the financing of the horror project. West Texan

Bill Parsley put up $60,000 for the picture, Kim Henkel's sister kicked in $1,000, an Austin attorney contributed $9,000, and "associate producer" Richard Saenza paid some $10,000 (in cash) as an investment (16). Essentially, these "add-ons" to the budget meant that the Vortex component of the film's financial backing was something less than fifty percent of the final cost of the film, which had an unfortunate cascade effect. The actors who had deferred their salaries actually had points *only* in the Vortex percentage of the investment (i.e. "half points"), a fact that some of the performers may not have understood and that even Henkel and Hooper may not have realized would affect people's pocketbooks in adverse ways.

Adding to the quagmire of financial difficulties, the eventual distributor of the Texas film, an organization called Bryanston, was controlled by an alleged crime family, the Perainos (of *Deep Throat* fame), and the company went bankrupt before a full and accurate accounting of the film's profits could ever be made. This meant that many investors, including the actors who deferred their salaries, felt cheated out of their money when *The Texas Chain Saw Massacre* became a worldwide success in the years following its release. As one might expect, lawsuits ensued. Simply put, the situation was a byzantine mess and, eventually, a highly publicized one.

But putting aside that conflict for the moment, Kim Henkel and Tobe Hooper succeeded in raising enough money to create their breakthrough picture. Various sources have listed the budget of the film as $93,000 (17), $105,000 (18), $140,000 (19), $160,000 (20) and $200,000 (21), but the bottom line was that the film was made very cheaply, even for 1973. Principal photography on *The Texas Chain Saw Massacre* thus began in and around Austin, Texas, in the very hot, very sticky, summer of 1973. The now-famous farmhouse, just outside of Round Rock on Quick Hill Road, was the location where filming commenced in mid July of 1973 and what followed was a grueling five-and-a-half-week shoot where the thermometer often topped out at 100 degrees and the working days sometimes stretched to 22 hours. Behind the scenes, Daniel Pearl, a noted documentarian (and later a collaborator on *Invaders from Mars* [1986]), was Hooper's inventive director of photography. He shot the film in 16 mm (later blown up to 35 mm for theatrical release), with Tobe Hooper backing him up on a second camera. Daniel Pearl's then wife, Dottie, served as the unit's make-up artist. Also in the 50 person crew (recruited mostly from the University of Texas) was art director Robert Burns, who was responsible for the terrifying and realistic "human bone" décor of the cannibal's farmhouse. These "props" were so effective that they were brought out of mothballs to decorate the Fairmont Hotel for the press announcement of the film in Dallas.

The film's cast consisted of talented unknowns from local circles, with the trim, beautiful Marilyn Burns (*Helter Skelter* [1975], *Future Kill* [1985]) portraying the film's screaming, much-tortured protagonist, Sally Hardesty, and Paul Partain performing as her highly annoying invalid brother, Franklin. The other "endangered teens" included Allen Danziger as Jerry, Teri McMinn as Pam and William Vail as Kirk. The bad guys—*the cannibals*—were played by Jim Siedow (Cook), John Dugan (Grandpa) and a twitchy, convincingly psychotic Edwin Neal as the Hitchhiker. Leatherface, the man who wore human flesh and played the chainsaw like a violin, was played by imposing Gunnar Hansen, a New Englander who had just completed his M.A. in Scandinavian studies at the University of Texas in 1973. When *The Texas Chain Saw Massacre* was rereleased on its 20th anniversary, *People Weekly* interviewed the 6 feet 4 inches tall and 275 pound (22)

Hansen about his audition for the part of the Leatherface:

> They [Henkel and Hooper] said "Are you violent?" I said no. "Are you crazy?" No. "Can you do it?" Yes [23].

Over the years, stories about the shooting of *The Texas Chain Saw Massacre* have become legendary in fan circles. Some are contradictory, some are apocryphal, and ferreting out the true story is not easy. Allegedly, Marilyn Burns was not particularly popular with her cast-mates at the time (in part because some people suspected she was associated with money man Parsley) and some accounts intimate she personally clashed with Edwin Neal and Paul Partain, among others. Interestingly, Tobe Hooper understood the relationship dynamics of his quarrelsome, put-upon performers and put them to use for the film's benefit, especially in some of the tenser dramatic moments:

> We were three to four weeks into the shoot ... and those two people [Burns & Partain] had gotten really sick of each other. The more takes we did ... the more irritated they got with each other.... I went off into a corner with each of them ... and started dropping ... clues that would fester the anger between them. Finally, they got very angry ... and to this day, on the last take when ... she grabbed for the flashlight, I don't know for sure where she grabbed him ... [24].

Other scenes were equally harrowing to capture on celluloid, particularly the centerpiece of the picture, an extended "last supper" (or "tea party," if you prefer), in which a hysterical Sally is bound, gagged and forced to break bread with the cannibal family. Edwin Neal described the scene to reporter Michael Goodwin for an article that appeared in *The Village Voice*:

> The heat was unbearable. It was 95 plus before they hit the lights, and ... there were two and a half-hour waits for individual shots.... That sequence took 36 hours to shoot. The animals on the table were filled with formaldehyde and they were literally rotting under the lights. There was a doctor giving anti-nausea pills, but they didn't help. As soon as they'd yell "Cut" we'd run to the windows and throw up. For 36 hours straight! [25].

Perhaps the most notorious scene in *The Texas Chain Saw Massacre* film involves Leatherface's capture of Pam. In a particularly brutal and unexpected moment, the killer appears to lift his victim directly onto a meat-hook and then she hangs there, with the cold, pointed metal ostensibly digging in her back. Gunnar Hansen explains how this disturbing—*and very realistic*—moment, was orchestrated:

> We actually put her [the victim] on a very small harness made out of nylon.... There's a shot over my shoulder as I ... lift her, we cut and do a shot from above, then we reversed the hook, so the point was pointing away. We threaded her on the harness, threaded the harness onto the hook and I picked her up so the harness was above the hook. I dropped her and the harness caught.... It happens so fast, you don't realize it's all done in cuts ... [26].

What Hansen doesn't note in the above-referenced quotation is that the nylon harness was incredibly uncomfortable, painful even, and that Terri McMinn was in real agony during that scene. In fact, each performer and crewmember of *Chain Saw* has recounted his or her own individual "horror" story about the making of the low-budget film.

Leatherface's mask afforded actor Hansen no peripheral vision, so he was constantly running (in high heels) into doorframes and walls during takes. He also performed difficult "running" stunts with a live chainsaw. For the sequence in which Marilyn Burns seeks help from Cook (Siedow) at his barbecue stand, Hooper had the actress do the scene some *seventeen* times despite bruised and bloodied knees.

In the "guess who is coming to dinner" finale, when slavering old Grandpa was to

Director Tobe Hooper (left) gives direction to Jim Siedow (Cook; far right) while a tortured Marilyn Burns (Sally; middle) prepares for another grueling take while shooting *The Texas Chain Saw Massacre* (1974). The cameraman is unidentified.

suck the blood from Sally's cut finger, Marilyn Burns' digit was *really* sliced open by a real knife. For his death scene, actor Edwin Neal had to lie face down on burning highway asphalt (a sequence eventually edited out of the final cut, but seen in the outtakes of the DVD collector's edition). There was a bonfire of animal carcasses behind the farmhouse and the associated fumes made most of the production sick. At one point, Dottie Pearl accidentally injected herself (in the knee) with a hypodermic of formaldehyde meant to preserve one of the dead animals used as set decoration. And, as Gunnar Hansen remembers, there was another irritant too:

> ... we all had only *one* set of clothes for the movie, it was too much of a risk to get them washed; the colors might change. So after a few weeks of shooting, it was a little more than "fright" that made us keep our distance from each other [27].

With these examples in mind, it is clear that *The Texas Chain Saw Massacre* represented guerrilla filmmaking of the most hardcore and dedicated variety. The mood of the film (harrowing, intense, and disturbing) seemed to mirror the mood of the set, but the results speak for themselves. There has never been another film like it. Not even Tobe Hooper escaped unscathed:

> I remarked, "wow, this is really incredible, we finished the movie ... and everybody got hurt except me." ... I leaned back, and the wooden boarding on the porch cracked ... and the chair slipped through it. I flew back into a pile of two-by-fours with six-inch heavy-duty nails ... and I was impaled.... But I ... thought of a line from the film: "Everything means something" [28].

But in 1974 the cast and crew's intense, trying efforts were vindicated in a way no one could have quite expected. The final edit, cut by Larry Carroll and overseen by Tobe Hooper (reportedly in his home), revealed a mastery of film technique and a "vitality" that most horror films had never managed to attain. *The Texas Chain Saw Massacre*, in addition to being unremittingly terrifying, was energetic and even artful, especially in its depiction of a universe where man was unimportant, unnoticed even, before the unblinking eye of the cosmos. At the same time the film broke ground with its revolutionary narrative structure — which gave the film's protagonists no insight into their plight — it was also wickedly funny, generating nervous laughter in its shocked audiences. During the film's premiere the week before Halloween of 1974, *The Texas Chain Saw Massacre* generated the kind of buzz that most Hollywood publicity agents would kill for. As film historian and scholar Danny Peary writes of the film's debut, in *Cult Movies*:

> ... it had been sneak-previewed at San Francisco's Empire Theater with ... *The Taking of Pelham One, Two Three* (1974), and ... the audience had no knowledge of the film's violent, stomach-turning content or even its forbidding title.... Soon unsuspecting viewers were seeing a huge man with a chain saw in a mask made out of what once was a human face, making mincemeat out of ... college-age kids. Some viewers threw up; others stormed the lobby to protest ... [29].

Around the country, audiences were tantalized. What was this bizarre-sounding movie and did it really go as far as newspaper reports seemed to indicate? Armed with a variety of titillating advertising lines (including "Who Will Survive, and What Will Be Left of Them?"), and a rave review from Rex Reed, who called *The Texas Chain Saw Massacre* "the most horrifying movie" he had ever seen, the film was well on its way to becoming a massive box office success. After a few weeks in release, the film was doing incredible business (grossing over $600,000 its first four days in Texas alone!) and taking America by storm. If that wasn't surprising enough, the film was promptly selected for the permanent collection at the Museum of Modern Art. Before it was finished, *The Texas Chain Saw Massacre* won "the outstanding film of the year" award at the London Film Festival and was even the "official selection" in the Director's Fortnight at the Cannes Film Festival. Judith Crist judged the film a new benchmark for the horror genre in her column in *New York*. By 2001, the film — *made for some figure less than $200,000 dollars in 1973* — had grossed more than $30 million (30) and some sources indicate upwards of $50 million (31). The put-upon actors, the clever behind-the-scenes personnel, and the dedicated Tobe Hooper had pulled a winner out of low budget hardship.

In 1975, *The Texas Chain Saw Massacre* was the third highest grossing film of the year, behind big budget mainstream efforts *Airport 75* and *The Odessa File*. Perhaps more impressively, it found a permanent niche with the young college audience, who embraced Hooper's nihilistic vision of an irrational universe. During September of '75 the film played to enthusiastic crowds at the Cinema Village Midnight Show (owned by Arista Theaters) and was even referred to as "The *Jaws* of Midnight Runs" (32). It was also a favorite on college campuses and heralded by critics as a perfect example of its under appreciated genre.

Even today, Tobe Hooper is surprised at the success and longevity of his breakthrough film:

> It's bigger than I ever imagined ... I had a good feeling about it at the time, about it being a film that would get lots of play dates and basically get another job for me. In that respect, I knew it was special because I knew that there was nothing like it ... but there was no way of anticipating that it would become a title as important as *Gone with the Wind* [33].

Yet taken in total, *The Texas Chain Saw*

Massacre experience has not been a totally pleasant one for Tobe Hooper either. Misperceived by guardians of morality, the film has been banned as an incitement to violence and as "indecent" in both Great Britain and France. Also, many of the cast members and crew of the film didn't receive the remuneration they felt they deserved because of the financing boondoggle involving the succession of investors and the film's ultimate distributor. When Bryanston Pictures went out of business in 1976, estimates were that the film had already made over six million dollars, but Edwin Neal and Bob Burns, among others, reportedly believed that they had been stiffed for their hard work and that Tobe Hooper and Vortex were at least partially responsible for that financial situation. In 1993, Hansen reported to *People Magazine* that his salary for *The Texas Chain Saw Massacre*, twenty years later, had come to a measly $2,800 (34). These are unfortunate situations to be sure, and Tobe Hooper was in the middle of it all.

Tobe Hooper Gets Eaten Alive by Hollywood

The Texas Chain Saw Massacre made quite a stir in Hollywood in the mid '70s and consequently Tobe Hooper had his calling card to the industry. Steven Spielberg, William Friedkin and Stephen King were just a few of the film's "fans" (along with critics Rex Reed, Vincent Canby and Judith Crist), but it still wasn't as easy finding work in L.A. as Texas boys Henkel and Hooper might have imagined. Though it was reported that Hooper and Henkel would next work on another horror film, entitled *Bleeding Hearts*, that project failed to materialize, as did Hooper's proposed collaboration with Friedkin and writer L.M. Kit Carson, on a film called *Dead and Alive*.

Instead, Hooper was offered the opportunity to direct *Death Trap* for Mardi Rustam, a low-budget exploitation producer (*Evils of the Night* [1985]). Though the idea informing the action of the film (that of a rundown hotel and its crazy clerk, Judd) was the notion of Alvin Fast and Rustam, the story was "adapted for the screen" by *Chain Saw* partners Kim Henkel and Tobe Hooper to fit their particular perspective. To wit: the film was set in a sleazy, dirtbag hotel in Florida. Hooper had grown up in the hotel business, even spending some of his youth in neighboring Louisiana, so one has to wonder if he was remembering a particularly unpleasant period from his youth, or merely turning his experience with regional hotels to his cinematic advantage.

Some sources have also indicated that the film's psychopath, Judd, was based on a real person (and his crime spree). A World War I medal winner (as Judd was a Vietnam War medal honoree in the film) named Ball, had gruesomely murdered many of the guests at his "Sociable Inn" in San Antonio, Texas, and fed the bodies to his pet alligators (35). This real-life character was an especially ironic one for actor Neville Brand to play because he was himself well known as one of the "most decorated" heroes of World War II (36). Though it was shot under the title *Death Trap*, this picture is more widely known as *Eaten Alive*. Other titles include *Starlight Slaughter*, *Murder in the Bayou*, *Horror Hotel Massacre*, and *Legend of the Bayou*.

With a reported budget of $600,000 (much of it reportedly raised on the guarantee of Hooper's participation), *Eaten Alive* boasted a great "B" movie cast. Marilyn Burns, that screaming alumnus of *Chain Saw*, appeared with Neville Brand (as the aforementioned psychopath), Stuart Whitman (of *Night of the Lepus* [1972] and *Ruby* [1977]), William Finley (of Brian De Palma's *Sisters* [1973]) and Carolyn Jones, Morticia of the *Addams Family* (1964-66) TV series. Also in this impressive mix was a promising young actor who, in the years to come, would make a name for himself as the greatest horror star of his generation, Robert Englund. An only child (whose father had developed the U-2 spy plane), Englund was a UCLA dropout (37) who had made it to the big time in movies such as *Buster and Billie* and *Stay Hungry*. In the years following his popular role as Freddy Krueger, the bogeyman of the *Nightmare on Elm Street* film franchise, Englund would work with Hooper again on three more occasions (the TV series *Freddy's Nightmares*, the direct-to-video feature *Tobe Hooper's Night Terrors* and *The Mangler*.)

If the film's cast was promising, Marshall Reed and Tobe Hooper's art direction was even more so. The Starlight Hotel—a seedy armpit of a structure—was built on a soundstage and it was a terrific, highly detailed southern gothic setting. The hotel interiors were even more remarkable; Judd's digs looked like a real dive, not Hollywood's sanitized conception of what a dive should look like. Cracked wallpaper, dirty toilets, torn upholstered furniture, rotting molding lumber, bad plumbing and other nasty touches made the Starlight as "real" (and disturbing) a world as *Chain Saw's* memorable cannibal farmhouse. Once again, Hooper was expressing the "inner" insanity of his villains with strange, outward trappings. And, contributing to the feeling of pure sleaze in *Eaten Alive*, several odd country songs seemed to drone on Judd's radio in the background of many scenes, some with truly bizarre lyrics. Welcome to backwater Hell!

Despite these production strengths and a totally audacious opening sequence featuring the immortal line "...Name's Buck, and I'm raring to fuck...," *Eaten Alive* didn't prove to be the sophomore success that might have catapulted Hooper to further fame. In fact, Hooper left the film before principal photography was complete on the project, and Carolyn Jones and the film's editor reportedly directed and oversaw the remaining editing of the picture. Some reports suggest that Rustam requested more nudity in the film and that Tobe Hooper had no desire to take the film in the direction of soft porn. Other stories indicate that Rustam viewed the film as a comedy, whereas Hooper was angling for a more serious, disturbing approach to the material. For whatever reason the creative breach occurred, Hooper didn't finish *Eaten Alive*. Nonetheless, the film was released with his name on it. As Robert Englund explained in an interview with *Fangoria*:

> Tobe left that movie under rather unpleasant circumstances. They raised close to a half million dollars on his name alone in Japan ... yet they pestered him more and more; they violated his sense of rhythm.... I got along terrifically with these people [producers] ... but of all things you need to pester Tobe about ... he's going to deliver. You have to let him delve into things his own way.... It was so disappointing when he left the project [38].

When it was released in 1976, *Eaten Alive* disappeared quickly from theaters only to be resurrected again and again under its various alternative titles in a last-ditch effort to make some of its cost back. Today, the critical community is polarized about the film. Some reviewers see it as pure exploitation, whereas others see it as a compellingly lurid companion piece to Hooper's work in *The Texas Chain Saw Massacre*. One thing is certain: like *The Texas Chain Saw Massacre* before it, *Eaten Alive* is no common horror movie. It boasts an atmosphere unlike any other movie's and even if it fails to reach the insane heights of its predecessor, it still features some truly spiky, bizarre moments. But, no doubt, *Eaten Alive* was not the feature Hooper hoped would follow his *Chain Saw* success.

Parking in Salem's Lot

After the disappointment of *Eaten Alive*, Tobe Hooper's luck in Hollywood took a disheartening turn for the worse. He prepped a low-budget science-fiction/horror film called *The Dark* for producer Edward Montoro (*Grizzly* [1976]), but abandoned the project after four days of principal photography over disagreements with Montoro in the style and direction of the film. He was replaced on the set by John Bud Cardos (*Kingdom of the Spiders* [1977] and *The Day Time Ended* [1979]) and the final film, released in 1979, was an unmitigated disaster. Hooper's decision to abandon ship was a smart career move and *The Dark* (starring Cathy Lee Crosby and William Devane) was savaged by critics, including the pre-eminent Roger Ebert in this review:

> This is without a doubt the dumbest, most inept, most maddeningly unsatisfactory thriller of the last five years. It's really bad; so bad, indeed, that it provides some sort of measuring tool against which to measure bad thrillers [39].

After dodging this particular bullet, Hooper still had a problem: what was to be his true encore to *The Texas Chain Saw Massacre*? As the summer of 1979 approached, the break at last came that would ultimately propel Tobe Hooper to Hollywood's A-List of directors. Warner Brothers had purchased the hot Stephen King property *Salem's Lot* (a story of a vampire invasion in a small New England town) in 1977 following the box office success of Brian De Palma's adaptation of *Carrie* (1976). Unfortunately, the studio had some trouble developing the lengthy, complex novel for film. At one point, Tobe Hooper was briefly attached to direct the project under the auspices of producer William Friedkin, but the problems in developing a script could never be licked because of the immense size of King's work. Sculpting a spare, two-hour movie out of the sprawling, epic tale of Ben Mears' battle with a vampire named Barlow was a difficult task, to the say the least. Consequently, the property bounced around to different writers, including Larry Cohen of *It's Alive* (1973) fame (40), and Stirling Silliphant (*Village of the Damned* [1960]). At various points, directors announced for the project included George Romero and Larry Cohen.

But then Richard Kobritz came aboard the stalled project as a producer and decided that *Salem's Lot* would work best not as a feature film, but as a mini-series running over an extended period of four hours. Kobritz's previous project, a suspenseful TV film entitled *Someone's Watching Me* (1978), had been a ratings knockout on television the year before, in no small part because of the writer/director he'd handpicked to vet the Hitchcock-style material: John Carpenter. *Someone's Watching Me* (shot immediately prior to *Halloween* [1978]), had been a fantastic success and Kobritz was eager to repeat the experience. After viewing a variety of horror films (including *Phantasm* [1979], with which he was reportedly unimpressed), Kobritz watched *The Texas Chain Saw Massacre* and, dazzled, realized that he'd found his director. Hooper, who had been on the verge of signing to direct an Italian low-budget quickie called *The Guyana Massacre*, came aboard the project, even though it promised to be a difficult shoot. Writer Paul Monash contributed the final screenplay, one which cut out some of the novel's peripheral characters yet retained the feeling of King's work.

There was little doubt that *Salem's Lot* represented Tobe Hooper's largest career challenge up to that point. He had just 37 days (but with six weeks of preparation time) to shoot a four hour screenplay featuring more characters and locations than *The Texas Chain Saw Massacre* and *Eaten Alive* combined. Fourteen of those critical 37 days would be spent on location in Ferndale, a town in Northern California doubling as Jerusalem's Lot. The mini-series was budgeted at four million dollars, a whopping amount compared even to *Eaten*

Alive's roughly half-a-million dollars. To put it in perspective, the cost of the Marsten House mock-up in *Salem's Lot* (and its corresponding interior sets), was roughly $160,000—the entire budget of *The Texas Chain Saw Massacre* back in 1973.

Further complicating matters, Hooper was to be responsible for two versions of the production: one that would pass muster with Standards and Practices at CBS, the other (with more graphic violence) for theatrical release in Europe. Notably, this was also Hooper's first exposure to prime time television and all its inherent limitations (including commercial breaks). The rushed schedule demanded 30-40 camera set-ups per day (41), a hectic pace for any director.

Cast in the picture as the primary villain, Barlow's henchman, Mr. Straker, was the legendary actor James Mason *(North by Northwest* [1959], *Journey to the Center of the Earth* [1959], *20,000 Leagues Under the Sea* [1954]). Opposing him as the hero of the piece was David Soul, late of *Starsky and Hutch* (1975-79). Others in the cast included Bonnie Bedelia (*Die Hard* [1988]), Lance Kerwin (*James at 15* [1977-78]), Kenneth McMillan (*Dune* [1984]), and Reggie Nalder (*Mark of the Devil* [1972], *The Dead Don't Die* [1974]) as the Nosferatu-like master vampire, Mr. Barlow. It was Nalder's job to emote under heavy make-up appliances, which took some two hours to apply. But with glowing contact lenses, vampire "fangs" and a skull-like headpiece (42), his Barlow remains one of the most frightening—and feral—screen vampires of all time (even if he doesn't at all resemble the Barlow of King's novel).

Principal photography on *Salem's Lot* commenced in July of 1979 and wrapped in August of 1979, on budget and on schedule. And, with Kobritz's blessing, Hooper fought for the production to evince something notably lacking from most TV efforts, *film style*:

Brian De Palma actually coined a phrase, "film grammar," which refers to the way particular shots are put together by particular directors in order to tell the story. It's not something you see evidenced very often on television. You build sequences, such as a shot of someone coming through a doorway who looks at a table across the room. On the table, there is a dagger, and as the subject approaches the dagger, the camera dollies back across the long room with the subject approaching the table. And then cutting to that person's point-of-view, which would be a moving shot traveling toward the table, getting closer and closer to the dagger ... that's grammar [43].

Hooper's decision (with Kobritz's blessing) to imbue *Salem's Lot* with film style made all the difference. When the mini-series aired (November 17 and 24, 1979) during sweeps, it achieved stellar numbers in the all-important Nielsen ratings. More importantly, audiences found the film remarkably scary and at least two of Hooper's staging choices became classics of the genre; one involves the sudden first appearance of the sinister Mr. Barlow (in close-up) in a quiet jail cell. The second depicts child vampires scratching malevolently at a window, hovering in the gloom of night (in reality, propped up in a harness attached to the arm of an invisible-on-film Apollo Chapman crane). With good performances from Soul, Bedelia, Kerwin and especially Mason, *Salem's Lot* works very, very well and is considered by most critics to be among the top three or four King adaptations yet filmed (*Carrie* [1976], *The Dead Zone* [1981] and *Misery* [1990] being the other contenders.) Indeed, this author's father-in-law, a genre buff and the former chair of the biology department at the University of Richmond, maintains to this day that *Salem's Lot* is the greatest horror film ever made, recalling with special fondness the night Mr. Barlow first appeared on his television set and literally scared him out of his seat. Even King himself was impressed with Hooper's craftsmanship, noting that *Salem's Lot* "exceeded" his expectations for what 'they could get away with on television" (44) and that he believed the film was "done quite well" (45).

For Hooper, *Salem's Lot* was a victory of another order. After the disappointments of *Eaten Alive* and *The Dark,* he had proven (again) his total professionalism and commitment to a directing career:

> This is a quantum leap for me.... It's a major studio production, I'm working with a fantastic cast and crew. And Kobritz is wonderful. This is a first for me.... Also, *Salem's Lot* does not rely on the same kind of dynamics as *Chainsaw*. It is scary, it is atmospheric, but in a different way [46].

That last point is an important one. *The Texas Chain Saw Massacre* was a brilliant film, but not a comfortable or mainstream one. With the polished *Salem's Lot*, Hooper established that he could work outside the savage "horror fringe" of *Eaten Alive* and his notorious Leatherface chronicle. *Salem's Lot* was a solid, traditional horror film, with bumps and jumps enough to satisfy mainstream and horror audiences, but there was nothing there that would be a lightning rod for controversy. Working on *Salem's Lot* with mainstream actors, a professional crew, a big budget and a producer who knew what he wanted, Tobe Hooper proved dramatically that he could deliver the goods: a stylish, entertaining, suspenseful (and if truth be told, complex) thriller. *The Texas Chain Saw Massacre* was no fluke and Tobe Hooper now had more than one "success" in his repertoire.

Things Afoot at *The Funhouse*

Had events been only slightly different, horror movie fans might today be debating a genre remake entitled *Tobe Hooper's The Thing*. In the late 1970s, while the remake of the Howard Hawks classic was under development at Universal Studios, Kim Henkel and Hooper were brought into the project by William Friedkin and assigned to write and direct the film for producer Stuart Cohen. Ultimately, they departed the adaptation of the 1951 Howard Hawks classic, leaving John Carpenter to develop the film (with screenwriter Bill Lancaster) into one of that auteur's greatest and most memorable works. It is an interesting coincidence: John Carpenter prepped *The Thing* for a release in 1982 and Universal Studios unveiled Tobe Hooper's *Poltergeist* in the same season. Both directors made terrific films and horror fans had much to celebrate in one summer.

With *The Thing* in John Carpenter's capable hands, Tobe Hooper learned that an old project he had once been attached to had suddenly gathered steam (as well as financial backing) following the success of *Salem's Lot* on television. The project was based on a screenplay by Lawrence Block entitled *The Funhouse*. Produced by Derek Power and *The Omen's* (1976) Mace Neufield, *The Funhouse* was the suspenseful tale of four rambunctious teens (Cooper Huckabee, Elizabeth Berridge, Miles Chapin, and Largo Woodruff) that elected to spend the night in a traveling carnival's funhouse only to be confronted with a deformed, murderous "carnie" (Wayne Doba) and his overprotective, money-grubbing father (Kevin Conway). Also in the cast was the solid William Finley, who had worked so well with Hooper on *Eaten Alive*. A standout in the film was young Berridge, a 5'2" actress reported in the press to be "terribly shy" and notable for "playing people younger than herself" (47). Like Jamie Lee Curtis in *Halloween*, Berridge gave the lead role of *The Funhouse* her all, imbuing the character with more humanity than is often evident in the genre, and later went on to greater success in Hollywood, playing Mozart's wife, Costanze, in *Amadeus* (1985).

More so than *Salem's Lot*, *The Fun-

house felt like a Tobe Hooper project from the get-go, since it focused on a world on the fringe of normal society (the twilight world of the carnival) and a twisted family's singular values. Like Leatherface's house in *The Texas Chain Saw Massacre* or Judd's hotel in *Eaten Alive,* the funhouse was a place that appeared normal on the surface, but underneath cloaked terrible secrets and horrors.

Shot on a smaller budget than *Salem's Lot,* but on virtually the same schedule of 30 days, *The Funhouse* also employed Rick Baker (*King Kong* [1976], *How The Grinch Stole Christmas* [2000], *Planet of the Apes* [2001]) and Craig Reardon to supply the make-up of the film's deformed "bogeyman." Another of *The Funhouse's* distinguishing features was its unusual setting. A 1940s era carnival was located in Akron, Ohio, packed up and subsequently rebuilt at Ivan Tors Studio in Florida for the duration of shooting. The creepy, "retro" look of the carnival (and some of its strange mechanical figures) added a whole new disturbing element of terror to the creepy film. By most accounts, it was a fast shoot, with some minor hold-ups involving overtime. Shooting ran seven days over schedule (thirty-seven days in all) and Hooper had to leave the country to helm *Venom* in England after toiling on a rough cut of the film (48).

About Hooper's involvement with *Venom* (starring Oliver Reed, Susan George, Klaus Kinski, Sterling Hayden, Sarah Miles and Nicol Williamson) there remain conflicting stories. Some accounts indicate that an illness in Hooper's family resulted in his return to the U.S. and his decision to turn over *Venom* to director Piers Haggard (*The Blood on Satan's Claw* [1971]). Other reports note that cost overruns and production problems plagued the film and that Hooper "failed to weather the storm" (49), consequently being replaced by Haggard. Regardless of which account is believed, Hooper subsequently returned stateside and oversaw editing on *The Funhouse,* which upon release was played with the droll ad line: "Pay to get in; pray to get out."

The Funhouse was released in March of 1981 to mostly positive reviews and modest box-office success. In some senses, it is, like *Eaten Alive,* another "lost" Tobe Hooper film because a sizable audience ignored it on its release, fearing it to be another *Halloween*-style slasher clone. By 1981, audiences had already been inundated with titles such as *Boogeyman* (1980), *Christmas Evil* (1980), *Don't Go in the House* (1980), *Friday the 13th* (1980), *Graduation Day* (1981), *Mother's Day* (1980), *Prom Night* (1980), *Terror Train* (1980), *Happy Birthday to Me* (1981), *He Knew You're Alone* (1981), *Madman* (1981) and *My Bloody Valentine* (1981), all of which inhabited the same dreary "teens in jeopardy mileu" also evident in Hooper's far more artful *The Funhouse*. To some extent, the film just got lost in this slasher glut (even though, technically, it is *not* a slasher film at all) and only when it was released onto the burgeoning home video market did *The Funhouse* start to garner its reputation as a frightening, well-crafted horror film. In that new secondary market it became a popular, profitable and perennial rental.

Ghost Director: Helming *Poltergeist*

Following post-production on *The Funhouse,* Tobe Hooper caught a break that would later prove to have serious repercussions for his directing career. He "was personally selected" by *wunderkind* Steven Spielberg "on the basis of *The Texas Chain Saw Massacre*" (50), to direct a new genre film. In particular, Spielberg—Hollywood's royal hitmaker with *Jaws* (1975), *Close Encounters of the Third Kind* (1977), and *Raiders of the Lost Ark* (1981) all to his recent credit—was interested in producing a horror movie that might be the flip side of *Close*

Encounters. It would focus not on the awe and wonder of first contact with extra-terrestrials, but on the dark, terrifying side of human interaction with aliens and flying saucers. The project, often referred to in the press as a sequel to *Close Encounters*, was titled *Night Skies* and it concerned an alien assault on an isolated farmhouse. The only problem was that Hooper didn't have an interest in directing an "alien invader" film, perhaps remembering his bad experience with *The Dark*, another tale of an evil extraterrestrial and one that had not been received warmly.

Hooper had a better idea. While overseeing the final stages of *The Funhouse*, he moved into director Robert Wise's old office at Universal Studios and found in Wise's desk a book about the occult, specifically poltergeists (a spooky element of his classic film *The Haunting* [1963]) (51). It was Hooper who suggested collaborating with Spielberg (out of the country at the time, filming *Raiders of the Lost Ark*) on a movie about ghosts and poltergeists rather than aliens and Spielberg was receptive to that notion (52). Hooper and Spielberg were both long-time admirers of *The Haunting* and together they researched the paranormal as a foundation for their partnership (53).

Furthermore, Hooper wanted to direct *Poltergeist*, a supernatural film about life after death, because of his unique personal experience with the subject matter:

> I actually had some poltergeist experiences after my father died, when I was seventeen. Water glasses, plates, and other stuff in the kitchen exploded, were replaced, and exploded again. For several weeks some very strange stuff went on. The experience left me with the desire to do a film about this phenomena [54].

Once the paranormal subject was settled upon, Spielberg wrote the script (with fellow writers Michael Grais and Mark Victor) with the intent that Hooper would direct and he would produce. And, at the same time *Poltergeist* was to be made, Spielberg planned to direct another feature for release in the summer of 1982, a little film called *E.T.—The Extra Terrestrial*. As most film buffs know, that sentimental (and beautifully directed) film went on to become the highest grossing movie of all time.

Production-wise, *Poltergeist* (which was budgeted at 9.5 million dollars but eventually cost closer to 11 million) represented another step-up into mainstream moviemaking for Tobe Hooper. The production was huge, stretching across three soundstages at MGM and featuring more than 100 optical effect shots. The special effects climax of the film, the spectacular implosion of a haunted house, was shot with a detailed (and highly convincing) miniature, six feet wide by four feet high (55). Not only was Hooper working with more complex visual effects than before, he was clearly shepherding an A-list, major studio release.

Cast in *Poltergeist* as the sympathetic Freelings, parents who were horrified to discover their house was haunted, were JoBeth Williams, who had been so memorable in the famous "fried chicken" exchange in *Kramer vs. Kramer* (1980), and Craig T. Nelson, an actor who early in his career had appeared in low-budget fare such as *The Return of Count Yorga* (1972). Portraying the terrorized children were Oliver Robbins, Heather O'Rourke, and Dominique Dunne.

With principal photography on *Poltergeist* in full swing, a controversy suddenly erupted and it involved Tobe Hooper, Steven Spielberg and the identity of the "real" director of *Poltergeist*. According to Hooper, a reporter from the *Los Angeles Times* arrived on location at Simi Valley as the first unit (helmed by Hooper) was filming one sequence (Oliver Robbins' encounter with a malevolent old tree) in the back yard of the film's suburban Questa Verde location. The second unit (overseen

Who's calling the shots? Producer Steven Spielberg (far left) and director Tobe Hooper (middle) discuss a shot with Craig T. Nelson (far right) on the set of *Poltergeist* (1982). Behind Nelson, Hooper regular James Karen (in suit) is visible.

by Spielberg) was simultaneously shooting pick-ups for the moment early in the film when mischievous children deploy remote-controlled cars to foul up a hurried football fan on a motorcycle (56).

Allegedly, the reporter returned to the newsroom with a unique story: that it was uncertain who was directing this film enterprise. And so began the long-standing legend that directorial "ownership" of *Poltergeist* was in question.

Of course, anyone who has ever worked on a movie set realizes that such an assertion, based on the described scenario, is utter nonsense. This author was on the set of a film called *Body Count* (1997) that shot at a prison near Charlotte, North Carolina, and during an eight- to ten-hour day was directed (quite ably) by an assistant director throughout. The actual director, an amiable enough fellow, didn't even *appear* to be on location until sometime late in the afternoon when the principal actors (Ving Rhames and Forest Whitaker) were put through their paces. This isn't a criticism of that director (who did, indeed, direct the film!), but rather an acknowledgment of the fact that it is no anomaly for an assistant director to work (at the express command of the director) on certain less-than-critical sequences. Steven Spielberg's presence on the set of *Poltergeist* easily fits into that category.

Here's another pertinent example that reveals the fallacy of trumpeting Spielberg over Hooper: producer Sean Cunningham has been acknowledged by Wes Craven as the director of at least one sequence of *A Nightmare on Elm Street,* a non-dialogue chase sequence (57) involving Freddy Krueger's assault on a teen named Tina in an alleyway. Yet, directorial ownership of that particular film has never been challenged, probably because the name Sean Cunningham doesn't have the same level of awareness and cachet in the press as does Steven Spielberg. Simply put, second units exist to pick up shots that go into the tapestry of a film, but which may not involve critical movements with lead actors or main locations. Second units exist to keep a film on schedule. Second units exist because assembling a film is a colossal task and a director, who must balance a million and one different factors, simply does not have time to personally shoot every frame of film himself. That anything was made of this at all on the set of *Poltergeist* is rather amazing, especially considering that Spielberg was the film's producer and thus a creative, powerful influence! He was already a frequent visitor to the set. How great a leap, then, was it for him to get behind a camera and direct one insert shot? Does the fact that he helmed such incidental material make him the director of *Poltergeist?* Not at all. In fact, there would be no *Poltergeist* to direct in the first place without Hooper's involvement because he suggested doing a film on ghosts in the first place, instead of *Night Skies*....

Unfortunately, many statements and actions made in the press didn't help to clarify the situation to Tobe Hooper's advantage. Some of Steven Spielberg's remarks to the press could be interpreted as subtle "nudges" affirming his ownership of the film were a reporter looking to support that particular story angle. When asked about working with child actors on horror films, for example, Spielberg seemed to indicate he was on equal footing with Hooper on the set, even calling out direction:

> Oliver ... became scared during the scene in which his big clown doll wraps its arms around him.... The arms became too tight and cut his wind off. I remember Oliver screaming, "I can't breathe." And Tobe Hooper and I thought it was great acting.... When I asked him to scream, he screamed better than Janet Leigh in *Psycho*. So here Tobe is yelling, "More! More!" and I'm saying "great, Oliver, look toward the camera!" and suddenly I saw his face turn crimson ... [58].

In another interview, Spielberg highlighted the importance of his own participation in the film, while simultaneously appearing reticent to discuss any specifics that might appear "hurtful" to any unnamed parties:

> All I can say about my involvement overall is.... I wrote the movie. I actually wrote *Poltergeist* but co-authored an earlier draft with Michael Grais and Mark Victor. I hired them to realize my original idea and ... did a complete rewrite.... And all I'll say about my involvement as ... line producer with Frank Marshall is that I designed the film. From the storyboards to post-production.... I was the David Selznick of this movie.... I functioned in a very strong way [59].

This quote, intentionally or not, pretty successfully minimizes Hooper's creative involvement in *Poltergeist* and that of other artists too. For instance Spielberg states that the original idea of the film was his, but wasn't the notion of filming a ghost story one that had allegedly come from Hooper? Spielberg had reportedly come to him with *Night Skies,* a film about hostile aliens! Secondly, Michael Grais and Mark Victor were awarded screenplay credit by the Writers Guild, right alongside Steven Spielberg, so *some* of their ideas, dialogue, characters, plotting must have played a role in the final film too. And, then there is the case of Paul Clemens and Bennet Michael Yelin, writers who filed a $37 million dollar lawsuit claiming that Spielberg appropriated elements of *Poltergeist* from a screenplay they penned in 1980 (60). The result was an out-of-court settlement allegedly in Clemens' favor (61). Similarly, Spielberg reportedly requested a videotape of *The Twilight Zone* episode "Little Girl Lost" from author Richard B. Matheson while preparing *Poltergeist* (62) and there are obvious and numerous similarities between that installment of the classic Rod Serling series and the Spielberg screenplay.

There is no doubt that Spielberg was instrumental in the making of *Poltergeist* (right down to casting decisions and his collaboration with Jerry Goldsmith on the score in post production), but film remains a collaborative art form. There were creative elements in the mix, including *director* Tobe Hooper.

In fairness to Spielberg, *Poltergeist* represented a new situation for him (producing and writing a film another man directed), and even he admitted it was not an easy or familiar process:

> ... turmoil is ... created by wanting to do it your own way and having to go through procedure.... I will never again *not* direct a film I write. It was frustrating for Tobe Hooper and it was frustrating for the actors, who were ... torn between my presence and his on the set every day. But rather than Tobe's saying "...get off the set," he'd laugh and I'd laugh. If he'd said, "I've got some ideas ... you're really not letting into this movie ... don't be on the set," I probably would have left [63].

The important word in that quotation may just be "probably."

The whole "who directed *Poltergeist*" issue got so out of hand that finally the Directors Guild of America intervened and launched an investigation to determine whether Hooper was "being demeaned by having his status as a director reduced to a mechanical rather than creative task" (64). This investigation came about when trailers for *Poltergeist* were released which showed Spielberg "directing" on the set and which advertised the picture as "A Steven Spielberg Film" while (in much smaller print) acknowledging Tobe Hooper as the actual director of the movie. Forced to respond, Hooper insisted that he had done "fully half" of the film's storyboards himself and totally directed the picture (a stance echoed by many of the cast of the film). He thus came to loggerheads with Spielberg, and the DGA sided with Hooper, fining Spielberg $15,000 (65) and demanding that the offending trailers be pulled on both coasts (66). The final judgment of arbiter Edward Mosk was that the trailers "denigrated the role of the director" (67).

But adding more fuel to the fire was Spielberg's strange wording in an ad in *Variety* (another condition of the arbitration), congratulating Hooper on their unique and successful collaboration (68). At the same time he wrote that Hooper had directed *Poltergeist* "wonderfully," he thanked Hooper for allowing him "as producer and writer," a "wide berth of creative involvement" (69). Some in the industry read the ad at face value: Spielberg and Hooper had created a wonderful film, with each contributing much to the project as a whole. More cynical industry watchers felt the ad was another way to reinforce the press's already implanted notion that Spielberg was the man, ultimately, calling the shots on the film.

When all was said and done, many in the film industry were infuriated by the situation because no matter how it had emerged in the first place, the real loser, in any final analysis, was Tobe Hooper. As an outspoken critic of Hollywood, science fiction writer Harlan Ellison assessed the situation in *Harlan Ellison's Watching* with his typical clarity and grace:

> ... [the] rumor [that Spielberg directed *Poltergeist*] has proved to be utterly false and destructive to Hooper's reputation ... no amount of setting the record straight will convince most people that Tobe Hooper, not Spielberg, directed *Poltergeist* [70].

Unfortunately, this issue is still not really settled today and some accounts of Spielberg's participation on the project have carefully glossed over the issue. In one biography of Spielberg, the writer commented only that Spielberg had "helped direct" (71) *Poltergeist* and, amazingly, even that he had chosen Tobe Hooper, "a little known director to whom Spielberg may have offered the position so that Spielberg could have as much control over the project as he wanted" (72).

If the issue of "who directed *Polter*-

geist" was the most fascinating industry debate of the summer of 1982, most Americans didn't seem to care. After the M.P.A.A. appeals process overturned a ruling that would have branded the picture with a dreaded "R" rating, thereby limiting the film's teenage audience, the movie went out with a "PG" rating (like *Jaws*) and became a monster hit. Opening against *Star Trek II: The Wrath of Khan* on June 4, 1982, the film racked up more than 6.8 million dollars in its first weekend. By the time of its Halloween reissue that October, *Poltergeist* had grossed more than 70 million dollars (73), and was soon to become the foundation of a franchise that would include two sequels (*Poltergeist II: The Other Side* [1985] and *Poltergeist III* [1988]) and the long-lived TV series *Poltergeist the Legacy* [1996–1999]). The film's most popular line, Heather O'Roarke's innocent (but ominous) exclamation "They're Heeeere..." became a pop culture catchphrase, exploited in endless commercials and even trailers for other films (like a sequel to *Revenge of the Nerds*). A critical darling too, the film was included as one of *Time Magazine's* prestigious ten best of 1982 (74). Only the late great Pauline Kael was curmudgeonly, terming the film a "dumb concoction" (75).

Interestingly, Joe Dante's "collaboration" with Steven Spielberg, *Gremlins* (1984), later referenced the whole *Poltergeist* controversy in an interesting if oblique manner, paying subtle homage to Tobe Hooper. In that film's climax, the mogwai villain, Spike, hides in a Montgomery Ward department store on Christmas Eve and uses—*surprise*—a chainsaw to attack protagonist Billy (Zach Galligan). The choice of department stores (Montgomery Ward) and weapon (the saw) clearly references Hooper's publicly acknowledged inspiration for making the landmark *Texas Chain Saw Massacre*: a holiday shopping excursion to that very retail store. Was this some kind of subtle apology from somebody? Or perhaps an acknowledgment from Dante that he too had gotten the "treatment" working on a Spielberg-produced film? It's a fascinating thing to speculate about and an interesting film reference, no matter how one chooses to interpret it.

Hooper's New Idol, and the Living Dead Return!

Over the years, a number of film directors have emerged from the ranks of music video production. McG (*Charlie's Angels* [2000]) and David Fincher (*Seven* [1995], *The Game* [1997], *Fight Club* [1999]) are just two prominent examples. In the early 1980s, however, there was another trend that helped to popularize the form of the music video. Hollywood's feature filmmakers began taking gigs as video directors. The first video (then known as "a clip") to employ "a known film director" was Billy Idol's "Dancing with Myself" (76), and the director was none other than Tobe Hooper! The "clip" was budgeted at $70,000 dollars and was shot by Hooper's director of photography on *The Texas Chain Saw Massacre*, Daniel Pearl, who had reportedly encouraged Hooper to take on the assignment. In 1983, this was quite a step for the burgeoning art form and Hooper's participation demonstrated to the world that videos could attract the kind of talent that had heretofore been reserved for features. For Hooper, a video was a perfect fit, since some twenty years earlier he had begun his career making "shorts" and "commercials," brethren to the newly popular music video format. Following *Invaders from Mars*, Hooper would direct another music video, this time for the Cars, entitled "Strap Me In."

On the movie front, there was some difficulty finding a satisfactory project to follow-up *Poltergeist* and for a time, Hooper's name was attached to *Return of the Living Dead* (1985), a sort of illegitimate "sequel"/parody of George Romero's cult classic

Night of the Living Dead (1968). The film once had roots in a serious-minded script by Romero's collaborators on that landmark film, John Russo, Russ Streiner and Rudi Ricci. But the property had been optioned by a producer named Tom Fox, who then attempted to get financing for the production from Hemdale films (77). There was a great deal of legal wrangling and Romero was quite concerned that audiences would confuse *Return of the Living Dead* for his upcoming zombie sequel *Day of the Dead* (1985). Lawsuits followed.

Dan O'Bannon (*Dark Star* [1975], *Alien* [1979]) was hired to write the script as the film project secured financing, and in 1983 Hooper waited to shoot the picture. As O'Bannon recalled of *Return of the Living Dead*, and Hooper's participation, in *Cinefantastique*:

> I scripted it more or less the way Tobe Hooper wanted it. He came up with some cute ideas, and I did too, but it was mainly geared toward his tastes. Then the backers, Hemdale, began having money problems because they were raising the cash on foreign distribution sales ... and it was taking ages [78].

Rather than sit and wait to direct a film that might never happen, Hooper moved on and Dan O'Bannon became the director of the film when it acquired financing. Instead, Hooper directed *Lifeforce,* with O'Bannon scripting that project as well!

One *Lifeforce* to Live

In the summer of 1983, Cannon Film's movie moguls, Manahem Golan and Yoram Globus, the self-described "world's leading purveyor[s] of B movies" (79), saw to it that a copy of Colin Wilson's 1976 genre novel, *The Space Vampires*, made it into the hands of their choice director, Tobe Hooper. They were preparing to finance a big budget adaptation of the film and Hooper was now considered a bankable commodity worldwide for the one-two-three punch of *The Texas Chain Saw Massacre, Salem's Lot* and *Poltergeist*. They quickly signed the director to a three-picture deal, an arrangement that would have a dramatic effect on Hooper's career. Acknowledged as having "single-handedly revitalized the Israeli film business in the seventies" (80) with films such as *Kazablan* (1974), *Operation Thunderbolt* (1977) and *Lemon Popsicle* (1979), this larger-than-life duo, owning a controlling share of Cannon, made larger-than-life movies and *Space Vampires* was to be part of the overarching plan.

Set in the latter half of the 21st century, Wilson's well-reviewed novel was the macabre tale of an expedition aboard the spaceship *Hermes* (commanded by Icelandic national Olof Carlsen) that investigated a strange derelict spaceship and its 30 alien inhabitants, "space vampires" from a highly advanced race called the Nioth-Korghai. One of the vampires appeared to be a beautiful woman (named G'room), who developed a telepathic contact with Carlsen. When returned to Earth with two of her male brethren, this "Space Girl" began to do what vampires of horror fiction have always done: seduce and devour victims. The twist this time was that the aliens were energy/vitality suckers rather than merely blood suckers.

In *Space Vampires*, G'room's subsequent spree of seduction, vampirism and rampant body hopping led to a heated and well-developed philosophical treatise about the nature of life. This information was presented by a Quatermass/VanHelsing type of character named Hans Fallada. A criminologist and the author of a work called *The Anatomy and Pathology of Vampirism,* Fallada proposed the notion that all creatures, even human beings, are vampires of one sort or another. After all, we eat the flesh of animals, don't we? The story climaxed when G'room was captured while inhabiting the body of a doctor (named Armstrong) and forced (while subdued by drugs) to recount the Nioth-Korghai's long story. The vampires had originally hailed from a planet near Rigel, but these peace lovers and philosophers became trapped near a black hole and were forced to resort to parasitism and vampirism, to survive. This group of renegades, known as the Ubbo-Sathla, then explored the universe looking for life-forms to exploit and even visited Earth in about 1500 B.C. As Carlsen and Fallada learned all of this information the "good" Nioth-Korghai arrived and, somewhat ashamed of their fallen comrades, recaptured G'room and her cohorts.

If this plot sounds complicated or awkward, it is probably because *Space Vampires* is heavy on exposition, not to mention unpronounceable proper names featuring apostrophes in the middle, the bane of the intrepid science fiction reader. Much of the book exists primarily as an intellectual give-and-take between Fallada and Carlsen about the nature of vampirism and it is undeniably fascinating philosophical stuff, if woefully lacking in cinematic imagery and frisson. The novel's climax, for instance, is an exposition-heavy meeting in the prime minister's office, in which everything comes together in sedate, lock-step and orderly fashion.

Yet the book was (and remains) an interesting film project because of several key "visual" components: an alien derelict spaceship (called *the Stranger* in the novel), a doomed space expedition, a beautiful *femme fatale*/siren who lures men to their deaths and the notion of a common "lifeforce" existing in all living things. Even without benefit of horror movie set pieces such as chases, vampire stakings and so on, the novel is a compelling read.

Hooper, a longtime fan of the British *Quatermass* TV series and film franchise of the '50s and '60s (including *The Creeping Unknown* [1956], *Enemy from Space* [1957], and *Five Million Years To Earth* [1968]), immediately appreciated the gothic tone of Wilson's atmospheric novel and saw how *Space Vampires* might be a homage to some of the favorite productions from his youth. At the same time, *Space Vampires* was designed to be a major production, filled with amazing special effects and complex sets, in essence a perfect follow-up to the complicated *Poltergeist*.

With Hooper signed on, the task of adapting *Space Vampires* was breached and promptly found to be filled with landmines. Dan O'Bannon was assigned to write the screenplay, but the futuristic setting of the novel, an Earth of "World Unity," moon bases and totally routine space travel, was thought to be too distancing, too remote, for a thriller of the horror genre. As Hooper understood, horror thrives on *immediacy*, on the capability of the audience to put itself in the shoes of the protagonist. If the setting is too remote, too out-of-the-norm, empathy becomes harder and scares more difficult to generate. Hooper explained his solution to this problem to interviewer Dennis Fischer, for *Starlog*:

> I think I came up with the lynchpin of making this story a contemporary piece, and that was to use Halley's Comet. Colin Wilson's novel is set in the distant future, and I feel that kind of story breaks the identification value that you have if it's contemporary. Once that line of identification has been broken, things aren't as suspenseful [81].

To foster identification, Hooper thus transported the events of *Space Vampires* to the year 1986—the very year that Halley's Comet would return close to Earth. This change not only landed audiences back in their familiar twentieth century, it also gave them a specific near-future event to dwell on, specifically the comet's return orbit. This change granted the story the immediacy the novel lacked and also landed it in the category of "what if" horror films like *Night of the Comet* (1986), ones that actively sought to generate fear out of the question: what "disaster" will come with the next comet?

After that decision, *Space Vampires* was well on its way towards fruition. With a more contemporary setting, the film was prepared with a then-whopping budget of 25 million dollars and a huge crew of some 400 artists (including a 40 man prosthetic team). Behind the scenes at Elstree Studios in England, where production of the Cannon film stretched over four giant soundstages, Hooper was teamed with cinematographer Alan Hume and special effects man John Dykstra, the Oscar-winning genius of *Star Wars* and the talent behind many effects on *Battlestar Galactica* (1978) and *Star Trek: The Motion Picture* (1979). In front of the cameras, the cast was headlined by Hooper's fellow countryman Steve Railsback of Dallas, Texas. Railsback had made a huge splash as Charles Manson in *Helter Skelter* (which co-starred Marilyn Burns!), as well as films such as *The Stunt Man*, but most modern genre audiences would probably recognize him first as "Duane Barry," the man who abducted FBI agent Dana Scully (Gillian Anderson) in the two-part *The X-Files* episodes "Duane Barry" and "Ascension."

The remainder of the cast included experienced British hands such as Peter Firth, Frank Finlay, Aubrey Morris and Patrick Stewart, later Captain Jean Luc Picard of *Star Trek: The Next Generation* (1987-94) and Professor Xavier of Bryan Singer's *The X-Men* (2000). Oddly, if there is one performer who will be forever associated with *Lifeforce*, it isn't Railsback or Stewart, but lovely Mathilda May. This beautiful, saturnine actress was cast as the alien Space Girl and promptly became the favorite "fantasy" pin-up of every adolescent sci-fi/horror fan boy the world around. Much of May's role required her to appear on-screen fully nude and in some circles *Lifeforce* has become notorious for so audaciously highlighting May's pulchritudinous charms. Once again, Hooper was pushing the envelope in mainstream film. But, just as many people misremember *The Texas Chain Saw Massacre* as gory and bloody, so did Hooper claim that *Lifeforce* actually featured the *intimation* of nudity more than graphic nudity itself:

> There is nudity, but there isn't a lot of nudity. The nudity ... was handled in the same way as the blood and gore we had in *The Texas Chainsaw Massacre*.... Most of it was in the mind's eye. It's there, but there are also shadows and motion that act as clothing, so you think you see much more than you do.... There was no way around the nudity.... We find ... humanoids in space and I couldn't ... rationalize finding them clothed [82].

Production on *Space Vampires* (not yet renamed *Lifeforce*) commenced in February of 1984 and lasted an incredible six months on over more than three dozen sets created especially for the film. The destruction of a London street was so massive a set piece that it reportedly took a month to lens the action. Other complex scenes included the simulation of weightless environments on the alien spaceship and aboard the space shuttle *Churchill* (replacing the *Hermes* of the novel). Apogee, John Dykstra's company, was charged with creating many revolutionary special effects, including the laser-like wisps that would come to be associated with the spontaneous release of human life forces. Bob Shepherd, an Apogee talent, explained the film's revolutionary effects, which were clearly one step beyond the creations of Hooper's *Poltergeist*.

> In many scenes, there is energy ... that is supposed to circulate around a room, or an actor.... Sometimes the lifeforce goes from one actor and goes out the door.... Sometimes it is ... an energy beam or energy source projected away from the actor to another actor.... I think that the way we used the laser in this picture represents something fresh. I don't know of anyone who used lasers in the way we're using them [83].

While Hooper mastered the technical effects of his sci-fi opus with the help of veterans at Apogee, his cast wasn't shy in singing his praises as a director. Steve Railsback, an actor who has never had a real fondness for science fiction or horror, felt the finalized film might help to settle some Hollywood scores:

> This film will prove that Tobe's a talented director who has unfairly taken some bum raps. *Lifeforce* will show people that he was the one who directed *Poltergeist* and that he is a filmmaker to be reckoned with [84].

When Patrick Stewart was promoted to captain of the U.S.S Enterprise, he had the opportunity to sound off to the media press about those prominent directors he had worked with in the genre, including David Lynch (*Dune* [1984]), John Boorman (*Excalibur* [1981]) and, inevitably, his *Lifeforce* compatriot, Tobe Hooper:

> ... of the movies we've been discussing, Tobe Hooper was the director to whom I got closest. I liked him very much and I admired his work. As compared with my experience with David Lynch and John Boorman, Tobe was much more accessible.... Tobe's an interesting man, very enthusiastic, very much a presence on the set. *Lifeforce* was one of the best experiences I've had as an actor [85].

Despite a set that by all accounts ran smoothly, *Space Vampires* was destined to strike trouble almost the minute principal production ended. It was decided by the powers that be at Cannon that the title *Space Vampires* sounded too exploitative and "low budget" and that a more appropriate title for the 25 million epic was ... *Lifeforce*. Hooper has gone on record in *Starlog, Fangoria, Cinemfantastique* and other periodicals stating his opinion that as a title *Lifeforce* sounded too pretentious, lacking the sense of fun that *Space Vampires* offered. On the other hand, *Lifeforce*, like *Poltergeist*, was a snappy one-word title of the variety that seemed to be all the rage in the genre in 1985 (*Cocoon* and *Explorers* are just two additional examples).

If the title switch wasn't disconcerting enough, Hooper's new film (which ran 116 minutes) was recut three times at Cannon without the director's final approval, resulting in an abbreviated 99 minute, R-rated release that pleased almost no one. Tri-Star distributed the picture and ran trailers for it before such fare as *Rambo: First Blood Part 2*, but few people in the summer of 1985 bothered to find out what the title actually meant. Disappointingly, the film tanked at the box office. Critics—never particularly kind to horror films anyway—were quick to write off its spectacular production values and dismiss the merits of the movie altogether.

The box office and critical reception of *Lifeforce* was disturbing to say the least, but even worse, some of those who had collaborated with Hooper on the film began a round of very public finger pointing and second-guessing about the movie's perceived failure. Prime among those who spoke out against *Lifeforce* was Colin Wilson, author of the source material, *Space Vampires*:

> *Lifeforce* was the worst film ever made.... If you launch into a film in the middle, there's nowhere to go, you've started too high. *King Kong* starts off nice and slowly and you don't see the monster until halfway through the movie ... well this thing has effects in the first five minutes. Just no good [86].

This was a peculiar criticism to make regarding Hooper's adaptation because the first half of the production rather closely mirrors the events of Wilson's book, including the discovery of the space ship, the expedition aboard *the Stranger*, the appearance of the Space Girl and her eventual escape from the Space Research Centre in London. Also, it would be mighty difficult to faithfully film Wilson's novel without effects "in the first five minutes" since all of the book's start-up action occurs in outer space, aboard space crafts such as *Hermes* and *The Stranger*! To feature no effects in the first five minutes would not only have been silly and untrue to the source material, but impossible. And, though some characters from the book were indeed eliminated in the film (including Carlsen's wife and a nosy reporter named Seth Adams), the tenor of the film and novel were otherwise very close. Much of the straight-faced dialogue featured in the film, so roundly excoriated by critics (such as "Use my body!" and "a naked girl won't get far..."), are actually transcribed word-for-word from the novel. Though Wilson is certainly entitled to voice his opinion on the matter, one wonders why he specifically faulted the first half of the film, which was rather faithful to his work, rather than the last half, which deviated seriously from the climax of *Space Vampires* with its focus on ambulatory zombies.

Others were able to look at *Lifeforce* with a bit more objectivity. Don Jakoby, co-writer of the film with O'Bannon, offered his carefully considered postmortem:

> *Lifeforce* has ... strong moments where it almost becomes lyrical, and that's to Tobe's credit. *Lifeforce* is a big movie and looks it. The film has ... intelligence as it moves over thin ice very swiftly. And that's a credit to the script. It tracks, it makes sense, and is very interesting for awhile, but then there are problems.... There are times when the actors rattle, overlapping their dialogue.... Tobe did a marvelous job with it, but it's not appropriate throughout [87].

Even John Dykstra, who had labored so hard and long on the film's amazing optical effects, found points of fault on *Lifeforce*. He was particularly upset by the lab's optical processing of his extraordinary visuals:

> *Lifeforce* was probably the worst patch-up job of timing ... in a movie I've ever seen in my life. Bad! Every print—the 70 mms were worse.... Terrible. There was stuff we had worked on for a long time that came out looking awful because they didn't time it right ... they paid good money for those effects and it's wrong for them to be destroyed by somebody's lack of concern [88].

In toto, *Lifeforce* ended up being slammed from all directions. Hollywood had apparently decided that Hooper needed a "comeback" after *Poltergeist* (which was a monster hit) because of the Spielberg rumors, but then quashed any chance that his follow-up, *Lifeforce*, would receive a fair shake. Cannon recut and retitled his work, the film laboratory mangled the film's spectacular effects and even the movie's story was criticized by its originator, though it was quite faithful to the source material. Only when the film finally arrived on home video did *Lifeforce* get the audience it deserved and begin gaining momentum—and a cult following. The film aired on the Sci Fi Channel on November 10, 2001.

In analyzing why *Lifeforce* failed to connect with critics at the time of its release, it isn't necessary to look far. For whatever reason—and it might even be dubbed "The Spielberg Effect"—some film critics in the '80s proved openly hostile to genre films that featured malevolent aliens. The new wave of "feel good" aliens seen in *Close Encounters*, *E.T.* and *Cocoon* had, apparently, spoiled them. As a result, two of the most interesting and finely crafted horror films of the decade, John Carpenter's *The Thing* and Tobe Hooper's *Lifeforce*, received criticism out of all proportion to their flaws. They were run out of theaters and badly maligned, but time has been their greatest vindicators. Like *The Thing*, *Lifeforce* has risen dramatically in critical estimation over the years, elevated even to the status of a classic. With its obsessive romance, blatant eroticism (unusual for a major genre release) and "disease metaphor" in the pattern of alien "infection," the film spoke more clearly about the dreads of the time (specifically the

Was it good for you? The Space Girl (Mathilda May) gets the point from Carlsen (Steve Railsback) in Tobe Hooper's *Lifeforce* (1984).

developing AIDS epidemic) than critics had heard on its original release. Today, even the film's detractors note the film's sense of pace, its gonzo-energetic direction and its go-for-the-throat, no-holds-barred set pieces. Still, that's slim comfort for Tobe Hooper, who had to wait a good fifteen years for the world to catch up with *Lifeforce*.

Return of the *Invaders from Mars*

In the late 1970s and 1980s, a new generation of baby boomer filmmakers dominated the American multiplexes like the Caesars of Rome. Importantly, it was a generation that had grown up on the genre films of the 1950s and loved them, even the productions that had been ignored by the mainstream. It is not surprising then that a rash of "sci-fi" remakes came along during the same span that brought these new artists, the "wise guys," to prominence. Philip Kauffman remade Don Siegel's *Invasion of the Body Snatchers* (1956) in 1978. John Carpenter remade Howard Hawks and Christian Nyby's *The Thing* (1951) in 1982. David Cronenberg remade *The Fly* (1958) in 1986. Chuck Russell remade *The Blob* (1958) in 1988 and Tobe Hooper directed a remake of William Cameron Menzies' *Invaders from Mars* (1953) in 1986. Ironically, the very people for whom the filmmakers had intended these remakes, specifically the boomer generation, attacked many of the revamps vociferously. By contrast, the younger audience (the one that didn't have a blind, generational devotion to the source material) responded more enthusiastically to the restructured, rethought material.

For the younger generation, Kauffman, Carpenter, Russell and Hooper drastically improved on the low-budget, B-movie material of the 1950s, but that's not an opinion likely to be heard so long as boomers continue to dominate media soapboxes.

At the risk of infuriating the genre old-timers, it is not hard to detect that William Cameron Menzies' original *Invaders from Mars* (1953) is one of the science fiction genre's sacred cows. It is a deeply flawed film rife with stilted performances, risible dialogue and oppressive use of stock and repeated footage (even at a sparse running time of 78 minutes). Yet the original *Invaders from Mars* is also a strikingly photographed and designed genre film, more interesting for how it looks and feels than how it actually plays. While noting its many flaws, genre critic John Baxter also praised it as a "remarkable exercise in sf cinema" (89). Similarly, it is listed as one of 20 greatest science fiction films in *Twenty All-Time Great Science Fiction Films*. Critics and audiences alike responded to Menzies' unique decision to film the movie from the psychological perspective of a disenfranchised child. Thus the film's main character (a boy who is "alienated" from his parents when Martians land in his backyard and turn them into soulless zombies) wanders about on oversize, minimalist sets that represent a child's isolation from the out-of-proportion adult world. This was a creative and inspired way to make a movie and few can deny the film's emotional power or visual appeal, a triumph of style and set design over substance.

Much like *The Texas Chain Saw Massacre*, the original *Invaders from Mars* feels like an unending nightmare and seems to prey on audiences on an almost subconscious level. That said, the make-up in the film is tacky (with zippers on the Martian drones blatantly obvious) and stock footage of the United States Army oppressively cut into the proceedings to bring the film up to an acceptable running time. Given the film's combination of flaws and strengths, it seemed a perfect venture to remake in the 1980s. After all, why remake a nearly perfect film (like *Planet of the Apes* [1968] or *The Haunting* [1963])? The only valid reason to mount a remake is to keep intact what was good about a production the first time around, whilst simultaneously avoiding the pitfalls of the original. If there are no pitfalls, what's the point?

When Tobe Hooper signed on to film the 12 million dollar remake of *Invaders from Mars*, the second film in his three-picture deal with Cannon, he was acutely aware of the challenges before him:

> I considered all of the possible remake pitfalls and then developed my own formula for this project that, at least in my mind, diffuses those dangers. The first thing is not to throw away the baby with the bath water and destroy what was really good in the original either in spirit or actuality [90].

That outline resulted in a film that was faithful in plot and character to the original, but quite different in tone. The basic story of *Invaders from Mars*, that of a boy isolated, was to remain intact, as was the film's dream-structure. But where Menzies had made the original *Invaders from Mars* a creep-fest of alienation and minimalism, Hooper opted for a satirical, fantastical approach. The boy's parents, when zombified, began to act like "yuppies" and the boy, a latch key kid used to fending for himself, had to save them. The creature and spaceship designs were to be the best money could buy, but more fantastical than creatures in such counterparts as James Cameron's gritty *Aliens*. In short, the Martians, part of the boy's adolescent dream perspective, were whacked out: all giant maws with serrated teeth, spindly legs and bulbous bodies. This was a good gamble because Hooper assumed that those who had seen the original movie would return to the remake with "grown-up" tastes. Instead of appealing to their "jolt" scare reflexes, he gave them something to think about instead, almost a parody, while the younger audience, unfamiliar with the source material, would find the paranoia trip a suspenseful one.

In keeping with his history of homage, Hooper also sought to honor the memory of director William Cameron Menzies and the original film, restaging much of the 1953 version's classic imagery, particularly the winding white fence and the sloping hill behind it, the secret hiding place of the Martians:

> The things that I loved about the first film were Menzies' things, things that burned holes in my brain as a child: the mother and the father going up the trail to the sandpit, the imagery of the house itself, the shots that emphasized the child's point of view. I didn't want to change the things I love about the film. It is, after all, partly a dedication to Menzies [91].

But if Hooper's mission statement was clear, getting it down on paper in script form proved to be a difficult task. *Lifeforce* scribes Don Jakoby and Dan O'Bannon were hired to write the original draft, which featured a flashback structure and had young David Gardner being a recent arrival in town, making his task of convincing the adult world of the Martian invasion doubly difficult. This draft was followed by a rewrite by Stuart Schoffman. In fact, there were three such rewrites by Schoffman. Then, complicating the matter further, two assistant directors, David Womark and David Lipman, also took a shot at the script (92). The final credits on the film noted the original screenplay by Richard Blake (from 1953) and acknowledged the team who had started on the project: Dan O'Bannon and Dan Jakoby.

Once the issue of the screenplay was settled, the cast was selected. Karen Black of *Easy Rider* (1969) joined Louise Fletcher of *One Flew Over the Cuckoo's Nest* (1975), Timothy Bottoms of *The Last Picture Show* (1971), *Saturday Night Live* (1975—) comedienne Laraine Newman, original *Invaders* star Jimmy Hunt and *Poltergeist* alumnus James Karen. Black's nine year old son with acclaimed writer L.M. Kit Carson, Hunter Carson, landed the starring role of the boy in crisis, David Gardner, after receiving great reviews for his role in Wim Wenders' *Paris, Texas* (1985). Carson, a straightforward and brilliant child who was still dealing with his parents' divorce (93), was to prove the heart of the film.

Production on *Invaders from Mars* commenced in Southern California. The Gardner home was located in Malibu Canyon State Park, but the creepy hillside scenes were all stage-bound interiors, filmed at Hollywood Center Stages, formerly the Zoetrope facility operated by Francis Ford Coppola. The interiors of the Martian ship, sweeping, massive sets with extraordinary music and video-like lighting called Vari-Lite, were filmed at Terminal island (94). Behind the camera, cinematographer Daniel Pearl, Hooper's comrade-in-arms on *The Texas Chain Saw Massacre* and the Billy Idol video "Dancing with Myself," was responsible for the picture's composition and worked closely with the director:

> There are several points in the picture where we go for shots very similar to those found in the first film. Hooper and I have an excellent rapport. Our minds frequently click on the same images and we tend to fall in love with them even though there's often pressure to abandon shots—especially trick shots—because they take up more time. But these are the types of shots that we both take delight in conceiving and executing [95].

Invaders from Mars wrapped up production on schedule and on budget, but fared badly when released in the summer of 1986 against the more adult, more intense *Aliens*. Like another casualty of that summer, John Carpenter's *Big Trouble in Little China*

(1986), the Hooper film had a lackluster advertising campaign and spotty distribution, and audiences stayed away in droves, despite glowing reviews from the *New York Times*, the *New York Post*, the *Los Angeles Times* and others. *Invaders from Mars* also found disfavor from its intended audience: science fiction aficionados, many of whom felt the film's humor and fantasy qualities didn't do service to the scariness they remembered in the original film. *Invaders* was nominated for the 1987 Razzie Award for worst supporting actress (for Louise Fletcher) and worst visual effects. But that was just part of the bad news. When the box office receipts were counted, Tobe Hooper's remake had grossed only 5 million dollars on its theatrical run, not even half the cost of the film. After *Lifeforce*, *Invaders from Mars* was Hooper's second very expensive financial failure.

Twice Upon a Texas Chainsaw....

Despite the failure of *Invaders from Mars*, Tobe Hooper remained a busy filmmaker in 1986. After finishing the editing of his Martian remake, Hooper was enlisted by Cannon's Golan and Globus to direct *The Texas Chainsaw Massacre Part 2,* the pre-sold (to more than a thousand theaters) sequel to his worldwide horror hit. At first, Hooper had intended only to produce the sequel, handing directing reins over to another artist, but Cannon wanted the film fast to cash in on the current horror boom exemplified by other successful "franchise" pictures in the *Nightmare on Elm Street* and *Friday the 13th* series. As a result of the crushing rush to usher the new *Chainsaw* (now one word) to theaters, there was almost no time for pre-production preparation and even less to write a script. Hooper's familiarity with the material became a paramount asset and he agreed to direct the picture himself.

In the thirteen years since *Chain Saw*'s release, the original film had gained genuine cult status and made a lot of money. However, it was also a project that left behind a sour residue for some of its more notable participants. Gunnar Hansen, Edwin Neal and others involved in the gruesome original felt under-rewarded for their fine work and agreed to return for a sequel only if they were well-compensated, not an unreasonable request considering their unique contributions to a great film. Hooper reportedly wanted the original actors back in the saddle too, despite bad blood and some battles in the press, but it was not to be. Instead, the sequel, if anything, just made the already aggravated situation much more bitter. The root of the problem was, as always, money. The new *Chainsaw* film, being made almost literally on the fly in a five-to-six week shoot, had a budget of only 2.5 million dollars (which reportedly skyrocketed to 6 million). Much of that funding was going to established star Dennis Hopper (playing a Texas Ranger), the film's only name player, and to make-up guru Tom Savini's creations, the best artist in the industry. Edwin Neal's agent reportedly asked for $45,000 dollars to cement Neal's participation and Gunnar Hansen was reportedly offered 10 percent *less* than industry scale by Cannon (96). In both situations, Cannon didn't come up with sufficient funds to return these, or cast members Marilyn Burns and John Dugan, to the fold. The picture was instead recast and made without them. The only *Chain Saw* veteran to return was Jim Siedow, who had appeared as Cook in the '73 film and was willing to reprise the role. In Hansen's (masked) place as Leatherface was Bill Johnson, and Neal's character, who had died in the original, was replaced by Chop Top (Bill Moseley), a sibling who had been stationed in Vietnam during the events concerning Sally Hardesty and her friends. Ken Evert assumed the role of Grandpa under a great deal of make-up.

Production on *The Texas Chainsaw Massacre Part 2* was not all smooth sailing. Writer L.M. Kit Carson, who had replaced Kim Henkel as the *Chainsaw* scribe in residence, was forced to rewrite on the set during many occasions and an inept second unit crew resulted in the scuttling of the film's major "blood" set-piece (a clan attack on yuppies, including Texas film critic Joe Bob Briggs, in a parking garage). Kerry O'Quinn, editor of *Starlog*, visited the set and made the following report on the conditions there:

> The pressure was on him [Tobe Hooper]. Cannon Films was demanding that lost time be made up and that the movie be ready for release by late August—a schedule that seemed impossible to me.... But Tobe was not barking at people and showed no visible signs of the 12-hour-a-day, seven-day-a-week marathon that he had lived since the first day of May. Tobe ... was a man totally in control of his production—aware of everything—answering questions—remembering things—helping, solving, creating [97].

The picture was finished on time, but another danger laid in wait. The M.P.A.A. refused to grant the intense sequel an R rating. Rather than go out with an X, the kiss of death for a commercial film, Cannon released *The Texas Chainsaw Massacre Part 2* without a rating, the same approach taken with *Dawn of the Dead* in 1979 and *Evil Dead 2: Dead by Dawn* in 1986. The only problem is that there are certain newspapers and certain movie theaters that refuse to go near an unrated film. That meant fewer theaters showing the picture, less advertisement, and so on. In the end, it also meant that *Texas Chainsaw Massacre 2* received less attention than it should have, though mainstream film critics tended to like it much in the manner they appreciated *Invaders from Mars*, as a genre parody, brimming with social commentary and unexpected humor. For horror fans that like their blood and guts pre-modern instead of post-modern, a smart, witty *Texas Chain Saw Massacre* wasn't exactly what they had in mind. Adding insult to injury, *The Texas Chainsaw Massacre* sequel was sent out to theaters in a form that Hooper didn't have the final say over:

> I haven't had final cut on a movie since the original *Chain Saw*. It disturbs me that, for the most part, my movies have not been shown the way they were intended because of someone's fantastic wisdom.... With *Chainsaw 2*, I felt the audience wanted and expected more than we had given them in 1974. Although I don't feel we went over the top, we still couldn't get a rating [98].

In 1998, more than ten years after the release of the second *Chainsaw*, reporter Marc Savlov for the *Austin Chronicle* asked Hooper about the making of the film. By then, Hooper had used the decade for reflection and was able to identify what worked in the bloody sequel and what didn't. In particular, he felt the film sought to obey two masters. On one hand, the story was funny and witty (at Hooper's behest), yet on the other, the gory special effects were incredibly realistic and disturbing. Those two points didn't necessarily fit together, as he explained:

> I'll be honest; I feel that the film came out of my frustration at the comedy in the first film not being appreciated or understood. And so I amplified the comedic aspects, but at the same time Tom Savini made everything so anatomically correct and cost so much, that, you know, the film ended up not even getting a rating. I like the film as this wacky, crazy, bizarre over-the-top comedy, but it missed its mark ... [99].

The Texas Chainsaw Massacre Part 2, the story of Texas Ranger Lefty Enright and his battle with the Leatherface clan, failed to live up to box office expectations, but worse, it seemed to seal the coffin on Tobe Hooper's film career. In the four years since *Poltergeist*, he'd directed three pricey feature films and had not even a single box office success. *Lifeforce* (cost: 25 million), *Invaders from Mars* (cost: 12 million) and *The Texas Chainsaw Massacre Part 2* (cost: 6 million) were financial disappointments, even though many critics had praised some of the efforts. It was a staggering blow to Hooper's opportunities in Hollywood and now he had a track record of disaster equal to his one-two-three track record of success (*Chain Saw*, *Salem's Lot* and *Poltergeist*). Hooper's three-picture deal with Cannon was mercifully finished and the days of that company were numbered. Thanks to several overblown, over budgeted failures such as *Superman IV: The Quest for Peace* (1986), *Masters of the Universe* (1987) and Sylvester Stallone's arm-wrestling opus *Over the Top* (1987), Golan and Globus was forced to declare Chapter 11 bankruptcy as the eighties gave way to the nineties.

Coming Soon to a Television Near You ...

For Tobe Hooper, the late 1980s were a time for serious contemplation, to reconnect with audiences, and he settled down to work on smaller projects. He directed the forty-fourth and final episode of Steven Spielberg's anthology series for NBC, *Amazing Stories*, an episode entitled "Miss Stardust." Some people in the press speculated that the assignment was designed to "mend fences" (100) between the two artists after the *Poltergeist* controversy. The episode, a zany installment about aliens in a beauty contest, aired on April 10, 1987 (101), and starred many of Hooper's movie entourage, including old friends Jim Siedow, Laraine Newman, and James Karen. Also in the cast was Weird Al Yankovic.

The following year, Hooper won accolades for an unusually sober contribution to a nongenre action-adventure series. On March 16, 1988, a Hooper-helmed episode of *The Equalizer* (1985-89) aired on CBS. The series, concerning an ex-secret agent named McCall (Edward Woodward of *The Wicker Man* [1971]) righting wrongs in New York City, had been on for some years at that point and had proven to be a successful bit of escapism cum vigilantism. Hooper's episode, however, was a deliberately provocative statement about an unemployed, homeless family facing victimization from criminals in the seamy Times Square of the late 1980s. Written by Robert Eisele, this installment of *The Equalizer* starred Michael Rooker, Matthew Stamm, Michael Lerner and recurring guest Keith Szarabajka; the episode was highlighted by the *New York Times*. Reviewer John J. O'Connor spotlighted Hooper in his review, noting that the episode was "directed leanly yet pointedly by Tobe Hooper" and that it was "tough" (102) in its commentary. It may not have been the kind of acknowledgment a feature film director longed for, but for an episode of an ongoing (and late in its run) series to be singled out by the most important newspaper in the world was no small deal either. For one thing, his work on *The Equalizer* demonstrated that Tobe Hooper could work outside the restrictions of the horror and sci-fi genres.

Late in 1988, Hooper received another honor. He was recruited by New Line Cinema and Warner Brothers Television to direct the first episode of a new syndicated series based on Wes Craven's *A Nightmare on Elm Street* icon, Freddy Krueger. The series was called *Freddy's Nightmares: A Nightmare on Elm Street, the Series* (1988–90) and Hooper's pilot "No More Mr. Nice Guy" was the Krueger story fans had longed to see since the first picture. The TV pilot depicted how the suburban town of Springwood performed its own "vigilante" justice on the criminal Krueger, transforming him from human monster (child molester and murderer) to inhuman, spiritual avenger. One of the few episodes of the series to actually focus on Freddy himself rather than feature him merely as host, "No More Mr. Nice Guy" aired the week of October 9, 1988, and starred Hooper's pal from *Eaten Alive* in 1976, Robert Englund. Hooper's episode, like most installments of the series, was made on the cheap (and looks as if it was shot on home video). Worse, the underwhelming teleplay by Michael De Luca, David Ehrman and Rhet Topham blatantly contradicted much of the Krueger history established by Craven's horror classic. Though Hooper executed some interesting shots, including some point-of-view subjective camera from Freddy's perspective, the episode is pretty weak by any objective standard. The series ran for 44 episodes (two seasons) and was never very popular. Hooper didn't return to helm additional stories, but found other "short form" outlets for his talents, including *Tales from the Crypt* (1991), and *John Carpenter Presents Body Bags* (1993)

Tobe Hooper *Spontaneously Combusts*

If *Freddy's Nightmares*' "No More Mr. Nice Guy" failed to adequately showcase Tobe Hooper's talents, his next feature film, *Spontaneous Combustion*, was an even worse vehicle, bordering on incoherent at times. The 1989 movie was budgeted at 6 million dollars, starred the talented Brad "Chucky" Dourif, Melinda Dillon, John Cypher and Dick Butkus, and concerned a man (Dourif) with the curious ability, courtesy of prenatal exposure to atomic radiation, to generate red-hot fire from his body. Featuring cameos by fellow director John Landis (who was afforded a show-stopping, fiery death scene) and Hooper himself (glimpsed in a restaurant bathroom), the movie was a difficult shoot, with much rewriting of the screenplay apparently done on the set. The final result was a picture featuring some extraordinary special effects, and some B-movie highs, but it pleased few critics. Re-

A publicity still from the CBS series *The Equalizer* starring Edward Woodward. Tobe Hooper directed a well-received episode of the series in early 1988.

ports are contradictory concerning the film's distribution. Some sources indicate it received a limited theatrical run while others note it was shunted directly to video. Brad Dourif discussed the movie, and its failings, with reporter Kyle Counts for *Fangoria*, shedding light on what went wrong:

> ... my feeling is, the producers destroyed it. Tobe could have made three different movies with the material he had, and each would have worked. But by the time he got it, it had changed from a love story to

a suspense thriller about my character's paranoid fantasy, to a 'guy goes crazy' film about this insane killer who becomes a destructive force that's going to wipe out mankind.... The beginning of the film was great, and a certain portion of my stuff was fine, but then it became stupid [103].

Though the film was a failure, mostly unnoticed, some prominent genre critics noted *Spontaneous Combustion*'s B movie zeal. John Stanley, author of the popular *Creatures Features Movie Guide* and one of the genre's most respected chroniclers, noted that the film was "intense" and that "one gets the feeling that writer-director Tobe Hooper was expressing his personal anger against Hollywood" (104). Overall, he gave the movie three stars. While it is true that the movie features some astonishing special effects work and intense pacing, its narrative clarity leaves much to be desired. Today, few people remember the film at all.

Following *Spontaneous Combustion*, Tobe Hooper directed Madchen Amick, Anthony Perkins, Dee Wallace Stone and R. Lee Ermey in the USA Network TV-movie entitled *I'm Dangerous Tonight*. Adapted from a short story by Cornell Woolrich and featuring a screenplay by *Buck Rogers* (1979-1981) producer Bruce Lansbury and Philip John Taylor, *I'm Dangerous Tonight* concerned an Aztec cloak possessed by the ancient evils of human sacrifice. Told in the "teens in jeopardy" mileu popularized so many years earlier by *The Texas Chain Saw Massacre* and *Halloween*, the film also mirrored the structure of Cinderella. Lead Madchen Amick, once possessed by the cloak-turned-party dress, became liberated from her "wicked" stepfamily. Other than a few interesting touches, the film was markedly routine and the same John Stanley who had praised *Spontaneous Combustion* noted that the TV film was a "low water mark" for Hooper (105). Perhaps, but that was the same year that Hooper directed a TV special entitled *Haunted Lives: True Ghost Stories*, another candidate for that title. This hour-long "based on fact" special featured a ghost inhabiting a toy store, one who had to be convinced to "go into the light" (just like in *Poltergeist*!) The other two stories in the TV show were run of the mill ghost stories, later the fodder of series such as *Sightings*, or *Encounters*.

Also in 1990, *The Texas Chainsaw Massacre* franchise went on without its original director. *Leatherface: The Texas Chainsaw Massacre Part III* was written by noted sci-fi author David Schow and directed by Jeff Burr. Viggo Mortenson (of 1998's *Psycho*), Kate Hodge (*She-Wolf of London* [1990]) and *Dawn of the Dead*'s Ken Foree starred in the film, and R.A. Mihailoff portrayed the title character, Leatherface. The film (clocking in at around 80 minutes) was badly cut up to merit an R-rating and didn't seem a good fit with the earlier two entries. Leatherface, still alive and well despite his disembowelling at the end of *Chainsaw 2*, had moved in with a new family of psychos and was up to his old tricks, cutting up unwary road trippers and burying the bones in a nearby swamp. In the new family, Leatherface even had a mother and a little sister! The film was violent but mostly lacking in the wit artists Kim Henkel, L.M. Kit Carson, Tobe Hooper, Edwin Neal, Jim Siedow and Bill Moseley had so skillfully brought to the long-standing Grand Guignol franchise. The most inventive aspects of the film were its ad line ("the saw is family") and the trailer, which aped John Boorman's 1981 Arthurian fantasy, *Excalibur*. In the brief teaser, a silver chainsaw emerges from a lake to take its rightful place in the hand ... of Leatherface.

Despite the continuation of his "baby" in the hands of new parents, the nineties were proving to be a less than stellar decade for Tobe Hooper following the failure of his latest feature film and the generic nature of *I'm Dangerous Tonight*. In 1991 he directed a segment of HBO's popular horror anthology *Tales from the Crypt* for executive producers Richard Donner, David Giler, Walter Hill, Joel Silver and Robert Zemeckis. His entry, "Dead Wait," came during the long-running show's third season and starred Whoopi Goldberg, John Rhys-Davies, James Remar and Vanity. The plot concerned "voodoo" and was written by series writers A.L. Katz and Gilbert Adler.

In 1992, Hooper took out time for fun, appearing in a cameo in Mick Garris's *Sleepwalkers* with fellow directors John Landis and Joe Dante, before teaming up with friend and horror legend John Carpenter for another cable TV project, Showtime's *John Carpenter Presents Body Bags*. The pilot for a proposed anthology (to compete with *Tales from the Crypt*) was a trilogy of short horror stories in the vein of the EC comics Hooper had enjoyed so much as a child. Produced by Dan Angel and Sandy King and written by Dan Angel and Billy Brown (later to create the Fox anthology *Night Visions* [2001]), *Body Bags* starred Carpenter as a ghoulish mortician. Tobe Hooper also appeared briefly as a surgeon to introduce the stories along with guest Tom Arnold. The cast of the film included fellow horror directors Sam Raimi, and Wes Craven (as the Pasty Faced Man) as well as performers Alex Datcher, David Naughton, Stacy Keach, and Deborah Harry. Carpenter opted to direct the first two installments, "The Gas Station" (about a serial killer outside of a town called Haddonfield) and a satire about vanity called "Hair." Hooper took the climactic story, "Eye," starring Mark Hamill, Twiggy, and John Agar. The story was an old chestnut, the evil transplant, but it was also the most serious of the troika.

John Carpenter explained to *Cinefantastique* why he had chosen Hooper to helm "Eye":

> I thought of Tobe for the last one because it's psychological, edgy horror, and I'm not sure if I'm best for it. He's bringing a real edge to it—it's some of the most powerful stuff he's done since *The Texas Chainsaw Massacre*. It's very strong [106].

Carpenter's instincts proved right and "Eye" was a good note for the horror trilogy to go out on, full of dread and angst and Biblical rants. One scene came perilously close to necrophilia (another taboo that only Hooper would break) and the ending was a kind of joke based on the Scripture passage that begins with the instruction "if the eye offends thee." Though *John Carpenter's Body Bags* never went to series after its broadcast in 1993, it quickly became popular as a video rental.

Mangled...

Things went from bad to worse in 1993 when legendary producer Harry Alan Towers (*The Face of Fu Manchu* [1965], *The Brides of Fu Manchu* [1966]) *Bram Stoker's Count Dracula* [1970], *Edge of Sanity* [1988]) recruited Tobe Hooper to replace the first director on a floundering horror project entitled *Night Screams*. A soft-porn/horror flick about the Marquis De Sade and a strange cult in Egypt, the film offered Hooper the opportunity to shoot a film in Israel, a great opportunity. Furthermore, the film gave him the chance to reteam with two of his favorite actors William Finley (*Eaten Alive, The Funhouse*) and Robert Englund (*Eaten Alive, Freddy's Nightmares*). Their reteaming proved to be less than stellar however and the project changed names again (to *Nightmare*) before becoming known as *Tobe Hooper's Night Terrors*. Though Zoe Trilling was game as the young woman in jeopardy from Englund's sadistic cult, the film was muddled and slow, crosscutting between scenes of De Sade (Englund) in prison and De Sade's descendant (Englund again) attempting to sacrifice

Trilling's innocent to some Gnostic god (?). Neither good erotica nor satisfactory horror, the film was a turgid bit of work that might have been better left buried with the Gnostic artifacts featured in the film. Cannon Pictures, still trying to make it in show business despite an earlier bankruptcy, had planned to release the movie theatrically, but it was dumped to video instead. The producers attempted to sell the picture based on Englund's presence (he was still riding high as the crowning king of horror, courtesy of his appearances in the *Nightmare on Elm Street* films) and Tobe Hooper's bankable name. The movie could have been *Night Terrors* or *Night Screams*, but savvy producers knew that distinguishing horror fans would seek out the title if it were associated with Tobe Hooper's fine work in the genre. For the most part the fans were sorry they had bothered. Critics who deigned to notice the direct-to-video flick were particularly caustic in their comments about it.

Although some media outlets reported that Tobe Hooper would next helm the direct-to-video feature *The Dentist* (starring Corbin Bernsen), the *Chain Saw* director instead sought relief from *Night Terrors* in an arena that had brought him luck once before. In 1979, desperate and willing even to direct an Italian horror quickie about Jonestown, Hooper had been recruited at the last minute to direct *Salem's Lot*, a miniseries based on the novel by Stephen King. In 1993–1994, Stephen King adaptations were still hot. *Misery* (1990) had done particularly well, *The Shawshank Redemption* (1994) was in production and Hooper had even appeared in the King screenplay-turned-film *Sleepwalkers* (1992). It was with some serendipity then that Hooper stumbled across a project called *The Mangler*, based on another Stephen King short story that had appeared in his *Night Shift* collection. This time, the King adventure told of a malevolent, hungry industrial laundry-folding machine. *The Lawnmower Man* (1992), based in name only on another King story, had been hot box office, but it had angered King for using his name and so drastically altering his story. When Kevin S. Tenney (of *Witchboard* [1986] and *Witchboard 2: The Devil's Doorway* [1993]) left the project, Hooper came aboard and solicited King's approval at every step to assure that the script met with the master of horror's approval. The screenplay went through some 40 drafts and began filming its eight-week shoot in 1993 (107).

Harry Alan Towers was producing again and the decision was made to shoot the film in South Africa to save money. Robert Englund was signed to headline in *The Mangler*, even though in *Night Shift*, his character Bill Gartley had been referred to but never actually seen. A hardened cop (Ted Levine of *The Silence of the Lambs* [1991] and *Switchback* [1996]) teamed up with a William Burroughs–like medical photographer (Jeremy Crutchley) and a friend with knowledge of the occult (Daniel Matmor) to save a 16 year old virgin (Vanessa Pike) from being spoon-fed to the Mangler by the diabolical Englund. The titular machine was designed and built by Hooper's son William and it was a masterpiece of art design. This giant machine, arcane, industrial, mammoth and terrifying, was a good centerpiece in the film's sweatshop locale. The only problem was that the film's heart-pounding, intense finale required the machine to sprout legs and chase after its victims. Hooper explained to *Sci Fi Entertainment* that such a stunt was easier to perform on paper than on the set:

> I had about three days of shooting left when we shot that [mechanical metamorphosis] and it just didn't work. The thing stood up and fell apart.... Luckily our back-up plan, to go with a computer graphics transformation, turned out better than I'd ever hoped. While they were doing the effects, I dropped in on them every day to make my suggestions, they'd take them and add to them — subtleties of

movement ... to just give that added dimension of reality [108].

Tobe Hooper, the low budget Texas filmmaker who had made his name on grainy filmstock and gritty filmmaking, had entered the digital age.

The Mangler was released on March 3, 1995, a particularly brutal period for horror movies and one that saw the financial smashing of films such as *Village of the Damned* (1995), *In The Mouth of Madness* (1995) and others. Hooper's effort was advertised with the ad-line: "From the three masters of horror, the ultimate tale of terror is about to begin." The idea that Hooper, King and Englund were collaborating on a horror film was not enough to draw in the audiences however, and critics were savage in their reviews of the picture. Though *The Mangler* was released in over 1000 theaters, its final box office tally was a pathetic $1,781,383 dollars (109), far less than the film's budget. *The Mangler* wasn't just a bomb, it was a full-fledged disaster, and many pundits predicted that its failure signaled the death of horror as a genre. In 1997, John Thonen wrote about *The Mangler's* nosedive at the box office for *Cinefantastique*:

> The film experienced one of the briefest and least successful major releases ... in recent memory.... The King franchise is justifiably dead but its damage to the genre lives on [110].

While critics predicted the death of the horror genre, *The Mangler* was released on video in an unrated "director's cut" with more gore and it was in this secondary format that the film began to gain some adherents. The picture, clearly no charmer, still had some interesting Hooper touches. But the writing was on the wall: Hooper had fallen from grace in the eyes of many, going from "hot" director to purveyor of bad B movies.

If Hooper found the mid–1990s to be a difficult time in his career, his partner on *The Texas Chain Saw Massacre*, Kim Henkel, was having no better time of it. He had directed the fourth installment of the franchise, *The Return of the Texas Chainsaw Massacre* (also known as *The Texas Chainsaw Massacre: The Next Generation*), but his film hadn't been released when he'd hoped, seemingly delayed forever in contractual and financial snares. Perhaps the hullabaloo had something to do with the fact that his two young stars, little-known Texans Matthew McConaughey and Renee Zellweger, had made it big in Hollywood since the picture's completion and the film didn't exactly fit the high profile of *Jerry Maguire* (1996) or *U571* (2000). After some hassle, Kim Henkel's film appeared on the video market in the late '90s and fans saw Leatherface co-habitating with his *third* family of patented Texas psychotics. Much superior to the lackluster third film in the series, Henkel's entry was directed with flair and good humor and featured some fine performances. One particularly hilarious sequence involved McConaughey's lame mechanical leg, which he controlled via a TV remote control. Zellweger, trying to escape him, got ahold of a TV remote, and before long it was a battle of clickers to see who could operate McConaughey's hydraulic knee. The scene ended with a spastic McConaughey unable to control his jerking leg. Critic Joe Bob Briggs loved these antics and called the newest *Chainsaw* "the best horror film of the 1990s," but, of course, that was before *The Blair Witch Project* was released to great acclaim.

Reborn on Television...

In the early 1990s, pre–*Scream,* horror films were dying en masse at the box office. The Stephen King "horror" adaptations (like *The Mangler*) were bombing. John Carpenter and Wes Craven movies (such as *Vampire in Brooklyn* [1995] and *In the*

Mouth of Madness [1995]) were tanking. Franchise pictures (such as *Tales from the Crypt: Demon Knight* [1995]) were virtually dead on arrival and things looked grim. Freddy, Jason and Chucky were dead, Michael Myers was on hiatus and Pinhead was circling the final ring of the toilet (along with stillborn features like *Dr. Giggles* [1993] and the atrocious *Leprechaun* [1993]). Some pundits pointed to the fact that America was finally recovering from the recession under the Clinton presidency and that, in a time of dawning prosperity, horror films were no longer "about" anything meaningful. After all, *The Texas Chain Saw Massacre* had grown out of 1970s zeitgeist, *A Nightmare on Elm Street* and *Poltergeist* out of the context of the 1980s. The 1990s were proving to be, by contrast, boring and placid. There were not yet any significant national nightmares (Columbine was still years off). Craven's *Scream* detected the detachment and violence of a generation in 1996, but that effort was still a ways off too.

Perhaps a more likely explanation for the genre's disfavor at the cinema in 1995 is that horror had found a new home: *television*. Nobody could have predicted it or expected it, but Chris Carter's superb series *The X-Files* (1993–2002) began airing good solid horror hours on the Fox Network week in and week out, starting in 1993. Not only were these efforts frightening and funny, they were better than most of the movies being made for theatrical release. The movies, which had become repetitive with stalkers and slashers and dream monsters, didn't have the advantage of this new TV series: it could change ghouls every week and never get boring. *The X-Files*, still a titan of television horror, became required viewing on Friday nights from 1993 to 1995. It was hardly worth it to shell out money at the local cinema to see inferior horror product when superior product was beaming onto the TV set for free.

It didn't take long for other TV networks to notice Fox's success with *The X-Files*. In 1995, new horror programs were being prepared to capitalize on the phenomenal drawing power of Carter's series, and Tobe Hooper, recognizing an opportunity, seized the moment. He quickly became known as the horror pilot director of choice and in two years his work launched two high-profile, expensive series, UPN's paranoia trip *Nowhere Man* starring Bruce Greenwood and, in 1996, *Dark Skies*, the story of alien abductions in America throughout the 1960s. Though each series lasted only a single season, the fact that they had gone beyond the pilot stage at all was a tribute to the talent of their director. In 1997, Hooper put his *Tales from the Crypt* and *Body Bags* experience to use directing "Panic," an episode of the short-lived HBO anthology entitled *Perversions of Science* (based on the William Gaine EC comic *Weird Science*). In the cast was his old friend from *Invaders from Mars* and "Miss Stardust," Laraine Newman.

In 1998, Hooper directed *The Apartment Complex*, a bizarre back-door pilot for the cable network Showtime. Starring Chad Lowe, Tyra Banks, R. Lee Ermey, and Patrick Warburton, the film, about a psychology graduate student encountering the strange denizens of a bizarre apartment complex, aired on Halloween of 1999. The show didn't make it to series, but it won positive notices.

In 2000, Hooper directed a white-knuckle adventure of the psychic series *The Others*, entitled "Souls on Board," again winning solid reviews for his feature-level direction in the maturing medium of television. The episode, set on a "haunted" plane in flight, was claustrophobic, stylish and of feature-film quality. In 2001, Hooper directed an episode of the new Fox anthology *Night Visions* created by *Body Bag* writers Billy Brown and Dan Angel. Hooper's entry, "Cargo" (about alien abduction), starred Jamie Kennedy of *Scream* fame and was scheduled to be aired on Thursday, September 13, 2001, but the terrorist attacks on the World Trade Center on the eleventh of the month resulted in around the clock news coverage that day. As of this writing, the episode has not been rescheduled and the series (also featuring the work of director and *Poltergeist* star JoBeth Williams) has been cancelled by Fox.

What a Croc!

Tobe Hooper's last feature film at the time of this book's publication was the direct-to-video feature *Crocodile,* a low-budget feature produced by Boaz Davidson (*Spiders* [2000]). Starring a cast of young, but game, unknowns facing off against an oversized crocodile on wild Lake Sobek, the film featured a combination of special effects styles, encompassing digital and old fashioned techniques. To shepherd this monster to the screen, KNB, the Rolls Royce of horror special effects houses, built the monster and simultaneously handled the computer generated imagery. On the set of the film, Hooper explained to *Fangoria* what had brought him back to "backwoods" horror after so many years away from chainsaws and crocodiles:

> It was the idea of doing a campfire tale again. That's basically what this is. It has this mythological background. There's a legend connected with it. Every town in America seems to have some story of a lake or woods with a monster in it. Or maybe something like the Blair Witch ... [111].

The film was released directly to video, lowering expectations for *Crocodile* significantly. But something unusual happened. The year 2000 turned out to be the year for crocodile movies. David E. Kelly had written the screenplay for a similarly themed film (about a giant crocodile on a lake) entitled *Lake Placid* (2000). That film failed at the box office and received terrible reviews. When *Crocodile* was released on video, several media circuits not only noticed the movie, they praised it, noting that the low-budget, direct-to-video effort was far superior in energy, humor and horror to the bigger budgeted Hollywood product. *Crocodile* may not be classic Tobe Hooper (in the class of *Chain Saw, The Funhouse, Salem's Lot, Poltergeist, Lifeforce, Invaders from Mars* or *Chainsaw 2*), but it is a fast-paced, fun film, a far cry from the more lugubrious, muddled efforts of the 1990s like *Night Terrors* and *The Mangler.* Horror fans, notoriously hard-headed and difficult to please, generally praised Hooper for making his crocodile picture such a fun romp (and referencing his older pictures like *Eaten Alive* and *Chain Saw*). Some of the CGI is cheesy, but the picture's insane vibe is pure Hooper. In 2001, *Crocodile* has aired on at least two occasions on the Sci Fi Channel and drawn solid ratings. It may not be the Tobe Hooper "comeback" so many admirers of the director have hoped for, but it is certainly a step in the right direction.

No Looking Back...

As the twenty-first century grows increasingly troubled and the United States launches itself into a war against terrorism, life continues after a fashion for the artists toiling in Hollywood. In 2003–04, Tobe Hooper will celebrate the thirtieth anniversary of his breakthrough movie, *The Texas Chain Saw Massacre.* His career since that blockbuster has been one of great highs and terrible lows, and even Hooper admits that his muse has not always guided him to the light. "I've made some wrong choices about what the public wanted to see" (112), he admitted candidly on one occasion.

Others have been far more harsh concerning the quality of his film output, fearing that the gory *Chainsaw 2* and *The Mangler* represent a weakening of his power and taste rather than the rigorous adherence to his stance of "no deal" with the audience, always taking the horror further:

> If gross-out is based on an aesthetic of challenge, with each new work daring to see how much more it may dare, then the mode itself must be ultimately self-consuming, reaching a point (best exemplified by some of the late Tobe Hooper) in which its challenges are so excessive they become self-defeating [113].

Indeed, the desire to constantly out-do himself seems, in some cases, to have led to a deep miscalculation in his work. *The Mangler* wasn't really very scary, but it was terribly graphic and its gore was too realistic (and sickening) for its own good. It was nausea provoking, but not fun in the manner of films like *Poltergeist* or even *Eaten Alive*. On the other hand, where is blame to be laid? Even the best director needs a judicious editor. And it is important to remember that Hooper has not frequently had control of the final shape of images in his films, and has been denied final edit on so many of them. Robert Englund, a longtime collaborator of Hooper's, believes it is this creative interference that has proven most damaging to Hooper's films and his reputation as a horror genius.

> I love Tobe—I just wish people would leave Tobe's films alone. You hire Tobe Hooper, you want to get Tobe Hooper. You don't want to shit on his creativity [114].

For Tobe Hooper the problem may simply be that he is, reportedly, the furthest thing from "the crazoid" Mansonite people expected when they saw *The Texas Chain Saw Massacre* and heard stories of the film's making:

> I've never been the kind of personality that people expect based on my earlier films. In terms of my career, I might have been better off if I was the son of a bitch people expected me to be [115].

And so, as the years pass, Hooper is left with much still undone, many visions yet to realize on film:

> I'd love to do comedy or something more mainstream, but it's a question of becoming a specialist in your field. I went through an internal war over this whole thing. I'd love to do *Dr. Zhivago*, and perhaps I will one day but once you're established as something it becomes increasingly difficult to switch. The business has long teeth. Had *Texas Chainsaw Massacre* not been as effective as it was, then who knows? [116].

Yet even if Hooper never gets to make his *Dr. Zhivago*, he has had quite a run in Hollywood. First of all he's managed the most important feat: he's *survived* three decades. And as of this writing, he's still working away (reportedly contemplating a *Chain Saw* remake with original scribe Henkel) and has a large enough (and consistent enough) body of work to merit book-length study. Many other genre directors are not nearly so fortunate, and Hooper is no flash in the pan.

Secondly, Hooper has seen his films achieve various, but valuable, tiers of success. Sure there have been the creative failures like *Spontaneous Combustion, The Mangler, Tobe Hooper's Night Terrors* and he's had those Cannon box office disappointments, but that's just not representative of the whole story. Tobe Hooper has undeniably shepherded one film masterpiece that will live as long as *Gone with the Wind* and *Casablanca* (*The Texas Chain Saw Massacre*). He's also had two mainstream successes of enduring and blockbuster status (*Salem's Lot* and *Poltergeist*) and three cult classics (*The Funhouse, Lifeforce, Eaten Alive*) and even had his share of those "intellectual" critical raves that reviewers are so stingy about writing (for *Chain Saw* and *Invaders from Mars*, particularly).

History already records Tobe Hooper as one of the giants of the genre, not just for *Chain Saw* but for his entire body of work.

Though one can wish that he might shepherd a cross-over hit like Craven's *Scream* or get the same deal Carpenter manages regularly (creative control, and a movie every two years, seemingly), it's important to remember that Hooper is still doing his thing with big budgets, solid actors and great stories. He's just doing it on TV (*Dark Skies, The Others, Night Visions*). This choice may be a critical one in the years to come when home entertainment, DVD, video, and cable come to finally eclipse adventures on the silver screen.

Whatever Hooper's final destiny (comeback kid of the twenty-first century or "merely" one of the great influences in the horror films of the '70s and '80s), his work features an admirable consistency in style and theme, and that's an accomplishment any artist can be proud to gaze back upon.

Part II
The Feature Films of Tobe Hooper

1. *The Texas Chain Saw Massacre* (1974)

Critical Reception

"There are films which skate right up to the border where 'art' ceases to exist in any form and exploitation begins, and these films are often the field's most striking successes. *The Texas Chainsaw Massacre* is one of these; in the hands of Tobe Hooper, the film satisfies the definition of art ... and I would happily testify to its redeeming social merit in any court in the country.... Hooper works in *Chainsaw Massacre*, in his own queerly apt way, with taste and conscience."
— Stephen King, *Danse Macabre*, Berkley Books, 1983, page 130.

"I think *The Texas Chainsaw Massacre* is one of the most brilliant and funny movies I've ever seen — truly an American classic ... Tobe Hooper ... really understood what he was doing."
— Robert Zemeckis, *Film Comment*, January-February 1995, page 66.

"...[T]he movie is some kind of weird, off-the-wall achievement. I can't imagine why anyone would want to make a movie like this, and yet it's well-made, well-acted and all too effective ... the movie is good technically and with its special effects ... there are bizarrely effective performances.... What we're left with is ... an effective production in the service of an unnecessary movie. *The Texas Chainsaw Massacre* belongs in the select company ... of films that are really a lot better than the genre requires."
— Roger Ebert, *Roger Ebert's Home Movie Companion*, 1993 Edition, page 656.

"Tobe Hooper's pic is well-made for an exploitation of its type ... has a professional look, with Hooper and cameraman Daniel Pearl making skillful and frequent use of dolly shots for atmospheric effect. Sharp sense of composition and careful accumulation of detail also help enliven the crude plot, and the acting is above par for this type of film."
— *Variety*, October 25, 1974.

"It is surely the most affecting gore thriller of all and, in a broader view, among the most effective horror films ever made."
— David J. Hogan, *Dark Romance — Sexuality in the Horror Film*, McFarland & Company, Inc., Publishers, 1986, page 247.

"...[A] truly distressing film, and it forces us to look at some pretty nasty truths, if not about ourselves exactly, then at least about our society ... it strips away just about every last vestige of civilized middle class values and gets right down to the pure, primal terror of being carved up by a maniac with a chainsaw...."
— Jake Horsley, *The Blood Poets: A Cinema of Savagery, 1958-1999*, Scarecrow Press, Inc., 1999, page 234-235.

"It touched that part of my brain, the primitive part, that made me realize that at some point the difference between the loving husband and doting father and a fellow with a chainsaw and evil intent, can be uncomfortably close.... It takes skill to make a wheelchair-bound victim unsympathetic, but this is managed early on, and quite soon the audience is eager to see a helpless cripple get his, even if his only crime is assholism."
— Joe R. Lansdale. *Cut! Horror Writers on Horror Films*, Berkley Books, 1992, page 149.

"...[A] landmark among horror films ... it shows a good deal of restraint, bringing style, craft and humor to the drive-in theaters ... forged with great suspense through director Tobe Hooper's expert pacing and use of humor as counterpoint ... an homage to unrestrained urges and the power of fear."
—Darrell Moore, *The Best, Worst and Most Unusual: Horror Films*, Beekman House, Publications International, Ltd., 1983, page 126.

"Despite a crippling low budget, it is even somewhat sophisticated, one of the few spawns of *Psycho* ... whose makers actually seem to have learned something from the master of suspense."
—John McCarty, *Psychos*, St. Martin's Press, 1986, page 133.

"What makes it an enduring classic is its ability to shock viewers without graphic gore. Using minimal resources to his advantage, director Tobe Hooper achieves the effect of a nightmare from which you can't wake up ... they don't make horror movies like this anymore."
—M. Faust, *Video Magazine*, December 1993, page 107.

"...[A] vile little piece of sick crap ... a film with literally nothing to recommend it: nothing but a hysterically paced, slapdash, imbecilic concoction of cannibalism, voodoo, astrology ... and unrelenting sadistic violence as extreme and hideous as a complete lack of imagination can possibly make it."
—Stephen Koch, *Harpers*: "Fashions in Pornography," November 1976, pages 108-111.

"...[D]espite its notorious and suggestive title, is not a visual bloodbath.... Rather *TCM 1* offers a clear example of ... uncanny horror: a disturbing and relentless vision of evil "out there" in the world ... the evil is localized in human form, but somehow it exceeds human instantiation and haunts the entire landscape."
—Cynthia A. Freeland, *Thinking Through Cinema. The Naked and the Undead: Evil and the Appeal of Horror*, Westview Press, 2000, page 244.

"A *reductio ad absurdium* of a horror movie ... 'unrelenting' is a good word to use here.... And yet the movie could have been more harrowing. As it stands, there's surprisingly little blood-and-gore evident. Hooper's film has a weird sort of tact. The director trusts his title and his hardware: you don't see what the awful chainsaw does. You don't need to ... the film is informed by a pristine viciousness."
—Gordon Willis, *Horror and Science Fiction Films II*, Scarecrow Press, 1982, page 393.

"Emphasizing claustrophobic terror and oppressive charnel-house atmosphere by filming everything with bloodless docudrama reality, Hooper established new levels of jaw-dropping macabre horror, forcing viewers to identify with victims as they're slaughtered...."
— *The BFI Companion to Horror*, BFI, 1996, edited by Kim Newman, page 311.

"This abattoir of a movie boasts sledgehammers, meat hooks and chainsaws, and the result, though not especially visceral, is noisy, relentless, and about as subtle as having your log sawed off without anaesthetic.... Pernicious stuff."
—Christ Petit, *Time Out Movie Guide*, Penguin, 1999, page 900.

"Unlike most of the quickie shockers, *Chain Saw* is well made. You may hate the content. I do. But it gets the job done, even if the job is to sicken you."
—Daniel Cohen, *Masters of Horror*, Clarion Books, 1984, page 111.

"Notorious, much banned, but highly influential exploitation piece whose occasional pretensions to style and humor make it seem even more revolting and sadistic."
—Howard Maxford, *The A to Z of Horror Films*, Indiana University Press, 1997, page 259.

"...[P]lot is virtually nonexistent and bloody 'special effects' are disgusting rather than frightening."
—Michael and Harry Medved, *The Golden Turkey Awards*, Perigree Books, 1980, page 219.

"Though certain puritanical critics have condemned it as a mindless exercise in gratuitous gore, the film is actually fueled by a fierce, almost Victorian, sense of morality. Rarely has a story about a grotesquely fat psychopath wearing a human skin mask while pursuing coeds with a chainsaw been depicted with such subtlety and finesse...."
—David Everett and Harold Schecter, *The Manly Movie Guide*, Boulevard Books, 1997, page 175.

"*The Texas Chainsaw Massacre* is an exemplary instance of the postmodern horror genre that constructs an unstable, open ended universe in

which categories collapse, violence constitutes everyday life, and the irrational prevails."
—Isabel Cristina Pinedo, *Recreational Terror: Women and the Pleasure of Horror Film Viewing*, State University of New York Press, 1997, page 48.

"Tobe Hooper's lurid classic combines primal Brothers Grimm and Police Gazette gore, and leaves us hooked and flailing, like one of Leatherface's victims."
—Glen Lovell, *Knight-Ridder/Tribune News Service*: "Here's my list of the 30 most thrilling movies of all time," June 11, 2001.

Cast and Crew

CAST: Marilyn Burns (Sally Hardesty); Allen Danziger (Jerry); Paul A. Partain (Franklin Hardesty); William Vail (Kirk); Teri McMinn (Pam); Edwin Neal (Hitchhiker); James Siedow (Old Man); Gunnar Hansen (Leatherface); John Dugan (Grandfather); Robert Courtin (Window Washer); William Creamer (Bearded Man); John Henry Faulk (Storyteller); Jerry Green (Cowboy); Ed Guinn (Cattle Truck Driver); Joe Bill Hogan (Drunk); Perry Lorenze (Pick-up Driver); John Larroquette (Narrator).

CREW: A Vortex/Henkel/Hooper Production. A film by Tobe Hooper. *Editors:* Sallye Richardson, Larry Carroll. *Cinematographer:* Daniel Pearl. *Production Manager*: Ronald Bozman. *Executive Producer:* Jay Parsley. *Story and Screenplay:* Kim Henkel and Tobe Hooper. *Produced and directed by:* Tobe Hooper. *Music Score:* Tobe Hooper and Wayne Bell. *Assistant Director:* Sallye Richardson. *Lighting:* Lynn Lochwood. *Assistant Cameraman:* Lou Perryman. *Location Sound Recorder:* Ted Alcolaou. *Post Production Sound/BoomMan*: Wayne Bell. *Art Director:* Robert A. Burns. *Titles and Opticals*: CFI. *Make-up:* Dorothy Pearl. *Camera Assistant:* J. Michael McClary. *Key Grip:* Linn Scherwitz. *Script Girl:* Mary Church. *Additional Photography:* Tobe Hooper. *Rerecording:* Paul Harrison. *Grip:* Rod Ponton. *Stunt Driver:* Perry Lorenz. *Stunts:* Mary Church. *Associate Producer:* Kim Henkel, Richard Saena. *Production Assistants:* Ray Spaw, Robert Pustejovski, N.E. Parsley, Sally Nicolaou, Paulette Gochnour, Paula Eaton, Charlie Loring, Jerry Bellnoski, Jim Crow, David Spaw, George Baotz, Tom Foote. *M.P.A.A. Rating*: R. *Running Time:* 84 minutes.

Advertising Lines

Who will survive, and what will be left of them?

What happened was true ... the most bizarre and brutal series of crimes in America. This is the movie that is just as real, just as close, just as terrifying as being there. After you stop screaming, you'll start talking about it....

Opening Card

The film which you are about to see is an account of the tragedy which befell a group of five youths, in particular Sally Hardesty and her invalid brother, Franklin. It is all the more tragic in that they were young. But had they lived very, very long lives, they could not have expected nor would they have wished to see as much of the mad and macabre as they were to see that day. For them, an idyllic summer afternoon became a nightmare. The events of that day were to lead to the discovery of one of the most bizarre crimes in the annals of American history, *The Texas Chain Saw Massacre*.

"You will have a disturbing and unpredictable day. There are moments when we can't believe what is happening is really true. Pinch yourself and you'll find it is."
—Franklin and Sally's foreboding "horrorscopes" in *The Texas Chain Saw Massacre* (1974).

Synopsis

On the sweltering day of August 18, 1973, young Sally Hardesty, her invalid brother Franklin, and three friends (Jerry, Pam and Kirk), drive out to rural Texas to check on the grave of Sally's grandfather. There has been a rash of grave desecrations in the area and Sally is concerned that her grandfather's grave may have been among those disturbed. After determining that there has been no tampering, the group leaves the cemetery and drives off in their green van. Inside, Pam reads from an astrology book, noting that Saturn—*a malefic force*—is in retrograde, and that its condition may impact the travelers negatively on that day.

Jerry's van passes a slaughterhouse on the road, one where Sally and Franklin's granddad used to sell cattle. The wheelchair-bound Franklin aggravates his friends by explaining, in nauseating detail, the methodology of slaughtering livestock, which includes the use of an air-gun that injects metal bolts into the brains of cattle. Not long after this conversation, Jerry stops the van to pick up a strange hitchhiker, an odd fellow with a facial disfiguration and several unsettling nervous tics. Unaware that this strange guest is actually the local grave desecrator, the kids engage the weirdo in conversation, amused. A former employee of the slaughterhouse, the Hitchhiker lost his job when the company updated the killing weapon from sledgehammer to the mechanical bolt gun described by Franklin. Now he's out of work.

The Hitchhiker grabs Franklin's favorite knife, cuts himself on his palm for no reason, and then snaps a photograph of the startled group with his Polaroid. Then he reveals a straight razor and asks to be taken to his house and paid for the photograph. The kids politely ask the increasingly erratic stranger to leave, but their visitor grows agitated and slices Franklin's arm with the rusty razor. Jerry and Kirk throw the strange Hitchhiker out of the van and continue on their way.

Unsettled, they stop for gas at an out-of-the-way barbecue and gas station. To their dismay, the cook at the establishment informs them that the station has no gas, and a transport truck won't arrive for a day or so. The kids buy some peculiar-shaped barbecue and ignore the cook's warning not to wander onto the property of the locals, who don't take kindly to strangers.

Bored, Sally and her friends decide to find the old Franklin place, the home that once belonged to their grandparents, and hang out there for the night. They drive out to a dilapidated old home on the side of the road and park in the overgrown front yard.

While Kirk, Jerry, Pam and Sally explore the house, Franklin grows angry that they have left him in the yard to fend for himself. After pushing himself up on the porch in his wheelchair, Franklin finds strange bone sculptures hanging about the old homestead. He is also disturbed because the Hitchhiker appears to have marked the van in blood.

Pam and Kirk head to the old swimming hole behind the remote Franklin place, and find it dried up. They explore a neighbor's property, thinking that they may have some spare gasoline to sell. Pam and Kirk approach an old white farmhouse. When they get no answer at the front door, Kirk opens the unlocked portal and goes inside to seek help. Pam waits outside, disturbed because she has found a human tooth on the porch.

Kirk searches the odd house for no more than a minute before a silver metal door to the kitchen slides open, and, without warning, a squealing, masked giant, Leatherface, attacks him. Leatherface smashes Kirk's head with a sledgehammer, killing him instantly. In the daze of a homicidal fever, Leatherface drags Kirk's body into the kitchen and slams the steel door behind him.

After a time, Pam follows Kirk into the house of horrors and is terrified by what she discovers. One bedroom upstairs is decorated with furniture made from human and animal bones and the way to the kitchen is decorated with a plethora of animal skulls. Alarmed to find another stranger in his house, Leatherface chases Pam, captures her, and then hangs her on a metal meat hook in the kitchen. Unluckily for her, she is still alive and conscious when Leatherface goes to work with his chainsaw, butchering Kirk like a slab of beef before her very eyes.

Back at the Franklin place, Jerry, Sally and Franklin wait for the others to return as dusk arrives. Jerry goes in search of his missing friends, leaving Franklin and Sally to quarrel about which of them last had possession of his missing knife. As sun sets, Jerry reaches the farmhouse and finds Pam's blanket there. He steps inside to investigate and finds Pam—*still alive*—stored in a large freezer. Before Jerry can save her, Leatherface clubs and kills him too.

In the pitch of night, Sally and Franklin wait at the van for any sign of their missing friends. With no keys to drive the van with and no sign of their errant companions, they go in search of Jerry and the others.

Sally grows agitated as she pushes Franklin and his heavy wheelchair through a thicket. There, the siblings are suddenly confronted by Leatherface ... who impales the crippled Franklin with the chainsaw. Sally runs for her life through the woods, chased by the mad-dog killer. She finds the farmhouse and locks Leatherface outside, but the maniac cuts down the door and pursues her relentlessly. Then Sally meets two apparently dead grandparents upstairs, perfectly positioned (and well preserved) in easy chairs.

Leatherface (Gunnar Hansen) grabs a terrified Pam (Teri McMinn) in one of the harrowing chase sequences in *The Texas Chain Saw Massacre* (1974).

She jumps out a window in horror and runs to the roadside barbecue stand for assistance. Desperate, she seeks out the helpful proprietor, but Cook is actually one of Leatherface's clan! He returns her to the house, where the crazy Hitchhiker is also returning home from a long day of grave robbing. Cook is especially upset because Leatherface has ruined the front door. He angrily wonders why Leatherface has no pride in his home.

Sally is invited to a "special" dinner in which she is to be the main course. She is tied up and gagged as an elderly—*but not quite dead yet*—Grandpa first drinks blood from her cut-up finger and then attempts to bludgeon her with a sledgehammer. At the slaughterhouse, Grandpa used to be the best killer of the bunch, but now he's past his prime, despite his family's unswerving support. Sally breaks free after Grandpa's fumbling with the killing implement and jumps through a first floor window. Bloodied but free, Sally runs for her life, making for the road beyond the farmhouse.

The Hitchhiker and Leatherface pursue Sally, and the Hitchhiker is run over by a passing truck. The truck driver, Black Maria, pauses to assist Sally, but Leatherface attacks the truck's cab with his weapon of choice, forcing Sally and her would-be savior to run for their lives. Leatherface cuts himself in the leg with the chainsaw when the truck driver strikes him in the head with a wrench.

Finally, a pickup truck stops and rescues Sally from the melee on the road. As she escapes down the highway, her grip on sanity finally shattered, the psychotic Leatherface fades away in the distance, twirling about insanely with his beloved chainsaw as the sun rises...

Commentary

Because movies are produced to appeal to the widest possible audience, truly terrifying films are difficult to make and come few and far between. In the long history of the genre, there are perhaps a half dozen productions that successfully chill and scare audiences again and again, even in the face of repeat viewing and new advances in film technology. Though taste is entirely subjective, few would argue that films on this select "best" and "most terrifying" list would likely include *The Exorcist* (1973), *Halloween* (1978), *Night of the Living Dead* (1968), *Rosemary's Baby* (1968), *Psycho* (1960) and *The Texas Chain Saw Massacre* (1973-74). Hooper's entry on the roster is one of the craziest and most intense horror films ever created, and no doubt one of the most finely crafted. It is visceral, vicious, invigorating, terrifying, and at times, quite funny (in a black sort of way). On a purely surface level, *Chain Saw* seems representative of the 1970s' "Savage Cinema" movement, a film of such hardcore, raw power (trumpeted by the title, even) that the audience recoils from the film's bluntness. Like its brethren of the "Savage Cinema," *Straw Dogs* (1971), *A Clockwork Orange* (1971), *The Last House on the Left* (1972) and *Deliverance* (1972), this is a film that cares little for sparing audience sensibilities, or about dodging dark human issues.

Yet on a much deeper level, there is an interesting method to director Tobe Hooper's madness in *Chain Saw*. Specifically, he exploits the language of film to foster the disturbing notion that man's world, his toils, his very existence, mean but little in the face of a vast, disordered and cruel cosmos. Hooper's victory is not just that he paces his film exquisitely, that his cinematographer, Daniel Pearl, is uncannily gifted with lighting and texture, or that the ghoulish details of this nightmare feel disturbingly right (courtesy of art director Robert Burns' macabre touches). On the contrary, *The Texas Chain Saw Massacre* succeeds most of all because it undercuts the traditional conventions of filmmaking, even while simultaneously understanding and exploiting the finer tenets of film grammar. Sometimes, it takes a fresh, enthusiastic voice to energize a genre, and that's the very talent Hooper brings to his breakthrough project. At the same time that he is clearly well-schooled in the arts of cutting, camera motion, staging, acting and the like, he is curious enough to prod at those techniques to see how those rules can be tweaked, stretched or shattered to surprise audiences. As a director, Hooper is akin to a "straight A" student finally released from the restrictive bounds of academia, free to go crazy and apply everything he's learned, but this time in new, exciting, and experimental ways.

Before the film proper commences, there is a title crawl and a voice-over (by *Night Court's* John Larroquette), solemnly informing the audience that the events it is about to witness are true. This claim of "truth" is the first weapon in Hooper's arsenal to unsettle viewers. He preps his audience that what it shall see "really happened," and the psychic effect of that warning is that viewers are immediately disturbed or at the very least, curious. The message is simple: *this can happen in our world, and in fact, it did*. Consciously or unconsciously, audiences respond to this statement of "fact" by identifying with the people they see on screen. These were *real* people; this *really* happened. Other films have used the same technique to foster identification, including *Last House on the Left* (1972), *The Hills Have Eyes* (1977), *The Amityville Horror* (1979) and even *The Blair Witch Project* (1999), and whatever the reason, audiences are always suckers for such (notoriously dubious) claims of verity. As Gunnar Hansen related on the DVD commentary of *Chain Saw*, for years people have stopped him and claimed that they knew "the real Leatherface." Residents of the farmhouse where the film was lensed have reported many incidents with curious tourists who want to know if their home is where "those crimes" were really committed. *The Texas Chain Saw Massacre* is *not* based on fact, but the claim that it is grants the film an immediate level of urgency and importance. It primes the audience.

Following the admittedly deceptive crawl, Hooper then plunges his viewers into complete blackness, and the soundtrack is dominated by the sounds of dirt crunching, a discordant whine (part of the music track) and then of periodic camera flashes "clicking" away. On screen, quick cuts of a rotting, decayed corpse are seen in close-up, surrounded by utter darkness. After a short span of these disgusting close-up "flashes," the first fully-lit, recognizable composition of the film is revealed: that of a body displayed atop a cemetery monument. A ghoulish work of art.

The camera originates the shot with a close-up of the corpse's goopy-looking face (replete with a full set of teeth, which gives the impression of a smile), and then pulls back to reveal that this dead body has been "posed," as if indeed a masterpiece of art. Behind and above the corpse hangs a marmalade sky, with the sun hanging low. In one sense, this sequence depicts the particulars of a grave robbing (from the shovel shifting the dirt above the corpse's plot, to the perpetrator proudly snapping photos of his handiwork), but in another, this opening gambit is evidence of Hooper's new world disorder.

The first real composition of *Chain Saw* is of the dead propped up, perched outside of a grave and positioned under the light of the sun, instead of below the earth, prostrate in the dark and gloom of the grave. The image of the posed corpse simultaneously suggests that madness reigns in this universe, and that the architect of the madness has an unconventional eye for beauty and art. For as certainly as the Hitchhiker and Leatherface are sick in their hobbies, they have an undeniable knack with arts and crafts.

At the same time that audiences are horrified at the mad world on screen, they are shaken that so many of the elements of that world reveal a new order superimposed over the predictable one. We expect wooden chairs or plastic lampshades, but in *The Texas Chain Saw Massacre*, madness has reshaped these common items into seats made of human skeletons and lamps made of human flesh. Madness has supplanted sanity. The corpse, so proudly decorating the land of the living, is the first clue that we are living in a mad, mad, mad world.

As the opening credits of *The Texas Chain Saw Massacre* roll, Hooper's camera focuses unexpectedly on close-ups of violent eruptions on the surface of our sun. The largest image in the frame is one of a red, boiling, almost "popping" sunspot. This fiery orb, randomly spitting fire and flame into space, is the next significant glimpse into Hooper's larger universe. It is not a cosmos of serenity and peace, but one of chaos and eruption. The red shade of the sun belies a kind of anger and that's also a running theme in the film. The universe is disordered, anarchic, even cruel. The sun might even be seen as one eye of the cosmos (the moon would be the other), because it is constantly "gazing" down on the activity of the film, watching from a distance. As we see in the earliest close-up of that "eye" it is disordered, explosive, red-hot and angry. Later in the film, a close-up of another orb (Sally's eyeball during the harrowing "dinner date" with Leatherface's family) reflects the same characteristics.

As the sun pops and sprays its energy millions of miles away from Earth (but in full-screen view), The *Texas Chain Saw's* oddball soundtrack reinforces the director's theme of disorder because it lacks melody of any sort. The music at this point in the film is distinctly unpleasant, all cymbal crashes and echoes; highly discordant and jarring. There is no lyrical theme running through the music, no recognizable *leitmotif*, only a jumble of ugly, seemingly random sounds strung together. Like the eruptions on the surface of the sun, the music reflects the absence of equilibrium, sanity, reason and order in this universe. Though radio news reports can be faintly heard at this point in the film, they are distinctly tertiary to the primary sound (the jarring music) and the imagery (of a sun burning hot in darkness).

Not surprisingly, the first shot of the film following the credits is yet another image that reveals how the ordered universe has become topsy-turvy. An armadillo (now only road kill) lies upside down on a hot asphalt highway, its dead arms reaching up towards the sky. Again, it can't be stressed enough that the armadillo is *overturned*, upside down, and that such a position is a long-time signifier of death in the language of cinema. More to the point perhaps, an animal shouldn't die on a road at all since the highway is a symbol of man's intelligence and his need to connect one place to another. But the animal *has* died there, because above and beyond man's sense of self-imposed order (the road), is the overriding chaos of the universe. Not long after the shot of the armadillo, a drunk is seen in the cemetery to be lying in the same position as the road kill. This strange fellow, who warns of dark secrets all around, lies with his back to the ground, his belly up to the sun. In fact, this is the movie's second "armadillo" shot: the drunk's face is upside down in the frame too, out of order, signifying again the death and horror to come.

By the time Hooper's camera finally introduces the main characters, occupying their van on the side of a Texas road, he has meaningfully undercut another sense of order. Since the birth of the medium, movies have possessed a thing called *decorum*; a specific manner of viewing things and people, and a specific methodology in storytelling. Audiences may flock to see horror films to experience fear and fright, but they never expect to see *truly* unpleasant, unappetizing or damaging things. That's why we always have in entertainment our lovely heroes and our hissable villains, our narrative resolution and closure and the ultimate defeat of evil. That's what is expected and even desired. Yet Hooper challenges such notions immediately, undercutting that sense of decorum, and film structure too.

The first scene featuring the film's young protagonists reveals the obnoxious invalid named Franklin perched in a wheelchair as he pisses into a cup on the side of the road. A truck roars by suddenly and the wind pushes this disabled youngster down a hill, where he lands flat on his face, piss can and all. On one hand, this is another overturning of order: the truck swoops in like a bird of prey and flips a human off his perch without so much as a warning. More importantly, however, the idea implied by this sequence is that Hooper's movie will feature no favorites, no bigger-than-life "stars," if you will, because that too would represent a kind of expected order; *cinematic* order. Imagine wheelchair-bound Jimmy Stewart in *Rear Window* facing such a humiliating situation. It just wouldn't happen. But here it can happen as Hooper makes abundantly plain in the staging. A disabled character takes an unceremonious spill, and the audience is shocked by such callous and surprising treatment. It is even encouraged to laugh! But regardless, the point is cleverly hammered home: these tiny, foolish people are not characters in some remote, carefully constructed drama of decorum. They are *us* and they dwell in a universe where terrible things can and do happen. Just as those things happen in real life too. Audiences are unnerved by this sequence because Hooper is laying down a challenge for them: whatever biases about movies you sat down with when you entered the theater will work against you here. Everything's up for grabs.

It is significant that Hooper has elected not to add music over Franklin's impromptu bathroom trip, but the steady sound of radio commentary instead. As Franklin sits on the precipice of a hill, trying to concentrate, on an authoritarian anchorman on the radio describes a series of discomforting news stories, all revealing a disordered, uncaring universe. A building has collapsed for no detectable reason and engineers are baffled. A double murder has occurred in Indiana and a man's genitals were removed during the crime. Foreign governments are waging violent battle over land rights. Police have arrested a couple in Dallas for locking their 18-month-old daughter in an attic. And so on. Every one of these accounts implies that a benevolent God is essentially missing in action. The universe (including the world of man) is without higher meaning, totally disordered, even cruel and monstrous. People kill each other and die for no sensible reason and the eye of the cosmos (that bubbling sun) doesn't even blink. These audio reports put Leatherface's murders into a common context beyond the borders of Texas. Violence, it seems, reigns everywhere—it is the law of the jungle, ubiquitous in man's universe.

Hooper also denies the audience their cinematic decorum (and hence order) in his choices of character executions. Kirk, the undeniable alpha male of the young protagonists, is the first person to succumb to Leatherface's sledgehammer. His early death denies the film a strong male hero figure for most of its running time. In some ways, this decision is more powerful than Hitchcock's choice to kill Janet Leigh's character in *Psycho*. Hitchcock believed in narrative structure (which Hooper flouts) and understood that he had to fill the audience's identification "gap" by creating Vera Miles and John Gavin as his new leads. Their characters were even able to experience a romance of sorts, giving the audience something to hope for and invest itself in following the death of Leigh's sympathetic Marion Crane. Hooper not only denies his audience a sentimental treatment of the disabled, he denies it a hero. The result is that the audience is put even more off balance than before. Kirk dies, and the audience almost instinctively grasps at straws. What about Jerry? He dies next and just as easily too. When he's gone, there is no "male" figure to cling to at all. Franklin is a whining weakling (and some reviews of the film have described him as a *castrato*) and so Sally is really and truly on her own. It's a grim prospect.

Hooper denies the audience something else in *The Texas Chain Saw Massacre*, something that most audiences probably aren't even consciously aware of. He denies his viewers the critical act of *learning*. Learning is essential to an understanding of a film's narrative, and an audience usually learns important facts from the story structure or through the expositional dialogue of the main characters. The narrative provides important clues even as protagonists expire, and learning continues as the plot develops. To utilize the *Psycho* example again, Janet Leigh's character died, to be sure, but along came Martin Balsam's private dick, Arbogast, to probe Norman Bates and develop the points of the plot. When he died, Loomis picked up the trail and the act of "learning" about the Bates mystery was again transferred to a new lead. There is no such learning in *The Texas Chain Saw Massacre*. Knowledge does not pass from one protagonist to the next and no acts are explained or even rationalized. Pam, Kirk, Jerry and Franklin — four of the film's five protagonists — fall to Leatherface's violence before they're even truly aware that they're in mortal danger. They are killed without learning anything, without realizing even that their friends are in danger, and so the audience doesn't learn anything either.

At the end of this film, no psychiatrist comes forward to explain that Leatherface, the Cook, the Hitchhiker and Grandpa are psychotic cannibals who form a dysfunctional family. In fact, the police don't even apprehend these lunatics and so there is no sense of closure (another form of cinematic order). *The Texas Chain Saw Massacre* denies audiences all such answers and explanation and so viewers are subconsciously troubled and frightened by this because all humans know (but deny) that life is really that way too. Why do planes crash? Why does a loved one die in a car accident? Why do bad things happen? That's the essence and the mystery of human life, and *The Texas Chain Saw Massacre*, by offering no answers, mirrors that uncomfortable reality. Again, the audience is left with the notion that *this is life*; this is real. It is an effective conceit, and a terrifying one.

Hooper's film technique reinforces these ideas in some innovative ways. Beautiful compositions of order overturned dominate many frames of *The Texas Chain Saw Massacre*. Upon entering the abandoned Franklin home, spiders are seen swarming in a corner of a ceiling. They have overrun their web, yet another symbol of order. Like the dead armadillo on the road, the image of another "road" (a spider's web) is shown marred by chaos (by teeming, skittering daddy-long-legs). Later, Pam and Kirk decide to go swimming, but instead of finding a watering hole, they discover only dry earth. Again, expectations are pointedly overturned. Where life should be is death instead, and events seem totally random. They go to the gas station expecting gas, but it's out of gas. They go to the swimming hole expecting water, but it's dry. They go to the friendly looking farmhouse down the lane expecting help but find only insanity and death. Those surprises are very important to understanding this remarkable film.

At other important points in *The Texas Chainsaw Massacre*, Hooper takes special pains to accentuate the vastness of the universe around his young characters. It is crit-

1. *The Texas Chain Saw Massacre* (1974)   59

The Hitchhiker (Edwin Neal) terrorizes Sally Hardesty (Marilyn Burns) with the farmhouse's ghoulish decoration in the background, in *The Texas Chain Saw Massacre* (1974).

ical to establish this because Hooper apparently sees Sally and her friends much as those very characters view the spiders in the web or the cows locked away in the slaughterhouse. They're little, meaningless creatures running around in their lives with a sort of tunnel vision, unable to see that they inhabit a much larger and terribly frightening domain. As human beings, we visit the bank, mow our lawns, eat dinner, or do a hundred "normal" and "routine" things ... while unaware that a tornado could be approaching, or that a serial killer could be roaming the very neighborhood where we live. But we impose a false sense of order (and hence security) in our everyday existence, and Tobe Hooper's *modus operandi* is to strip all that away and reveal that nothing separates us from the cows or the spiders, or the armadillos. We're victims of a universe that unfolds randomly. There's a brief montage of the cows in the slaughterhouse, some of them staring accusingly at the camera. Do they know what fate awaits them? Do we know what fate awaits us?

The universe has a plan, one might say, but humans don't know what it is, or even if they're important to it. Take for instance, an early shot in the film that explores this notion. Under the uncaring eye of the distant sun, Jerry's van picks up the Hitchhiker. This event is staged in an extreme long shot. Under a giant blue sky, the Hitchhiker and the van itself might as well be ants on a hill or cows in the slaughterhouse, and to Hooper they are. All humanity is dwarfed beside the vastness of creation. The sky is what matters, the activity below it only background noise.

Later, there's a beautifully composed tracking shot of Pam and Kirk as they approach the farmhouse where they will meet their grim fates. The camera is positioned at a low angle and the sun is visible all throughout the shot, glaring down on the oblivious characters like an unblinking eye. As Pam and Kirk move, so the camera tracks them, but, importantly, the sun remains positioned in its orbit—*unmoving*. The ants are transitory, even our very eye (the camera lens) is transitory, but the universe moves for no creature. It is callous and unconcerned with the life teeming on a tiny world.

Hooper repeats this marvelously executed tracking shot when Pam first goes into the cannibal house. Again, there is a lot of blue sky visible above her, as if it is a player, or at least observer in the drama. These are instances in which Hooper and cinematographer Pearl make inventive use of the low angle perspective. Hooper is not revealing the strength of his protagonists (as the low angle is usually designed to depict). Instead, he is revealing the inherent hierarchy (or disorder) of the universe. High above his oblivious characters stand outer space, suns, and galaxies. And those cosmic entities could not care less that five teens are about to meet their makers in a backwater corner of some place called Texas.

The film's dialogue reinforces many of these themes. Franklin's horoscope reads: "you will have a disturbing and unpredictable day." Sally reads her own horoscope, and it is equally as frightening. "There are moments when we can't believe what is happening is really true. Pinch yourself and you'll find it is." The horoscope (and astrology in general) represents a man-made method of imposing some kind of understandable order on the universe. After all, astrology charts the manner in which the planets or the universe at large affect man on a daily basis, but it is a "science" not that different from clinical psychology because it attempts to find reason and order behind man's behavior or misbehavior. Hooper's point is not that astrology is a credible and valuable tool, it is that life is totally random and that on this horrible day, the horoscopes just happen to be right. That's as much a cosmic joke as the notion that five teens should happen to run out of gas on the very day, on the very road, where a deranged grave robber is seeking new prey. Thus *The Texas Chain Saw Massacre* tells us that as tiny ants with tunnel vision, our actions, our mistakes, our choices have unforeseen results, especially in a universe of chaos, eruptions and anger. You might wake up one morning, go on a trip, and have no inkling that you will die at the hands of a mad cannibal before the sun sets.

Ultimately, the very nature of Leatherface's villainy is a prominent part of Hooper's thesis about the universe too. Leatherface is a creature who apparently sees human beings as nothing more than meat and spare parts for his unusual culinary brews. He doesn't want to have sex with the lovely Sally, he doesn't want to know her as a "person" and he doesn't want her money, either. He simply desires to clobber her with a sledgehammer, cook her up, and eat her for supper. If he can get a nice face mask out of her soft flesh, that's all the better. In this regard, Hooper's film might be viewed as some kind of twisted vegan anthem or fantasy. Leatherface and his family see no difference between Sally, a rabbit, or a cow. To the cannibals, they're all merely ingredients. That's part of the crazy universe too; it doesn't make moral distinctions. On this hot day in August, Sally Hardesty learns that she is no different from the cows in the slaughterhouse where her granddad once worked. Animal flesh is animal flesh, and meat is meat. If cows can be slaughtered and served up for dinner, so then can Sally. It is highly disturbing, but *The Texas Chainsaw Massacre*, like no other film ever made, makes us sympathize with the cows, or the lambs, or any other animal that is slaughtered as food. Hooper's film makes us adopt the perspective of the slaughtered, and that's troubling for audiences because it challenges another one of their key assumptions: that the meat on their supper table is not a result of murder. Well, of course it is. And the people who kill the cows do so with the same cold detachment and lack of compassion that Leatherface, Cook and Hitchhiker embody in their pursuit of Sally and her friends. Watching this movie will make you want to give up beef...

The Texas Chainsaw Massacre is a terrifying film because it surrounds the audience with a universe we dare not contemplate. The heavens don't care about us as "thinking" human beings. Each and every one of us will die one day, and yet the Earth will stay in its orbit. We can be hunted down, treated as cattle, and exposed to every atrocity imaginable, but the sky won't fall, or even protest such terrible treatment. That's an important and terrifying realization because as human beings we all have egos. We see the world through our own eyes, not through the eyes of others. The universe, we think, revolves around our wants and needs. *The Texas Chainsaw Massacre*, by creating villains who see their fellow man as ingredients for barbecue, reminds us that our perception of life isn't accurate.

There's a strange equation to films like *The Texas Chainsaw Massacre* and Tobe Hooper understands it. Insanity is so pronounced in a movie like this that the horror sometimes gives way to nervous laughter. At the same time that the cannibal family is awful, it is also distinctly funny. Sure, the family possesses values different from most, but it also reveals universal elements of family life and we want to laugh at that. Brothers don't always get along (just like Leatherface and the Hitchhiker). Grandpa is past his prime, but nonetheless encouraged by his progeny. The Cook is upset by the rising cost of electricity, and so forth. It's a twisted view of the American family, yet still a view of that family anyway. We laugh because we recognize that, despite strange appetites, this family could be ours. After all, the cannibals gather around the dinner table too—it's just what they eat that differentiates them from us.

And table manners play an important part in this film. The last act of *The Texas Chain Saw Massacre* involves the family "inviting" Sally to their dinner table for a meal. What's so unusual about this set piece is that the setting, blocking and character dynamics of the sequence resemble Chapter VII of *Alice's Adventures in Wonderland*, entitled "A Mad Tea Party." In that chapter of Lewis Carroll's famous tale, the March Hare, the Mad Hatter and the Dormouse share tea with a girl named Alice, who is obviously an outsider to their ways, not sharing in their manner of behaving and interacting. In *The Texas Chain Saw Massacre*, it is Cook, Leatherface and the Hitchhiker who befuddle their female guest, this time Sally, around a table. The scene, at least on a superficial level, is staged identically. Carroll wrote: "the table was a large one, but the three were all crowded together at one corner of it" (1). In other words, at a long table, there was a visible and substantial division: the Hatter and his cohorts at one end and Alice at the other. Hooper stages *Chain Saw*'s mad tea party with Grandpa, Cook, Leatherface and Hitchhiker similarly (and quite oddly) massed around one end of a long table while the outsider in their midst, Sally, sits alone at the far end.

The tenor of the two sequences is quite similar as well. Alice/Sally is disturbed and bewildered by the manners and habits of her table mates in both circumstances. In *Alice's Adventures in Wonderland*, the Dormouse recounts a silly story and all the unusual characters seem to talk at opposite ends from Alice. In *Chain Saw*, Sally is clearly in much more grievous danger than Alice ever was, but she likewise finds herself unable to effectively communicate with those around her, many of whom have strange affectations. Instead of an affinity for hats, Leatherface wears human skins. Instead of insisting that he had "the *best* butter" (page 75), as the March Hare does so proudly, the Hitchhiker repeats continually that Grandpa is the "*best*" of the lot of them at killing. In both sequences, language and culture are barriers to understanding and communication, and in both sequences there is a sense of a topsy-turvy, mad world. In the end, both Sally and Alice move on in "disgust" (Sally by jumping through a window; Alice by finding a tree with a door in it), leaving the other partygoers to their strange games.

Some may argue that the connection between *Texas Chain Saw* and *Alice's Adventures in Wonderland* is a tenuous one, but both tea party scenes are over-the-top and clearly indicative of a crazed, disordered world (though to varying degrees). Others who prefer a more literal, socially minded explanation of that dinner table sequence might simply note that it is the dinner table where American families get together to discuss the most important topics in their lives. Eating is a form of emotional bonding and meals offer an opportunity for family members to communicate with one another. In *Chain Saw*, however, Sally sees the dark side of that ritual, the dark underneath of the American family.

In fact, much of the *Texas Chain Saw Massacre* concerns (and satirizes) the idea of the modern American family. Much as Wes Craven did in *The Last House on the Left* and *The Hills Have Eyes*, Tobe Hooper sets up his horror film as a pointed contrast between two families, one supposedly civilized, one savage. In *The Last House on the Left* it was the middle class Collingwoods against the evil, crass Krugs. In *Hills* it was the white-bread Carter family in deadly conflict with Papa Jupe's cannibal clan. In *The Texas Chain Saw Massacre*, the Hardestys and the cannibal clan, once neighbors and co-workers at the slaughterhouse, now duke it out for supremacy. It's interesting that in both families, there is a pronounced sense of sibling rivalry. Sally and Franklin can barely stand one another, and likewise, Leatherface and Hitchhiker seem to have a competitive relationship to win the affection of Grandpa. Franklin Hardesty and Leatherface might even be described as two sides of the same coin. Both are crippled (one physically, one mentally), both are overweight, both covet weapons (a knife and a chainsaw respectively) and both are cared for by a more responsible sibling (Sally and the Hitchhiker, respectively). Is Leatherface the living embodiment of Franklin's id? Doing the terrible things to Sally's friends in revenge for their treatment of Franklin? Where Franklin is impotent,

1. *The Texas Chain Saw Massacre* (1974)

A family portrait. From top to bottom and left to right: Leatherface (Gunnar Hansen), Cook (Jim Siedow), the Hitchhiker (Edwin Neal), Granpa (John Dugan) and the corpse that is Grandma. From *The Texas Chain Saw Massacre* (1974).

crippled, Leatherface is almost "super-potent," especially if one is inclined to view the chain saw as an out-of-control phallic symbol. Even if this connection sounds far-fetched, the two families are clearly mirror images of one another.

Tony Williams, author of *Hearths of Darkness: The Family in the American Horror Film*, has carefully analyzed *The Texas Chain Saw Massacre* and writes persuasively that the two families dramatized in the film represent two opposite sides of a significant economic breach. The Hardestys have "made it," while the cannibals, put out of work by new technology in the slaughterhouse, have devolved into savagery and are waiting to revolt:

> Sally and Franklin Hardesty are the successful products of "getting ahead," benefiting from a process that has destroyed the Frontier.... The Hardesty business involved meat, built upon the physical and mental exploitation of the slaughterhouse family. A group of selfish and bickering youngsters venture out and encounter their repressed counterparts in America's most violent state. Like H.G. Wells's Morlocks, the slaughterhouse family emerge and take bloody vengeance on 20th century Eloi beneficiaries of their economic exploitation ... [2].

This interpretation works well with the details of the film, which tend to support the idea that unemployment, poverty and a barren area of land all contributed to the cannibal family's fall from civilization and grace.

It couldn't have been easy making a living in that area of Texas wasteland after the lay-offs at the slaughterhouse, and so the cannibals had to use what they could get their hands on (including passersby) to stay alive. When food was short, they took to eating human beings. When supplies were short, they used that "human" food to service their business, a barbecue stand. When they couldn't afford new furniture or luxuries like new lampshades, they again exploited the material they had on hand, once more of human origin.

Instead of sticking it out through the tough times, the Hardestys moved away from that region of Texas (leaving their home behind), and consequently prospered. Contrarily, the clan learned to stick together and exploit their region, whereas Sally, Franklin and their friends have been fattened and made easy prey by their wealth. Notice that there is enough gasoline available to power the farmhouse generator, Cook's truck and Leatherface's chainsaw, but importantly *not* enough to propel Sally's van out of the dangerous territory. In becoming the "upper class," Sally and her friends have come to depend on others, on an American lower class, to provide them the services that sustain their class privileges. In this case, that fact proves fatal because predators (the cannibal family) hold all the cards, owning the local gas station and having a home nearby. This class split is also evident in the Hitchhiker's grave robbing ventures. Notice that his own kin, such as Grandpa, are revered, while the kin of Sally and the other folks who left the area are disrespected, desecrated. It's another form of revenge against those who helped to put the Hitchhiker and his family out of work.

Lending further support to the idea that the Hardestys and Leatherface's clan represent opposite sides of the same coin (the "haves" and "the have nots") is the fact that the defining moment in both families seems to be the downsizing at the slaughterhouse. Both Franklin and the Hitchhiker seem to be obsessed with the era of their "grandpa," the time when either wealth or poverty was cemented, depending on the individual family. Those were the good old days, when times were good, before the economic slowdown of the 1970s and the threat of automation destroyed livelihoods.

The Texas Chain Saw Massacre has also often been studied under the microscope of sexual, rather than familial politics too. And again, further analysis reveals that the film is deeper contextually than its lurid title suggests at first glance. Some factions found much to take issue with in the film, and in a review of the film in *An Album of Modern Horror Films*, Frank Manchel wrote:

> Less than 90 minutes long, the film managed to offend anyone who took it seriously. Feminists, in particular, were outraged by Hooper's apparent endorsement of male supremacy and his calculated torture of the two women in the film [3].

Cynthia Freeland, author of *Thinking Through Cinema: The Naked and the Undead: Evil and the Appeal of Horror,* was particularly fascinated with the film's unique approach to gender and sex roles, but she didn't view the film as misogynistic or in any way anti-woman. Her approach was more reasonable than some:

> [*The Texas Chain Saw Massacre*] presents ambiguous views on gender. There is no hero to protect the young damsel in distress. Instead, the chief patriarchal figure is mad and abusive. The cannibal family includes only men. Given the entirely decrepit Grandpa, we could conclude that patriarchy has run aground. Yet the apparent heroine (or chief victim), Sally, has almost no personality other than wanting to be with her boyfriend. Her only merit is sympathy for her brother Franklin. She is not especially strong, brave, or resourceful ... [4].

Freeland seems to have struck on something important here. Firstly, the film dispatches its two male heroes (Jerry and Kirk) without a second glance, leaving only Franklin—a sexual impotent—to represent "maleness" on the side of the so-called normal people. Oppositely, all of the insane people in the film are males (Cook, Hitchhiker, Leatherface, Grandpa), and they are all ridiculous figures to one degree or another. Not one of the "boys" shows a sexual interest in a woman (Sally in particular) and when she offers her body to them in desperation, their response is one of confusion and bewilderment. They can't even imagine what the hell she's suggesting. It would not be until *The Texas Chainsaw Massacre Part 2* that Leatherface would actively demonstrate an interest in the opposite sex, and Cook would directly address it (as a "swindle").

If anything, *The Texas Chain Saw Massacre* seems determined to avoid the issue of sex in relation to its crimes (and this may be part of the taste Stephen King ascribes to Tobe Hooper). Were the killers in the film given visible and obvious sexual hungers and tastes, the film would have been truly debauched, not to mention far more predictable.

The film is revolutionary because, unlike *Psycho* or *Halloween*, *The Texas Chain Saw Massacre* unlinks sex and death. If the cannibals wanted sex, they could have gotten it from Pam or Sally at any time, since the women are held captive for long periods. But that not only would have made for a misogynistic picture about rape, it would have made this film less powerful. It is much more frightening to be faced with killers who have no recognizable human motivation than to be confronted with merely horny ones.

On the subject of Sally, one can't really make the claim that she survives the film because she is a woman. Again, one senses that sex is not important in this film, that Hooper was trying to unwrap the cinema's long-standing but unhealthy (and not necessarily realistic) association between sex and violence. Any serious reading of the film reveals that Sally survives her night of terror simply because of circumstances. It is true that she is not particularly resourceful (like Laurie Strode in *Halloween* or Nancy Thompson in *A Nightmare on Elm Street* [1984]), smart or brave. The truth is, she's just lucky. And that fact also makes the film stronger on its thematic level. Remember, this is a disordered, random and chaotic universe. Sally *happens* to get a break, to escape the crazies and make it to the road beyond the farmhouse but none of that is part of a design or intentional strategy on her part. It's just the law of averages: Leatherface and his kin go after five hapless travelers one day, and one happens to escape their grasp. There's no magic to it because Sally is "a woman" or better than anyone else. Indeed, Freeland is wrong about Sally being sympathetic to Franklin. To this writer's eyes, she is downright horrible to him, so she has no moral high ground to claim whatsoever.

Again, it is interesting to note, however, that *The Texas Chainsaw Massacre Part 2* would choose a different path in its study of gender and sex. The heroine in that film, Stretch, is clearly a 1980s woman, able to defend and fight for herself. She survives because she takes action, and is resourceful. Sally isn't the same at all, but one might argue she lives in a less-traditional movie universe. Stretch is of the same universe as Ripley in *Aliens* (1986) or Laurie Strode in *H20* (1998): one that rewards smarts, stamina, and strategy. Sally lives in a universe where none of those things would have mattered one way or the other, or as L.M. Kit Carson would no doubt remind us, there's "no deal." And besides, one can also make the argument that Sally didn't really survive intact: her sanity is in serious question at the end of *Chain Saw*. The Leatherface clan is kind of like a nuclear strike, it's almost better to die during the initial blast, than wait around for the fallout (or in their case, the dinner table). One can easily support the argument that Sally actually gets it worse than any of the other characters in the film, being forced to watch her brother die and then endure a night of total madness.

Much has been written of *Chain Saw's* "nightmarish" texture. Despite the film's grainy documentary look and appeal, it contrarily boasts the rhythms and feel of a terrible dream. Danny Peary, the acclaimed author of *Cult Movies*, notes that the film "perfectly reproduces our worst nightmare" (5) and Michael Goodwin for *The Village Voice* explains that it captures "the syntax and structure of a nightmare with astonishing fidelity" (6). By recreating the particulars of a dreamscape, Hooper is clearly adhering to Breton's tenets of surrealism. The film's illogical structure (no learning; a disordered universe; the blending of comedy and horror; the juxtaposition of the very real with the totally *unreal*) trades on what Breton termed "neglected associations," and a "superior reality" where dreams are "omnipotent."

The act of watching a movie has long been associated with the act of dreaming (except the former is performed with eyes open, the latter with eyes shut). *The Texas Chain Saw Massacre* is a fantasy of such compelling and irrational proportions that the audience almost literally *can't* look away (much as how a dreamer often can't wake up immediately from a disturbing dream). For 84 minutes, Hooper's adherence to surrealism results in a waking vision of horror that treads on the conscious and subconscious mind in insidious and powerful ways. The endless circular chases, which always seem to begin and end with the farmhouse, the gruesome monster from the id (an irrational killer who speaks only in animalistic grunts), and the sense that there is no escape and no help, all contribute to the film's nightmare/dream associations.

Whether one prefers to view *The Texas Chain Saw Massacre* as representative of class warfare, a treatise on vegetarianism, a study of sex roles, a peek into the surreal, or merely an extremely effective exercise in terror in which Hooper undercuts every bit of audience security by fostering the notion of a disordered universe, the film stands up to the heaviest scrutiny. Although many positive aspects of the film have been noted in this review, there are other fine points worth mentioning. As a student of the horror genre, this author especially appreciated the manner in which the camera so often viewed Pam's sexy, bare back in the early part of the film, only to have that very part of her body perforated by Leatherface's meat hook. The audience, so titillated by that fine looking back, was acutely aware of how attractive and *naked* it was, and it was a masterstroke decision to make that very noticeable and *noticed* portion of her anatomy the centerpiece of a death scene. In the same sequence, there's a terrific shot of Pam standing just outside the farmhouse screen door, and a horizontal black decoration is visible on it, symbolically cutting her off at the neck. This is a nice visual foreshadowing of the character's doom.

Also interesting is Hooper's appropriate use of signage at just the right times to provide the audience subconscious clues about the horror to come. At the gas station, there is a sign reading "Gulf," quite an appropriate brand for a half-way place between two regions, in this case the normal and the insane. Shortly thereafter, another sign reads "STOP" as the protagonists near the old Franklin place, a visual warning that is ultimately ignored.

The Texas Chain Saw Massacre is really a director's film. It succeeds or fails on how well Hooper is able to marshal all the film's elements into a cohesive, fast-paced nightmare. Still, it would seem unfair not to mention that he had extremely able support from technicians such as Larry Carroll (editor), and Daniel Pearl (cinematographer). Kim Henkel also wrote a screenplay with a fascinating, nontraditional structure and which evidences no tact whatsoever in describing the thoroughly nauseating process of slaughtering cows or listing what ingredients, precisely, go into the making of head cheese. If the script were not so unsettling and provocative in and of itself, Hooper would have had no new ground to explore.

Also, the cast deserves recognition for undergoing from what, by all accounts, was a torturous shoot. In movies like this, the acting needs to be almost invisible for the effects to work. The first sign of overacting would have killed the reality of this picture, and Edwin Neal, Gunnar Hansen, and Jim Siedow all deserve kudos for creating memorable, frightening lunatics without overdoing the funny business and breaking the picture's spell. Of the leads, Paul Partain and Marilyn Burns make the most impact. Partain is tremendously irritating, but interesting, as Franklin, easily the most "individual" and recognizable of all the film's characters, and Marilyn Burns is the cinema's greatest screamer since Faye Wray. Every one of these artists contributed to Hooper's vision of a universe spiked with disorder and chaos and each did their job with the talent of a seasoned professional, not new kids on the block.

The Texas Chain Saw Massacre is Tobe Hooper's masterpiece, a film that hovers between unrelenting horror and nervous laughs and is possessed of more raw energy than a dozen low budget horror films combined. Hooper has brilliantly created a universe without order and without hope. It is a universe where madmen roam freely and the skies above just turn a blind eye. It's chilling, bizarre and unlike any other movie ever made. It has some obvious (and funny) didacticism (don't pick up hitchhikers; don't play with your food) but more than that it effectively terrorizes and assaults the psyche. The bottom line is that *The Texas Chain Saw Massacre* is scary because it makes audiences face the truths it would rather deny; that random, meaningless death could be around the corner for any of us, and in the scheme of the universe, that fate would hardly matter.

2. *Eaten Alive* (1976)

Critical Reception

"From *The Texas Chainsaw Massacre* director Tobe Hooper comes this creepy sophomore effort.... Blackly comic elements do little to blunt the unsettling aura created by the garish lighting and intense dentist drill 'score' ... Grade: B-."
— Doug Brod, *Entertainment Weekly*, March 10, 2000, page 53.

"At its best, the film's lurid tone matches the evocative gloom of the EC horror comics of the '50s, in particular the amazing swamp stories drawn by 'Ghastly' Graham Inglis. Otherwise it's trite and unconvincing."
— David Pirie, *Time Out Film Guide*, page 214.

"Zero-budget schlock horror which isn't even good exploitation."
— Howard Maxford, *The A to Z of Horror Films*, page 54.

"*Eaten Alive* definitely has its high tension moments, but overall they just weren't as effective as *TCM*.... One thing Tobe Hooper always seems to accomplish is having villains that are just plain psycho. Neville Brand ... did a terrific job on the character."
— Horrordvds.com, "Eaten Alive," January 30, 2000 *(www.horrordvds.com)*

"*Eaten Alive* is completely ridiculous, but it's *brilliantly* ridiculous. It's one of the most outlandish horror films I've ever seen.... The plot is twisted ... the majority of the film is madness. We've come to expect this from Tobe Hooper...."
— Dan Lopez, Digitallyobsessed.com :"Eaten Alive," August 4, 2000 *(www.digitallyobsessed.com)*

Cast and Crew

CAST: Marilyn Burns (Faye); William Finley (Roy); Stuart Whitman (Sheriff Martin); Roberta Collins (Clara); Kyle Richards (Angie); Robert Englund (Buck); Crystin Sinclaire (Libby Wood); Janus Blyth (Lynette); Betty Cole (Ruby); Sig Sakowicz (Deputy Girth); Ronald W. David (Country boy); David Hayward (The Cowboy); David "Goat" Carson ("Marlo"); Lincoln Kibbee (First Guy in Bar); James Galanis (Second Guy in Bar); Dog (Snoopy); **WITH:** Tarja Leena Halinen, Caren White, Valerie Lukeart, Jerome Reichart.

CREW: A Virgo International Pictures Release, a Mars Production. Mardi Rustam presents *Eaten Alive*. *Executive Producer:* Mohammed Rustam. *Associate Producer:* Samir Rustam, Larry Huly, Robert Kanto. *Co-produced by:* Alvin L. Fast. *Music composed, conducted and arranged by:* Tobe Hooper, Wayne Bell. *Written by:* Alvin L. Fast, and Mardi Rustam. *Adapted for the screen by:* Kim Henkel. *Produced by:* Mardi Rusam. *Directed by:* Tobe Hooper. *Director of Photography:* Robert Caramico. *Editor:* Michael Brown. *Casting:* Eddie Morse. *Sound Effects:* Echo Film Services, Bill Manger. *Music Editor:* Lee Osborne. *Assistant Editor:* Andy Ruben. *Second Assistant Directors:* Jeff Kibbee, Laurie Lawless. *Script Supervisor:* John D'Amato. *Second Unit Cameraman:* Jack Beckett. *Art Director/Set Designer:* Marshall Reed. *Set Decorator* Mike Wiegant. *Wardrobe:* Greg Tittinger, Jane Mancbach. *Make-up/Hair:* Craig Reardon, Beth Rogers. *Special Effects:* A & A. Stunt Coordinator: Von Deminy. *Radio Songs by:* Rick Casual, Eddie Barles, Cam King, Lisa Casady, Jay White, Rick Smith, Oscar De Leon, Napleon Colombo, Al Bolt. *Mechanical alligator and crocodile furnished by*: Bob Mattey. *Dog trainer:* Lou Schumacher. *M.P.A.A. Rating:* R. *Running time*: 88 minutes.

"I've seen all the things I want to see. I've been all the things I want to be."
— Song lyrics heard in the background "atmosphere" of Judd's grim hotel in *Eaten Alive* (1976).

Synopsis

A young hooker at Miss Hatty's brothel in Florida protests vehemently when Buck, a regular customer, pays to have anal sex with her. Miss Hatty appeases Buck with two free girls and throws the uncooperative girl out of her place of business, but a friendly domestic spares her some cash and instructs her to stay at the nearby Starlight, a local fleabag hotel, until she can get out of town. The downtrodden hooker rents a room from the strange clerk there, a babbling war veteran named Judd. When Judd learns his new guest is a whore, he kills her with a pitchfork and feeds her to his pet crocodile in the swamp.

Sometime later, a middle-class family on a long road trip stops by at the establishment for some respite. The family's pet poodle, Snoopy, is unceremoniously devoured by the crocodile, and the little daughter, Angie, promptly goes into shock. When Angie's father, Roy, attempts to kill the murderous swamp predator, Judd stabs him with a scythe. Roy manages to shoot Judd in the foot before dying, but Judd has a false leg and is uninjured. Then Judd ties up the beautiful Faye, Roy's long-suffering wife, and attempts to kill the little girl. Angie hides under the rotting hotel foundation, and temporarily evades capture.

The same night, a businessman, Mr. Wood and his grown daughter, Libby, come to the Starlight seeking the dead prostitute, actually Libby's estranged sister. Mr. Wood requests the help of Sheriff Martin on the case, and the law enforcement official takes him to see Miss Hatty. The madam claims never to have seen Mr. Wood's daughter, a bald-faced lie. A despondent Mr. Wood returns to the hotel while Libby dates the sheriff. When Mr. Wood hears Angie crying nearby and plans to investigate, Judd slices him with his scythe, committing another murder.

Sheriff Martin escorts Libby to a local bar, where redneck Buck is busy raising hell. Martin runs him off, and Buck takes his underage girlfriend to the Starlight Hotel. When they make love there, Judd is aroused, and makes advances toward Faye ... still strapped to a bed. Buck hears her screams and tries to save her, but Judd pushes Buck into the swamp and the crocodile kills him too. Then Judd chases Buck's little chickie through the swamp, but she escapes.

Libby returns to the hotel and rescues Faye and her daughter, Angie, from the madman of the bayou. Judd pursues the women, but is eventually eaten by his own carnivorous pet.

Commentary

As even a cursory viewing will reveal, *Eaten Alive* is not a great film, but boy is it an *interesting* one. There are many factors in the film's favor (particularly the stellar art and set design and Tobe Hooper's trademark, low-budget sense of energy and enthusiasm), but probably just as many elements dragging the movie down. It is a film that captures the feeling of a seedy, forgotten corner of the world better than just about any horror movie ever made. No Hollywood artifice here, thank you. The movie also powerfully evokes the randomness of madness, and the role coincidence can play in bringing people together (to die) in an out-of-the-way hellhole. There's an "Ed Gein" sense of reality and power to *Eaten Alive* that's hard to deny too. People like Miss Hatty (proprietor of the local whorehouse) and the sheriff (a stolid Stuart Whitman) know Judd as one of their own, part of their community, but fail to detect his murderous predilections. To them, he's just a little strange, a little off, but to visitors he's much worse: a murderous, deranged predator.

When contemplating the notion of insanity dwelling on the border of normality, *Eaten Alive* feels authentic, a worthy heir to the themes first expressed by Hooper in *The Texas Chain Saw Massacre*. Yet, in the final analysis, *Eaten Alive* may be too much of a good (or bad...) thing. It highlights a very sleazy world, and is populated by too many unlikable characters to win it (or Hooper) wide accolades. The editing is downright jagged in *Eaten Alive*, the transitions are rough, and the picture doesn't quite feel professional. And that's the paradox of this movie. Those very raw qualities, the ones that make the film feel amateurish, like a slice of redneck life, are the same ones that keep it oddly viewable. It feels like we're watching Judd's story happen to us, not like we're watching a glossy, entertaining product from the protected environment of a movie theater. The film is simultaneously distancing and compelling; you want to turn away from it all, but something keeps your eyes glued to the lurid action on screen.

As with *The Texas Chain Saw Massacre*, *Eaten Alive* is a film in which Tobe Hooper willfully preserves none of the audience's sensibilities. There's no covenant with the audience that Hooper won't break to achieve his effects and so this film starts (after a shot of the moon in the night sky) with a lascivious close-up of Robert Englund's jeans as he pulls down his zipper. "Name's Buck ... rarin' to fuck," we hear him utter, and then—*in a truly debauched manipulation of film grammar that establishes cause and effect within one frame*—a chastened hooker's frightened face is superimposed over the offending, garbed-in-blue-jeans crotch. As if that isn't bad enough, Englund's character then states his intention to penetrate the hooker anally ("turn over and get on your knees.... I'm gonna ride you like you've never been rid before..."). When the hooker protests Buck's peculiar idea of a good time, the scene then degenerates into a disturbing and all-too-real appearing near-rape, a struggle on a bed between a powerful man and a victimized female that puts the endangered, scantily-clad woman and her exploiter into frightening physical confrontation. The setting is a shabby-looking bedroom, the tone is desperation, and the atmosphere borders on truly dangerous. Welcome to the fun-filled world of *Eaten Alive*...

From the opening scene of the film, the underlying message is clear: we're not in Hollywood. This isn't *Pretty Woman*, where beautiful hookers frolic about in expensive clothes and meet good-looking, rich clients in fancy hotel rooms. On the contrary, this is real; this is *sleaze*; this is a $20 sex transaction between a desperate young woman and a redneck lout. It isn't fun, it isn't nice, and it certainly isn't candy-coated. It's sickening and compelling in a nasty way, and, the performances are better than are required (with Englund particularly slimy and menacing; a smirking testament to backwoods ignorance and lust). *Eaten Alive* is a title that may pointedly refer to the fact that Judd's crocodile devours victims, but it is also about the death of innocence (for the hooker and the audience).

After this opening, Hooper doesn't shy away from intentionally shattering other long-held film conventions. Before the film is over a cute little puppy named Snoopy is devoured by a crocodile, a little girl named Angie is continuously placed in grievous danger, and murder is depicted as a messy and difficult act. The hooker's death (by pitchfork) is a gruesome encounter replete with splattering blood and ear-shattering screams, but it is Mr. Wood's death that best expresses the movie's ethos. Judd plants a scythe in Woods' neck, but this intended deathblow is as much a botch as punctuation. The weapon sticks ingloriously in the victim's soft flesh, and neither Judd nor Mr. Wood is able to remove it for a good few seconds. It's a really, really gross moment, but it acknowledges a fact most horror movies gloss over: flesh doesn't always oblige. This isn't a movie where a simple stabbing will bloodlessly end a life. Pitchforks, scythes, and other implements used by Judd make for very sloppy kills, and it's a revelation because film doesn't usually go so far in depicting violence.

What's interesting about this (and other death scenes) in *Eaten Alive*, is that they become strangely funny because of their elaborate messiness, a grotesque comedy of errors. They are so over-the-top, dis-

Judd (Neville Brand, with scythe) attacks the long-suffering Faye (Marilyn Burns) in *Eaten Alive* (1976).

gusting and ineptly handled (by Judd, not the moviemakers) that there is a strange black humor to them. That is Hooper's niche, and so he breaks another long-held taboo in the film: that the death of a main character should be a serious moment, filled with gravity and noble intent. Instead, Hooper stages the death scenes so they are simultaneously frightening, and able to invite a laugh. It's in bad taste, no doubt, but humorous just the same. Some people will think it's wrong, even immoral, but the distinct personality of the death scenes in *Eaten Alive* (and in *Chain Saw*, for that matter) humanize Hooper's early work to a very strong degree. In *Chain Saw*, one gets that sense that Leatherface is baffled by the fact that these people keep showing up at his house, and he has to kill them. Likewise, Judd in *Eaten Alive* is a dimwit and a bungler, and his killing sprees reflect that truth. He's a temperamental mad dog, driven by his own psychoses, not a cold-blooded killer who plans out his attacks with mechanical precision (like Hannibal Lecter). These characters are not monsters that invite us to see how different they are from the rest of mankind, but flawed human beings who remind of us ourselves. Our worst selves.

The thing about Tobe Hooper's films, *Eaten Alive* included, that no critic can deny is that the madness in his work feels spontaneous and real, not rehearsed and made palatable for mass consumption. Is this approach morally valuable? Perhaps, perhaps not, but it is scary because Hooper's *modus operandi* leaves viewers distinctly unsettled. In his films the audience never feels safe. That was an effect Hitchcock was able to achieve as well (particularly in *Psycho*), but a generation later, audiences aren't shocked as easily, and Hooper goes further down the road of "surprise" and "shock" than Hitchcock ever did, and in much more visceral fashion. Depending on taste, this will be seen as either a logical step in a world where movie-goers expect (and demand) more and more intense experiences, or a sign that as American morals have relaxed film has been given too much leeway to depict disturbing imagery. No matter which side of the debate one lands on, Hooper's artistry is apparent. It's an interesting alchemy of film movement, pace, and sense of place that even Hooper himself is not always able to successfully conjure (as in *Night Terrors*). But when he achieves the right mix, the horror genre gets another masterpiece.

One of the strongest elements of *Eaten Alive* is its sense of place. The Starlight Hotel certainly ranks with the family farmhouse of *The Texas Chain Saw Massacre*, though it reeks more of neglect than it does of out-and-out horror. And that's effective too. Unlike the rural clan of *Chain Saw*, Judd dwells in a place where guests are expected, so his madness bubbles over in ways not as immediately apparent as bone furniture and lamps made of human skin. There's a terrific scene in which the lonely Judd sits in his room, singing to himself, as he models a bunch of eyeglasses from a large box. Clearly, those glasses have come from people Judd has killed, but it is an interesting quirk that he would keep souvenirs of these atrocious acts amongst his personal belongings. One gets the feeling it isn't so much to gloat over his murderous accomplishments, but rather simply to avoid boredom. It's an interesting insight into Judd and one could probably make the argument that the Starlight Hotel is an external representation of Judd's interior: all rotten and sickly, barely holding together.

Audiences who appreciate art design will love the Starlight Hotel in *Eaten Alive*. The toilet in the bathroom is filthy, with dried brown leakage evident on one side. The sofas in the lobby appear worn and threadbare (and are probably filled with fleas), lamp shades are grimy and stained, and wallpaper is cracking and peeling off the walls. This is definitely one place where you don't want to know how long it's been since the sheets have been changed.

Another nice touch is the second story railing, which appears to have been added many years after the hotel was built, since it is a different style, and minimalist in construction to say the least. One can intuit that the old, more regal balcony collapsed (perhaps during one of Judd's rages), and this makeshift, unattractive replacement was added in its stead. Basically, all of these really nasty touches bespeak one thing: history. There's a strong sense in *Eaten Alive* that the Starlight Hotel is a real place, probably 30 or 40 years past its prime, and that it has existed and degenerated all that time. It doesn't appear to be a fresh "new" movie set, designed just for this picture (although that's exactly what it is; a soundstage creation).

Judd's surroundings may be the most interesting aspect of *Eaten Alive,* but the characters are not lacking unique facets either. Neville Brand's Judd is not that distant in character from Anthony Perkins' conception of Norman Bates. He runs a hotel (rather than a motel), and seems to have some serious sexual hang-ups, though not, apparently, involving Mom. Of course, Judd is a Vietnam veteran and a babbler, two distinctions that separate him from his spiritual cinematic grandfather. More interesting than the characters, however, is what they represent in the film. A large portion of the *dramatis personae* seem to signify base desires and instinct. Judd goes crazy when exposed to sex, allowing his murderous "instincts" loose. Buck is lusty, and representative of another primal instinct (rape). Conversely, the women (Faye, Libby, the prostitute, *et al.*) are the objects of desire that result in the release of male gutter instincts. Consider that even the sheriff is given a romantic partner, in the form of Libby: It's as if everyone in the film is in some way obsessed with lust and carnal pleasure. When Judd apologizes for his crocodile's murderous behavior early in the film, he notes that the murder of Snoopy was committed "according to" the creature's "instincts" and one senses that he could be speaking of himself, or apologizing for his own actions.

What differentiates Judd from the cannibals of *The Texas Chain Saw Massacre* is, indeed, the strong sexual component of *Eaten Alive*. *Chain Saw* was revolutionary because the killers escaped the logic of our culture. Audiences expected that the murderers would see the beautiful Sally Hardesty (Marilyn Burns) in sexual terms, but they never did. She was just meat and bone, that's all. That fact allowed *Chain Saw* to escape some cries of misogyny. Sure, a woman's life is in danger throughout the picture, but at least she wasn't an object of lust or sexual degradation. She's just dinner (as her cohorts—*male and female*—were appetizers). Instead, *Eaten Alive* treads on the timeworn yet nonetheless controversial movie conceit of a sexual dysfunction's fostering homicidal impulses. So Judd despises fornicating, but has no problem with violence (a metaphor perhaps for the standards of the M.P.A.A.?). He kills those who arouse him and he believes himself moral, not monstrous. To some, the addition of sexuality matures Hooper's vision, but to others it merely muddies the waters. Interestingly, *The Texas Chainsaw Massacre Part 2* would also sexualize its predator, Leatherface, resulting in a character development most fans of the original did not approve of.

As interesting as *Eaten Alive* is, there is also plenty of evidence to suggest that the film represents a "sophomore slump" for Tobe Hooper. Since he left the picture before it was finished, one can never know for sure how it might have been different with his editorial input, but as it stands, it bears obvious flaws. The film's plot has some problems of credibility because the Starlight is such a sewer that no self-respecting person would stay there (especially since Huntsville is described as being just "an hour away"). Also, it's a little strange how an out-of-the-way fleapit like Judd's place gets so much business in one night. A prostitute, a traveling family (replete with pooch), a businessman and his daughter, and Buck all arrive within the span of one short night. In hindsight, that may just strain believability too much. With its sagging foundation and poorly kept rooms (not to mention out-of-the-way location), one might imagine Judd getting one or two visitors a month, and certainly not of the variety who wear jackets and ties.

On other fronts, Judd's crocodile is pretty phony looking and the film doesn't quite achieve the sustained intensity and pace of *The Texas Chain Saw Massacre*. One chase through the swamp evokes Leatherface's hair-raising pursuit of Sally through the thicket from that watershed horror picture, but it feels more like a visual quote than a successful keynote of *Eaten Alive*. Marilyn Burns—who's obviously got what it takes as a solid actress—is sidelined (strapped to a bed and gagged) for much of the picture, and *Eaten Alive* would have benefited from more screen time in her interesting, unique presence. Neville Brand is charismatic, but overly cryptic as Judd, and finally, the film just isn't that entertaining. It accomplishes the task of being sleazy, disturbing and compelling, but it never entertains.

One of the best reasons to watch *Eaten Alive* is to visit the Starlight. This seedy hotel, where country music seems to be piped in from the *Twilight Zone* is a truly unique corner of horror history. This aging, dilapidated setting reflects the crumbling psyche of the film's homicidal protagonist, an interesting idea also evident in Hooper efforts such as *Salem's Lot*, *The Texas Chain Saw Massacre*, and *The Mangler*. In the final analysis, any tour of Tobe Hooper's cinematic career would find some tantalizing clues about the filmmaker's sensibilities by taking a one-time detour to *Eaten Alive*. Just be sure to take a shower after staying there...

3. *The Funhouse* (1981)

Critical Reception

"The cinematic intelligence of Tobe Hooper, who radically made over the horror genre in *The Texas Chainsaw Massacre*, is reasserted with *The Funhouse*.... [E]qually important is his ... method of architecting each film as one long, relentless build of tension.... *The Funhouse* is spiked with the same sort of irresistibly anarchic and black humor as *Chainsaw* ... an eminently satisfying piece of film work."
—Cynthia Rose, *Monthly Film Bulletin*, April 1981, page 66.

"Which is socially acceptable—to love Tobe Hooper movies for their perverse but stubborn puritanism, or to love them for the incredible way they decoy your attention with stylish homage to other horror classics then spring on you new and inventive means of scaring you out of your seat? ... It's not every day the fright genre produces a film capable of commenting on epic subjects like the ties that bind and the disintegration of the modern family, the foolishness of dabbling voyeuristically in others' pain and the possible detrimental effect of the Polaroid Instamatic on American moral fibre ... while doing its proper job of providing plenty of cheap thrills. It's rare that any film follows through its chosen themes with such attention to detail, much less leavening the package with a truly anarchic blend of black humor."
—Cynthia Rose, *Time Out Film Guide*, page 325.

"On this lively shocker [*The Funhouse*], Hooper combined traits of Roger Corman and Dario Argento and just let rip on a story of four youngsters who stay after closing time at the funhouse for a dirty night out.... Most of what follows is formula shock, although noisier, better-paced and better-edited than most; the sort of film William Castle might have been making had he lived. The finale in the engine-room is really imaginative and throws in everything but the kitchen sink, and the pace leaves no one time to go to the loo."
—David Quinlan, *The Illustrated Guide to Film Directors,* Barnes and Nobles Books, 1983, page 145.

"*The Funhouse* doesn't trade on gratuitous and graphic gore, but it doesn't have to. In little ways and using the traditional tried and true devices of the genre ... it skillfully heightens expectations ... [and] nicely evokes the chiller of a bygone era as it pays respect to Hitchcock and James Whale...."
—Alex Keneas, *Newsday*, March 13, 1981, page 7.

"To put it diplomatically, *The Funhouse* suggests that Hooper's flair for the horror genre was exhausted by that notorious hit [*The Texas Chainsaw Massacre*].... As Hooper guides *The Funhouse* through its listless, perfunctory motions, it's difficult to resist the impression that the filmmaker himself is short of enthusiasm.... [H]orror freaks who care enough to discriminate between attractions could make the first smart move by giving *The Funhouse* a prompt pass."
—Gary Arnold, *Washington Post* "This Funhouse Is Condemned," March 18, 1981, page B4.

"*The Funhouse* is a horror movie, not a really good one, but considering that its central horror is a standard monster ... who pursues four standard teenagers, it is not really a bad movie either. Tobe Hooper, the director, was in there trying.... Mr. Hooper almost persuades us that he is up to more than just gore, creepiness and trauma. He has photographed a carnival ... with a sense of style. The carnival is a small vision of

Middle America gone sour ... and it is not bad while it lasts."
—John Corry, *New York Times*, March 14, 1981.

"While the director, Tobe (*The Texas Chainsaw Massacre*) Hooper ought to have moved on to better things, he is the master of this gore-and-sadism genre.... The film features an excruciatingly tense final confrontation...."
—*People Weekly*, April 27, 1981.

Cast and Crew

CAST: Cooper Huckabee (Buzz); Miles Chapin (Richie); Largo Woodruff (Liz); Sylvia Miles (Madame Zena); William Finley (Mario the Magnificent); Elizabeth Berridge (Amy); Kevin Conway (The Barker); Wayne Doba (The Monster); Shawn Carson (Joey Harper); Jeanne Austin (Mrs. Harper); Jack McDermott (Mr. Harper); David Carson (Geek); Sonia Zomina (Bag Lady); Ralph Marino (Truck Driver); Herb Robins (Carnival Manager); Susie Malniki (Carmella); Sid Raymond (Strip Show M.C.); Larry Ross (Heckler-Girlie Show); Frank Grimes (Strip Show Voyeur); Frank Schuller (Poker Player); Peter Domrad (Midget with Tall Lady); Glen Lawrence (Spectator); Shawn McAllister (Garbage Collector #1); Sandy Mielke (Garbage Collector #2); Mike Montalvo (Spectator); FEATURING: Jeanne Austin, Jack McDermott, Sonia Zomina.

CREW: Universal, an MCA Company, Presents a Mace Neufeld Production in Association with Derek Power, a Tobe Hooper film. *Casting:* Fern Champion, Pamela Basker. *Associate Producer:* Brad Neufeld. *Music:* John Beal. *Film Editor:* Jack Hofstra. *Production Designer:* Morton Rabinowitz. *Director of Photography:* Andrew Laszlo. *Executive Producers:* Mace Neufeld, Mark L. Lester. *Written by:* Larry Block. *Produced by:* Derek Power, Steven Bernhardt. *Directed by:* Tobe Hooper. *Unit Production Manager/First Assistant Director:* Norman Cohen. *Second Assistant Director:* Adrienne Bourbeau. *Post-Production Supervisor:* John Orland. *Set Decorator:* Tom Coll. *Art Director:* Jose Du Arte. *Special Makeup Design:* Rick Baker. *Special Make-up Execution:* Craig Reardon. *Location Editor:* Angelo Ross. *Assistant Editor:* Robert Leader. *Sound Editor:* Dale Johnston, David Whittaker. *Post-Production Assistant:* Vicki Hiatt. *Music Supervisor:* Tom Catalano. *Music Editor:* Ken Johnson. *Camera Operator:* James Pergola. *First Assistant Camera Operator:* John Winner. *Gaffers:* Rusty Engles, Walter Morris, Jr. *Key Grip:* Eddie Knott, Jr. *Best boy:* Eddie Kammerer. *Construction Coordinator:* Howard Collins. *Property Master:* Nick Romanac. *Make-up:* Marlana May. *Hairstylist:* Donisia McGowan. *Wardrobe:* Linda Benedict, Andre Lavery, Harold Richter. *Special Effects:* J.B. Jones. *Sound Mixer:* Jack Dalton, Sr. *Rerecording Mixers:* Robert Hoyt, Earl Madery, John Stephens. *Script Supervisor:* Susan Preston. *Production Coordinator:* De Dee Winner, Cynthia Steit. *Production Assistants:* Jeff Stacey, Melanie Grefe, Don Gilman, Arnold Leibowitz. *Assistant to Mr. Hooper:* Daphne Stacey. *Miami Casting:* Bob Gordon, Susie Feldott, Jonathan Lane. *Still Photographer:* Robert De Stolfe. *Production Accountant:* Roberta Rose. *Animal Figures:* Animal Display Creations Ltd. *M.P.A.A. Rating:* R. *Running time:* 95 minutes.

"You were born with a knowledge of the occult ... do you have premonitions that often come true?"
—Fortune teller Madame Zena probes Amy's future, exposing another method of prognostication (like the astrology in *Chain Saw*), in the works of Tobe Hooper. From *The Funhouse* (1981).

Synopsis

Little Joey Harper frightens his older sister, Amy, while she showers by dressing as a masked maniac. Angry, she tells the boy she won't take him to the carnival passing through town. Though her parents warn Amy not to go to the carnival because there was trouble at it in a nearby town, Amy goes anyway with older boyfriend, Buzz. Together with pot-smoking friends Liz and Ritchie, Buzz and Amy head to the fair while Joey sneaks out of the house and walks to the carnival to spy on his older sister.

The four teens visit the Freak Show and see a two-headed cow and a mutant fetus corpse. They watch a magic show in which an audience member is seemingly impaled, but it is just a trick. Next up, the foursome visits an old fortune teller, Madame Zena. The strange woman warns Amy that her hand has a break in the "fate" line and that a tall, dark stranger will change her life. Amy is disturbed by the prediction, especially when Zena's crystal ball seems to roll to the fortune teller of its own volition, but the other teens mock the reading.

Next up is a tantalizing stripper show. Buzz and Ritchie cut a hole into the women's tent and peep while the annoyed girls wait none too patiently.

Amy and her friends decide to spend the night in the funhouse, an attraction overseen by a strange fellow wearing a Frankenstein monster mask. They sneak inside the funhouse, hop out of their funhouse ride car, and wait in secret for the carnival to close down for the night. Outside, Joey waits for Amy and her pals to come out of the funhouse, and grows worried when they don't. He begins to nose around the carnival.

Inside the bizarre funhouse chamber, the teens begin to make out, but stop when they hear a noise nearby. They gaze down through a grate in the floor, and see the living quarters of the ubiquitous and sleazy Barker and the Frankenstein Monster. They watch as the masked man pays for the sexual services of Madame Zena, the fortune teller. The strange masked man ejaculates prematurely and wants his money back, but Zena refuses. The carnie flies into a rage and kills Zena. After witnessing the crime, the kids attempt to escape but find all the doors to the outside world locked. In search of a way out of the funhouse, they stumble upon the quarters where Zena was murdered, and Ritchie steals the Barker's hard-earned money from a lockbox. Unable to escape, they return to their previous perch above the living quarters.

Amy and her friends watch in fear as the Barker and his masked son dispose of Zena's body. The carnies realize before long that their money is missing. When Ritchie's lighter falls down through the floor into their habitat, the dangerous carnies realize that the culprit is still in their funhouse.

Worse, underneath the mask, the Frankenstein monster is a terrible deformed mutant, the savage, drooling sibling of the dead freak show fetus.

The Barker and his mutant son go on the offensive, killing Ritchie. Meanwhile, Joey's parents find him at the carnival and take him home, even as their daughter faces danger in the funhouse, just yards away. Inside, Liz falls down through a trap door and finds herself in a vent shaft with the angry, sex-starved mutant. She pretends as though she intends to seduce the monster but then stabs him with a knife. Angry and betrayed, the mutant kills her.

Upstairs, the barker confronts Amy and Buzz, armed with a pistol. Buzz and the Barker wrestle for possession of the weapon and in the ensuing scuffle both men are killed. Then the mutant arrives and chases Amy into the bowels of the carnival's funhouse. Amy retreats into a corner and defends herself with a crowbar. After a hair-raising confrontation with the monster, the mutant is electrocuted when his head is caught in the gears of the funhouse ride.

In shock, Amy escapes alone in the morning light.

Commentary

In the late 1970s and early 1980s, horror films took a cheap, disappointing downturn in quality. Any hack with a camera and $50,000 could make a profit from what critic Roger Ebert dubbed "the dead teenager" movie: films in which scantily clad adolescent girls were graphically murdered by unstoppable (and usually unimaginative) serial killers. Inspired by the incredible financial success of John Carpenter's brilliant *Halloween* (1978), some five dozen "dead teenager" movies came out between 1979 and 1983. Though some of these efforts were harmless date movies that are remembered today with the warmth of nostalgia (this is particularly true of the not very good *Friday the 13th* [1980]), others caused real damage to the genre, proving that good acting, solid direction, a coherent plot, convincing character motivation and other long honored elements of the horror film were no longer really required. All these films needed to make money was show some teenage T & A and lots of blood and gore. *The Burning* (1982), *Curtains* (1982), *Dorm that Dripped Blood* (1981), *The Driller Killer* (1979), *Girls School Screamers* (1984), *Graduation Day* (1981), *Happy Birthday to Me* (1983), *Graduation Day* (1981), *Mother's Day* (1980), *My Bloody Valentine* (1981), *New Year's Evil* (1982)*, Slumber Party Massacre* (1982), *The Toolbox Murders* (1979) and *You Better Watch Out* (1980) are just a few of the titles that evoke the bad memories of this trend, this slump in creative horror aesthetics.

Amidst this sea of detritus, however, many good films were understandably lost or missed. Critics saw a P.O.V. "stalk" shot, teenagers and a masked killer and they automatically checked out. In at least one case, that of Tobe Hooper's 1981 entry, *The Funhouse*, that oversight was a real mistake. Along with *Halloween* and perhaps one or two others, such as *When a Stranger Calls* (1979), *The Funhouse* is a great horror film of the period, one which remains powerful and frightening twenty years after its production. Though it lacks the "buzz" surrounding *The Texas Chain Saw Massacre* and the Spielberg cachet of the megahit *Poltergeist*, *The Funhouse* is nonetheless one of Hooper's best films and one of the finest horror entries of the early 1980s.

The Funhouse, sometimes known as *Carnival of Terror*, is a reflexive horror movie before such things were popular with audiences. Though Hooper's fellow horror maven Wes Craven is generally acknowledged as the genre's Pirandello, shattering the fourth wall in *Shocker* (1989), *Wes Craven's New Nightmare* (1994) and the *Scream* trilogy (1996-1999), Tobe Hooper also architected one of the masterpieces of self-reflexive horror in *The Funhouse*, a film that knowingly and cleverly dances on two levels of meaning. On its basic "surface" level, *The Funhouse* is a dead teenager movie like *Halloween, Scream* or *I Know What You Did Last Summer* (1997). On a deeper and more meaningful thematic level, however, this is a film *about* horror films in general and in particular about the glut of "dead teenagers" inhabiting American cinemas in the early eighties. Accordingly, the film's plot mirrors the sub-genre: four teenagers (two girls; two guys; only moderately likeable, even distinguishable) visit a traveling carnival and decide to spend the night in a spooky funhouse. Unfortunately, they meddle with the carnies and witness a murder, forcing the malevolent Barker and his deformed son to hunt them down and kill them one at a time. It sounds like a simple premise, and it is. And yet that "under" level is present too, that reflexive one. This thematic layer finds voice in the fact that the film follows these teenagers from carnival attraction to carnival attraction for a long time (roughly 20 minutes), in essence sending them to the on-screen equivalent of a horror movie. That gives Hooper the opportunity to make a horror entertainment about horror entertainment.

Sometimes the teens are frightened by what they see (at a magic show seemingly gone bad), sometimes they are stimulated by the sights (at a stripper's tent) and sometimes they are amused and mystified (at the fortune teller's tent). But by sending his protagonists on this extended odyssey of entertainment, Tobe Hooper is mirroring the moviegoing experience and, with jolts in all the right places, the horror movie experience in particular.

So many of Hooper's films involve a double image, the so-called normal world and the creepy, dangerous "world underneath" that exist side by side. In some ways, the world of moviemaking is similarly bifurcated by a double image: the twin pillars of reality and illusion. Images on film appear one way (real) but are actually false. Actors read lines and live real lives beyond the screen yet for ninety minutes appear to be "characters" in a play. In *The Funhouse*, the carnival, like the moviemaking process, is a collision of illusions and reality. In the opening scene (following the credits), the camera adopts the subjective point of view of a stalker. This unseen killer puts on a clown mask, grabs a butcher knife and proceeds to hunt his prey, a girl in the shower. This beginning is clearly designed as homage to the opening scene of *Halloween* (Michael Myers' murder of his older sister), but it is much more than that. When the killer, whose eyes the audience shares, attacks young protagonist Amy in the shower (yet another homage, this time to the genre's progenitor, Alfred Hitchcock's *Psycho*), the point of view vantage is abandoned and the audience sees that the "killer" is just a child, Amy's brother, pulling a devious prank. The knife is rubber, the boy's intent not homicidal, merely jovial. The audience subconsciously relaxes, in on the joke, but the point is made: it is not always easy to discern reality from illusion, especially in movies. This will prove critical for many of the characters in the film as the story develops.

The Funhouse is packed with such revelations. An adult stranger in a pick-up truck offers Joey a ride to the carnival, then pulls a rifle on the boy. Then he laughs and drives away, leaving the boy unharmed. Like Joey, he is a trickster too, appearing kindly one moment, then dangerous, and finally harmless again. What is the truth? The audience isn't certain and so the scene comes off as unsettling, unpredictable, full of ominous foreboding. Once at the carnival, *The Funhouse* continues this reflexive structure, taking its characters to a horror movie within a larger horror movie. To wit, they visit a freak show with deformed, two-headed cows and the corpse of a mutant fetus. The teens laugh at these anomalies: they're behind ropes or in containers and thus, like the remote images displayed on the silver screen, deemed harmless. At the magic show, a carnie dressed as a vampire (*Eaten Alive's* William Finley) seemingly kills a young girl, an audience volunteer, when he drives a wooden stake through her heart. But this only appears to be so (as do the carefully orchestrated, graphic deaths in movies such as *Friday the 13th*). The girl is actually the magician's assistant, in the know the whole time, and the blood is merely makeup, the stake but a prop. In these sequences of perceived reality turning "safely" to entertainment, the viewer of the film (like the four teens at the carnival) gets suckered into relaxing, into a kind of comfort zone. Nothing here is real. Nothing here can hurt you.

And then and only then does Hooper deliver his whammy. He flips a switch and suddenly the seemingly safe becomes rigorously unsafe. The turning point is Madame Zena's tent. Amy has her fortune revealed there and the gypsy woman speaks in a flowery, stereotypical fortune teller–style accent. But when angered by her customers, Zena lets the artifice slip and becomes her true self: a venomous, nasty woman of low accent and filthy vocabulary. Here it is the performance of geniality that is a sham. It is the illusion that is safe; the truth that is so dangerous. The scene ends terrifyingly when Zena's crystal ball, of its own volition, rolls to her hands. The implication is that her affability is an act but her strange abilities are not. Scarily, she has noted that Amy has knowledge of the occult, and naturally, it is Amy all along who sees terror in the reappearing face of the Barker.

From this point in the film, everything that should be safe is merely an illusion and the danger to the teens transforms into reality. The Barker's son wears a Frankenstein monster mask, a symbol of horror homog-

3. *The Funhouse* (1981)

Terror in the shower! A masked killer confronts a frightened Amy (Elizabeth Berridge) in *The Funhouse* (1981).

enized and made acceptable in American culture. It is a safe, familiar image, seen in old movies, on TV reruns, and lampooned throughout our culture. Underneath it, however, reality is much worse than this mainstream visage of horror seems to indicate. Or, as Bruce Kawin, film scholar wrote:

> ... the monster has been wearing a Frankenstein mask, a downright brilliant gesture, not just because the Frankenstein monster is the correct prototype (the child rejected by his creator and looking for love) but because with the mask on he appears part of the normal world, the world that includes horror images as elements in its playground. Now the father criticizes him so harshly that the son tears off his mask and confronts him with what he is. The horror, the audience discovers, is real [1].

In other words, a mass market, cultural image of acceptable horror (of a long-lived, famous monster) has been used to cloak a real terror, to lull the living into a sense of false security. In the ultimate reversal of reality and illusion, three of the nosy teens are killed in the funhouse, becoming part of the rides and attractions inside the chamber, taking their places beside the "safe" animatronic horror of the carnival. After Richie is killed, he is purposefully displayed on a rolling funhouse car, an axe jutting out of his head. He's become part of the scenery, like the macabre ghouls who bend and speak and wave their mechanical arms in an attempt to scare visitors to the fair. Hooper's point is that this is no longer a joke, no longer artifice. Reality is terrifying, illusion comforting, but each can be misperceived.

By mirroring the dichotomy of the movies (artifice substituting for reality) Hooper offers an important comment about film and in particular the "dead teenager" kind of film. These movies feature gruesome imagery, blood and gore galore and vicious violence, yet their producers hide behind the notion that these entertainments are not real, that they are merely playing at being real. But real or not, what do these graphic and disturbing images do to the young viewers who were exposed to them? Roger Ebert was one critic who feared that the glut of gory, bad "dead teen" movies would cause real children to formulate a "world view in which the primary function of teenagers is to be hacked to death" (2). In response to that fear, Hooper, a responsible horror director, seems to be saying with *The Funhouse* that filmmakers ought to choose their disturbing images carefully, especially if they intend to depict death and other horrors. It is something that should be done with meaning, not merely as a carnival freak show.

It is important that Hooper is not a censor, in any way advocating censorship, or attempting to curtail horror output; he is only trying to return it to the more "meaningful" genre it had always been, pre–1978 (with films such *Night of the Living Dead, The Exorcist* [1973], *Don't Look Now* [1973] and even his own *Chain Saw* representing high points). The self-reflexive nature of *The Funhouse* lets the audience in on that feeling. We should be careful what we laugh at, mindful of what we write off as "harmless," because, in fact, it could be harmful to some. It is a voice of responsibility and one Hooper would hone in his next film, *Poltergeist*, a picture that made much the same remark about the ubiquity of television in American households.

The Funhouse is also a reflexive film in another very specific way. It draws a direct parallel to the Frankenstein mythos in that images of the popular, revered monster appear virtually everywhere. There is a poster of the monster in Joey's bedroom. He plays with a Frankenstein monster action-figure. *Bride of Frankenstein* is playing on TV in Amy's living room and, of course, the carnie mutant wears a mask of the famous horror icon. All these references are apt for different reasons. In his affection for horror movies and "scary" moments, Joey has been made a monster, himself: pulling nasty tricks on his unsuspecting older sister. He is associated with the Frankenstein Monster twice: in his choice of bedroom decoration and his selection of toys. Like others in the film then (including the often-misled audience), Joey seems to have some difficulty in separating reality from illusion. For him, the monster is a hero, but he learns in his encounter with a real monster (the mutant cloaked as the Frankenstein monster) that such creatures are not to be admired.

As for Amy, in a very real way she becomes the bride of Frankenstein as the film unspools. She is the only survivor of the beast's murderous onslaught and her prized status as a virgin makes her the only suitable object for the mutant's affections. He may be attracted to seductresses like Liz (who tricks him using sex) or Madame Zena (whom he pays for sex) but it is the virgin Amy whom he lavishes his most special attention on. Accordingly, throughout the film violence is associated with the mutant's sexual desires. He prematurely ejaculates with Zena (a scene replayed with Leatherface and a chainsaw in Hooper's *Chainsaw 2* [1986]) and in his rage damages a fuse box, causing electricity to course through the room. These ejaculatory sparks bring animatronic figures to life and physically embody his rage. The same thing happens again when he confronts Amy during the film's climax. When he dies in pursuit of her it is practically an orgasm of electricity that jolts the underground chamber. This is an important link to Mary Shelley's creation because in the Frankenstein myth (and movies), it is electricity that brings life to the terrible monster in the first place. In *The Funhouse*, electrical discharge is likewise associated with life and death, a physical side effect of the creature's lustful desires.

Amy has something else in common with the frightening and deformed antagonist of *The Funhouse*. She is his "bride" because she is, like him, the unhappy child of dysfunctional parents. Like the monster, she is a virgin, desiring to experience (with Buzz) the joys of sex while simultaneously afraid of the power sex has over her. The Frankenstein motif thus links protagonist and antagonist much in the way Laurie Strode's desires for a "man" in *Halloween* link her to Michael Myers. In some senses these characters (Amy and the monster) are two sides of the same coin, only Amy grew up in a so-called normal family while the mutant grew up in a less stable, mobile, abnormal one. But both want more than what their parents can give them (jobs, life in a small town, and so on). Just as *The Texas Chain Saw Massacre* depicted mirror images of American families (the Hardestys and the Leatherface clan), so do *The Funhouse* show a similar reflection by putting Amy in opposition with the mutant monster.

Besides the unusual bond between Amy and her mirror image, the monster, *The Funhouse* features relationships that are often highlighted in Hooper's work. The bickering siblings, Amy and Joey, are a slightly less extreme version of the unhappy siblings Franklin and Sally in *The Texas Chain Saw Massacre,* and in both cases it is the male of the duo who needs protecting and comes off as taunting and immature. In a later Hooper production, *Poltergeist,* the sibling rivalry between a younger boy and his teen sister is similarly revived in the relationship Oliver Robbins and the late Dominique Dunne share. Perhaps of more interest to avid Hooper scholars is the double villainy of *The Funhouse.* In much of his filmed work, Hooper likes his "evil" to be shared by two characters, a duo of danger (and sometimes, even a full family). One of the main baddies is always, to outward appearances, normal, while the other is somehow grotesque or abnormal. It is the "normal" human-looking evil that enables the "abnormal" evil to thrive.

In *Chain Saw*, Cook provides the raw material for Leatherface's cannibalistic cooking. In *Salem's Lot* it is the urbane, clever, well-dressed Straker (James Mason) who procures victims for the feral, green-skinned vampire named Barlow (Reggie Nalder). Likewise in *The Funhouse*: the seedy, sinister Barker (Kevin Conway) protects and kills for his deformed son (Wayne Doba). And, like Cook in the *Chainsaw* films, this enabler claims to honor family values above all else, and even says that "blood is thicker than water." Although he is upset that his wayward son has killed Zena, a member of his extended carnival family, he stands by the boy when push comes to shove. This dedication may arise in part because, like Cook, the Barker also clearly exploits his family ties. The Barker runs the funhouse and makes money off his boy (an able assistant) much as Cook runs a barbecue and later a catering business with Leatherface as his butcher. These "employees" must be protected at all costs or economic freedom will be sacrificed.

The reflexive structure of *The Funhouse* and the interesting character dynamics are only part of Hooper's overall tapestry. Visually and atmospherically, *The Funhouse* is one of the director's most creepy ventures. The images accompanying the opening credits are what the hecklers of *Mystery Science Theater 3000* politely refer to as "good old fashioned nightmare fodder." In particular, the names of the film's contributors are seen side by side with creepy carnival automatons (straight from the 1940s and 1950s). There's one such robot swinging endlessly in a rocking chair, a chattering woman, a malevolent clown (later a symbol of fear in *Poltergeist*), a Humpty-Dumpy, a gorilla, an obese woman, and so forth, all pictured in irises and wipes and accompanied by horrific carnival music. It's a distinctly disturbing note to open on, and a highly effective one.

Another nice visual touch is that all of the carnival barkers are portrayed (with light make-up alterations) by Kevin Conway, implying that there has been some pretty heavy in-breeding at this traveling fair. It might also be an indication that "greedy evil" has but one, sleazy face.

Two of the most effective visuals in the film occur late in the action. The first comes as the funhouse and the surrounding carnival tents are shut down for the night. The animatronic figures cycle down slowly and then grind to a halt. Lights turn off, giving way to ebony night, and the notion of being alone in the dark at that locale, among those freaky figures, is a terrifying one to contemplate. To heighten these feelings of doom and danger, Hooper stages a long, elaborate pull back from the funhouse. This is a long, steady shot, composed with stately elegance and chilly perfection. The camera eventually retracts so far that it reaches the carnival parking lot and captures the patrons as they get in their cars and drive home. The feeling of being left behind in the dark, in the company of evil, is palpable.

The climax is also quite powerful, and it is a sequence almost universally praised by critics. The scene builds to a fever pitch and ends on another note of reflexivity. As the monstrous mutant is finally killed, he joins the funhouse rides themselves. Chains and hooks move across the ceiling, big gears spin and the mutant is pulled apart by the ugly machinery, just another animatronic cog in an amusement park attraction. This sequence (bathed in a chilly blue light and peppered with white flashes of electricity) is some kind of genre highwater mark of intensity, as ghoulish, disturbing and amusing as anything seen in *The Texas Chain Saw Massacre* or *Poltergeist*.

Seen on its own merits, *The Funhouse* is a great horror film, every bit the equal of *Halloween* or *The Texas Chain Saw Massacre* in meaning and use of effective film technique. But seen in the context of Hooper's career, it gains even more steam. The childhood obsession with magic and monsters, a facet of Hooper's life characterized in *Poltergeist*, *Salem's Lot* and *Invaders from Mars*, plays a big role here, particularly in Joey's bedroom accouterments. The homages evident in the film (to *Psycho*, to *Frankenstein*, to *Halloween*) are a near constant refrain in Hooper's oeuvre. And though the film does feature randy teenagers making out and taking off their clothes (you have to satisfy your core demographic, after all), it artfully examines and condemns the glut of dead teenager movies that it was accused of "ripping off." It's an accomplished film that captures the raw edge of early Hooper (exemplified by *Eaten Alive* and *The Texas Chain Saw Massacre*) as well as the new, more disciplined Hooper (exemplified by the pristine *Salem's Lot*). The burgeoning DVD market has brought this title out of obscurity and back to please horror fans, and *The Funhouse* is finally receiving the reevaluation it has so long deserved.

4. *Poltergeist* (1982)

Critical Reception

"My favorite film from the Spielberg factory is, oddly enough, an associational item, as is *Gremlins*; the vastly underrated and strangely unsung *Poltergeist*, which I view as a Tobe Hooper film, influenced by Spielberg."
—*Harlan Ellison's Watching*, Underwood Miller, 1989, page 193.

4. *Poltergeist* (1982)

"It's one of the flashiest, most dazzling ghost stories ever made, yet it lacks any real element of fear.... *Poltergeist* is a treat. It's a simple entertainment, though not a great horror film in the way that *The Thing* or ... *The Texas Chainsaw Massacre* are great horror films."
—Darrell Moore, *The Best, The Worst, the Most Unusual: Horror Films*, pgs. 90-91.

"Director Tobe Hooper ... has a nice visceral touch for what scares kids at night. Anyone who has jumped in one bound from door to the bed to avoid the Three Billy Goats Gruff under the bed will empathize with young Robbie, who must keep an eye on that relentlessly fake-looking tree, and watch his life-size clown in the dark at the same time. Unfortunately, Spielberg has used a lot of these moments before—and better in *Close Encounters* when their power was fresh.... These details from every boy's ... life are fine, even if this is roughly the 872nd leering clown doll to appear.... (It may be a Hooper trademark; his *Funhouse* had a midway clown apparition, I seem to remember.)
—Sheila Benson, *Los Angeles Times*, June 4, 1982.

"Under Tobe Hooper's direction, Jobeth Williams and Craig T. Nelson shine as the dogged Mom and the heroic-in-spite-of-himself dad."
—*Time Magazine*: "Best of '82," January 3, 1983, page 82.

"...[A] marvelously spooky ghost story that may possibly scare the wits out of very small children ... full of creepy, crawly, slimy things that jump out from the shadows.... *Poltergeist* is a thoroughly enjoyable nightmare.... It's also witty in a fashion that Alfred Hitchcock might appreciate."
—Vincent Canby, *The New York Times*, June 4, 1982.

"I do not think the alleged tension between the two [Spielberg and Hooper] hurt *Poltergeist* unduly. I can honestly report that I was shaken from the ends of my hair to the tips of my toes by this stirring fable of love, fear, and rebirth."
—Andrew Sarris, *The Village Voice*, June 15, 1982, page 59.

"At first and final glance, *Poltergeist* is simply a riveting demonstration of the movie's power to scare the sophistication out of any viewers. It creates honest thrills within the confines of a PG rating ... the picture can also be seen as a sly comedy supporting the proposition that violence on TV ... or precisely, in it, can have an influence on children who watch it."
—Richard Corliss, *Time Magazine*: "Steve's Summer Magic," page 56.

"...[N]arrative flaws are mitigated ... by the film's sheer momentum, its technical virtuosity, and the convention that a horror film need not always explain cause and effect."
—Marc Mancini, *Magill's Cinema Annual 1983*, page 266.

"Spielberg is credited as producer of *Poltergeist*, with the directing credit going to Tobe Hooper, a technically talented filmmaker whose best-known work is the notorious *Texas Chain Saw Massacre*. Yet the energetic Spielberg appears to have provided the basic vision of the film. By his own account, he served as a 'strong, David O. Selznick-type' producer and was active on the set every day."
—David Sterritt, *Christian Science Monitor*, June 17, 1982, page 18.

"The film plays more for laughs and chuckles than anything else. Perhaps director Tobe Hooper, of the *Texas Chainsaw Massacre* fame, should have had a freer hand."
—Kenneth M. Chanko, *Films in Review*, August 9, 1982, page 430.

"As a horror film, *Poltergeist* is sadly disappointing, conventional, predictable. But as a case study, it is fascinating, given that the project's originator and producer (Steven Spielberg) and its director (Tobe Hooper) come from such different traditions—the former from Disney, suburbia and TV; the latter from Gothic and the campus film scene (University of Texas). *Poltergeist* is also a practical test of authorship. Though Hooper 'directed', the team with which he worked ... was Spielberg's. After rumors that Hooper had effectively been fired from the set and that Spielberg had shot much of the material, the latter put an advertisement in *Variety* congratulating his director on their 'unique' creative relationship—which merely added fuel to the gossip."
—Chris Auty, *Monthly Film Bulletin*, September 1982, page 205.

"Tobe Hooper, director of that creeps' delight *The Texas Chainsaw Massacre*, may be formally credited with the direction of the latest haunted house movie, *Poltergeist*, but the thing is stamped all over with the obsessions of Steven Spielberg."
—John Coleman, *New Statesman*, September 17, 1982, page 26.

"The authorship of this movie will be much debated. There are a few horror-film touches—disintegrating faces and the like—that are similar to things done in the past by Hooper.... But there are also a variety of unmistakable Spielberg obsessions.... The movie has got to be more Spielberg's than Hooper's."
—David Denby, *New York*, June 7, 1982, page 71.

"Although Tobe Hooper is credited with the direction, Spielberg was reportedly almost constantly on the set and giving expert advice.... In *Poltergeist* two distinct voices seem to come from behind the camera screen also. Horror specialist Hooper, director of the notorious *Texas Chainsaw Massacre* ... highlights the gory and gothic aspects of the plot. More characteristic of Spielberg is the stress on the imagination of the children and the resourcefulness of the mother, the quizzical attitudes to television.... In the end, the Spielberg predominates because *Poltergeist* is more genial than gruesome."
—Neil Sinyard, *The Films of Steven Spielberg*, Bison Books Ltd, London, 1986.

Cast and Crew

CAST: Craig T. Nelson (Steve Freeling); Jo Beth Williams (Diane Freeling); Beatrice Straight (Dr. Lash); Dominique Dunne (Dana Freeling); Oliver Robbins (Robbie Freeling); Heather O'Rourke (Carol Anne Freeling); Michael McManus (Ben Tuthill); Virginia Kiser (Mrs. Tuthill); Martin Casella (Marty); Richard Lawson (Ryan); Zelda Rubenstein (Tangina); James Karen (Mr. Teague); Lou Perry (Pugsley); Dirk Blocker (Jeff Shaw); Clair Leucart (Bulldozer); Allan Graff (Sam); Joseph R. Walsh (Joey); Helen Baron (Woman Buyer); Neal Conlon (Husband); Robert Broyles (Pool Worker # 1); Sonny Landham (Pool Worker # 2); Bill Vail (Implosion Man); Jeffrey Bannister (Implosion Man); Phil Stone (Football Announcer).

CREW: MGM Presents a Tobe Hooper Film, a Steven Spielberg Production, *Poltergeist*. *Music:* Jerry Goldsmith. *Director of Photography:* Matthew Leonetti. *Editor:* Michael Kahn. *Production Designer:* James H. Spencer. *Screenplay:* Steven Spielberg, Michael Grais, Mark Victor. *Story:* Steven Spielberg. *Directed by:* Tobe Hooper. *Associate Producer:* Kathleen Kennedy. *Visual Effects:* Richard Edlund. *Production Manager:* Dennis Jones. *First Assistant Director:* Pat Kehoe. *Second Assistant Director:* Bob Roe. *Casting:* Mike Fenton, Jane Feinberg, Marci Liroff. *Production Coordinator:* Beverly Webb. *Script Supervisor:* Marion Tumen. *Location Manager:* Paul Pav. *Camera Operator:* Dennis Matsuda. *First Assistant Cameraman:* John Leonetti. *Set Decorator:* Cheryal Kearney. *Sound Mixer:* Art Rochester. *Property Master:* Craig Raiche. *Make-up:* Dottie Pearl. *Hairdresser:* Toni Walker. *Special Effects Make-up:* Craig Reardon. *Special Effects Supervisor:* Mike Wood. *Costume Supervisor:* Ann Lambert. *Mechanical Effect Supervisor:* Jeff Jarvis. *Visual Effects Coordinator:* Mitch Suskin. *Stunt Coordinator:* Glen Randall Jr. *Stunts:* Cindy Folkeson, Dana Gendian, Jami Gendian, Beth Nufer, Felix Silla, George Wilbur, Jean Epper, Bob Yerkes, Bob Herron. *Associate Editor:* R. Fields. *Music Editor:* Ken Hall. *Special Sound Effects:* Alan Howarth. *Special Visual Effects Produced at:* Industrial Light and Magic. *M.P.A.A. Rating:* PG. *Running time:* 115 minutes.

"Some people believe that when you die, your soul goes to Heaven.... Some people believe that when people die there's a wonderful light as bright as the sun, but it doesn't hurt to look into it. All the answers to all the questions you ever want to know are inside that light. And when you walk to it, you become a part of it forever. And then some people die but don't know that they're gone ... maybe they didn't want to die, maybe they weren't ready, maybe they hadn't lived fully, or they'd lived a long, long time and they still wanted more life. They resist going into that light, however hard the light wants them. They just hang around, watch TV. Watch their friends grow up, feeling unhappy and jealous. Those feelings are bad, they hurt. And some people just get lost on the way to the light and they need someone to guide them to it."
—Dr. Lesh's stirring description of "ghosts" in Tobe Hooper's *Poltergeist* (1982).

Synopsis

In suburban Questa Verde, little Carol Anne Freeling alarms her family by communicating with people she says inhabit the television. Then, one morning, Carol Anne's pet bird, Tweety, dies, and brother Robbie is troubled by the gnarled old tree outside his bedroom window because he thinks it is staring at him. By night, a storm

It Knows What Scares You. Steve Freeling (Craig T. Nelson) is about to face a monster from "the other side" in *Poltergeist* (1982).

rolls in, and Mrs. Freeling puts the children to bed. Robbie is frightened by the strange-looking toy clown figure in his bedroom and the thunder outside. As Diane and Steve Freeling smoke pot in their bedroom and discuss the children, their revels are disrupted by an unsettled Robbie. Steve takes care of the boy, easing his fears about the approaching storm and the tree outside his window. His efforts to soothe the child fail and little Robbie and Carol Anne spend the night in the parents' bed.

In the middle of the night, a force of malevolent energy exits from the television (to the strains of the National Anthem), and rocks the house. The family wakes, thinking an earthquake has struck, but Carol Anne calmly and ominously announces "*they're here.*" At the breakfast table the next morning, the "TV people" begin to make mischief, bending the silverware, and moving the chairs at the kitchen table. When Steve comes home from work, Diane shows him how a chair moves across the floor without being touched by living hands. Next, Carol Anne is pushed across the floor by the same strange invisible force. Steve is flabbergasted.

That night, another storm rocks the suburb of Questa Verde. The weather turns violent, and the creepy old tree breaks into the Freeling house and pulls Robbie outside. As Diane and Steve race to save him from the grasping tree and an oncoming twister, a powerful force drags Carol Ann into her bedroom closet and transports her out of our reality, into another dimension. Diane and Steve save Robbie after much difficulty, but return inside to learn that Carol Anne has vanished without a trace.

Together with their older daughter, Dana, the entire family searches the house from top to bottom. Steve even searches the half-finished swimming pool in the backyard, which is now overflowing with rain water. Then Robbie hears Carol Anne's voice emanating from the TV. The Freelings are stunned: their little girl has been taken away by spirits.

Steve takes leave from his job as a real estate sales man and consults with parapsychologist Dr. Lesh and a team of two assistants. They agree to come to the house to observe the phenomena, but Steve just wants his daughter found. Once in the Freeling home, Dr. Lesh and her team find Carol Anne's room a swirling hotbed of psychotronic energy. Toys fly around the room of their own volition, forming a kind of psychic madhouse. Diane calls to Carol Anne in the presence of the parapsychologists, and to their amazement, she responds via the TV. She reports that she is afraid of a bright white light. Dr. Lesh quickly orders that Diane command Carol Anne to stay away from the light at all costs.

Next, a grab bag of objects such as old watches and jewelry suddenly falls down from the grand room ceiling, and weirder yet, Carol Anne detects some kind of evil presence within the nether region. Dr. Lesh determines that the ceiling may be a portal from which Carol Anne can escape, but the dark thing in the other dimension seems to be holding her back.

That night, the house's spirits respond with hostility to Dr. Lesh's investigative team. One member of the duo imagines his face peeling off. Later, video cameras register a parade of spectral entities descending the home's main staircase. Diane feels Carol Anne's soul flash through her in an instant. The next morning, a fearful Diane and Steve send Robbie and the family dog off to stay with Diane's mother, concerned that the spirit manifestations are escalating in intensity. Meanwhile, Lesh examines more closely the objects dropped through the dimensional portal. Most are personal belongings, but of widely different eras, some old and some new.

Steve's boss, Mr. Teague, visits the house to ask why his star salesman has missed so much work of late. Since Teague wants to keep his best sales generator on staff, he takes Steve to the newest phase of the real estate development. He wants to build over an old hilltop cemetery, and Steve isn't sure that it's a good idea. Teague insists that the graves will be moved to a new location, and offhandedly remarks that he's relocated graves before—under Questa Verde!

Back at the house, Dr. Lesh brings a diminutive medium, Tangina, to cleanse the Freeling home of spirits. She determines that the opening to the other dimension is the closet in Carol Anne's bedroom, and that the exit is the portal in the great room ceiling. She also verifies Carol Anne's report of a frightening presence on "the other side"—one filled with rage. Diane and Steve contact Carol Anne at Tangina's urging, and tell her to run away from the dark presence. They order her to run to the light, which represents another plane of existence that the ghosts are assiduously avoiding. Then they order her to stop before going in, lest she "cross over" to the place beyond death. Attached to our dimension by a rope around her waist, Diane goes after her daughter, into the limbo dimension, while Steve holds onto the rope. He attempts to pull her back too soon, however, and a terrifying spirit faces him. Frightened, he releases the rope, sending an untethered Diane and Carol Anne plummeting through the nether region, out the portal exit in the great room. Covered in a bizarre, slimy afterbirth, Diane and Carol Anne are shaken, but alive. Tangina pronounces the house clean.

Later, the Freelings pack up their belongings and plan to move out of the house.

While Steve finishes up some work at the office, Diane stays with Robbie and Carol Anne at the Questa Verde house. As Diane naps in a bathtub, the malevolent spirits return with a vengeance, seeking their missing prize, Carol Anne. Robbie's clown doll comes to malevolent life to throttle the boy. Another spirit makes sexual advances on Diane, pushing her up to the ceiling and attempting to peel off her clothes! Diane frees herself and attempts to save the children, but is repelled from their room by a skeletal monster. The monster's force propels her out of the house and into the backyard pool, where skeletons in coffins start to push their way out of the ground. She is rescued by her perplexed neighbors. Then Diane races back inside to save her children from a hellish, organic maw.

Meanwhile, Steve returns home to see all hell breaking loose. He realizes at last, as caskets burst up from the Earth, that Mr. Teague never moved the graves when he built here, he just moved the headstones! The wronged spirits are now protesting in full force. As Diane escapes with the children, Steve and Dana join them, and they drive away from Questa Verde, even as their house folds up on itself and vanishes to a nether realm. Later, the Freelings arrive at a motel room and make sure to push the television set out of their suite.

Commentary

In an unusual irony, the supernatural thriller *Poltergeist* is probably the best known of all Tobe Hooper's films. Yet, those who know the film tend to associate it not with Hooper, but with its producer-writer, Steven Spielberg. Even the *TV Guide* "blurb" credits the film to Spielberg, reinforcing the idea that it is "his" film. Though ownership of *Poltergeist* is much debated, in the final analysis the film is a terrifying concoction of horror thrills and chills that, upon close inspection, more closely resembles the work of Hooper than it does the film fantasies of Spielberg.

If someone were to ask this author to give just one argument why *Poltergeist* feels like a Hooper film, not a Spielberg one, it would be simple to pinpoint the central point of debate: *tone*. In addition to being a balls-out horror film, *Poltergeist* is, on a deeper level, satire about American values in general and the role of TV in our society in particular. Now, Spielberg is a gifted filmmaker, to be certain, a wonder even. But a satirist he is not. Steven Spielberg is, above all else, a *sincere* filmmaker. His work is usually apolitical (or politically correct) and very much "on the nose," not humorous jibes at real life people, politics or trends. If he wants to issue a valuable societal point about the treatment of veterans (*Saving Private Ryan* [1998]), slavery (*Amistad* [1998]) or the Holocaust (*Schindler's List* [1994]), he directs an accomplished, emotionally honest motion picture revolving around the very serious topic of choice.

Similarly, *E.T.* (1982) is a straight-faced film about boyhood friendships, *Raiders of the Lost Ark* (1981), though droll, an updating and *cherishing* of 1930s cliffhangers. Yet *Poltergeist* is a different animal altogether. Like another Spielberg-produced film, *Gremlins* (directed by Joe Dante), it is blatantly and unabashedly satirical. It is a film that, without reservation, equates the television with evil. To state the matter succinctly, the TV gets turned on in the Freeling house and promptly exposes the family to evil. The first and the last images of the film involve television as a portal for terror and the Freelings' last act before the end credits roll is to kick the offending TV set out of their motel room! There's no way around it.

Poltergeist commences with an extreme close-up of a television. The set is playing the national anthem, but the images are not pristine, not clear. United States icons like the flag and the Capitol building are seen as

Diane Freeling (JoBeth Williams) is thrown to the ceiling by invisible (and amorous) spirits in *Poltergeist* (1982).

grainy and indistinct and then they change, devolving to static almost at once. Later in the film, the playing of the national anthem on television recurs, undeniably tying TV and America together in a tight bond. This union seems to indicate that America's future, in Hooper's eyes, is as a TV-obsessed nation. Liberty, freedom, and ideals have become fuzzy, blurred (like the static-ridden picture) before the unblinking eye of a TV that sells fast food, cars and other luxuries twenty four hours a day. The metaphor extends even to the Freelings: Mr. Freeling wants to sell real estate and get rich, regardless of what demographic (the spirits of the dead!) he might have to trample to make his fortune.

This satirical undercurrent is an important facet of *Poltergeist*'s narrative tapestry and it is not likely one envisioned by Spielberg. In his work as a director, he rarely, if ever, speaks with tongue in cheek and he *never* bites the hand that feeds him. Consider that *Poltergeist*, in its indictment of television and 1980s consumer culture (i.e., the yuppie mentality), runs totally counter to the mentality that would permit such blatant product placement in a work of art (*Reeses Pieces* and *E.T.*—perfect together!). Contrarily, Hooper has always utilized horror films as a vehicle for satire and making socially valuable "points." *The Texas Chain Saw Massacre* was in some ways about the gas shortage and job layoffs of the early 1970s. *The Funhouse* concerned the adverse impact of bad but profitable "dead teenager" movies so popular at the time of the film's release. *The Texas Chainsaw Masacre Part 2* satirized yuppies and small business owners, and *Invaders from Mars* equated the "don't worry, be happy" 1980s with the conformist 1950s. The mode of *Poltergeist*, satire, is therefore Hooper's typical manner of expression.

It is no coincidence in *Poltergeist* that the strobing light of the television is constantly reflected on the face of the film's principals, and that the self-same coloring and lighting scheme is used to render the closet doorway to the nether region. Both the blue light in the closet and the blue light of the TV set represent the same thing: portals to places that can steal your children away. Both venues can overtake your life (especially if *Temptation Island* is on) and both can be evil if allowed to run rampant. The only way to get rid of the nasty spirits in *Poltergeist* is to throw away your "tainted" material wealth (your house, your belongings, your television set) and reject the values of a culture obsessed with greed. That's why the final images of *Poltergeist* are so important: a family is reunited, dependent and trusting each other, and their first act, post haunting, is to kick the TV to the curb. They have no TV now, no house in the suburbs, no corporate sponsors. What they do have, at long last, is family togetherness.

For the satire to work correctly, *Poltergeist* must define the culture of its characters as corrupt, and that is exactly what the film does. Steve Freeling is a consummate schmoozer, a protypical yuppie. He's a salesman (ugh) and a real-estate agent (double ugh), who is slick, insincere and more concerned about career advancement and making money than in doing the right thing. "The grass grows greener on *every* side," he slickly tells a prospective client, kissing ass and hoping to make a deal simultaneously. Similarly Steven is shown at one point in the film to be reading *Reagan: The Man, the President.* This choice of reading is important because Ronald Reagan's revolution, his very values, are directly responsible for the horrors that occur at Questa Verde.

Reagan's trademark as president was to offer simple answers to complex problems. Kids doing drugs? "Just say no!" Crime on the rise? Stress "family values." The economy in the tanker? Resort to voodoo economics and take the country deeper into debt while cutting taxes for the rich. *Poltergeist* mirrors these surface solutions to complex social problems. Want to start a new urban development, but a cemetery is in the way? Just move the headstones! Don't worry about ghosts or deficits, just worry about taking what you want and making more money. But what *Poltergeist* (accurately) forecasts is that budgetary deficits, like angry spirits, rise up and bite you on the ass eventually, as Reagan's inept successor George Bush learned in the recession of 1991-92. *Poltergeist* not only punishes the greedy, the real estate tycoon played by James Karen, it punishes those who benefit from the greed and moral lassitude of others. The Freelings go through hell not because they did anything *really* wrong themselves, but because they have inadvertently prospered by the unseemly business practices of Steve's firm! Even Steve's choice of heroes (Reagan) is at issue.

Again, there is no precedent for such veiled commentary in the works of Steven Spielberg. If anything, his films (particularly *Close Encounters* and *E.T.*) seem to laud the middle-class American lifestyle of conspicuous consumption. As film scholar Morris Dickstein wrote in *Love and Hisses: Steven Spielberg and George Lucas on Peter Panavision*:

> The suburban worlds of these [Spielberg] movies strikes me as dim, stereotyped, and pretty much interchangeable. He loves suburbia too much to examine it closely … his vision of the nuclear family, presided [over] by loving guardians, is not far removed from *Father Knows Best* [1].

In casting blame on the middle class for the greed and business practices of corporations, *Poltergeist* is pretty serious business, even harsh. Hardly the stuff of an artist who admires suburbia and benefits from mass merchandising and product placement, and whose vision of America is so close to 1950s sitcoms. Again, these pointed comments are quite in keeping with Tobe Hooper's film record. He criticized yuppies and small business owners with satiric good humor in *Chainsaw 2* and despised the "latch key kid," "TV as babysitter" phenomenon of the 1980s in *Invaders from Mars*. Spielberg is a visual and emotional genius, but his work doesn't reveal the kind of wit that dominates Hooper's films, and the important issue of tone is one that clearly lands *Poltergeist* under Hooper's banner. Spielberg is whitebread (in a good, patriotic, stirring way) in never-never land, and Hooper, coming out of the underground film movement, is subversive, perverse, reactionary, over the top. The critique of television culture and a then-sitting president in *Poltergeist* are definitely in keeping with Hooper's record, especially since he lampooned suburbia in pictures as diverse as *The Funhouse* and *Invaders from Mars*.

Another feature of *Poltergeist* that marks the film as a Hooper piece is its narrative U turns. Midway through the picture, one of Dr. Lesh's associates goes to the bathroom and proceeds to peel his face off.

Squishy maggots push a juicy steak across a counter too. These are phantasms (imagined moments) not externally perceived by others. They are not quantifiable phenomena, as are the rest of the occurrences in *Poltergeist*. Therefore, they don't really fit in with the spectral wisps and flashing lights, and one suspects such horrific, gory images were included just to unsettle. Remember, Hooper is the "no-deal" kid. The moments with the disposable face and the worm-infested steak represent an early warning that Hooper intends to obey no rules, not even the tenets of parapsychology, in scaring the hell out of his audience.

Perhaps more importantly is the fact that *Poltergeist* has two distinct climaxes. One arises logically out of the plot, the other is pure rollercoaster. Near the end of the film, Steve and Diane band together and rescue the abducted Carol Anne from the afterlife. The family comes together, and Tangina pronounces "this house is clean." Well, *beg to differ*. The house is not clean (even though, logically, it should be), and that sets the way for the over-the-top action/horror finale of the film. If this were a Spielberg film, one can see how it might have played out. Carol Anne is restored (as little Barry was restored to his mother in *Close Encounters of the Third Kind*), the restless, unhappy spirits find the light (*E.T.* phones home and hitches a ride back to the stars) and normal life resumes for the Freelings (as normal life resumes for Brody once the menace of the great white shark is dispatched in *Jaws*). But Hooper isn't usually satisfied with that kind of closure and so he tags a very personal ending onto *Poltergeist,* one that is as vicious and intense as any Hooper trademark scenes in *The Funhouse* or *The Texas Chain Saw Massacre*.

A clown (a figure of terror also featured in *The Funhouse*) is animated to violent life, strangling a helpless child. We know Hooper is fascinated by animism, the everyday objects rendered living, because at least two of his films feature animism prominently (*I'm Dangerous Tonight* and *The Mangler*). But more to the point, this manifestation (like the face peel) is one of unadulterated horror. There is no wonder, no feeling of awe or enlightenment, just terror. Then, an unseen ghost tries to rape Mrs. Freeling and again, this is beyond the previous scope of the film. The restless spirits have been defined as playful, grasping, dangerous even, but nothing could have prepared the audience for the intensity of this sexual attack (one that, literally, has Diane Freeling climbing the walls).

Then all hell explodes (much like the finale of *The Funhouse* in the gear room) and Hooper throws in everything but the kitchen sink. A swimming pool of corpses. An organic, tentacled maw leading straight to Hell. An imploding house, even! It isn't difficult to discern that the film is a rollercoaster ride pure and simple, an amusement park attraction that takes audiences on a jolting rip. It isn't comforting (like *E.T.* or *Close Encounters*), it isn't a victorious triumph (like *Raiders of the Lost Ark*), it is purely and simply intense and horrific. And, as a side note to this argument, Hooper's conceit works: the climax of *Poltergeist* is adrenaline inducing, even if it isn't narratively valuable. After all, shouldn't the Freelings get their money back from Tangina? (And, oddly, the first thing they do in the sequel is get the medium in again. It's not like she did a very thorough job the first time...)

This author would argue that as a filmmaker, Tobe Hooper has always made an effort to take his climaxes over the top, regardless of the consequences to the narrative. The monster in *The Funhouse* isn't only killed, he's bashed, electrocuted, and caught in the gears of a carnival ride. A "possessed" machine is exorcised in *The Mangler*, but the exorcism doesn't take and the machine sprouts legs and starts to run after its enemies. In *The Texas Chain Saw Massacre*, the heroine escapes but, again, there is no conventional narrative ending. Leatherface dances with his chainsaw on the side of a highway as the sun comes up and the girl is left a bloodied, raving maniac. In all these cases, the movies end on unconventional yet high notes, just like *Poltergeist*. A victory is overturned; a villain unexpectedly survives;

Grave problems: Diane (JoBeth Williams) falls into a pool of corpses during the harrowing climax of *Poltergeist* (1982).

incident piles upon incident until the audience is left breathless, and so on. This seems far more evocative of Hooper, the former magician and "scare you at all costs" director than it does Steven Spielberg, a brilliant man who prides himself on lyrical and emotional "storytelling" (with all of its requisite conventions, like narrative resolution.) Hooper's endings are super real (surreal), over the top and, sometimes, virtually independent (or even contradictory) to narrative expectations.

At a very basic, gut level, Tobe Hooper's movies have always concerned death, the fear and ugliness of death. Though ostensibly more upbeat than the nihilistic *Texas Chain Saw Massacre* or *Eaten Alive*, *Poltergeist* likewise finds itself obsessed with encroaching death. What is more remarkable (and again suggestive that the film was not directed by Spielberg) is that he lands the fear of encroaching death into an arena where it is easily ignored, suburbia. The Questa Verde of *Poltergeist* is a decaying place where death is just around every corner. The suburban streets are dotted with trees, but they are lifeless, leafless trees. They look sad, out of place, because real estate development has run rampant and killed off nature. Then Carol Anne's little bird Tweety dies unexpectedly, shattering the illusion that life in suburbia is undending bliss and safety. Mortality is still a real issue here, as the colossal graveyards dotting the nearby hills testify. Finally, dark clouds roll in over head, signaling the insurrection of the unsettled spirits, and Hooper's message is clearly rendered. The suburbs, even with all their luxuries, all their remote controls and TV sets, do not elevate humanity beyond the level where it must fear death. No place, not even middle class America, is insulated from the stench of death. These images are less visceral perhaps than the cast-off belongings of the dead accumulated by Judd in *Eaten Alive*, the embalmed and contained corpse of an embryo in *The Funhouse,* or the ubiquitous bone furniture of the cannibal farmhouse in *The Texas Chain Saw Massacre*, but nonetheless representative of a continuing theme in Hooper's work. Death is a companion that we see everywhere (like the road kill of *Chain Saw*), and we ignore this predator at our own peril.

When *Poltergeist* debuted, movie critics fell all over themselves noting that the film seemed to have more in common with Steven Spielberg's body of work than Tobe Hooper's. Twenty years later, it seems time to seriously examine that assertion. Spielberg had a dyanamic, powerful influence over *Poltergeist* as its co-writer and producer and it would be foolish and irresponsible to claim otherwise. But this film is so much more "down" on American pillars (like government, commerce, the family, suburbia) than Spielberg would likely permit. Remember that Spielberg is often considered the champion of the middle-class family, but only two of his films have actually been set against that background: *Close Encounters of the Third Kind* and *E.T.* In both cases, the families depicted were single-parent homes, lacking fathers. Oppositely, Tobe Hooper's work has also involved the middle-class family (*The Funhouse, Invaders from Mars*) and in both cases, they were two-parent households, as in *Poltergeist*. So, *Poltergeist*'s setting alone doesn't automatically reference Spielberg's other films.

Preadolescent boys are figures of interest in Spielberg films *Close Encounters of the Third Kind* and *E.T.*, both of which feature a boy's bedroom and all of his fancy toys. Ditto with Tobe Hooper: the same bedrooms (down to the obsessive detailing of toys, posters, so on) appear in *Salem's Lot, Invaders from Mars* and *The Funhouse*. Critics associated this, and other touches, with Spielberg, not Hooper, simply because Spielberg was better known. A more familiar commodity.

And, for those who say Spielberg has a

special relationship with children in his films, they might want to watch *Salem's Lot* to see Hooper's deft handling of the child performers there. Finally, there's the pot, the marijuana. In *Poltergeist*, Diane Freeling and Steve Freeling are depicted using illegal drugs in their bedroom. In what Spielberg film have heroic (not comedic) characters *ever* used illegal drugs? In Hooper's *The Funhouse,* several characters are seen smoking marijuana before the terror begins, just like in *Poltergeist*. Hallucinogenic drugs also play a part in Tobe Hooper's *Night Terrors* and *Crocodile* (with teenagers smoking pot around a campfire). Spielberg is much too respectable to go for that and Hooper's subversive film works, including *The Texas Chain Saw Massacre*, are often equated with a "bad trip" for their surreal, disturbing qualities.

All this debate about "ownership" only serves to cloak the obvious: Steven Spielberg (as producer and co-writer) and Tobe Hooper (as director) collaborated to create a terrifying, socially valuable film that has withstood the test of time. Along with Wise's *The Haunting*, *Poltergeist* is probably the best (and most perpetually frightening) haunted house film Hollywood has ever produced. The film is hair-raising, amusing and brilliantly paced, and it satirizes the trends and values of the early 1980s. It as an accomplished, skilled work of art that founded a film and TV franchise. Controversies aside, *Poltergeist*'s legacy should be that it brought terror home to middle-class suburbia, and made yuppies "see the light" about television. At least until the Fox News Network came around.

5. *Lifeforce* (1985)

Critical Reception

"*Lifeforce* may come to be considered a noteworthy science-fiction film precisely because it is so relentlessly unsentimental and edgy. This film displays a sensibility so odd, so unfamiliar, that it may prove one of the most subtly original sf films of the 1980s.... [T]he film has something to offend almost everyone but offers much for serious analysis."
—Brooks Landon, *The New Encyclopedia of Science Fiction*, 1988, page 276.

"...Tobe Hooper did sci-fi fans the supreme favor of combining a stylish and haunting space-opera with a good old-fashioned blood-sucker epic when he helmed his classic vampire hybrid, *Lifeforce*.... With *Lifeforce,* Hooper has taken the tried and true A.I.P. style, complete with a futuristic Van Helsing type, and beefed it up with zombie gore and plenty of eye-popping nudity.... After nine years the film has weathered unusually well...."
—R.T. St. Claire. *Sci-Fi Universe:* "13 Vampire Movies that Don't Suck," October/November 1994, page 24.

"*Lifeforce* may be the last great science fiction film to come out of England.... Director Tobe Hooper moves the action along briskly, and the movie quickly fills up with effects.... The restraint of the British players helps immensely until the end, when London is transformed into a pit of seething horror and the movie nearly comes apart. But what a ride!"
—Bruce Eder, *Video Magazine*, May 1995, page 55.

"Clearly inspired by Nigel Kneale's splendid Quatermass adventures, screenwriters Dan O'Bannon and Don Jakoby got the spectacle and weirdness right, but the film lacks a much needed sense of humor.... [T]he overheated, confusing climax is a real jaw-dropper."
—Bill Warren and Bill Thomas, *American Film*: "Great Balls of Fire," March 1986, page 70.

"*Lifeforce* ... fails completely to translate the horror of the original to the screen, despite the sophisticated optics and miniature sets of effects wizard John Dykstra.... Hooper would have done better to stick more closely to Wilson's original, which at least made sense."
—*Futurevisions*, page 186.

"*Lifeforce* ... has a few ... comic flashes, but most of it is painfully solemn. Both the leading men

... snap out their lines without a trace of real enthusiasm. The screenplay by Dan O'Bannon and Don Jakoby, from a novel by Colin Wilson, flings together elements ... but the results are nonetheless sterile. And Mr. Hooper, despite *The Texas Chainsaw Massacre* to his credit, doesn't even make it scary."
—Janet Maslin, *New York Times*: "Zombies on Parade," June 21, 1985.

"Apart from a few lively shock scenes, an object lesson in failure. Merges Colin Wilson's taut, austere, un-pulpy novel *Space Vampires* (the antithesis of this lurid mess despite the title change) with Richard Matheson's *I Am Vampire* [sic].... Excluding Frank Finlay, everyone is miscast. The effects are good...."
—Bill Kelley, *Cinefantastique*, Volume 15, Number 4, page 44, October 1985.

"Hooper, director of *Poltergeist* and the respected cult film *The Texas Chainsaw Massacre*, is bursting with energy, and maybe with talent. But he needs a more cleanly crafted outlet than the top-heavy *Lifeforce* can provide.
—David Sterritt, *Christian Science Monitor*, June 27, 1985, page 26.

"Anyone noting that this film was directed by Tobe Hooper, whose credits include *The Texas Chainsaw Massacre* and *Poltergeist*, will not expect *Lifeforce* to be *Little Women*. Hooper has, though, developed a reputation for doing things with style, however brutal and frenetic—and that's one thing lacking in this film.... Some of its special effects by John *(Star Wars)* Dykstra are flashy—but the lightshow excesses become reminiscent of *Ghostbusters*.... Hooper tries to get mileage out of parading newcomer Mathilda May around nude. But May, like the cadaverous extras, gets tiresome."
—Ralph Novak, *People Weekly*, July 15, 1985, page 11.

Cast and Credits

CAST: Steve Railsback (Commander Tom Carlsen); Peter Firth (Inspector Caine); Frank Finlay (Dr. Hans Fallada); Patrick Stewart (Dr. Armstrong); Michael Gothard (Bukovsky); Nicholas Ball (Derebridge); Aubrey Morris (Sir Percy); Nancy Paul (Ellen); Jim Hallam (Lamson); John Keegan (Guard); Mathilda May (Space Girl); Christopher Jagger (First Vampire); Bill Mallin (Second Vampire); Jerome Willis (Pathologist); Derek Benfield (Physician); Derek Benfield (Physician); John Woodnutt (Metalurgist); James Forbes-Robertson (The Minister); Peter Porteous (Prime Minister); Katherine Schofield (Prime Minister's Secretary); Owen Holder (First Scientist); Jamie Roberts (Rawlings); Russell Sommers (Navigation Officer); Patrick Conner (Fatherly Guard); Sidney Kean (Brash Guard); Paul Cooper (Second Guard); Chris Sullivan (Kelly); Milton Cadman (First Soldier); Rupert Baker (Second Soldier); Gary Hildreth (Police Sergeant); Edward Evans (Doctor); Nicholas Donnelly (Police Inspector); Peter Lovstrum (First Boy in Park); Julian Firth (Second Boy in Park); Carl Rigg (First Radar Technician); Elizabeth Morton (Second Radar Technician); Geoffrey Frederick (Communications Officer); David English (First Crewman); Emma Jacobs (Second Crewperson); Michael John Paliotti (Third Crewperson); Brian Carroll (Fourth Crewperson); Richard Oldfield (Mission Leader); Christopher Barr (Trajectory Officer); Burnell Tucker (NASA Man); Thom Booker (First NASA Officer); Michael Fitzpatrick (Second NASA Officer); Richard Sharpe (Rescue Ship Crewman); John Golightly (Colonel); William Lindsay (Colonel's Aide); David Beckett (Soldier); Sydney Livingstone (Beckett); Ken Parry (Sykes); John Edmunds (BBC Commentaries); Hadyn Wood (Helicopter Pilot).

CREDITS: Cannon Group Presents a Golan-Globus Production of a Tobe Hooper Production, *Lifeforce*. *Costume Designer:* Carin Hooper. *Costume Supervisor:* Tiny Nicholls. *Special Visual Effects:* John Dykstra. *Prosthetic Make-Up Effects:* Nick Maley. *Special Effects:* John Gant. *Editor:* John Grover. *Director of Photography:* Alan Hume. *Production Designer:* John Graysmark. *Music:* Henry Mancini. *Performed by:* London Symphony Orchestra. *Associate Producer:* Michael Kagan. *Based on the novel* The Space Vampires *by:* Colin Wilson. *Screenplay by:* Dan O'Bannon, Don Jakoby. *Produced by:* Manahem Golan and Yoram Globus. *Directed by:* Tobe Hooper. *Mime Artists:* Adrian Hedley, Corrinne Bougaard, Cal McCrystal, Bob Goody, Paul Antony-Barber, Kristine Landon-Smith. *Stunt Artists:* Roy Alon, John Lees, Michael Law, Frank Henson, Nick Hobbs, Reg Harding, Doug Robinson, Stuart Fell, Gareth Milne, Alf Joint, Dinny Powell, Del Baker, Tip Tipping, Dickie Beer, Andy Bradford, Chris Webb, Stuart St. Paul, Denise Ryan, Tracy Eddon, Saide Eddon, Dorothy Ford, Ray Ford, Graeme Crowther, Terry Furrestal, Fred Haggerty, Malcolm Weaver, Dave Brandon. *Production Man-*

ager: Basil Summer. *Production Accountant:* Len Cave. *Production Coordinator:* Marlene Butland. *Unit Manager:* Terry Lens. *Location Manager:* Geoff Austin. *Models Location Manager:* Roy Parkinson. *Production Company Liaison:* Michael Hartman. *Production Secretary:* Felicity Newton. *First Assistant and Second Unit Director:* Derek Cracknell. *Camera Operator:* Mike Frift. *Sound Recordist:* George Stephenson. *Continuity:* Cheryl Leigh, Carol Snook. *Stunt Arranger:* Peter Diamond. *Casting:* Maude Spector, Ann Stanborough. *Unit Publicist:* June Broom. *Stills Photography:* Bob Penn, Douglas Luke. *Art Directors:* Alan Tomkins, Bob Cartwright, Tony Reading, Terry Knight. *Set Decorator:* Simon Wakefield, Dennis Exshaw. *Make-up:* Derek Mills, Michael Morris, Sandra Exelby. *Hairdresser:* Pat Kirkman. *Assistant Directors:* Richard Hoult, Melvin Lind, Tim Reed, Tony Aherne, Paul Lowin. *Focus:* Simon Hume. *Focus:* David Litchfield. *Technical Advisor:* Brendan Alimo, Alexander Beetham. *Sound Designer:* Vernon Messenger. *Dialogue Editor:* Nigel Galt. *Music Editor:* Bob Hathaway. *Music Mixed by:* Eric Tomlinson. *Musical Advisor:* Jack Fishman. *Boom Operator:* Colin Wood. *Special Effects Editor:* Richard Hiscott. *Special Visual Effects Produced by:* Apogee. *Property Master:* Eddie Francis. *M.P.A.A. Rating:* R. *Running time:* 116 minutes.

> "It was always intended you should find us and bring us to Earth. The web of destiny carries your blood and soul back to the genesis of my lifeform."
> —The Space Girl (Mathilda May) tells Carlsen (Steve Railsback) of the "way of things" in Tobe Hooper's *Lifeforce*, 1985, a double-barreled homage to Great Britain's Quatermass saga and *Night of the Living Dead*.

Synopsis

On August 4th, at 2:30 P.M., the space shuttle *Churchill*, with a joint American-British team of astronauts aboard, is set to intercept and study Halley's Comet as it nears earth. On board the *Churchill*, technicians discover a gigantic anomaly in the head of the comet, an artificial object, a derelict spaceship some 150 miles long. Unable to confer with his superiors on Earth, American commander Tom Carlsen opts to study the vehicle, realizing it will be seventy-six years before there is another chance to learn its secrets.

With Carlsen in the lead, a team of astronauts from the *Churchill* execute an extra-vehicular maneuver to board the strange derelict. The outside of the vessel is scarred and pitted and the interior is a vast, womb-like corridor. At the end of a long passageway, the Churchill explorers discover the corpses of the ship's occupants: hundreds of desiccated bat-like alien creatures. They bag one of the dead with the specimen net (to bring back to the *Churchill*) when suddenly the derelict deploys a massive, umbrella-like structure and a doorway to another passage is revealed. Carlsen and his men explore the new chamber and find three human bodies—*one female and two males*—perfectly preserved in crystalline chambers. Immediately, Carlsen feels drawn to the beautiful, naked sleeping woman, but tries to shake off the strangely powerful sexual desires. He orders all three of the humans brought back to the ship.

Thirty days later, mission control in England tracks the shuttle *Churchill* as it returns to Earth orbit, apparently out of control. The *Columbia* is launched to intercept the *Churchill*. The *Columbia* soft-docks with the *Churchill* and the crew finds Carlsen's ship burned up and gutted. The crew is found burned and dead. There is one other discovery: three perfectly preserved human bodies. These three alien humanoids—from the derelict—are brought down to Earth for further examination.

The three aliens are transported to the European Space and Research Center in London. There, the Space Girl's chamber opens, but she appears dead. Dr. Fallada, a brilliant scientist fascinated with death, isn't sure that any of the alien humanoids are truly dead, but okays an autopsy. At close to 2:00 A.M., a lonely guard approaches the Space Girl's body and is drawn by unusual forces to touch her. She opens her eyes and mesmerizes the guard. When she kisses him, she drains the "lifeforce" from his body. By stealing this powerful energy, the Space Girl leaves the guard a rotting, withered husk. Dr. Fallada interrupts before the alien female can claim another victim, but she escapes from the center (still naked) when security is unable to stop her—even with machine guns!

Colonel Caine from the SAS arrives at the Space Centre to investigate the dangerous situation, and Dr. Fallada tells him he believes that the alien girl drained the lifeforce energy from the guard like some kind of mythical vampire. Meanwhile, the two male aliens awaken and attempt to break free from captivity. They are shot dead by security, but they only die "physically." Unbeknownst to any Earth authority, the vampiric males have jumped bodies and are remaining hidden for the time being.

An autopsy of the drained guard is conducted, but he's not dead at all. He awakens on the operating table and, now a vampire, drains the life energy from the operating pathologist. This revives the guard, but leaves the poor doctor a desiccated shell! Not long after this unusual turn of events, a dead girl is found in Hyde Park in the same desiccated condition as the pathologist, indicating that the Space Girl is continuing to drain the lifeforce of human beings out in the real world. This is a problem, because after two hours the victims of the vampires come back to life as vampires themselves, and further spread the "disease" of soul vampirism. A plague could erupt in London if the girl isn't stopped.

As authorities in London attempt to stop the spread of the vampire plague, *Churchill*'s escape pod, with Commander Carlsen aboard, lands in Texas. Carlsen is shuttled to London to help Caine and Fallada deal with the aliens. He recounts the last days aboard the *Churchill*, when someone sabotaged the communication equipment and freed the alien woman. Once she was freed, crewmembers began to die, drained and desiccated. Rather than expose

"I feel like I've been here before!" The astronauts of the space shuttle *Churchill* enter the giant, womblike chamber of the space vampires in *Lifeforce* (1984).

5. *Lifeforce* (1985)

Earth to these alien monsters, Carlsen set a fire aboard his own ship and fled the *Churchill* in an escape pod. Exhausted after telling his story, Carlsen is permitted to sleep for a time, but soon it is reported that a massive alien ship has been detected on scanners. The vampire vessel has left its perch near Halley's Comet and is making for Earth orbit...

Later, Carlsen dreams of the Space Girl, and Fallada and Caine realize the American has a psychic link with the alien, a link that can be used to their advantage. Fallada hypnotizes Carlsen, and he reports that he can see the alien in his mind's eye. She has changed bodies, and hidden her original body somewhere important. With some explicit details from the telepathic link, Carlsen and Caine track down the Space Girl to an insane asylum, where she is hiding in the body of a masochistic nurse named Ellen. Carlsen interrogates Ellen and learns that the vampire has fled again, into the body of staid Dr. Armstrong. Carlsen and Caine tranquilize Armstrong and hypnotize him into cooperating. While being interrogated, the Space Girl reveals that she is the "feminine" in Carlsen's mind, and that she took her form based on his deepest thoughts and desires. Unfortunately, this is all but a carefully constructed distraction, for when Carlsen and Caine return to London, the vampire plague has reached epidemic proportions. If it is to be stopped, the male vampires, still alive, and the Space Girl, back in her original body, must be destroyed. Fallada reveals to Caine that he has killed one of the male vampires with an iron sword, not through the heart, but through the energy center directly below it. Apparently, vampire legend came from these creatures, who visited Earth long, long ago.

Carlsen reveals that he was the person who released the Space Girl in the first place, and that he therefore must be the one to destroy her. Now, she is calling him, even as London burns out of control with a zombie plague. Carlsen and Caine seek reinforcements, but quickly learn that the prime minister is already a vampire. Overhead, the alien ship is collecting human souls, pulling the lifeforce energy into its power cells. The Space Girl is the conduit in this unusual procedure, the receptacle through which all souls must pass. Carlsen confronts her in the cathedral while Caine meets with Fallada, who has also succumbed to vampirism. After dispatching the transformed doctor, Caine takes the traditional weapon—*the iron sword*—to kill the girl and stop the massive soul transfer. He braves the city of the vampires and kills the surviving male vampire. Then, Caine throws Carlsen the sword, and Carlsen runs the Space Girl—*and himself*—through with the implement to stop the soul collector. The Space Girl and Carlsen are spirited away to the vampire spaceship as it pulls away into deepest space, leaving a London in flames, but Earth safe.

Commentary

Lifeforce, Tobe Hooper's big budget 1985 entry in the sci-fi/horror blockbuster sweepstakes, is a nightmare about the consequences of sex in all its sizes, shapes and forms. That may sound like unusual (and bold) territory for a mainstream film but the concept fits in with Hooper's other movies. His villains are vampires (shades of *Salem's Lot*), he twists his narrative in unusual knots (shades of *Poltergeist*), stages a whole portion of the film as homage (the *Halloween-* and *Psycho*-inspired opening of *The Funhouse*) and shatters screen taboos (*The Texas Chain Saw Massacre*). Most importantly, the "evil" in the story arises from a specific context. In *Chain Saw* the context was the gas shortage and the unemployment of the post-hippie 1970s. In *The Funhouse* the context was the advent of cheap, rotten "dead teenager" movies. In *Poltergeist* and *Invaders from Mars* the context was the growing immorality of the yuppie 1980s. Even *The Mangler*, with its sweat shop conditions and exploited workers, reflects a contemporary issue, the post–NAFTA age, mid 1990s. In *Lifeforce*, the rising "gay plague," a dangerous sexually transmitted disease of the early 1980s later identified as AIDS and recognized as an epidemic, is the subject informing so much of the terror.

It's unusual to consider it, but both John Carpenter and Tobe Hooper have made critically reviled (but later appreciated) horror films in which a shape-shifting evil is passed from person to person much like a sexually transmitted disease. Both *The Thing* and *Lifeforce*, of course, were produced in the early 1980s when this issue was coming to the forefront of public attention with the mysterious deaths of gay men in a kind of insidious "slimming disease." Invisible to detection, the alien infection in these films subverts people, unbeknownst to their neighbors. Affected people appear normal to outward appearances, healthy even, but in fact they are carriers of a secret death. In both films, that strange death is represented as malevolent alien extra terrestrials that want to subvert the human form to its own needs.

John Carpenter's *The Thing* and Tobe Hooper's *Lifeforce* parallel the development of AIDS in another way: both have a serious homosexual undercurrent. In *The Thing*, a deadly plague passes in the blood from person to person in an exclusively male population (at an Antarctic base). In *Lifeforce,* there is more than a single-sex grouping of victims (and the beautiful Mathilda May makes a fetching feminine evil), but there is nonetheless an emphasis on male-to-male infection. First, there is the jarring and impassioned kiss between Carlsen (Steve Railsback) and Armstrong (Patrick Stewart), an embrace that is inarguably homosexual in form (even though May's Space Girl mentally inhabits Armstrong). Secondly, a male victim of the Space Girl awakens on the operating table early in the film and "mesmerizes" his male pathologist (a gay man?), converting the poor doctor into one of the sick "transmitters" of the disease. Or, as Edward Guerrero describes the scene in his article "AIDS as Monster in Science Fiction and Horror Cinema":

> The film foregrounds homosexual transmission by focusing on the ravished bodies of male victims and by depicting in a key, horrific autopsy scene, an emaciated young male corpse who ... with outstretched arms hypnotically draws one of the male pathologists into a fatal, energy draining, homoerotic embrace and kiss.... [T]he camera moves through ... close-ups of the faces of the doctors trapped in the surgery as they register various reactions to the act and its gay proclamations, ranging from frozen panic and disavowal to ambivalent fascination [1].

Guerrero also writes that *Lifeforce*'s grisly corpses, which receive considerable camera attention, are depicted as young and starkly emaciated, resonant with the media's description of the "wasting" effects of the then so-called gay plague. Yet *Lifeforce* is not an indictment of homosexuality so much as it is a warning against succumbing to *all* manner of sexual urges. The film plays no favorites, and homosexuality is just one aspect of the human sexual equation. In point of fact, *Lifeforce* is as bold about depicting sexual issues as *The Texas Chain Saw Massacre* is about recording horrid, graphic violence. Throughout the film, Hooper uses one powerful symbol to represent the wanton lust of the human being: the Space Girl (Mathilda May). Hooper parades her about naked throughout the film, a groundbreaking decision in a mainstream entertainment, but her purpose, in essence, is to take the viewer on a tour of sexual issues.

When Carlsen boards the alien spaceship early in the film, he finds the interior of the spaceship to be something akin to a massive womb. The similarity is so telling that Carlsen states unequivocally, "I feel like

I've been here before." The tiny astronauts, probing deep into the long tunnel to the hidden chamber, might well be the tiny sperm navigating a woman's uterus. When they reach the hidden' (egg?) chamber, they discover May there, and their instant lust for her brings her to life. When she is returned to Earth, this creature of lust, "the feminine" in Carlsen's mind, begins her exploration of human sexuality. She

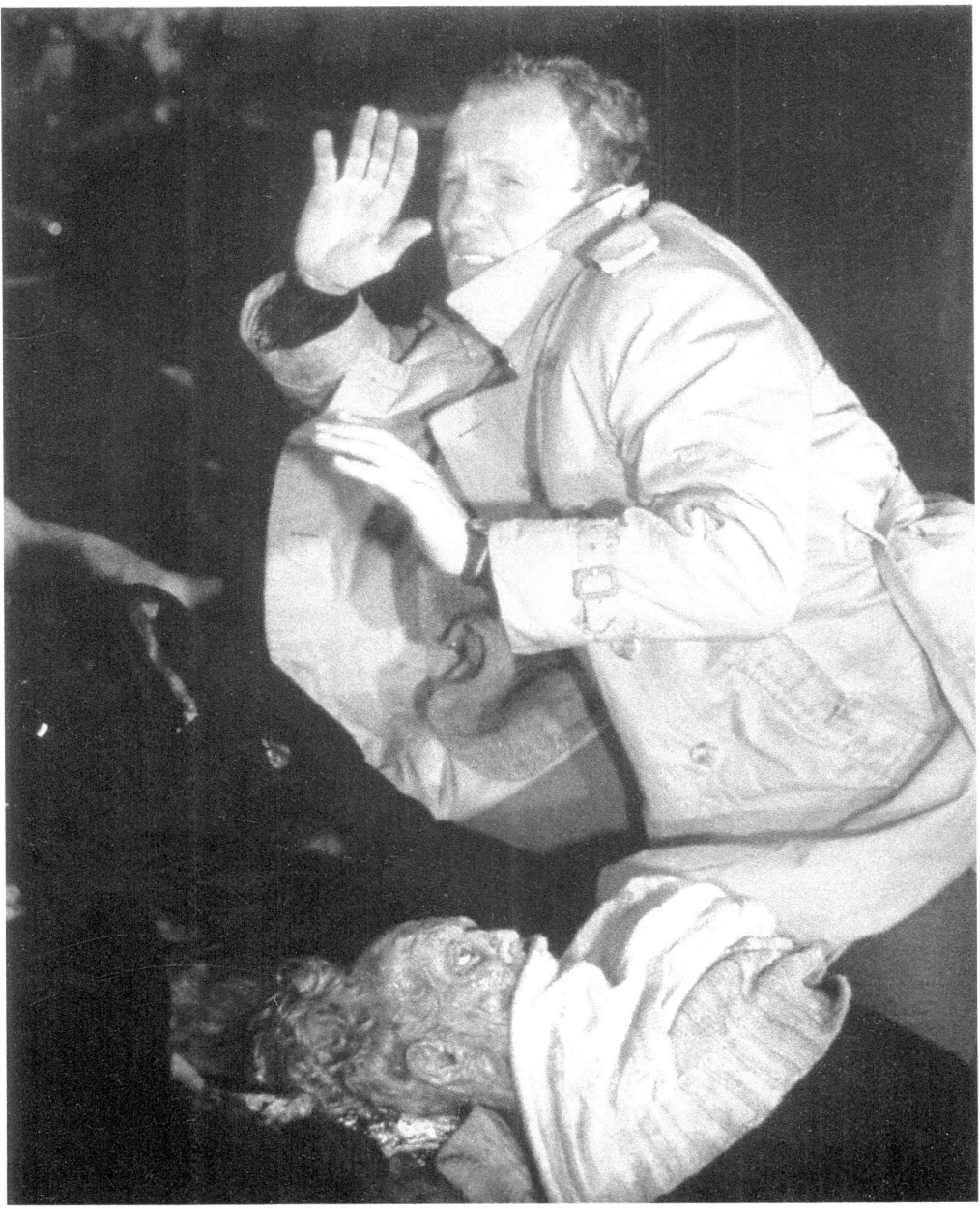

Inspector Caine (Peter Firth) recoils in horror, zombies at his feet, during the climax of *Lifeforce* (1985).

encounters sex as *infidelity* (with a married man in a parked car); she experiences *male-to-male* contact in the body of Armstrong and his homosexual kiss with Carlsen. For a time, her consciousness enters the body of a nurse who is a devoted *masochist*. This woman takes great joy in the fact that Carlsen has to beat information out of her, and Inspector Caine acknowledges his own sexual side when he notes that he is a *voyeur*. Even sex as grounds for political scandal is touched upon briefly when the film's prime minister spreads the sexual infection to his unsuspecting secretary. Beyond this *Alice in Wonderland* tour of human sexuality, there is all the fiery *heterosexual coupling* between Railsback and May, a devastating relationship that ends in a double penetration (by sexual organs and by a fatal stab from a sword blade).

Considering the wide breadth of indiscriminate sexual behavior that *Lifeforce* covers, it is no surprise that the film relies on vampires as the ostensible villains. After all, vampires are the sexiest of all screen monsters. They are alluring, magnetic and filled with strange, unsated appetites. They thrive on a body fluid, blood, and they can "transmit" their sickness to unaware victims. Their kiss, their caress, brings death. But the space vampires of the film steal souls, not blood and that's an important distinction in Hooper's allegory about the perils of promiscuous sex.

The film ends, appropriately enough, in a grand British cathedral, a sanctuary for the pious. There, the infected bodies of the sexually depleted await their judgment, spent and sick. Their souls have been carried away on a beam of light which focuses on the altar (God's vengeance?), and these souls have been dispatched to a nether realm, the alien spaceship, a place apparently equivalent to Hell. This is a moral conclusion, no doubt, a literalization of Christian puritanism. Indulge in indiscriminate sex and if it doesn't kill you outright, it'll make you sick with a plague! The end result is that you'll lose your soul and dwell forever afterwards in Hell. It's a harsh comment, but given the decadent sexual proclivities of the 1970s, and the reckoning period of AIDS awareness from the early 1980s onward, an entirely appropriate one for a horror film.

If *Lifeforce* is an examination (and condemnation) of promiscuous, rampant sexuality, it is also a supreme entertainment that doesn't hammer its points home with a heavy hand. In some ways, *Lifeforce* is Tobe Hooper's grandest and most accomplished film (at least for its first two-thirds). It boasts more pure spectacle and excitement in its first seventeen minutes that most genre films can pack into two hours. A space shuttle's approach to a comet, the exploration of an alien derelict's eerie interior, and an outer space docking of two earthships, are all highlighted as the first quarter hour ticks by rapidly. For some critics at the time, this dynamic, fast-paced opening represented the movie's biggest problem: After a slam-bang introduction, the film degenerates into a slow mystery and most movies take exactly the opposite approach, building up to a fever rather than starting there.

Still, one thing is for certain: *Lifeforce* opens on a high note. As Henry Mancini's martial-sounding, rousing main theme begins, the camera sweeps up and up over a rocky, mountainous planet surface and the effect is one of breathless anticipation. The dramatic percussion-driven score coupled with the visual conceit of constant movement generates a feeling of unfettered excitement in the audience, and Hooper adroitly uses that sense of danger and adventure by next introducing the object hiding in Halley's Comet. Here his direction is splendid: expositional dialogue comes fast and furious, but in appropriate proportions, as Carlsen and his team venture into the alien spacecraft, a wonder of art design. This sequence involves actors suspended on wires, tiny puppets, miniature sets, blue screens and full-scale "flying effect's' (a la *Superman* [1978]) and every last detail comes off beautifully. These opening sequences are brash, confident, brawny even in their ability to convince.

The scenes that follow, those that take place on Earth, are equally compelling but for another reason. Following a careful, almost scientific progression, Hooper patiently charts the progression of the alien disease from one victim to the next. These scenes are not overtly spectacular (like the scenes in space), but intimate and riveting pieces of a puzzle, and again the special effects are great. The corpse puppets that substitute for the wasted victims of the Space Girl were terrifyingly real and convincing in 1985 (so much so that many theater patrons, disgusted beyond belief, had to excuse themselves from showings). Today these "dummies" are obviously fully articulated puppets and easy to spot as fakes, and in that way the film has not aged well. Still, a film must be judged in its context, not outside it, and these effects, like Dykstra's outer space work, were stunning and terrifying in 1985.

Inevitably, however, the film falters in its last act. The opening acts of *Lifeforce* are good, buttressed by rapid-fire dialogue, spectacular action, Mathilda May's nudity, the novel's literate beginning and Hooper's steadfast determination to honor the British tradition of the Quatermass saga, the ongoing adventures of an English scientist confronted with extra-terrestrials, popular in England in the 1950s and 1960s. There is more than enough flair in Hooper's direction, in the performances, in the special effects, the set-pieces and in the film's sexual underpinnings to give *Lifeforce* great excitement. But Hooper, usually so canny about pacing and audience needs, then sets off on one of his patented narrative U turns in the last act. Despite the grand scale of the film, *Lifeforce*, up until the last half-hour, is a relatively personal story about a man (Carlsen) hunting a monster that he both hates and loves. But then, echoing the over-the-top ending of *Poltergeist*, Hooper leaves the conventional narrative for an admittedly impressive, but ridiculous (and overlong) set piece in London in which the entire populace is turned into raving, hungry zombies. Though narrative twists are common, even expected in the Hooper oeuvre, as are homages to favorite films, this scene's resemblance to George Romero's *Night of the Living Dead* and other zombie films only succeeds in diffusing the considerable tension so skillfully built up to that point.

Part of the problem is the look of the zombies. In their tattered, raggy clothes and with their shambling, familiar gait, it indeed looks as though these characters have wandered off the Pittsburgh set of Romero's latest horror picture. While it's true that 1985 was the year of the zombie (they were featured in *Day of the Dead* [1985] and *Return of the Living Dead* [1985] too), their presence in *Lifeforce* feels wrong. These creatures, these zombies, are meant to represent the same wasted victims of the space vampires as the film has depicted throughout (usually by the articulated puppets). But these zombies do not at all move or resemble those creatures, so a confused audience is left with the unmistakable perception that these zombies are somehow a different phenomenon arising from the vampire disease, a new and unexplained wrinkle. Old-fashioned, flesh-eating zombies have no place in *Lifeforce*; in it, the creatures are just hungry, soul-draining individuals, not undead monstrosities, and so the ending doesn't track as it should.

Also, the grand scale of this set piece, admittedly spectacular, feels wrong after the careful layering of the personal story. Though the film eventually wanders its way back to Carlsen and the Space Girl in the cathedral, it loses them in zombified London for a while, and it is too long a diversion. The immediacy drips out of *Lifeforce* until it's just a showcase for gross make-up, great miniatures, fantastic opticals and other special effects miracles. It's an over-the-top Hooper U turn all the way, but this time one can argue that it simply doesn't work, that it proves less satisfying than the intense (if intimate) sting in *Poltergeist*'s tail. Here the plot matters more: this is a more serious, scientific world and a far more "global" problem than the one encountered by the beleaguered Freelings. Even the science is pretty convincing up to this point, so it seems a shame to throw it all away on a visually beautiful, but dramatically unsatisfying show of fire and light.

Another problem weighing down *Lifeforce*'s prospects is its total and utter lack of humor. Tobe Hooper's films always have real wit and style (and humor) to spare, but one senses that the massive scope and expense of this project may have short-circuited that sensibility. Worse, Hooper is saddled with a totally humorless cast. The Brits pull off the serious scenes brilliantly, effortlessly spouting their technical dialogue and making it sound believable. But what a stiff, humorless bunch! Patrick Stewart is probably the most humorless actor on Earth and, even after fifteen years in the captain's chair on *Star Trek: The Next Generation*, has failed to carry off a humorous scene with anything approaching a laugh (witness his really lame "mamba" moment in 1998's *Insurrection*). The others, Finlay, Firth, Gothard and Morris, nail their characters' professional characteristics, but fail to give the project the slightest inkling of humor. And, without humor there is no humanity.

Contrarily, Railsback probably goes too far in his dramatic scenes, to the point that his intensity becomes kind of funny. His kissing scene with the reserved Patrick Stewart is uncomfortable, and it is hard to

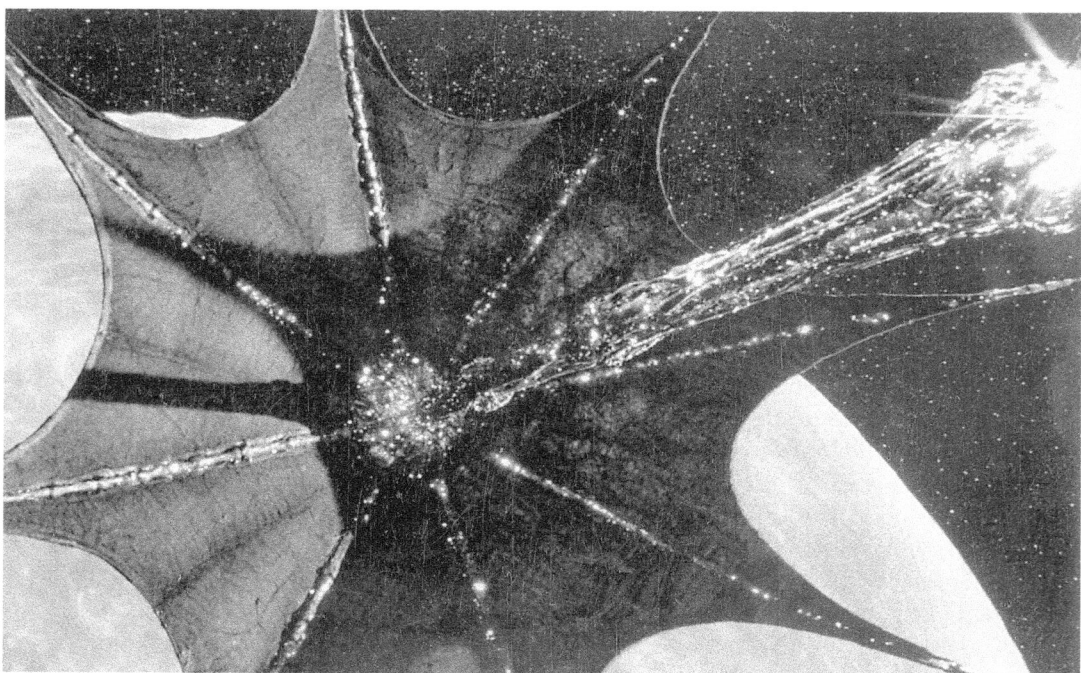

A detailed view of the spectacular vampire spaceship near Earth's moon. From the conclusion of *Lifeforce* (1984).

tell if the reason is because the actors, hot and cold, just don't mesh, or simply because audiences then (and now) aren't familiar or comfortable with images of two men kissing. It's very possible that the "nervous laughter" often erupting from this scene is a result of discomfort, of the fact that it treads so heavily on screen taboo. And, Hooper doesn't shy from showing it all in close-shot. There's no last minute cut away to something more palatable.

There can be little debate that *Lifeforce* is Tobe Hooper's biggest film. It was a massive production, involved a colossal scope and the most complex, state-of-the-art special effects available. The underlying theme, a dread of rampant, promiscuous sex in the age of AIDS, is particularly well enunciated, and the film motors like a freight train for much of its running time. *Lifeforce* is undeniably a much better picture than most critics noted at the time of its release, and an acknowledged cult classic for good reasons (like May's angel of death, the story's mythological nature, and so on), but some aspects during the last half hour of *Lifeforce* just don't gel, even if they are consistent with Hooper's other films (narrative U turns, homage galore).

When one thinks of Hooper, one can't help but remember the raw, "organic" vistas of his other film work. The bowel-like alien spaceship of *Invaders from Mars*, the bone-rooms of *The Texas Chain Saw Massacre*, the earthen tunnels of *Chainsaw 2*, the slimy ectoplasm of *Poltergeist*, the dank, steaming walls and wet floors of the laundry room in the industrialized *The Mangler*, and so forth. *Lifeforce* is visually impressive and appropriate, but it still feels slightly out of step with that other work. The high-tech gloss, the white lights, the reliance on science and focus on intellectual debate are interesting, but kind of remote. This is especially true when one remembers that Hooper is a meatier, more immediate guy than any of these Kubrickian *2001* touches indicate. As impressive as *Lifeforce* remains (particularly the first half) it is too restrained to win the title of Tobe Hooper's masterpiece away from the original *Chain Saw*. A very good, very deep, very dense film, yes. But not the jewel in the crown. Now, a down-and-dirty Tobe Hooper film about sexual politics, one as base and brutal and blunt as *The Texas Chain Saw Massacre*, that *really* would have been something to see.

6. *Invaders from Mars* (1986)

Critical Reception

"Tobe Hooper ... knows how to construct a horror film so it builds to a fever pitch. He shoots many of his images from below, to give the view a child might have, and deftly manipulates the audience to feel the growing menace. He is helped by an excellent cast ... Karen Black is terrific ... Hunter Carson ... gives a remarkably honest performance ... completely lacking in childhood affectation.... Mr. Hooper has done more than make a remake of *Invaders from Mars*. He has shot a tribute to it and the science fiction genre."
—Nina Darnton, *New York Times*, June 6, 1986, page C14.

"...[It] hangs together effectively, thanks to the directorial skill of Tobe Hooper.... Both as science fiction thriller and nightmare visions of a child, *Invaders from Mars* turns out to be a superior sample of its genre. Realistic backdrops and fairly believable performances are matched with fantastic creatures that spring out of the mind untethered."
—Archer Winston, *New York Post*, June 6, 1986, page 24.

"Hooper remakes the film faithfully. He doesn't really try to update it or refashion it.... He simply does the movie over again—with a vaster budget, a modern perspective, and a lot of reflexive inside humor.... Hooper is trying to make a more self-referential, self-conscious ver-

sion of *Invaders*—his ideal version.... When Hooper and his collaborators get the languorously empty paranoid '50s feel they want, this film verges on hysterically funny."
—Michael Wilmington, *Los Angeles Times*, June 5, 1986, page 1.

"This remake is surely a spoof. *Invaders from Mars* doesn't take itself seriously and acknowledges the absurdity of its plot. As a consequence, it is one of the year's funniest films."
—Jim Welsh, *Films in Review*, October 1986, page 483.

"Sincere remake ... with writers Dan O'Bannon and Don Jakoby ... and director Tobe Hooper trying to recapture what made the original so memorable to the young. In ways they do a better job of capturing the paranoia of a lad who sees everyone being turned into zombies.... The film is simple and fast-moving with cliff-hangers and visual delights...."
—John Stanley, *Creature Features Strikes Again,* Creatures at Large Press, 1994, page 199.

"Some directors stoke the trend with camp updates of olden turkeys. In Tobe Hooper's remake of the 1950s *Invaders from Mars*, you can see tongues burrowing into cheeks on both sides of the camera. Sometimes though, directors can outsmart themselves. *Invaders from Mars* is so good at mimicking '50s mediocrity, it's bad."
—Richard Corliss, *Time Magazine*, July 14, 1987, page 62.

"It has cinematographer Daniel Pearl's hypnotically fluid, roving camera, imparting a dreamlike quality to the action. It has effectively stylized sets by Lester Dilley.... It has a good cast, with young Hunter Carson just right as David Gardner.... Finally *Invaders from Mars* has screenwriters ... and a director who are knowledgeable in the genre and have solid track records. *Invaders from Mars* has everything. Except one thing. Originality."
—Douglas Borton, *Cinefantastique*, Volume 16, Number 4/5: "*Invaders from Mars,*" October 1986, page 107.

"This remake by director Tobe (*Poltergeist*) Hooper does not seem seriously intent on scaring anyone. Neither is it enough of a send-up to be funny.... Fletcher and Black are especially hammy, broadly overacting as if to make sure everyone knows that they'd really rather be doing *Macbeth*.... Maybe when the real Martians finally come, they at least will get something out of this movie: a thrill, a chuckle, a light snack, whatever."
—Ralph Novak, *People Weekly*, July 23, 1986.

Cast and Crew

CAST: Karen Black (Linda); Hunter Carson (David Gardner); Timothy Bottoms (George); Laraine Newman (Ellen); James Karen (General "Mad Dog" Wilson); Bud Cort (Young NASA Scientist); Louise Fletcher (Mrs. McKellch); Eric Pierpoint (Sgt. Rinaldi); Christopher Allport (Captain Curtis); Donald Hotton (Old NASA Scientist); Kenneth Kimmins (Officer Kenny); Charles Dell (Mr. Cross); Jimmy Hunt (Police Chief); William Bassett (NASA Scientist); Virginia Keehne (Heather); Chris Hebert (Kevin); Mason Nupuf (Doug); Joseph Brutsman (MP # 1); Eric Norris (MP # 2); Debra Berger (Corporal Walker); Eddy Donno (Hollis); Mark Giardano (Johnson); Dale Dye (Squad Leader); Douglas Simpson (Lieutenant); Lonny Low (Communications Officer); Scott Wulf (Young Marine); Frederick Menslage, Michael McGrady, Lawrence Poindexter, J. Acheson, Matt Bennett, Aaron Scott Bernard (Marines); Steve Lambert (Demolition Man); Debbie Carrington, Joe Anthony Cox, Matt Bennett, Douglas Simpson, Margarite Fernandez, Salvatore Fondacaro, Lonny Low, Scott Wulf (Drones).

CREW: The Cannon Group, Inc., Presents a Golan-Globus Production of a Tobe Hooper film, *Invaders from Mars. Associate Producers:* Edward L. Alperson, Jr., Wade Williams. *Production Designer:* Leslie Dilley. *Director of Photography:* Daniel Pearl. *Editor:* Alan Jakubowicz. *First Assistant Director:* David Womack. *Second Assistant Director:* David Lipman. *Special Visual Effects:* John Dykstra. *Invader Creatures Designed and Created by:* Stan Winston. *Costume Designer:* Carin Hooper. *Music:* Christopher Young. *Based on a screenplay by:* Richard Blake. *Screenplay:* Dan O'Bannon, Dan Jakoby. *Produced by:* Menahem Golan, Yoram Globus. *Directed by:* Tobe Hooper. *Stunt Coordinators:* Steve Lambert, Eddy Donno. *Stunt Players:* Tim Davison, Diane Hitfield, R.H. Fransworth, Ken Lesco, Richard Washington. *Executive in charge of production:* Mati Raz. *Casting:* Robert MacDonald, Perry Bullington. *Art Director:* Craig Stearns. *Set Designer:* Randy Moore. *Set Decorator:* Cricket Rowland. *Set Dresser:* Portia Iveson. *Production Coordinator:* Iya Labanka. *Camera Operator:*

Bruce Pasternack. *Sound Mixer:* Russell Williams II. *Boom Operator:* Mary Jo Devenny. *Key Grip:* Michael Popovich. *Storyboard Artist:* Keith Crossley. *Concept Artist:* William Stout. *Property Master:* Doug Fox. *Costume Supervisor:* Dana Lyman, Louis Valadez. *Make-up and Hair Supervisor:* Mony Mansano. *Key Make-up:* Dee Mansano. *Make-up and Hair:* Lisa Schulze, Vered Hochman. *Location Manager:* Allen Alsobrook. *Script Supervisor:* Marion Webb. *Assistant to Mr. Hooper:* Peter Combs. *Post-Production Supervisor:* Michael R. Sloan. *Additional Editing:* Daniel Loewenthal. *Supervising Sound Editor:* David Bartlett. *Music Supervisor:* Paula Erickson. *Music Editor:* Jack Tiller. *Title Design:* Wenden K. Baldwin, Kyle Seidenbaum. *Titles and Opticals:* Pacific Title. *Second Unit Director:* John Dykstra. *Second Unit Director of Photography:* J. Michael McClary. *Producer of Special Effects:* Robert Shepherd. *Art Department Coordinator (Creature Effects):* Alec Gillis. *Creature Crew:* Robert Kurtzman, Kevin Yagher, Howard Berger, Matt Rose, Scott Wheeler, Steve Wang, Mark Williams. *Special Visual Effects by:* Apogee, Inc. Louma Crane by Panavision. *M.P.A.A. Rating:* PG. *Running time:* 103 minutes.

"Marines have no qualms about killing Martians!"
—James Karen's famous refrain as General Wilson, from *Invaders from Mars* (1986).

Synopsis

In quiet, suburban Middle America in the 1980s, little David Gardner awakes in the middle of the night and sees a colorful, but terrifying orb-shaped UFO burrow into the field beyond his home. The next morning, his dad, George, walks up to Copper Hill to investigate his son's story and returns strangely changed, somehow less than human. David goes to school with concern, evading his Dad's insistent offer to show him "what's up there."

After a day at Menzies Elementary School that involves a run-in with the nasty old science teacher Mrs. McKellch and a visit to the pretty school nurse, Linda Magnuson, David returns home and informs his mom that he feels there's something weird going on with his father. David's mother calls the police when George doesn't return home after work. After checking out Copper Hill for themselves, the police also return—similarly changed. Then George shows up with another man, a fellow from the phone company who works for the "switching" department, and makes some lame excuse for his absence. That night, George sneaks into David's room, steals his penny jar, and takes Mom up to Copper Hill by cover of darkness...

The next morning, David awakes to find his mother changed too, and now both parents are insistent about taking David up to the hill. He escapes to school instead, only to surreptitiously witness Mrs. McKellch eating a frog. He turns to nurse Linda for help, telling her the story and making special note of the fact that everybody who has been "changed" following the arrival of the UFO seems to bear a strange mark on their necks. The story makes more sense when Linda sees a bandage on the old school marm's neck. Concerned, Linda sends David to her house, but he is waylaid in the parking lot and forced to hide in Mrs. McKellch's van. Unaware of his presence, she drives up to Copper Hill and follows a path to a strange sandy cave. David follows her into the subterranean tunnel, where she enters the interior of a massive, strangely organic, alien spacecraft. David sees a grotesque alien brain—*The Martian Supreme Intelligence*—and its toothy inhuman drones. He escapes from the ship and reteams with Linda, even as Miss McKellch takes his unsuspecting classmates to be "converted" by the Martians.

Linda and David hide in the school boiler room and are nearly captured by the converted police. They escape when a Martian drilling machine unexpectedly breaks through the ground, inadvertently offering a diversion. David and Linda then race to a military base run by kindly General Wilson. They tell him their incredible story while George Gardiner and other human conspirators plot to sabotage a NASA space flight to Mars. General Wilson orders a security check and two conspirators are found—though they promptly self-destruct. The Martians blow up the Mars probe, even as they steal copper wire from the base to power their ship.

Retaliating, Wilson and the marines, with David and Linda in tow, wage war on the Martians at the sandpit on Copper Hill. Down in the tunnels, it is close-quarters combat between man and Martian, and the marines learn that the Martians use copper as an energy source. David and Linda veer off on their own in the underground labyrinth in search of David's parents, but are captured. David is granted an audience before the Supreme Martian Intelligence, and begs for mercy for Linda and his parents, but his pleas are mocked by the cold-hearted ruler.

David escapes from the throne room, and the Martians swallow Mrs. McKellch whole for bringing the little mischief maker into their lives. General Wilson and his troops battle the Martians with machine guns and plant explosive charges in the throne room. General Wilson and David save Linda from the conversion chamber, and then use one of the Martian weapons to break their way back to the surface. All the way up, David's parents give relentless chase. The soldiers, David, Linda, and the Gardners escape to Copper Hill as the Martian ship lifts off and explodes in mid-air.

David Gardner awakens suddenly: the whole encounter has been a nightmare. His parents soothe him and explain that his bad dream was just the result of his day—thinking about his penny jar, General Wilson's visit to the school, and so forth. David accepts this explanation and hunkers down for a good night's sleep. Then, the still of the night is shattered as flashing lights from the sky descend towards Copper Hill ... and the Martians begin their invasion in earnest.

Commentary

The Martians are coming in Tobe Hooper's 1986 remake of *Invaders from Mars* (1953), but they have faces only a mother could love. And that, in a strange way, is the movie's point. From start to finish, this film represents the phantasm of a slightly isolated, slightly "spaced" (in the words of his schoolmates) preteen boy who has seen too many 1980s blockbusters such as *Gremlins* (1984), *The Goonies* (1985), *Indiana Jones and the Temple of Doom* (1985) and *Poltergeist* (1982). Like the 1950s version it emulates so carefully, Hooper's *Invaders from Mars* is a film seen entirely through the filter of childhood, but this time it is a *media-saturated* 1980s childhood rather than one based on the conformist, communist-baiting 1950s. Hooper's film is careful to note the similarities of the 1950s and the 1980s, as well as the differences, and *Invaders from Mars* is his third social commentary about the media's impact on youth after *The Funhouse* and *Poltergeist*.

Adhering to the idea that the film is being told via a child's point of view, adults in *Invaders from Mars* are depicted as frightening, contradictory and remote automatons, perspectives reinforced by Hooper's frequent use of the low-angle shot in compositions involving David's parents, teachers, and local policemen. Worse than the strange and thoughtless behavior of the adults, however, Dad takes away Mom's attentions (with something insidious called "sex"?), transforming her into a thoughtless zombie in the process. Also evoking the sensibilities of a child, the U.S. army is apparently "cool" beyond belief (and also working hand in hand with NASA) and the aliens are slobbering, fantastical monsters that none but the young could possibly imagine (let alone combat). Young David Gardner's subconscious (dreaming) mind, imagines his elaborate adventure with the Martians, and his fantasy is based in no

The Martians are coming! The Martians are coming! Little David McLean (Jimmy Hunt, center) prepares to blast space invaders while the American military watches. From the original Menzies film *Invaders from Mars* (1953).

small part on the popular movies he has seen at his local cinema or on television (probably without supervision). Even the décor of his bedroom reinforces the impact these 1980s productions have had on his tortured psyche: his bed sheets, wallpaper and toys are all merchandising tie-ins for space operas, movies and TV shows, packed with robots and spaceships galore.

By maintaining the original film's focus on a "boy's life" and one kid's childish perceptions of a less-than-welcoming adult world, director Tobe Hooper honors the 1953 source material. But in casting the events of the film three decades later, he takes the source material further, modernizing the invasion for a more savvy generation. He enriches the film with startling new images and technologies (particularly in the realms of special effects, lighting and make-ups) that are markedly different from any-

thing Menzies would or could have contemplated in the early 1950s. But rather than taking viewers into a dark, minimalist tunnel without hope, Hooper leavens the package with humor, topical references and satire, a far cry from the grim, desperate feeling of the Menzies film. Today's "realism"-minded audiences (weaned on intense, suspenseful actioners like the *Alien* and *Predator* films) may not enjoy the fanciful, child-like innocence of this homage-minded, almost whimsical remake, but perhaps that is more a statement about the state of contemporary culture than Hooper's directorial skills. *Invaders from Mars* (1986) is droll entertainment for adults and a totally engaging one for children. It has moments of high fear and nightmarish imagery, but no more so than *Lord of the Rings, The Hobbit, A Wrinkle in Time, The Lion the Witch and the Wardrobe* or other dark fantasies that have enraptured America's young for decades.

At the core of the new *Invaders from Mars* is a meditation on childhood and an examination of one child in particular, the character of David Gardner. This is a boy who feels disenfranchised from the adult world all around him. His nightmare about invading Martians is symbolic of the forces and relationships in his life and the film makes that point in a number of interesting ways. One dark night, Daddy Gardner takes Mom up to Copper Hill, his arm around her in an embrace, and she returns from the (off-screen) experience drastically changed, "possessed" by the Martians, and much less concerned with her son's happiness or well-being. David sees her go, walking arm in arm with her husband, and immediately understands the danger. He fearfully cries out for her to stop before it is too late, a pointed telescope (one of many phallic symbols in the film) at his side. This element of the story, the abandonment by Mother Gardner, is no doubt an explicit reference to sex and the fear of a child that the sexual, spousal relationship could become more valued to the all-important Mother Figure than is the nurturing, maternal one. Thus it is no accident that the "evil" that transforms Mom in Tobe Hooper's *Invaders from Mars* comes at the end of a massive, phallus-like mechanism that "penetrates" her neck. Even the Martian control device it implants there (itself another phallus) is a tool (i.e., the penis) that takes Mommy's attention away from her child.

Similarly, it is important that late in the film a Martian drone speaks to David in his father's voice. David has equated his father with the enemy, the competitor for his mother's affections. In one terrifying sequence, David lies cringing in his bed and his father (seen only from the neck down) approaches, silent and dangerous, motives uncertain. David is unsure what horror is to follow, a beating, an attack, even molestation, but his father eventually leaves him unharmed, taking only his coin collection. Still, the fear and helplessness of a child in his bed is captured with chilling efficiency.

Tobe Hooper's use of film language in *Invaders from Mars* is the most impressive it has been since *The Texas Chain Saw Massacre*. His always-on-the-prowl camera not only records David's nightmare of alien invasion, it successfully expresses his situation, his mood and his feelings of isolation. The opening shot of the movie, that of David and his Dad lying flat on their backs in the grass, stargazing, should be a peaceful, idyllic one. Instead, forecasting the horror to come, the high angle perspective (always the harbinger of doom in the cinematic lexicon) grows increasingly disturbed. As the camera nears its objects, it commences a fast spin, rolling over and over as it nears David and his Dad. This spin reveals that David Gardner's world is about to be turned upside down, and that below the surface of perfect suburbia trouble exists.

Throughout the film, Hooper's well-placed camera continues to express the plight of the film's dreaming protagonist. On the school playground, David is framed inside a metal jungle jim, a surrogate jail cell of sorts, and the message is clear: he's trapped like a caged animal. Of all the children on the playground, only David is "trapped" in this fashion, simultaneously indicating his special status (as the star of his own dream) as well as his knowledge and his isolation. Later, David is literally surrounded by cages, by stuffed, mounted animals in miniature cages in his teacher's van, and the blocking is very much the same, expressing the identical point: this is a nightmare David cannot escape from. In the original film, Menzies staged many shots, nay, *entire sequences*, in minimalist, oversized sets to achieve similar results: feelings of entrapment and isolation. Instead of relying on art design, Hooper falls back on his thorough understanding of film grammar, *mise en scène* and cutting. And, not unlike John Carpenter, Hooper is quite expert at using the background and foregrounds of shots to convey important, frightening information. Once the evil has suffused the town, David is stalked by his school bus and it prowls silently behind him in an impressive sequence. Even more frightening is a scene in which David, mesmerized by the TV, fails to notice shadows stirring on a staircase in the background. These details may sound small, but taken together they are part of the tapestry, part of a perfectly composed horror film.

Since *Invaders from Mars* is the story of David's fear of alienation from his own mother (who is busy going to school as an accountant and tending to her husband), it is no wonder that much of the film's screenplay involves the boy's "courting" of a more appropriate mother surrogate, the kindly and beautiful school nurse portrayed by Hunter Carson's real mother, Karen Black. Linda Magnuson frequently relies on David's judgment, is often rescued by him, and even cowers under his protection. Some audiences found this scenario blatantly unbelievable, but one must always remember that this is a film seen through David's pre-adolescent eyes. In his dream, he is ever the hero, and many events in the film that seem unrealistic become recognizable instead as personal fantasy. Rather than showing skepticism for a child's claim that Martians have landed, the U.S. government and armed forces demonstrate total faith and support in the boy. They even go so far as to permit David to take part in the assault against the alien spaceship and to fire a Martian cannon.

David's two-dimensional view of his teacher, Mrs. McKellch (Louise Fletcher), is also the stuff of a juvenile fantasy. David just knows that this teacher has it in for him and, of course, she does. She couldn't possibly have concerns about David because of his work habits or behavior in school because children don't think in anything but the most egocentric terms. Therefore, the only way to explain McKellch's hostility is to write her off as a Martian stooge, a villain. David's rationalization about Mrs. McKellch's behavior, casting her as a monster in his dream, also signifies David's special status within his own world. He is not only a misbehaving child, but the *one* soul in all creation who can foil the Martian invasion and see the adults for what they really are.

Unlike *Aliens* (1986) or *Independence Day* (1996), the alien invasion of Hooper's film is the kind of tactic imagined by a child. How else to explain that the aliens arrive on Earth in search of copper, just as Gardner's class goes there on a field trip, studying copper? It all dovetails neatly because it is the dream of a single, prepubescent mind.

When reviewing any film, it is useful to ask what goal the movie sets out to reach and then judge whether or not it meets those ambitions. It isn't really very smart (or particularly useful) to go into a film called *Invaders from Mars* expecting Ibsen or Shakespeare. Instead, one can look at Hooper's purpose, to retell for the 1980s a child's nightmare that he found meaningful during his formative years in the 1950s, and judge the results. In striving for a faithful revamp of a famous story, Hooper uses another favorite trick from his magician's bag: the homage. Thus *Invaders from Mars* is not merely David's fantasy, but an amalgamation, a synthesis, of all such 1950s films that Hooper has enjoyed over the years. When Dr. Weinstein of SETI attempts to communicate with the Martians and is then killed by the malevolent drones, his ill-fated plea for peace references a similar moment in Howard Hawks' *The Thing* (1951) and George Pal's *War of the Worlds* (1953). In the 1950s sci-fi/horror cinema, there was always some namby-pamby, peace-loving scientist (read: Communist) willing to welcome (read: collaborate with) the aliens. But in the end, no accommodation could be reached with the monsters, and the stupid scientists paid the price for their appeasing behavior. Dr. Weinstein's blatantly ridiculous peace attempt, in the presence of a fang-faced Martian monster, recalls this tradition and gently mocks it. None but an idiot would attempt to peaceful co-existence with a set of teeth on legs! Likewise, when another character in the film exclaims "Great Scott!" he is purposefully echoing 1950s, *not 1980s*, slang, thus reminding the viewer of the epoch that gave rise to these alien invader films.

And, of course, Hooper goes to great lengths to reference the Menzies film in particular. Jimmy Hunt (who played the dreaming child in the original film) returns here as an adult, muttering "Gee, I haven't been up here since I was a kid," as he walks to his doom beyond the white side-rail fence. David's school is named Menzies Elementary, and the first film's Supreme Leader is glimpsed briefly in the school basement (alongside a pod from the original *Invasion of the Body Snatchers* [1954]). All these references let audiences know that (a) the director honors his filmic predecessors and (b) that this picture need not be taken as a serious polemic about alien invasions. It isn't an *Aliens*, *Star Wars* or even *Poltergeist*, but rather a post-modern, reflexive variation on a popular theme. It's designed to be fun.

The sci-fi fans who find Tobe Hooper's *Invaders from Mars* unsatisfactory might ask themselves if Hooper could have made a serious alien invasion film instead, if that was his intent. The answer to that query is affirmative. In fact, the Hooper project immediately preceding *Invaders from Mars* was

A new invasion for a new generation. David Gardner (Hunter Carson) steels himself against attacking aliens, and alienated parents, in Tobe Hooper's remake of ***Invaders from Mars*** (1986).

Lifeforce, just such a story! Obviously, Hooper opted to make a very different kind of movie this time behind the camera, one that was a tribute to the flawed but beloved genre films of his childhood. Those who don't like the movie sometimes fail to see that it isn't "childish" in execution, but told from the viewpoint of a child. That's a critical difference.

Beyond the entrapment imagery, the interesting perspective and multiple instances of homage, *Invaders from Mars* is interesting and provocative because of its many touches of humor. Even before the decade was finished, Hooper was already lampooning Reagan's 1980s. In *Poltergeist*, a Reagan biography found its way into the hands of an admiring yuppie. In his next picture after *Invaders*, *The Texas Chainsaw Massacre Part 2*, he poked fun at the "greed is good" yuppie values of the business-oriented Reagan era. But in *Invaders from Mars* he crafts a wicked satire by comparing the prosperous but empty-headed decade of Reagan to that of Eisenhower's similarly vapid 1950s, the very decade that gave rise to the alien invasion genre as well as the boomer generation of Spielberg, Carpenter, Lucas and Hooper himself! The Gardner family life in *Invaders from Mars* is thus pure *Ozzy and Harriet* (1952–1966). In that sense, the parents are conformist drones even before the Martians arrive to spoil things for David! The scenes between Timothy Bottoms and Laraine Newman are two-dimensional in the extreme, but intentionally so. Hooper has his actors play these scenes tongue in cheek, like *Father Knows Best* (1954-1963) on acid, and his subversive approach is illuminating.

The 1950s and the 1980s are alike in many ways, including resurgent patriotism, paternal (read: old) presidents and escalations of defense spending to win the Cold War. Both decades are often viewed as a "return" to simple American values, and thus quite unlike the turbulent '60s or complex '70s. More to the point, every little David Gardner in 1980s America longs for the existence of the 1950s set-up: a world where parents lived together in bliss, in sitcom perfection, to nurture the children. It is no mistake that as the Martians arrive, their first act is to split up the parents (read: divorce) and thereby transform David into that modern phenomenon, the latch-key child who must go it alone because the parents are too busy with careers or whatever to be home at the end of the school day. Especially relevant is one particular sequence early on in which David Gardner comes home from school to find his house empty, save for the eternal babysitter: the television. He turns it on, and it is showing Hooper's own *Lifeforce!* This passing reference is more than simple homage. This is a deliberate stab at the culture that provides violent entertainment for children under the umbrella of PG-13, yet simultaneously allows no at-home parents to protect the exposed child. It's no wonder that Gardner experiences a violent, disturbing nightmare: the media is saturated with violence (like *Lifeforce*) and there is no parental figure to shepherd him through it and protect "family values." Once again (as in *Poltergeist*), the TV is a portal that lets evil into the American household.

The reshaping of the 1980s into the 1950s works wonders for *Invaders from Mars*, as does its *Alice in Wonderland* template. Little David Gardner, a latter-day Alice, falls down a hole into the world underneath and as usual for Hooper, the new realm turns out to be a surreal place. In one egregious example of Hooper's daring, the new Martian Supreme Intelligence is seen emerging and retracting from a hole in the wall that can only be described as a bio-mechanical *anus*. Another surreal moment involves the humorous death of Louise Fletcher's character, always so properly dressed as a 1950s-style school marm. She is devoured by a Martian drone in precisely the same manner that David earlier saw her eat a frog! Head and body are gulped down, leaving dangling legs, then nothing. It's a funny visual joke that many viewers missed. Another wonderful tongue-in-cheek moment is James Karen's declaration that "Marines have no qualms about killing Martians!"

Though very well received by mainstream critics, *Invaders from Mars* was met with some scorn by those for whom it was intended in the first place: the sci-fi community. The backlash may have been caused by Hooper's decision to recast the Martians as fanciful and bizarre creatures from a child's nightmare, like a terror one might find in *Willie Wonka* or *The Wizard of Oz*, rather than as a "believable" alien threat. But one can hardly condemn Hooper for having a clear vision and for recasting a very weak story into a post-modern, hip mode. Some viewers also seem to object to Hunter Carson's central performance, judging it to be overly emphatic and lacking subtlety. In regards to that jibe, one can only write that children are not creatures known for subtlety in any regard and this is, after all, a child's adventure. Carson may be no Haley Joel Osment, but he is not a Jake Lloyd either.

Overall, *Invaders from Mars* accomplishes exactly what it sets out to do, to recount a crazy adventure from the viewpoint of a slightly off-kilter, smart aleck, media-exposed kid. Hooper's camerawork is laudable, his pacing is good, and his tongue is planted firmly in check. At times, when the picture involves the shadowy and unfriendly faces of whispering adults plotting secret matters, *Invaders from Mars* evokes the isolation and discontentment of childhood in a very tangible way. Along with *The Texas Chainsaw Massacre Part 2*, *Invaders from Mars* represents one of the most interesting phases of Tobe Hooper's career. He's gone beyond the stylish gut-wrenching terror of his early work (*The Texas Chain Saw Massacre, Eaten Alive, The Funhouse*), left mainstream roller coasters and special effects shows (*Salem's Lot, Poltergeist, Lifeforce*) and plunged into the hallowed—*but challenging*—land of post-modern entertainment. Here irony and humor are as important as the scares, and it's a good fit for Hooper.

7. *The Texas Chainsaw Massacre Part 2* (1986)

Critical Reception

"This is one horror movie that delivers the goods—and then some. It's the kind of movie where good taste isn't merely thrown out the window, but shredded, stomped, and spit on. But it's done with such style and energy, such bursts of red-hot invention and anarchic, madly irreverent satire that it almost scorches you out of your seat. Kit Carson's screenplay—defying anyone's notions of proper slasher-movie sequels—is a wicked send-up, not only of some half-mad Texas byways, but of horror movies in particular, and modern American culture in general."

—Michael Wilmington,
Los Angeles Times, August 23, 1986.

"...[A] longer, better made, more elaborate, better acted film that actually bested its predecessor in both nastiness and sick humor. Of course, by 1986 the myth of the Family Unit was in full swing and it afforded Hooper and screenwriter L.M. 'Kit' Carson almost bottomless material for truly vicious satire.... As a blistering indictment of Reaganism and the 'Me' generation, *Chainsaw 2* is even more to the point than David Lynch's more famous portrait of the nastiness beneath the delusion, *Blue Velvet*, made the same year."

—Ken Hanke, *A Critical Guide to Horror Film Series*, 1991, pages 266-268.

The last half of the film ... abounds in nonstop scenes of visual excess. There is a *tour de force* sequence where Stretch runs along an endless maze of hallways lit by Christmas lights and decorated by tableaux of corpses and other body parts. The swift tracking shots are brilliantly executed (they are particularly stunning on the big screen). The static and eerie visual displays of *TCM 1* are

replaced in the sequel by a completely over-the-top (and appropriate) amusement park style of dynamic filmmaking. Just as the (defunct) amusement park recreated scenes of past glory (and blood) at the Alamo, so this movie recreates the scenes of *TCM 1* as demonstrable fakes through the use of grotesque parody."
—Cynthia Freeland, *Thinking Through Cinema: The Naked and the Undead: Evil and The Appeal of Horror*, Westview Press, 2000, pages 249, 50.

"If you don't like slasher movies, you won't like *Saw 2*—it's too gruesome. And if you do like slasher movies, you won't like *Saw 2* either—it's too funny."
—Jami Bernard, *New York Post*, August 23, 1986, page 14.

"...[H]as a lot of blood and disembowelment, to be sure, but it doesn't have the terror of the original.... This movie goes flat-out from one end to the other, never spending any time on pacing, on timing, on the anticipation of horror. It doesn't even pause to establish the characters...."
—Roger Ebert, *Chicago Sun Times*, August 25, 1986.

"A plodding example of the ultimate in stupid behavior by one person after another, all underscored by inappropriately Hitchcockian music.... The effect sequences by Savini are a lot better than the rest of the film. The makeup set-piece is the skinning of a body that turns out not to be dead...."
—Judith P. Harris, *Cinefantastique*, Volume 17, Number 1, January 1987, page 52.

Cast and Credits

CAST: Dennis Hopper (Lieutenant "Lefty" Enright); Caroline Williams (Stretch); Jim Siedow (Cook); Bill Moseley (Chop-Top); Bill Johnson (Leatherface); Ken Evert (Grandpa); Harlan Jordan (Patrolman); Kirk Sisco (Detective); James N. Harrelli (Cut-Rite Manager); Lou Perry (L.G. McPeters); Barry Kinyon (Mercedes Driver); Chris Douridas (Gunner); Judy Kelly (Gourmet Yuppette); John Martin Ivey (Yuppie); Kinky Friedman (Sports Anchorman); Wirt Cain (Anchorman); Dan Jenkins (TV Commentator); Joe Bob Briggs (Gonzo Moviegoer).

CREW: The Cannon Group, Inc Presents a Golan-Globus Production of a Tobe Hooper Film, *The Texas Chainsaw Massacre 2*. *Special Make-up Effects:* Tom Savini. *Costume Designer:* Carin Hooper. *Music:* Tobe Hooper and Jerry Lambert. *Unit Production Manager:* Henry Kline. *First Assistant Director:* Richard Espinoza. *Second Assistant Director:* Mark Lyon. *Production Designer:* Cary White. *Director of Photography:* Richard Kooris. *Film Editor:* Alain Jakubowicz. *Associate Producer:* L.M. Kit Carson. *Co-Producer:* Tobe Hooper. *Executive Producer:* Henry Holmes, James Jorgenson. *Written by:* L.M. Kit Carson. *Produced by:* Manahem Golan, Yoram Globus. *Directed by:* Tobe Hooper. *Stunt Coordinator:* John Moio. *Stuntmen:* Daniel Barringer, Bob Elmore, Larry Hold, Tom Morga, Beth Nufer, Jim Stephan, Allen Wyatt, Jr. *Assistant Art Director:* Daniel Miller. *Leadperson Art:* Jay Rymond. *Set Decorator:* Michael Pearl. *First Assistant Cameraman:* Ralph Watson. *Boom Operator:* Henry Miller. *Sound Mixer:* Wayne Bell. *Video Assistant Operator:* Samuel Crowther. *Property Master:* Michael O'Sullivan. *Property Assistant:* Anita Dalls, Terry Evans. *Best Boy Electric:* Jon Lewis. *Key Grip:* Ferrell Shinnick. *Dolly Grip:* Bobby Lewallen. *Gaffer:* Phillip Curry. *Rigging Gaffer:* Doug Sutton. *Rigging Best Boy:* Dwight Cary. *Costume Supervisor:* Julia Combert. *Costumer:* Karen Miller. *Make-up:* Candi Duke. *Hair Stylist:* Denise Carfagno. *Special Effects Make-up Crew:* Jon Vulich, Mitchell Devane, Gino Crognale, Shawn McEnroe, Bart Mixor, Gabe Bartalos. *Model Maker:* Tony Hooper. *Production Coordinator:* Tamara Carlisle. *Location Manager:* Sjon Ueckert. *Script Supervisor:* Laura Debolt Kooris. *Unit Publicist:* Scott Holton. *Special Effects Coordinator:* Eddie Surkin. *Special Effects Leadman:* Joshua Hakian. *Special Effects Crew:* Gerald McClanahan, Todd Smiley, Ray Bietz, Joe Quinlivan. *Mechanical Special Effects:* Daniel f. Morris. *Post-Production Supervisor:* Michael R. Sloan. *First Assistant Editors:* Koby Dagan, Anne Cook. *Title Design:* Wenden H. Baldwin, Kyle Seidenbaum. *Main Titles and Opticals:* Freeze Frame. *Second Unit Directors:* Newt Arnold, John Moio. *Music Supervisor:* Paula Erickson. *Music Editor:* Michael Linn. "Shame on You" *Performed by* Timbuk 3, *written by* Pat and Barbara McDonald. "Goo Goo Muck" *performed by* the Cramps, *written by* Ronnie Cook. "No One Lives Forever" *performed by* Oingo Boingo, *written by* Danny Elfman. "Life is Hard" *performed by* Timbuk 3, *written by* Pat McDonald. "Over the Shoulder" *performed by* Concrete Blond, *written by* Johnette Napolitano, Jim Mankey. "Crazy Crazy Mama" *performed and written by* Roky Erickson. "Haunted Head" *performed by* the Lords of the New

Church, *written by* Stiv Bator and Brian James. *"Strange Things Happen" performed and written by* Stewart Copeland. Based on the motion picture *The Texas Chainsaw Massacre*, a Vortex/Henkel/Hooper production of a film by Tobe Hooper. *M.P.A.A. Rating:* Unrated. *Running time:* 101 minutes.

Opening Card

On the afternoon of August 18, 1973, five young people in a Volkswagen van ran out of gas on a farm road in South Texas. Four of them were never seen again. The next morning the one survivor, Sally Hardesty-Enright, was picked up on a roadside. Bloodcaked and screaming murder.... The girl babbled a mad tale: a cannibal family in an isolated farmhouse ... chain sawed fingers and bones ... her brother, her friends hacked up for barbecue ... chairs made of human skeletons.... Then she sank into catatonia. Texas lawmen mounted a month-long manhunt but could not locate the macabre farmhouse. They could find no killers and no victims.... Officially, on the records, the Texas Chainsaw Massacre never happened.... But during the last 13 years ... reports of bizarre grisly murders have persisted across the state of Texas....

"The saw is family."
—Cook (Jim Siedow) reasserts his family values in *The Texas Chain Saw Massacre Part 2* (1986).

Synopsis

In 1986, on the big Texas vs. O.U. football weekend, two preppie high school students in a Mercedes are target-shooting road signs as they drive the highway. The obnoxious kids call up Stretch, the D.J. at the Red River Rock and Roll Request Line, and harass her for a time. While on the phone with Stretch, the teens play chicken with an approaching pick-up truck and then run it off the road. That night, the

Stretch (Caroline Williams) spreads 'em while Leatherface (Bill Johnson) shows off the size of his ... chainsaw. From *The Texas Chainsaw Massacre Part 2* (1986).

preps cross a bridge only to be confronted by the same pick-up truck, now angling for revenge. The gruesome Leatherface pops out of the vehicle, cuts up the Mercedes with a chainsaw and viciously murders the boys even as their deaths are recorded on Stretch's radio line.

The next morning, Texas Ranger "Lefty" Enright, Sally and Frank Hardesty's slightly unhinged uncle, investigates the crime scene where the Mercedes crashed and the boys were killed. He finds evidence of chainsaw damage on the ruined vehicle and is convinced that this "accident" is related to the notorious crimes that resulted in the death of his nephew, Franklin, some thirteen years earlier. He is now obsessed with catching the bizarre perpetrators. He gets his story out in a local newspaper in hopes of finding a witness to this crime. In no time he gets one: Stretch. The D.J. visits Enright in his hotel room, and tells him that she has recorded the murder.

Later, Stretch and her friend at the station, cowboy L.G., cover a chili-cooking contest. The winner of the contest is strange Drayton Sawyer, the cook of the deadly Leatherface clan! Meanwhile, Lefty familiarizes himself with the weapon of his unseen enemy—the chainsaw. He "test drives" several chainsaws and purchases three of them. Later, he asks Stretch to broadcast the preppie slaughter on the radio, in hopes of drawing out more witnesses and making a legitimate case that all the disappearances and accidents across Texas are actually ghoulish murders perpetrated by a roving band of killers.

Unfortunately, when Stretch transmits the chaotic sounds of the murders over the air, she only succeeds in drawing out the worried Sawyers. Cook orders Leatherface and his deranged brother, Chop-Top, to silence the broadcast before his lucrative chili concession is threatened by scandal. At midnight, Chop-Top and Leatherface arrive at the radio station and beat L.G. to within an inch of his life. Then they terrorize Stretch. Unbeknownst to Chop-Top, Leatherface feels sexual stirrings for Stretch and lets her live. After the bizarre killers leave the station with L.G.'s bloody, unconscious body in tow, Stretch follows them to their bizarre underground home in a defunct amusement park called Texas Battle Land. Lefty follows Stretch there, but is not in time to save her from falling down a trap door into the strange lair of the Sawyers. She ends up in Leatherface's bloody abattoir, where he has sliced off L.G.'s face and started carving into his body with an electric knife. Still barely alive, the cowboy frees Stretch from Leatherface, who has hidden the girl from the rest of his family.

Enraged when he discovers Franklin's skeleton in the Sawyer place, Lefty becomes demented and sets about with his chainsaws to bring the whole fetid place down. Meanwhile, Stretch attempts to escape the strange underworld, but is chased down by Chop-Top, Cook and Leatherface. Leatherface is ordered to kill the girl, but still has feelings for her, and Chop-Top taunts him for having a girlfriend. A concerned Cook warns Leatherface that he can either have sex or the saw ... and the saw is family. At this warning, Leatherface straightens up and Stretch is promptly invited to a Sawyer family dinner. There, the boys encourage 137-year-old Grandpa—once the fastest killer in the slaughterhouse—to club Stretch to death. Unfortunately, Grandpa is nearly catatonic and his reflexes aren't what they used to be.

Stretch escapes her grim fate when Lefty arrives and challenges Leatherface to a duel by chainsaw. With the Texas Battle Land park and his business in ruins, Cook blows up the hellhole with a grenade. Lefty, Cook, Grandpa and Leatherface perish in the explosion, but Chop-Top chases Stretch out of the subterranean hell and up into a mountain cave attraction. There, Stretch finds the corpse of Grandma Sawyer. Stretch

A family reunion. Left to right: Cook (Jim Siedow), Grandpa (Ken Evert), Chop-Top (Bill Moseley) and Leatherface (Bill Johnson) as they appeared in *The Texas Chainsaw Massacre Part 2* (1986).

pulls a chainsaw from Grandma's hands and goes at Chop-Top with it, wounding him badly and sending him careening back into the hell of the underground cavern. Then, chainsaw in hand, Stretch swirls about in a victory dance.

Commentary

The 1980s were good to Leatherface and his Sawyer family and to their chronicler, Tobe Hooper. Since 1973, Hooper and the Sawyers had both made successful bids for respectability, moving up the ladder in their professions (movies and meat, respectively). *The Texas Chainsaw Massacre Part 2*, 1986's unrated family reunion, revels in a decade's worth of change, revealing a Hooper and a Sawyer family funnier and more confident in their ghoulish enterprises.

In the original *Texas Chain Saw Massacre*, Hooper unexpectedly landed audiences in a terrifying, bizarre, surreal world from which it could not escape. The sequel, though equally intense and startling, is not so straight-faced in its machinations. Instead, director Hooper and screenwriter Carson employ the distancing techniques of comedy and subversive wit to create an odyssey that can only be described as a thinking man's horror movie. Contrarily, and to the film's ultimate detriment, Hooper's camera also focuses intently on extremely graphic, extremely convincing blood and gore. These twin approaches, comedy and nausea, never seem to gel adequately, and that may be the reason why the film is ultimately considered less powerful, less artful than its notorious predecessor.

The humorous, pointed satirical elements of *The Texas Chainsaw Massacre Part 2* work very well, resulting in an often amusing, often uproarious movie. The bulk of the comedy material involves the so-called "yuppification" of the cannibal family, now identified as the Sawyers (the *Saw*yers, get it?). The family has survived Nixon, Ford and Jimmy Carter's malaise days of the 1970s (no gas, no trust in government, no jobs…) and found new success in Reagan's economic boom of the 1980s. In particular, the local yokels, led by the business-minded Cook, have become successful entrepreneurs, the self-employed owners of "the Last Round-Up," an appropriately named mobile barbecue and chili catering company. This popular small business has won a chili cook-off contest two years running, but Cook still isn't happy, mainly because of his Schedule C expenses and the general ineptitude of his less business-minded partners in crime, Chop-Top and Leatherface. "Man builds a good solid trade by hookin' and crookin'," he complains, "and the Gods just kick him right in the balls." Other relevant *bon mots* include his dissatisfaction that "Damn property taxes fuck up everything" and that "the small businessman gets it in the ass every time."

In admittedly less colorful language, it is clear that Drayton (Cook) has joined the mainstream and become part of the economy. He is thus the Willie Loman of horror movies, his death that of a cannibalistic chili cook. All of these moments (most revolving around Cook and the business) are played at a perfect pitch and the viewer comes away with the notion that "making a killing" doesn't necessarily have two distinct meanings for this particular family. They kill other people to make a killing financially. The killings are connected!

Some of the other humor in the film also involves Chop-Top and his "retro" (but oh so fashionable) fascination with the 1960s and the Vietnam war. In fact, Chop-Top's main obsession in the movie isn't meat or his family's murderous trade, it's his own shot at financial independence! He's developed a "business plan" of sorts for "*Nam Land*," an amusement park based on his Vietnam experience. 'It's what the people want!" he declares, and again one senses that Hooper and Carson have very carefully gauged the times. The mid 1980s were, after all, the time of nostalgia for all things '60s, from the Beatles to the rehabilitation of Richard Nixon, to the Vietnam War. In the mid '80s, there were no less than four major Vietnam War movies produced (*Platoon, Full Metal Jacket, Hamburger Hill, The Hanoi Hilton*), and though *The Texas Chainsaw Massacre Part 2* was at the beginning of that tidal wave, its creators seemed to sense that the public was turning the war, like everything else in the 1960s, into toothless nostalgia fodder. Chop-Top, primed to cash in on that wave, sees Nam Land as his opportunity to create financial freedom.

These amusing touches automatically elevate *The Texas Chainsaw Massacre Part 2* over any average sequel, or any average horror film for that matter, and nicely reference the time the picture was created. The 1980s was the decade of Gordon Gekko, "greed is good," the corporatization and businessification of middle America, and everything that the yuppie movement stands for is thus skewered. The Gipper's revolution, it seems, even struck ass backwards Texas and the most notorious of nutcases. The Sawyers, murderers all, still fit in with their society: valuing wealth above conventional morality. And, again like yuppies, they don't care who they have to grease to get ahead.

And, in its support (and mocking) of Leatherface's amorous advances towards the beautiful D.J. Stretch, the film also reflects that other 1980s political myth: a return to so-called family values. In Chainsaw World, Grandma and Grandpa are beloved and revered (despite the fact that they're mostly dead) and the family that slays together stays together. Leatherface flirts with the idea of romance but soon learns (from Cook and from Stretch) that sex is a "swindle" and that only "the saw is family." In genuflecting to American trends and making note of them in his film, Hooper acknowledges that he's a director concerned with more than the traditionally narrow confines of the

"Bring it all down!" Lefty Enright (Dennis Hopper) saws down Texas Battle Land with extreme prejudice during the final battle of *The Texas Chainsaw Massacre Part 2* (1986).

genre. But unlike Wes Craven, who occasionally comes off as heavy-handed, Hooper's insane brand of humor carries the day, making the film's socially relevant comments with a light and wacky grace.

Contrarily, *The Texas Chainsaw Massacre Part 2* goes too far and is too heavy with the thick red stuff. There was very little blood in the original film, a factor that makes it timeless in some senses. The film was so powerful, so raw, it didn't need to show a lot of blood. At its heightened pace, audiences filled in the "blanks" with gore of their own imagining. Alas, the sequel is not so cleverly crafted in this regard, going all-out for the on-screen gross-out factor. Unfortunately, this choice diminishes the film's lovingly created comedy sequences. The butchering scene wherein Leatherface cuts off L.G.'s face, in particular, is completely convincing and harrowing from a realism standpoint. This is a bad miscalculation and the excessive grue smothers the humor of what might have been a funny sequence (L.G., still alive, spits out his tobacco.) As a rule, audiences can't laugh while they're gagging. This has been Tobe Hooper's greatest miscalculation of late, repeated in *The Mangler* (1995): blood drowns out the wit, and the audience, sickened, misses the messages (and values) in his work.

One of the most interesting elements of the original *Chain Saw* was its total and utter lack of overt sexual politics. Sally Hardesty and her hippie friends represented only meat, raw ingredients, to the deranged Sawyers. *Chainsaw 2* moves into new territory by making the chainsaw an obvious phallic symbol, one representative of Leatherface's new adolescence. When Leatherface attacks Stretch in the radio station, he plunges his saw between her legs, into a freezer full of ice. Unable to remove the weapon from the material, Leatherface pumps and grinds. Later, when he nearly strokes Stretch's attractive, naked legs with the saw, he prematurely ejaculates in his pants, thrusting and retracting his hips with a sexual savagery that is frightening and simultaneously pitiful. Though this plot development infuriated some fans of the original film, it is nonetheless in keeping with Hooper's always-on-display love of nostalgia and homage factor. The love affair between Stretch and Leatherface harks back to the cinema's famous beauty and the beast couples such as King Kong and Fay Wray, Dracula and Lucy, The Phantom of the Opera and his starlet, and other "classic" relationships of the genre. In his specific work, the premature ejaculation was a moment of equal horror in *The Funhouse*.

In *Chainsaw 2*, the relationship between Stretch and Leatherface works because it is so unexpected. A sequel's biggest stumbling block is always predictability. If you've seen the first entry in a movie series, you've basically seen the blueprint for all the follow-ups. Not so with *The Texas Chainsaw Massacre Part 2*, an unpredictable, unconventional sequel.

In *Chainsaw 2*, Hooper artfully shatters all the covenants of the sequel. The first *Chain Saw* was pure out-and-out horror, devoid of post-modern humor and even conventional narrative. The sequel is almost the opposite, relying on funny barbs at contemporary society and a traditional narrative structure involving the fallen lawman (Dennis Hopper's Enright) and his long bid for revenge against those who have shattered his family. There was no acknowledgment of sex in the original film, but it becomes a focus of the second picture. There was almost no blood and guts in the 1974 chapter of the legend, yet the 1986 follow-up is drenched in it. *Chainsaw 2* even undercuts its own conventions. Dennis Hopper's law-enforcement character starts out as a hero figure, but ultimately emerges as a full-blown loony-tunes, offering relatively little help to the film's intended victim, Stretch. Only in the slavish restaging of the *Alice in Wonderland*–like tea party scene does Hooper rely on old, predictable material, and it is consequently the least interesting aspect of the movie.

Including the repeat "tea party" sequence, *The Texas Chainsaw Massacre Part 2* is also the most blatantly reminiscent of *Alice in Wonderland* of all Hooper's canon. Besides the dinner sequence, there's the crazy subterranean world and the girl (Stretch) who falls into it. Carroll's description of Alice's arrival in Wonderland clearly informs Stretch's fall into Texas Battle Land:

> The rabbit hole went straight on like a tunnel for some way, and then dipped suddenly down, so suddenly that Alice had not a moment to think about stopping herself before she found herself falling down what seemed to be a very deep well [1].

The tunnel in *Chainsaw 2* is different in just one important regard: it is lined with human skulls and bones. Viewers familiar with Hooper's work remember his fascination for the "world underneath," so the inclusion of it in this film should be no surprise. The carnival had a horrific underside in *The Funhouse*. The Martian spaceship in *Invaders from Mars* burrowed underground, there were womb-like labyrinths and interiors in pictures such as *Lifeforce* and *The Mangler*. Yet nowhere is the *Alice in Wonderland* "underworld" so memorably rendered as in the lunatic final portion of *Chainsaw Part 2*. Part amusement park, part wax museum, part butcher shop, it is a world never before imagined in the horror cinema. Even the name "stretch" is a reference to Carroll's Alice in a sense, a reminder that the lead girl in Carroll's adventure was constantly changing her size from small to large, "stretching" as it were. In *Chainsaw 2*, Stretch "stretches" from pesky D.J., to Leatherface love interest, to full-fledged heroine.

Beyond the humor, the homage to the horror classics and an ongoing reference to the surreal world of *Alice in Wonderland*, *The Texas Chainsaw Massacre Part 2* is notable mainly for Hooper's penchant for edgy (and disgusting) character touches. In particular, Chop-Top has a nasty bit of business that could only find a home in a Hooper production. He heats up a wire hanger with a lighter, scratches his head with the heated implement (at the edge of his metal skull plate) and then eats the detritus he has managed to scrape off. Like Judd in *Eaten Alive*, Leatherface in the original *Chain Saw*, or *The Funhouse* mutant, Chop-Top is a patented psycho, a glimpse of true, unrestricted insanity. As such he is a valuable addition to Hooper's bogeyman pantheon.

The Texas Chainsaw Massacre Part 2's larger budget allows its director the freedom to use the world of the chainsaw, and the chainsaw itself, to its fullest potential, tearing up a radio station, jutting dangerously through walls and so forth, but the picture's real strength comes not in the glorious, expensive destruction, but in the moment when Hooper goes beyond the pale with his surprises, alternately scary and funny. Leatherface's appearance in the radio station is a splendid example of the former, Dennis Hopper's ironic visit to a chainsaw outlet the latter. The film also gains some credibility from its smart opening: there's no need to resurrect the *Chain Saw* villains in some half-assed way (as has been done with Pinhead, Freddy, Jason, Chucky, the Leprechaun, Michael Myers and just about every other horror icon), since they've just been operating under the radar for 13 years.

Even more impressive is the film's conclusion: Stretch's victorious chainsaw dance, a clear reminder of Leatherface's famous twirl in *Chain Saw*'s coda, is reimagined for the era of Sigourney Weaver's Ripley. You've come a long way baby.

The Texas Chainsaw Massacre 2 is a very good, very smart horror film about more than killing yuppies, dueling chainsaws and gallows humor. Underneath the surface, the film concerns itself with American economics and "family value" sensibilities. A family "downsized" by the job layoffs of the 1970s sticks together through the tough times and rises as a self-made success in the eighties, profiting from the Reagan revolution despite or perhaps because of their unusual predilection for cannibalism. The only thing that undercuts this fast and furious (and smart and funny) sequel is the focus on the blood and gore effects. It's a bad misstep in an otherwise provocative sequel to a classic.

8. *Spontaneous Combustion* (1989)

Cast and Crew

CAST: Brad Dourif (David "Sam" Bell); Cynthia Bain (Lisa); Jon Cypher (Dr. Marsh); William Prince (Lew Orlander); Melinda Dillon (Nina); Dey Young (Rachel); Tegan West (Springer); Michael Keys Hall (Dr. Cagney); Dale Dye (General); Dick Butkus (Lieutenant General); Joe Mays (Dr. Persons); Stacy Edwards (Peggy Bell); Brian Bremer (Brian Bell); Frank Whitman (Young Orlander); Judy Prescott (Student Director); Judy Behr (School Nurse); Betsy Thomas (Nurse at Hospital); John Landis (Radio Technician); Jamie Alba (Waiter); Mark Roberts (Dr. Simpson); Richard Warlock (Mr. Fitzpatrick); Judith Jones (Jennifer); Bill Forward (Scientist); Ron Blair (Maitre-D); Mimi Wearm (Vicki); Sandy Ignon (Doctor in 1950s); Nick Gambella (Student in Theater); Patricia Gallagher Layton (Maid); Barbara Leary (Amy Whitaker); Paul Barresi (Hospital Guard); George "Buck" Flower (Preacher on the Radio).

CREW: Tobe Hooper/Henry Bushkin present a Jim Rogers Production of a Tobe Hooper film, *Spontaneous Combustion*. *Executive Producers:* Henry Bushkin, Arthur Sarkissan. *Music:* Graeme Revell. *Special Visual Effects:* Stephen Brooks. *Edited by:* David Kern. *Director of Photography:* Levie Isaacks. *Associate Producer:* Sanford Hampton. *Co-Produced by:* Jerrold W. Lambert. *Story by:* Tobe Hooper. *Screenplay by:* Tobe Hooper and Howard Goldberg. *Produced by:* Jim Rogers. *Directed by:* Tobe Hooper. *Casting:* Carol Lewis. *Costume Designer:* Carin Hooper. *Production Designer:* Gene Abel. *Stunt Coordinators:* Greg Gault, Rick Barker. *Stunts:* Richard Warlock, Monty Cox, Don Pike, Paula Moody, Glory Fioramonti, Debbie Ross. *Production Manager:* Sanford Hampton. *First Assistant Director:* Paul Moen. *Second Assistant Director:* Kristi Kat Morias, Michael Looney. *Production Executive:* Glenn Sobel. *Production Coordinator:* Rochell Goodrich. *Script Supervisor:* Nancy Karlin. *Set Dresser:* Timothy Keating. *Property Master:* Frank Bertolino, Bill Roberts. *Special Make-up Effects Created by:* Steve Neill. *Pyrotechnic and Floor Effects:* Guy Faria. *Assistant Pyrotechnic Effects:* Duncan W.

Puett, Pat Patterson, Lou Carlucci, Panacus Callas. *Special Mechanic Effects:* Tony Hooper. *Sound Mixer:* Craig Felburg, Cameron Hamza. *Costume Supervisor:* Julia Gombert. *Costumer:* Janet Sobel. *Make-up Artist:* Bill Miller-Jones. *Hairstylist:* Kerry Mendenhall. *Special Visual Effects Produced at:* Apogee Productions, Inc. *Special Effects Consultant:* John Dykstra. *Running time:* 97 minutes.

Synopsis

In 1955 at the Nevada Desert Hydrogen Bomb Testing Site, Brian and Peggy Bell—*known as America's first "nuclear family"*—live in a reinforced bomb shelter as the H-Bomb called "Samson" is test detonated. They survive the blast thanks to the shelter, but avoid radiation poisoning courtesy of a series of "anti-radiation" injections developed by a pharmaceutical company owned by the shadowy Lew Orlander. Peggy and Brian are toasted by the military for their success during the ordeal, but happiness quickly turns to fear when it is learned that Peggy is pregnant. A beautiful baby boy, David, is delivered nine months later. The only sign that he is not right is a birthmark on his hand: a perfect circle. In a bit of atomic irony, David is born on the tenth anniversary of the Hiroshima bombing. But while a doctor named Nina tends to David and Peggy, something goes horribly wrong. Peggy and Brian spontaneously combust, leaving a young David to be adopted by the shadowy Lew Orlander.

Thirty years later, David is divorced from Rachel, Orlander's granddaughter, and dating a girl named Lisa in his new home at Trinidad Beach. David and Lisa are both adamant in their opposition to nukes and have been protesting the opening of a new nuclear plant in the region. Oddly, the supervisor of the new facility, Amy Whittaker, turns up burned to a crisp in her bed one morning, after David has been in close contact with her.

On David's birthday, he visits with his ex-wife and her lover, Dr. Marsh, and his anger with Rachel unexpectedly causes one of his fingers to expel flame. David goes to see Dr. Simpson, but there is no explanation for this strange phenomenon. Shortly after studying David, Dr. Simpson also spontaneously combusts. Before long, David begins to experience strange flashbacks of his natural parents. The birthmark on his hand expands and David begins to explore the mysteries of his origins. On a local radio show, his old doctor, Nina, attempts to contact him, but an irritating radio technician prevents the *tête-à-tête*. David causes the technician to spontaneously combust, even though he is miles away. At the same time, however, David's arm expels flame and Lisa takes him to see Dr. Marsh at the local hospital.

Unbeknownst to David, Dr. Marsh is part of a conspiracy orchestrated by Lew Orlander. David's marriage to Rachel and even his relationship with Lisa are all part of Orlander's plan to develop and harness David's unusual powers. In particular, David's ability to burn up his enemies—*even across vast distances*—provides for the cleanest kills Orlander has ever seen. He knows David could be a formidable weapon, and Lisa—*born after a nuclear test in 1965*—is of a similar breed. His plan is for the two mutants to mate and provide "nuclear" offspring. Dr. Marsh, however, fears that the experiment has gotten out of control and systematically begins to kill those people who are aware of David's existence and the secret experiment. After David finds Nina and learns some of the secrets of his past, Marsh kills the kindly doctor.

Realizing he has been controlled and manipulated throughout his whole life, David confronts Lew and determines that he doesn't like the destiny that Orlander has planned for him. At the same time that the Trinidad Beach Nuclear Facility is to go on-line, David becomes a nuclear power: blowing up Orlander, searing off most of his own epidermis, and causing a power surge to rage across the countryside. When Marsh attempts to kill Lisa, who really loves David, David comes to her rescue. Seeing that her atomic powers are also developing, David's last act is one of compassion. Before transforming into a radioactive puddle of energy, David reaches out and absorbs Lisa's energy, preventing her from combusting and suffering his own fate.

Commentary

Tobe Hooper's *Spontaneous Combustion* commences on a high note, but then goes down in flames. Like his best film work (*The Texas Chain Saw Massacre*), the film relies strongly on the director's *outré* sense of humor. And, like his weakest efforts (*Night Terrors*, *The Mangler*), features a muddy narrative and pretty uninteresting characters. Hooper, ever the 1950s nostalgia buff, clearly has a ball in *Spontaneous Combustion* by ribbing that decade's sense of naivete regarding atomic power in a splendid, humorous and perfectly-pitched prologue. And the film often evokes the pleasant feeling of a 1950s sci-fi B picture like Bert I. Gordon's *The Amazing Colossal Man* (1957). Yet for an artist who began his feature film career by revolutionizing the genre, this project is an immense disappointment. A faithful Hooper viewer gets the distinct impression with *Spontaneous Combustion* that the genius of *The Texas Chain Saw Massacre* has faltered badly, going from genre innovator to mere king of the B's. The material he vets in *Spontaneous Combustion* is weak by any accounting, and his handling of it (following the artful prologue) leaves much to be desired. If anything, this movie seems to spontaneously combust before the audience's eyes.

And yet *Spontaneous Combustion* starts so very powerfully. Rippling balls of flame flower across the screen between the opening credits and the raw, powerful nature of fire is dramatized. How beautiful fire can be and yet how dangerous. That's some marvelous terrain to open a horror film on, and it promises that Hooper is on track to show his audience something really interesting and disturbing this time out.

From there, the film follows an H-bomb test at dawn and then turns into a delightful 1950s era propaganda short about America's first "nuclear family," Brian and Peggy Bell. This is where Hooper's genius is readily evident. His pervasive and subversive sense of humor coupled with his innate skill as a "documentary" style filmmaker couples to create a genuinely funny (and unnerving) sequence. Brian and Peggy hunker down in their deluxe, government-constructed bomb shelter (equipped with food for seven days) as the military detonates the bomb, named Samson. As the propaganda film continues to unspool, depicting the preparations of the young married couple, it joyfully and enthusiastically glosses over the inherent danger involved in this unusual enterprise. The blindly patriotic, naïve and optimistic texture of the conservative 1950s is humorously and brilliantly expressed. Hooper, as per his gift, makes the audience laugh and gasp at the same time, and his ironic use of the tune "I Don't Want to Set the World on Fire" played over the H-bomb test is nothing short of a masterstroke.

The writing is good here too. The H-bomb is described euphemistically as a "new tool" given to mankind and the reinforced shelter is "guaranteed to take the anxiety out of the atomic age!" This super-strong shelter (*cuz* "That's how we build it in the USA!") can really "take it!" These ridiculous, horn-blowing statements about American ingenuity are voiced in upbeat narration over black and white documentary-like footage, and artfully reveal the government/military's hypocrisy. Propaganda promises that Americans will survive and even flourish in a nuclear bombardment when — *as Brian and Peggy soon learn so dramatically* — nothing could be further from the truth.

8. *Spontaneous Combustion* (1989)

This ten minute opening sequence reveals a synthesis of that old Hooper magic. With zeal and humor, his story and theme (about the danger of nukes) come across beautifully. He has recaptured the vapid, propagandistic images of an age and simultaneously paid homage to the genre films of his youth. Just as atomic bomb testing spurs disaster in *The Amazing Colossal Man*, *Them* (1954) and even *Godzilla* (1954), so it is here the catalyst for an experiment in terror. As the film develops, Brad Dourif's David (or "Sam," depending on the scene) begins to transform into a monster, again not unlike the heroes of such '50s fare as *The Fly* (1958) and *The Amazing Colossal Man* (1957).

And, like those film protagonists, Dourif's character retains after his transformation a rudimentary sense of his own humanity. In the end, even as Sam has morphed into a blue puddle of neon radioactive energy, he remembers enough of his previous life to save his girlfriend, Lisa, from a determined assassin. As Hooper recollects his personal childhood of magic and monsters in *Salem's Lot* and *The Funhouse*, so does he in *Spontaneous Combustion* remember the feel of that era's entertainment. *Spontaneous Combustion* is a big 1950s B-movie about a man who, because of the military's testing of nukes and "tampering in God's domain," becomes a terrible monster. This theme fits in well with Hooper's career-long obsession with the decade of his youth. *Invaders from Mars* was a remake of a beloved 1950s film, *Body Bags* featured 1950s genre icons like Roger Corman and John Agar, and *Spontaneous Combustion*, at least for ten minutes, inhabits that decade.

Unfortunately, *Spontaneous Combustion* lacks the grace to remain in the 1950s. Once the film arrives in the present (the late 1980s), it sacrifices virtually every grain of narrative clarity and purpose. The characters are not even introduced successfully, leaving audiences confused and irritated. The scene at a restaurant in which Sam's ex-wife tells him of Amy Whittaker's unusual death (by spontaneous combustion) is a perfect example. At this point, the audience has no idea who Amy Whittaker is, why she is important, or how she is related to Sam. It is significant information, referring to a new nuclear plant going on line, yet the connection to Sam and his ex-wife is tenuous at best.

Another misconceived sequence involves Sam's flashbacks of his mom and dad—when his mom was still carrying Sam in her womb! That's incredibly silly, and nearly as ridiculous as the scene in Wes Craven's *The Hills Have Eyes II* (1985) when a dog has a flashback to events from the first *Hills* feature in 1977. The longer *Spontaneous Combustion* remains in the 1980s, the more ridiculous and unsatisfactory it seems. This author was particularly amused by the moment when Sam's girlfriend (a double agent of sorts) reported to Lew Orlander (the nefarious mastermind of the movie's conspiracy) that Sam had just telephoned her "and fire came out of the phone...." That's the kind of thing you don't hear at the movies every day.

For much of *Spontaneous Combustion*'s running time it is needlessly complicated. There is a long-lasting plot to control Sam, run by a variety of ill-defined characters including his doctor, his girlfriend, his ex-wife, and Lew Orlander. But a major flaw here is that none of the conspirators seem to move about according to a coherent plan. Why is Jon Cypher's Dr. Marsh suddenly a dangerous assassin? Why would Orlander permit his only granddaughter to marry a person as dangerous as Sam turns out to be? And so forth. This is a movie where, from moment to moment, there seems to be no motivation for characters to act as they do.

Following the ten minute opening sequence in 1955, there is precious little to enjoy or actually comprehend in *Spontaneous Combustion*. Melinda Dillon of *Close Encounters* (1977) and *Magnolia* (1999) makes a brief, but engaging appearance as a compassionate scientist who knows Sam's lineage and history (as the son of Brian and Peggy Bell). Directors John Landis (*The Twilight Zone: The Movie* [1983], *An American Werewolf in London* [1981]) and Tobe Hooper himself make funny cameos. It should also probably be noted that *Spontaneous Combustion* deploys state of the art special effects for its time. The fiery, brutal demise of Landis' radio technician is not easily forgotten. Nor the instances when Dourif's strange body chemistry causes jets of flame to spit out of his fingers and arms. These moments are expertly directed and quite shocking. But notably, the most effective death scene in the picture comes early, when Brian and Peggy Bell spontaneously combust. The audience feels for this sympathetic couple. They've bought into the American dream and the military's promises, and tried to be responsible citizens ("American heroes for America's future!"). Then they are nastily betrayed. Though goofy and naïve, this Ozzie and Harriet couple (who dream of living in a post–World War II community called Atom City) are more sympathetic and more clearly characterized than any other players in the film.

There have been allegations about constant rewriting on the set of *Spontaneous Combustion*, as well as other production problems, including creative interference, so perhaps it is not surprising that the film, overall, is pretty weak. Hooper has certainly done better, but he's rarely done worse. Fans of the director are advised to watch the first ten minutes of *Spontaneous Combustion*, groove on Hooper's humor and homage to the 1950s, then promptly turn off the VCR. Viewing the whole picture will only leave viewers with a handful of ashes.

9. *Tobe Hooper's Night Terrors* (1993)

Critical Reception

"While it was inevitable that someone would merge the sensibilities of the two video Kings, Zalman and Stephen, the project shouldn't necessarily have been attempted by the stars and director of 1976's *Eaten Alive*. Englund ... shows up as the Marquis ... for reasons that ... only serve to further pad the already meandering storyline."

—JRT, *Entertainment Weekly*, September 15, 1995.

"...[A]n ugly piece of crap ... this whole movie sucks."

—John Stanley, *Creature Features Movie Guide: The Science Fiction, Fantasy and Horror Movie Guide*, Boulevard Books, 1997, page 517.

Cast and Crew

CAST: Robert Englund (The Marquis de Sade/Paul Chevalier); Zoe Trilling (Genie); Alona Kimhi (Sabina); Julianno Merr (Mahnoud); Chandra West (Beth); William Finley (Dr. Matteson); Irit Sneleg (Fatima); Niv Cohen (Chuck); Doran Barbi (Ali); Howard Ripp (Harry Matteson's Assistant); Tsachi Noy (Chuck's Father); Dafna Armoni (Marzille); Yaakov Bana (Chevalier's Servants); Uri Gavriel (Yzutul); Yosef Shiloa (Hardy); Moti Bootbooi (Black Taxi Driver); Tamar Shamit (Snake Woman); Babi Noeman (Gnostic Leader); Daniel E. Matmor (Priest); Dmitri Phillips (Duval); Duvi Cohen (Warden); Gregory Tal (Warden's Assistant); Adam Zilberman, Didi Lukov (Prisoners); Shmuel Arzer (Market Vendor); Fitcho Ben-Zur (Blind Beggar); Charli Buzoglo (Mirage Servant); Atzmon Itshak (Sabina's Sevant); The Allo Alaev Family (Arab Band); Liz Fachima (Gnostic Woman); Amiram Gavriel (Akim); Racheli Hanig (Arab Girl); Harry Ringer (de Sade's Double); Anna Perelman (Genie's Double), David Macnehm, Yonatan Cherci, Shmuel Omani, Dar Ben.

CREW: Yoram Globus and Christopher Pearce Present a Global Pictures Production of a Tobe Hooper Film, *Tobe Hooper's Night Terrors*. *Make-up Effects Created by:* David B. Miller. *Music:* Dov Seltzer. *Edited by:* Alain

Jakubowicz. *Director of Photography:* Amnon Solamon. *Written by:* Daniel Matmor, Rom Globus. *Associate Producer:* Anita Hope. *Line Producers:* Allan Greenblatt, Michael Sharfstein. *Executive Producers:* Yoram Globus and Christopher Pearce. *Produced by:* Harry Alan Towers. *Directed by:* Tobe Hooper. *Production Manager:* Amitan Manelson. *First Assistant Director:* Assaf Amir. *Second Assistant Director:* Avichai Henig. *Executive Consultant:* Rita Bartlett. *Art Director:* Yossi Peled. *Camera Operator:* Amnon Solomon. *Script Supervisor:* Guy Leder. *Dialogue Coach:* Michael Rush. *Local Casting:* Cheli Goldenberg. *Production Coordinators:* Ruth Lustig-Dassa, Dorit Kfir. *Location Manager:* Shemi Shoenfeld. *Make-up Artist:* Maskit Koren. *Make-up Effects:* Lou Lazzara. *Make-up Assistant:* Dalit Davidov-Pridan. *Hairdresser:* Nancy Balwin. *Property Master:* Zviki Aloni. *Set Decorator:* David Varod. *Set Dresser:* Amiran Lichter. *Special Effects:* Bashir Abu-Rabea. *Special Effects Assistant:* Jeanne Voslod. *Titles and Opticals:* Film Opticals, Toronto. 1993 Surge Productions. *M.P.A.A. Rating:* NA. *Running time:* 98 minutes.

Synopsis

In Alexandria, Egypt, in 1993, archaeologist Dr. Madison greets his freewheeling daughter Jeannie at the airport. He brings her to his luxurious home, which is close to an important dig he is working at, and they share their first meal together in six months. He tells her of the Gnostic ruins he has unearthed, but she is more interested in catching up with her friend Beth. They make plans to go the horse races in a few days.

Jeannie has trouble adapting to the restrictions of the Arab world. She wears skimpy, provocative clothes to a local bazaar and is nearly raped by swarthy locals. She is rescued from this fate by a beautiful friend of her father's named Sabina. The seductive Sabina invites Jeannie to her apartment, and it is there that Jeannie sees a portrait of a courtesan who resembles her a bit too closely. Oddly, this is the very courtesan who betrayed the Marquis de Sade a century earlier, and had him sent to prison for hi debauchery.

Noting her interest, Sabina lends Jeannie a book by de Sade, but Jeannie's father is furious to learn she has been with Sabina. He claims she is a woman of "bad reputation."

That night, Jeannie flouts her father's instructions and goes out on the town with Sabina. They party at a strange club, and the gathering quickly descends into topless dancing, and orgies. Jeannie, high on drugs, experiences disturbing visions of wriggling snakes while Sabina makes love to a servant boy. The following morning, a hung-over Jeannie goes out to the races in the desert with Beth. Still sick from the night before, she collapses in a faint (again experiencing visions of snakes). She is tended to by a handsome Arab noble named Mahnoud. Jeannie is taken home by her friends to recuperate and given a protective amulet by her father's superstitious housekeeper, Fatima.

The following day at the bazaar, Jeannie runs into Mahnoud. He invites her to go riding with him in the desert. They spend time together and she learns he's a well-traveled man who loves the desert. She makes love to him by twilight. After this romantic encounter, Jeannie starts to read the tantalizing works of de Sade, even as Sabina invites her to a strange costume ball. At the party, Jeannie meets Paul Chevalier, the host of the event. She learns he is a direct descendant of de Sade himself!

Beth also attends the party with her boyfriend, but finds it depraved and perverted. She warns Jeannie that Sabina and Chevalier, as well as many of the partygoers, are part of a dangerous cult. She urges Jeannie not to get too close. After issuing this warning, Beth is stalked through the city by a taunting, unseen murderer and eventually killed.

Meanwhile, Dr. Madison and his staff find a secret subterranean chamber at the archaeological site. This discovery keeps Madison away from Alexandria and the vulnerable Jennie. While Madison digs into the

Gnostic past, an assassin arrives and slits his throat. Back in the city, Jeannie is terrified when she finds Beth's severed head in her father's refrigerator and Fatima hanged! She runs through the streets seeking help and makes her way to Sabina's apartment. Sabina offers to help, but in fact drugs Jeannie and takes her to Chevalier's dungeon, where the girl is strung up and prepared for torture. Sabina and Chevalier await a third visitor before beginning their sadistic pleasure with the American. He arrives, and Jeannie is shocked to see that the third conspirator is Mahnoud, who wants to join Chevalier's strange cult.

Chevalier and Sabina tell Jeannie that all the horror is concerned with her. They have gone to great lengths to pervert and degrade her. Then, they show her Dr. Madison's severed head, a "souvenir" according to Chevalier. Without warning, Chevalier then turns on Mahnoud, killing him because he feels accomplices are "dangerous." Then, Chevalier's evil pleasures are interrupted again when another cultist insists on seeing him upstairs. There, he informs Chevalier that Beth was a diplomat's daughter and that questions are being asked by officials in Alexandria.

Jeannie seizes this opportunity to trick Sabina into releasing her. When Chevalier returns to the dungeon, he uses an ancient Gnostic artifact to reinforce his belief in a vengeful, violent God rather than a Christian one. But when he opens the artifact, a small box, he only finds a scale. Sabina has stirrings of disloyalty and challenges Chevalier. She stabs him in the back before he can pluck out Jeannie's eyes. Weakened but not defeated, Chevalier murders Sabina, then pursues Jeannie as she escapes from the dungeon. But Paul Chevalier has a nasty shock in store: ghostly Gnostics weigh the scales of justice against him and determine him unworthy. Jeannie escapes and the evil of Chevalier and the Marquis de Sade dies.

Commentary

Quills (1999), this isn't. Instead, *Tobe Hooper's Night Terrors* is a project that could generate terror in even the most devoted fan of the director's film output: a heavy-handed, turgid muddle of a movie that isn't thrilling or even particularly erotic (though it has been dubbed an "erotic thriller"). This film is atypical of Hooper as a filmmaker because there's no sign of his infectious sense of humor (which so dominates the *Texas Chainsaw Massacre Part 2*, *Invaders from Mars* and *Poltergeist*), or even his unflagging energy. Instead, the film is 90 minutes of pure nonsense about an heir to the Marquis de Sade's evil and his cult's planned sacrifice of a sexy American woman (played by fetching Zoe Trilling).

The Marquis de Sade (1740–1818) is a fascinating historical figure and a great subject for a Tobe Hooper film. There are many, many questions about de Sade that are still being debated today. Was he a great writer, or merely a pornographer? Did he debauch the world with his depictions of wild sex, or liberate it from the repression of his era? Was he a hero/martyr or a self-serving opportunist? Was he a flagrant misogynist (because his work often featured the torture and rape of women), or an early feminist (because he was the first author who was willing to view women outside their reproductive/biological role as child bearers)? Any one of these subjects would have been fascinating fodder for a film about de Sade and Hooper is the perfect director to tackle such a project. Why? Well, de Sade was an early surrealist for one thing, and author Francine Du Plessix Gray considers him to be an artist who:

> ... gave free reign to those darker inclinations, to the impulses that can compel us to regress, if only in our fantasies, to an archaic, animal-like stage liberated from even the most fundamental taboos,—incest, cannibalism—imposed by civilization [1].

That sounds suspiciously like a review of *The Texas Chain Saw Massacre*, or any other Hooper opus that features violence, fantastic imagery, and shatters taboos. In *Chain Saw*, cannibalism was the bugaboo. The specter of anal sex popped up (briefly) in *Eaten Alive*, and the first quarter of *Lifeforce* featured extensive female nudity, another taboo (of the film industry) shattered.

Du Plessix Gray also wrote that:

> For those who take to Sade's work, his fascination comes from the dual movement of attraction and repulsion he exacts on us, a relationship that foregoes all traditional narrative "pleasure" [2].

Again, consider how Hooper takes away the act of learning in the *Texas Chain Saw Massacre*, stealing the viewer's sense of narrative comfort and "pleasure." Likewise in *Poltergeist*, wherein the resolution of one plot is followed by a structurally unrelated coda of some lengthy duration.

Also, Hooper's subject matter in many films (sexually transmitted infection in *Lifeforce*, cannibalism in the *Chain Saws*, sexual dysfunction in *Eaten Alive* and *The Funhouse*, vampirism in *Salem's Lot*) are simultaneously compelling to watch and distasteful, frightening and repellant (as all horror movies strive to be).

None of this intellectual gamesmanship is meant to suggest that Tobe Hooper is a closet sadist, only that de Sade and this filmmaker have in common a commitment to the surreal, and to subject matter which is considered controversial. Given that common ground, the notion of Robert Englund and Tobe Hooper collaborating on a film about the Marquis de Sade sounds like a dream come true. After all, Englund is probably the most versatile actor working in horror in the last thirty years, capable of playing a low-grade human sleaze-ball in *Eaten Alive*, a larger-than-life "supernatural avenger" in the *Nightmare on Elm Street* films, and even an innocent and naïve extraterrestrial in *V* (1985). Frankly, there's little that Englund can't do well and the opportunity to see him as de Sade is full of potential.

Unfortunately, Englund seems no more engaged by the film's weak material than does Hooper. Englund's scenes as the Marquis are pretty unnecessary to *Night Terror*'s narrative thrust, as if they were piped in from an unfinished project instead. Even given the restrictions of the script, Englund tends to ham it up as de Sade, and show almost no subtlety as the modern version of the sadist, Chevalier. He makes far too much of moments that should be underplayed (such as the character's enjoyment of classical music). Basically, Englund plays Chevalier as though he were a modern day James Bond villain: impeccably dressed, light, charming and not terribly menacing. As de Sade, Englund is under about as much face make-up as he'd have to endure had he chosen to play Freddy Krueger again instead. Under a foppish wig (and boasting a blinded, white eye), Englund's de Sade's is an unpleasant face to watch and for some reason Englund plays the Marquis with a constant sense of amusement and enjoyment. He's the only one, audience included, who experiences that sensation in *Night Terrors*.

On the Tobe Hooper scale of quality, *Night Terrors* is really pretty weak. No bones about it. It drones on endlessly, cutting between de Sade in the past and Trilling's character in Alexandria in the present. Neither story is very interesting, though Trilling has significant screen presence and good looks. Her body is on display a lot in the film and since there are simulated sex scenes, this might qualify as Tobe Hooper's first soft core sex movie.

For die-hard Hooper fans, there are some commonalities in *Night Terrors* with his other (and better) films. First, this is his third collaboration with William Finley and Robert Englund. Second, on a thematic level, the film resurrects the horny boyfriend (always a useful cliché in horror movies) familiar from *Eaten Alive, The Funhouse, Salem's Lot,* and *I'm Dangerous Tonight.* The film also features "strange locals" (Chevalier, Sabina, the cult), operating on the fringes of normal society and threatening so-called regular folks. Like Cook in *The Texas Chain Saw Massacre,* Judd in *Eaten Alive,* or the carnies in *The Funhouse,* these people appear normal on the surface, but cloak hidden desires and anti-social behavior. How Hooper exploits these common touches is a lot less interesting than one might expect from the artist behind *The Texas Chain Saw Massacre* and *Lifeforce.*

Even the film's advertising is misleading. The video box depicts snake and frogs erupting out of Robert Englund's face. Nothing so picturesque occurs in the actual movie, unless one counts a few trippy dream sequences (another bow to surrealism) involving snakes and crucifixes, as well as the unexpected appearance of ghostly Gnostics.

Sometimes, the best of directors come up empty-handed, and there's no shame in admitting that *Tobe Hooper's Night Terrors* is one of those incidents. George Lucas made *Howard the Duck* and directed *The Phantom Menace.* Wes Craven directed *Deadly Friend,* William Friedkin directed *The Guardian* and Tim Burton oversaw the ill-advised remake of *Planet of the Apes.* It's sad to see good directors blow it and in this case it's downright depressing to see this particular energetic, inventive innovator waste his time (and ours) on so weak a picture.

10. *The Mangler* (1995)

Critical Reception

"Director Tobe Hooper's directing career has been in decline since the popular *Poltergeist,* but this over-the-top chiller shows he still has a brawny visual imagination. Also present is his propensity for gratuitous gore, putting the picture way off limits for the squeamish."
—David Sterritt, *Christian Science Monitor,* August 25, 1995, page 14.

"The film scores high on production finesse: new digital editing techniques give many of the cast amputated fingers, the gore is viscerally convincing, and the sequence where the 40-foot machine becomes a kind of giant mechanical bullfrog is well done. Yet all this fails to add up to a frightening movie...."
—Philip Strick, *Sight and Sound,* July 1995, page 50.

"The best part of the movie is the fetid, oppressive atmosphere Hooper works up inside the sweatshop that evocatively serves as an industrial hell. *The Mangler* itself is an imposing creation, and its gory activities ... pack an occasional chill."
—Michal Gingold, *The 1996 Motion Picture Annual Guide,* 1996, page 199.

"The teaming of director Tobe Hooper, actor Robert Englund and author Stephen King would seem to offer a horror trifecta, but that's not the result in *The Mangler,* the latest King-inspired debacle to hit the big screen.... *The Mangler* is ludicrous from start to finish: Its plot lines dangle, its effects fail to dazzle and the acting and directing are uniformly bad. The movie looks as if it's gone through its namesake.... Even the least demanding genre fans will be hard-pressed to tremble in its presence."
—Richard Harrington, *Washington Post,* March 5, 1995.

"...[O]nce the set-up is established, the movie, like so many other horror films, quickly fizzles.... [T]he climactic man-machine battle is one of the sloppier mini–Armageddons to hit the screen in awhile ... the horror-movie equivalent of visual and verbal gibberish."
—Stephen Holden, *New York Times:* "Dirty Work at the Blue Ribbon Laundry," March 4, 1995.

"...[T]his cheapo horror flick lacks a whit of sense — narrative coherence is mangled more than anything else.... [I]t's a glum, lackluster affair ... call it 'The Bungler.'"
—David Kronke, *Los Angeles Times,* March 6, 1995, page 7.

"There's naught to recommend in *The Mangler* ... other than—and you should be ashamed if this is what you want—its many gory shots of arms, heads and bodies being crushed and, my personal favorite, a dying man hocking bloody sputum directly into the camera lens."
—Leah Rozen, *People Weekly*,
March 27, 1995, page 18.

"...[A] mess, trying to mix too many horror genres and succeeding at none.... [T]here are some effective set designs here ... but the script kills any potential they have to scare."
—Bill Hoffman, *New York Post*,
March 4, 1995, page 15.

Cast and Crew

CAST: Robert Englund (Bill Gartley); Ted Levine (Johnny Hunton); Daniel Matmor (Mark Jackson); Jeremy Crutchley (Pictureman); Vanessa Pike (Sherry Ouelette); Demetre Phillips (Stanner); Lisa Morris (Lin Sue); Vera Blacker (Mrs. Frawley); Ashley Hayden (Annette Gillian); Danny Keogh (Herb Diment); Ted Liplat (Dr. Ramos); Todd Jensen (Roger Marlin); Jeremy Crutchley (Mortician); Sean Taylor (Derrick Gates); Gerrit Schoonhoven (Aaron Rodriguez); Nan Hamilton (Ms. Ellenshaw); Adrian Waldron (Mr. Ellenshaw); Norman Coombes (Judge Bishop); Larry Taylor (Sheriff Hughes); Irene Trangs (Mrs. Smith); Megan Wilson (Ginny Jason); Odile Rault (Alberta); Ron Smerczak (Officer Steele).

CREW: New Line Cinema and Anant Singh Presents A Distant Horizon Production in Association with Filmex Ltd. and Allied Film Productions, a Tobe Hooper Film, *The Mangler*. *Directed by:* Tobe Hooper. *Produced by:* Anant Singh. *Screenplay by:* Tobe Hooper, Stephen Brooks and Peter Welbeck. *Based on a short story by:* Stephen King. *Director of Photography:* Amnon Salomon. *Production Design:* Dave Barkham. *Edited by:* David Heitner. *Music Composed and Conducted by:* Barrington Pheloung. *Executive Producers:* Helena Spring, Harry Alan Towers, Sudhir Pragjee, Sanjeev Sing. *Visual Effects Supervisor:* Stephen Brooks. *Make-up Effects:* Scott Wheeler. *The Mangler Created by:* William Hooper. *Associate Producer:* Rita Marie Bartlett. *Unit Production Manager:* Genevieve Hormeyn. *First Assistant Director:* Graham Hickson. *Post-Production Supervisor:* Lesley Fox. *Co–Second Assistant Directors:* Philip Mosofu, Gavin Joubert, Shane Mohaber, Diane McCarthy. *Production Coordinator:* Sandra Mazzotti. *Unit Production Manager:* Michael Snell. *Script Supervisor:* Maureen Conway. *Dialogue Coach:* Cathy Plewman. *Focus Puller:* Ewen Bogle. *Second Unit Director:* Stephen Brooks. *Second Unit Cameraman:* Clive Lawrie, Vincent Cox. *Set Dresser:* Jeanne Henn, Hamid Croukamp. *Property Master:* Shane Bruce. *Special Effects:* Maximum Effects. *Special Effects Coordinator:* Max Poolman. *M.P.A.A. Rating:* R. *Running time:* 106 minutes.

"Don't suppose you know anything about industrial laundries?"
"You know, I used to work in an industrial laundry...."
—A typical dialogue exchange
from *The Mangler* (1995).

Synopsis

At the Blue Ribbon Laundry in Riker's Valley, a young worker named Sherry is injured while working on the Hadley-Wilson press machine, affectionately known by toilers in the industry as "the Mangler," when two men transporting an old ice box to its new owner bump into the machine. A strange burst of energy is released from the Mangler, and Sherry is left with a bloodied hand. The cruel taskmaster at Blue Ribbon, Bill Gartley, is unaffected by sixteen-year-old Sherry's plight, even though she is his legal ward. Later, the refrigerator deliverymen nearly have a second accident when they almost run police detective Johnny Hunton off the road.

Back at Blue Ribbon Laundry, a kindly old worker, Ms. Frawley, gets chewed up in the Mangler and dies horribly. Hunton is assigned to investigate the accident, but when he sees what's left of the corpse he vomits and leaves the scene. Shortly thereafter, the local judge and sheriff test the Mangler for flaws and declare it safe during an "official" inquest, and reopen the laundry. Hunton believes the investigation is a whitewash and can't let it go.

At home that night, Hunton meets with his friend Mark, who has a propensity to believe in anything paranormal. A former employee at another industrial laundry, Mark tells Johnny that the Mangler couldn't malfunction in the way it did because of the safety bar, and Johnny remains convinced that the town elders conspired to reopen Gartley's operation before an adequate investigation could be completed.

Meanwhile, Gartley, an old cripple, becomes intimate with Lin Sue, one of the more attractive young laundry workers, and lets her in on the secret of his power. Before long, another accident has occurred at the Blue Ribbon, this one involving a nice girl named Annette Gillian. Johnny visits her at the hospital, where she reports that everything went bad when Sherry's blood first touched the Mangler. On hearing this, Mark becomes convinced that the machine is haunted, or perhaps possessed, though Hunton is skeptical. Mark researches his theory and comes to believe that a demonic pact is being organized in Riker's Valley, one that requires the blood of a young virgin. Mark suspects 16-year-old Sherry, Gartley's ward, is being set-up for an unpleasant fate. He and Johnny visit her at Gartley's mansion and she tells them about the icebox that struck the Mangler, and the strange burst of light that followed.

The ice box turns out to be very important. When it struck the Mangler during the accident, it became infused with the Mangler's evil. Now it has killed an innocent child and a furious Hunton smashes it with a sledgehammer. Oddly, this act of destruction vanquishes the demon inside, releasing an odd blue energy into the night air. Now, Hunton isn't so skeptical about Mark's beliefs in the supernatural. Mark recommends a rite of exorcism on the Mangler before the blood of a virgin gives the machine additional power.

Johnny goes to the morgue to examine Ms. Frawley's belongings, and runs into his friend there, an elderly crime scene photographer. The photographer is old and dying, claiming he is "eaten up" inside, but nonetheless provides the important final pieces in this puzzle. His scrapbook reveals that the town elders of Riker's Valley have all "lost" their daughters when they turned sixteen. Hunton understands that the children didn't disappear or die in accidents ... they were sacrificed to the Mangler, and in return for this "gift," the Elders were promised immortality and power. Hunton confronts Gartley at the plant, but Gartley has the town elders on his side, and sees to it that Hunton is fired from the police force.

While Hunton licks his wounds, Gartley and his protégée, Lin Sue, abduct Sherry and prepare to feed her to the Mangler. Johnny and Mark arrive in time to save Sherry, but must fight Lin Sue and Gartley. After a violent scuffle, Gartley and his lover both end up dying in their beloved machine. Johnny, Sherry and Mark perform an exorcism and feed the Mangler a crucifix and a Bible. The machine comes to life, sheds its mechanical skin, and turns into a living demon. It chases Hunton, Sherry and Mark down a long corridor and into a labyrinth below the laundry. The machine is finally destroyed, but not before Mark is killed.

Evil is not destroyed, however. When Hunton visits the Blue Ribbon Laundry the following day, he sees that the Mangler is back in business and that Sherry is possessed by the spirit of Gartley. Disgusted, Johnny drives away from Riker's Valley for good.

Commentary

The Mangler first entered the public consciousness as a short story in a 1972 issue of the periodical *Cavalier*, but it gained a wider readership, no doubt, as part of Stephen King's 1979 *Night Shift* collection. It's a twenty-four-page story about a possessed laundry machine and the veteran cop who opposes the bloody thing. It's an involving tale at two dozen pages, yet hardly the stuff of a successful feature-length film.

Perhaps that's part of the problem. By the mid '90s, when producer Harry Alan Tower, director Tobe Hooper and actor Robert Englund were reteaming after *Night Terrors* to adapt the King tale, all of the most promising King stories had already been adapted for film or television. John Carpenter had taken his swing at *Christine* in 1983, Stanley Kubrick had directed *The Shining* in 1980, and David Cronenberg had shot *The Dead Zone* in 1981. De Palma's *Carrie* (1976) was another King high-water mark and even Hooper himself had done well by King's scary material with his ratings-grabbing TV adaptation of *Salem's Lot*. But for every victory like *Carrie*, *The Shining* or *Salem's Lot*, there was a King failure too. King's *Maximum Overdrive* (1985) was a bomb, George Romero's adaptation of *The Dark Half* (1991) was instantly forgettable, and then there was the pure dreck like *Silver Bullet* (1985), *Children of the Corn* (1984) and so on. King's work isn't easily adaptable to film in any regard, and many good directors have failed to translate his powerful, literate work into box office gold. Though *The Mangler* is a good short story, adapting it to film is, in some senses, akin to all of those *Saturday Night Live* sketches that have become feature films—like *Ladies Man* (2000) *Superstar* (2000) or *A Night at the Roxbury* (1999). Over ninety minutes, the material becomes thin, whereas at five minutes or in the case of *The Mangler*, 25 pages, it works just fine.

On the surface, Hooper and co-writers Brooks and Welbeck have been true to the King source material. Their main character is a fourteen-year veteran of the police force named Hunton and the villain of the piece is a possessed Hadley-Watson Model Six Speed Iron and Folder affectionately dubbed "the Mangler." Sherry Ouelette is the virgin whose blood the Mangler first tastes, kindly old Miss Frawley is the Blue Ribbon employee who gets gulped down by the machine and Stanner is the floor supervisor who loses an arm to the industrial tool. The differences are mostly cosmetic. In the short story, for instance, a police officer tells a story about a demonic icebox, but it is a tale unrelated to the Hadley-Watson. In the movie, for clarity's sake, the icebox is possessed by the same evil as the Mangler when the two appliances "touch" during the opening scene. In both the film and short story, Hunton and English professor Mark Jackson face off against the Mangler, but in the film, the Mangler is the tool of Bill Gartley (Robert Englund) whereas in the story it is merely a "random possession" that causes all the trouble.

In the short story, Bill Gartley is named as the owner of the Blue Ribbon Laundry, but is not present for any of the action. In the film, he has become the primary villain, and one feels this was done to accommodate star Robert Englund. At the time the film was made, Englund was still the eminent horror icon of the silver screen—having starred in seven *Nightmare on Elm Street* films, not to mention *Phantom of the Opera* (1990) and the like. His name on the marquee seemingly promised an added draw (plus Hooper—director of the infamous *Chain Saw Massacre*, and Stephen King—the king of horror). So, *The Mangler* grafts on a conspiracy to King's story. Gartley feeds or "sacrifices" people to the Mangler so that he, presumably, is permitted immortality and wealth. The problem with this conspiracy is that the benefits Gartley gets out of the deal with the devil, the contract of ownership with the Mangler, are never really clear. Englund walks throughout the film in old age make-up, in leg and arm braces. He is a cripple with one blind eye and no "whole" limbs … so it seems he's participating in a fool's bargain. If he were to remain young and beautiful, well then, it would be clear why he sacrificed his daughter to the lean, mean pressing

"You gotta make sacrifices!" Bill Gartley (Robert Englund) and Lin Sue (Lisa Morris) prepare to feed an unsuspecting victim to a possessed laundry machine in *The Mangler* (1995).

machine. Still, it is typical of Hooper to showcase material in which there is more than one villain. The carnie and his dad in *The Funhouse*, Straker and Barlow in *Salem's Lot*, Leatherface and his family in *Chain Saw*. *The Mangler* adds to that tradition, also dramatizing a relationship in which one evil (Gartley) allows the evil of another (the possessed laundry press).

Also, the climax of King's short story has been changed for the film. In the printed version, Hunton and Jackson exorcise the demonic Mangler but the spiritual cleansing doesn't work. After killing Jackson, the Mangler follows Hunton home to his wife (who is deceased in the film), and the inference is Hunton will be the next to go the way of all flesh. In the film, the Mangler sprouts legs, chases down Hunton and Sherry, but is finally stopped. Sherry becomes part of the town-wide conspiracy, the Mangler returns to its evil ways, and Gartley lives on in Sherry's body, leaving a disillusioned Hunton to drive away from Riker's Valley, presumably never to return. The film's ending is inferior for the simple reason that it is not clear why the Mangler stops pursuing Sherry and Hunton in the first place. It chases them through a long subterranean corridor, down a spiral subterranean staircase, and into a sewer, and then there is an explosion and it retreats—for no clear narrative reason. It just stops, and the audience is left to wonder why. It may be a failure of the special effects, or a narrative lapse, but the ending of *The Mangler* simply fails to track.

The other primary difference between short story and film is that Stephen King can get away with, in printed form, describing horrid things that are simply disgusting on film. In the short story, King chillingly describes how the machine eats Miss Frawley. It is frightening and disgusting, but the images of blood and death are just phantasms, pictures conjured in the mind. On film, this moment is thoroughly nauseating as mashed flesh, innards and torrents of blood are folded and sprayed everywhere. This is the same problem that plagued Tobe Hooper in *The Texas Chainsaw Massacre Part 2*. In that film, the tone was satirical, but the bloody aspects of the picture were so realistic and so carefully scrutinized that humor became impossible. You can't laugh while you're gagging. The same is true of *The Mangler*. The very idea of a possessed laundry machine is inherently ridiculous, but the Hooper who found humor in the macabre (and sometimes ridiculous) incidents of *The Texas Chain Saw Massacre* and *Poltergeist* is completely somber and straightforward here. His camera dwells on crushed human body parts for no reason other than the gross-out factor. As if that isn't bad enough, he follows up the gore with scenes of the main character Hunton regurgitating on camera. It isn't a pleasant sequence, and much of the film is like that—unpleasant and heavy.

To be fair to Hooper, one can note that *The Mangler* boasts some brilliant art direction. The look of the laundry is particularly good, like some 1940s or early '50s industrial nightmare. As the movie opens, a long pan establishes the grimy, inhuman dimension of the laundry machine with its tank-like tread, twisting gears and steaming motor. Hooper's visuals reveal with instant efficacy that this machine isn't user friendly. And neither, for that matter, is the Blue Ribbon laundry. Sweat, steam and sheets co-mingle in the misery of a great factory building reminiscent of old-fashioned sweatshops. It's weird that the costumes and cars are modern, while the laundry is a beacon from the past. Still, it's an appropriate touch: the laundry reflects the past because Gartley has artificially, or rather *supernaturally*, been elongating his life span. He's a product of the 1950s and even in the '90s that hasn't changed because he's prolonged his existence. The Mangler, like Gartley, is a giant old machine, a dinosaur of the pre-computer pre-miniaturization age. In Gartley's private office, there's even a telephone with a switchboard device, as if Ma Bell is still in business.

All these art-design touches work to the film's advantage, and Blue Ribbon laundry, where workers seem to endure 24-hour shifts, steam burns, high temperatures and headache-inducing heat, is a nightmare realm worthy of a more interesting movie.

Though it may be ill advised to search for subtext in *The Mangler*, an ambitious critic could note that the film arrives almost immediately post–NAFTA. This is a time when many Americans were afraid of losing their jobs to overseas workers or seeing their wages cut to compete with Mexicans or others in foreign lands that would work more cheaply. And, in 1992, Bill Clinton had won the presidency by remembering the mantra, "It's the economy, stupid." Both of those factors seem at play in *The Mangler*, which arrived in theaters in 1995. Throughout the picture, Gartley is pressing his workers on, grumbling about being behind, struggling to keep his cash cow (the industrial laundry) making money. He is exploiting his workers physically while at the same time taking advantage of them spiritually: he is feeding their bodies to his business not just for riches, but for eternal life. What counts is money and wealth (it's the economy, stupid), and working conditions need not be safe when there's always a new worker around to replace a "mangled" one.

This thematic strand is not nearly strong enough, however, to gloss over the failures of *The Mangler*. The film was shot in South Africa, and that may be part of the problem. Though the movie is ostensibly set in Riker's Valley, Maine, every character seems to speak in a different accent, and some of the dialogue seems just a little bit off. This doesn't feel like America, it feels like Americana as seen through the filter of a foreign film company, and it's off-putting. Also, this author would be remiss if he didn't note that the script is pretty dreadful.

Though Hooper and his co-writers have carefully utilized dialogue right out of King's novel, the main problem is in the development of the characters. Hunton and Mark are not very interesting leads, and there is no real emotional attachment forged to them. Their performances are adequate at best, and their characters bland in an almost embarrassing way. We're on the outside looking in at these heroes, rather than being on the inside with them. In *Poltergeist*, *The Funhouse*, *Salem's Lot* and *The Texas Chain Saw Massacre*, Hooper managed to — *more or less* — put us into the brains of his protagonists. We identified with the characters and their travails. The people of *The Mangler* are too cold for that identification to be engendered here, and Ted Levine, so effective as Buffalo Bill in *Silence of the Lambs*, makes for a very remote, very cold lead.

The Mangler just doesn't hold together very well, for a variety of reasons. Stephen King's story has a major flaw in it, but one can gloss over it in 20 or so pages. That flaw is, simply, that if you're afraid of a possessed laundry machine, *just don't go to the laundry*. Avoid the bloody thing! Stretched out over 90 minutes, that flaw is inescapable. Why do characters, again and again, willingly put themselves in close proximity to the flesh mangling iron press? That they do this repeatedly hinders identification with the already lackluster protagonists. They're just not very smart people.

Another question involves the sacrifices Gartley makes. If he's already sacrificed his daughter, why does he have to feed Sherry to the machine? Are there term limits on demonic sacrifices? Again, one isn't sure why this is such a good deal for Gartley, considering his physical impairments and the emotional attachments he is forced to forego for the Mangler.

The Mangler's greatest flaw, however, is that the film never develops King's idea that the machine is a personality: a vile, monstrous thing. He wrote, for instance:

I will tell you one thing, Hunton, since you seem to have taken this case to heart. If you mention it to anyone else, I'll deny I said it. But I didn't like that machine. It seemed ... almost to be mocking us. I've inspected over a dozen speed ironers in the last five years on a regular basis. Some of them are in such bad shape that I wouldn't leave a dog unleashed around them — the state law is lamentably lax. But they were only machines for all that. But this one ... it's a spook. I don't know why, but it is [1].

This and other passages reveal that the Mangler is conscious, aware of the harm it is doing. Yet in the film it comes across as little more than a tool that Gartley uses to keep his high life. By adding Gartley to the story as the primary villain, Hooper and his co-writers have done their title character, the Mangler, a grave injustice. Its villainy has been made secondary to Gartley's. It is no longer a hungry maw wantonly pulling people inside its jaws, just because it can. Instead, it is a leashed dog at the service of a bad man who throws it scraps. This is a structural flaw that results, again, from the casting of Englund. A significant part had to be made for an icon of his stature and so the original story was twisted to accommodate his presence. This is especially silly because Englund could easily have portrayed Hunton or Mark, both protagonists, without altering the fundamental nature of Stephen King's villain. Still, on film, the two-faced villainy of Gartley and the Mangler does evoke earlier Hooper films.

The Mangler was a bomb, the film that finally killed the Stephen King film adaptations. It played in over a thousand theaters, but grossed less than a million dollars. It is also Tobe Hooper's last theatrical release as of this writing (*Crocodile* was a direct-to-video effort). It failed for many reasons, but basically it had a hopeless draw. Who wants to go to the theater just to see people get ripped apart in industrial machinery? There's nothing romantic or engaging about that premise and even worse, the "villain," unlike a great white shark, an unstoppable serial killer or even a crocodile, is stationary, so the characters have to repeatedly go to it and consciously land themselves in danger. That's just too much for even the least discriminating horror fan to bear. *The Mangler* is a failed project, and if anything, it mangled Tobe Hooper's film career and the future aspirations of directors looking to adapt King's literary works.

For students of Hooper looking for consistency in his filmed work, *The Mangler* is of moderate interest. It represents Hooper's fourth teaming with Englund, his second adaptation of a Stephen King tale, and his second rumination on animism (the first being the 1990 TV movie *I'm Dangerous Tonight*). Like many of Hooper's films, *The Mangler* features a world underneath the regular world—here the Satanic-sponsored Blue Ribbon Laundry in Riker's Valley—and exhibits his fascination with the era of his youth, the 1950s. Robert Englund and the Mangler form another duo of evil, one human and powerful (like *Salem's Lot*'s Barlow), the other hideous, feral and hungry. But there's a lack of consistency in quality. *The Mangler*, like *Night Terrors* and *Spontaneous Combustion*, has little in common with the satirical *Poltergeist, Invaders from Mars, Chainsaw 2*, the reflexive *The Funhouse*, or the intense *Texas Chain Saw Massacre*.

11. *Crocodile* (2000)

Critical Reception

"*Crocodile* brackets schlock in quote marks with a loud, Troma-like self-consciousness. Since Hooper helped popularize the teens-in-jeopardy approach, he figures he's allowed to push it far past silliness now.... Young lovers fuss while their friends become bait. Inbred rubes mumble through black teeth. A white poodle proves remarkably crocodile resistant."
—Jerry Bokamper, *Dallas Morning News*: "Giant Reptile chews the scenery and much more in Crocodile," December 25, 2000.

"*Crocodile* is a throwback to monster films of the anything-goes-gore of the 1970s, with the requisite humor and over-the-top acting ... a fang-toothed hoot ... and those who remember director Tobe Hooper ... know what he can do when he is focused on mayhem."
—Dan Bennett, *Video Store*: "Crocodile," November 26, 2000.

"Everywhere *Lake Placid* failed, this film managed to succeed ... a well-crafted and thrilling little film."
—Ted Geoghegan, *The Diabolical Domain*: "Crocodile," 2000. (www.diabolical-domain.com).

"Hooper takes a limited budget, an inexperienced cast and a wild idea and binds them together as a fun and exciting film."
—Fusion 3600, *DVDauthority*.com: "Crocodile," 2000. (www.dvdauthority.com).

"Adolescents of both sexes, as depicted here, are a loud, obnoxious, unethical lot, and deserve whatever they get. I was always rooting for the crocodile ... the second half of the film has a few good thrills and amusing ideas."
—Roy Frumkes, *Films in Review*: DVD Review—"Crocodile," 2000. (www.filmsinreview.com).

"*Crocodile* is a thoroughly routine, predictable and anachronistic low-budget shocker, devoid of genuine suspense and impaired by laughably cheap, unconvincing special effects.... Hooper doesn't seem to take the film seriously, and you should urge potential renters ... to approach it with a similar mindset."
—Ed Hulse, *Video Business*, November 20, 2000, page 19.

"Pretty much all of Hooper's early films showed what great promise the director had.... Somewhere along the way.... Hooper decided that he would make standard direct-to-video horror fare nowhere near as worthy as his early films.... Hooper sets up his camera with all the thrill and excitement of a history teacher trying to explain Manifest Destiny."
—Brian Matherly, *Jackson Film Journal*: "Crocodile," (*www.jaxfilmjournal.com*).

"Hooper is retreading some territory that he covered in *Eaten Alive*, a superior croc-related movie that served as his follow-up to *Texas*. While that movie had great atmosphere, this film looks like a TV movie."
—www.*esplatter*.com "Crocodile," 2000. (www.esplatter.com).

Cast and Crew

CAST: Mark McLouchlin (Brady Turner); Caitlin Martin (Claire); Chris Solari (Duncan McKay); Doug Reiser (Kit); Julie Mintz (Annabella); Sommer Knight (Sunny); Rhett Jordan (Foster); Greg Wayne (Hubs); Harrison Young (Sheriff Bowman); T. Evans (Shurkin); R. Vern Crofoot (Harvey); Larry Udy (Arnold); Adam Redmon (Lester); Kip Adotta (Stanley the Fisherman); Crystal Atkins (Blond Bikini Girl); Mark Watters (Helicopter Pilot); Miles (Princess).

CREW: Nu Image Presents a De Martini/Davidson Production of a Tobe Hooper film. *Casting:* Cathy Henderson Martin, Dori Zuckerman, Rebecca Quiroz. *Princess Trained by:* Steven Ritt. *Production Designer:* W. Brooke Wheeler. *Special Effects:* Robert Kurtzman, Gregory Nicotero, Howard Berger. *Music:* Serge Colbert. *Edited by:* Alan Jakubowicz. *Director of Photography:* Eliot Rockett. *Associate Producer:* Lee Lazarow, R. Vern Crofoot. *Co-Executive Producer:* Eddy Chamichian. *Executive Producer:* Avi Lerner, Danny Limbert, Trevor Short. *Story:* Boaz Davidson. *Screenplay:* Michael D. Weiss, Adam Gierasch, Jace Anderson. *Produced by:* Boaz Davidson, Frank DeMartini, Danny Lerner. *Directed by:* Tobe Hooper. *Stunts:* Tamilynn Lane, Carin Berger, Maximillian D. Day. *Unit Production Manager:* Dwayne L. Shattuck. *First Assistant Director:* Thomas McAuley Burke. *Second Assistant Directors:* Kevin Anthony, Maximillian M. Day. *Visual Effects Producer:* Teresa Rowlee. *Assistant to Tobe Hooper:* George Higginson. *Art Director:* John Marshall, David Leiceister. *Storyboard Artist:* Jonathan B. Woods. *Set Decorator:* Mae Brunken. *Houseboat Design by:* Peter Kanter. *Property Master:* Lee Lazarow. *Special Effects Coordinator:* George Phillips. *Pyrotechnican:* Rick Hill. *Key Make-up:* Philip Rico. *Key-Hair:* Sergio Lopenz. *Location Manager:* T.J. Greidanus. *Costume Designer:* Carin Berger. *Wardrobe Supervisor:* Karen Baker. Alligator appearance courtesy of Brockett's Film Fauna. *Alligator Wrangler:* Jim Brockett. *Animal Trainer:* Dennis R. Crisco. *Second Unit Director:* Sam Firstenberry. *Second Unit Director of Photography:* Eduardo Flores. *Visual Effects Supervisor:* Karin O'Neill. *Special Visual Effects Created by:* Flat Earth Products, Inc. *M.P.A.A Rating:* NA. *Running Time:* 94 minutes.

Synopsis

A group of college friends, including the straight-arrow Brady and his wise-cracking buddy Duncan, go on vacation at Lake Sobek for Spring Break. Also along for the ride is Sunny, a trashy girl whom Brady slept with once. Her presence is a special problem because Brady's longtime girlfriend, Claire, is also vacationing with the group and is unaware of Brady's infidelity. Claire also strongly dislikes Duncan, because she blames him for the fact that Brady was thrown out of school for cheating. Other co-ed vacationers on this trip to Sobek include Hubs, the responsible Kit, and Annabella, who dotes on her dog, Princess. Together, this group purchases some beer at a local grocery store and runs afoul of the stern local sheriff, Bowman. After he warns them to mind their manners on the weekend, they head out onto the lake in a houseboat.

Close by the young vacationers, two local yokels discover a nest of crocodile eggs. Plastered, they play with the oversized eggs and proceed to destroy a bunch of them. In response, a giant crocodile emerges from Lake Sobek and devours them. Then, the crocodile pushes their car under water, covering its murderous tracks.

The next morning, the college kids frolic in the lake and happen upon the remains of the crocodile nest. They mess with the eggs too, especially the disrespectful Duncan. Hubs steals an egg and hides it in Claire's bag, thinking that his tomfoolery will make for a great practical joke. Around a campfire that night, the teens get really wasted, and a drunk Sunny reveals to Claire that she slept with Brady. An angry Claire storms off to the boat, leaving Brady to ponder his infidelity. While the teens sleep off their hangovers, Hubs remains on land in a catatonic stupor. He awakens in the wee hours of the night, untethers the houseboat, and is promptly devoured by the mammoth crocodile. Aboard the houseboat, the other teens sleep, unaware that their vessel is drifting aimlessly on the lake and that one of their number is dead.

The hung-over teens awaken the next morning to discover that Kit's houseboat has run aground on a mucky shore. They are unable to free the vehicle, and Kit worries. Not far from their perch, Sheriff Bowman investigates the disappearance of the local yokels, flying to and fro around Lake Sobek by helicopter. He finds the splintered pier where the crocodile crunched Hubs and the boat's tether, and then the destroyed remains of the crocodile nest. Disturbed, he pays a visit to a nearby alligator farm, afraid that one of the barracked beasties has broken loose. The strange old proprietor of the farm, a coot named Shurkin, warns that a giant crocodile called "the Flat Dog" is roaming the lake. The Flat Dog is famous in these parts and rumored to be mightily pissed off. The croc killed Shurkin's "grandpappy" and so Shurkin swears to help Bowman stop it before it can kill again. He is unaware that his dimwitted assistant has been covertly feeding the crocodile and plotting to kill him. The plan goes badly wrong, however, when the dimwit is himself devoured by the roaming crocodile.

Back at the houseboat, Kit is having precious little luck getting the vessel back on the lake. Brady attempts to reconcile with Claire, but she will have none of it. Sensing an opportunity, Sunny attempts to seduce Brady. While they frolic in the water, the crocodile attacks and chases them back to the houseboat. The oversized lizard demolishes the boat and devours one of the teenagers. The survivors flee for land, unaware that Claire's bag still contains the object of the crocodile's quest: the egg. As night falls, the crocodile attacks the teenagers in the woods, and Sunny loses her way. After she is eaten by the crocodile, the survivors (Kit, Annabella, Brady, Claire, Duncan and the poodle, Princess) find shelter in an out-of-the-way convenience store. They hide there for a time, call the police, and try to arm themselves. Brady finds a shotgun and Duncan's weapon of choice is a chain saw. While Annabella sits in the bathroom crying, the crocodile breaks into the lavatory and gobbles her up. Terrified, Kit runs for a parked pick-up truck outside, but the crocodile inadvertently starts a fire, and the truck and the gas station beyond explode. Duncan is wounded by the croc, leaving Brady and Claire (with Princess in tow) to drag him about in a wheelbarrow. The surviving teens make for the shore and are rescued by Sheriff Bowman and Shurkin the next morning. Not surprisingly, the crocodile attacks again, eating Shurkin and swallowing the sheriff whole.

Desperate, Duncan, Claire and Brady make it back to shore. They discover the egg in Claire's backpack and decide to use it as bait. Angry, they fight the persistent croc. During the dangerous final battle, Princess comes to the rescue, distracting the beast when Brady is vulnerable. Duncan attempts to blind the crocodile, but it swallows him whole. Luckily, Duncan is carrying a spray bottle of bug repellant with him, which the monster finds indigestible. The crocodile regurgitates Duncan, and Claire holds it off with the egg. The egg starts to hatch and a little crocodile emerges. The Flat Dog takes the baby carefully in its mouth and departs the scene happily, leaving a relieved Brady, Claire, Duncan and Princess to renew their friendship.

Commentary

The low-budget, direct-to-video feature *Crocodile* is an unassuming little horror picture that reveals a Tobe Hooper tanned, rested and ready for action. This grade-B variation of *Anaconda* (1997) boasts a ludicrous screenplay, characters as thin as cardboard and some effective, but cheap computer generated special effects. The most important thing about *Crocodile* is that it moves, and moves well. It has the pace and thrusting inevitability of *The Texas Chain Saw Massacre*, in particular. A re-energized Hooper has apparently thrown caution and restraint to the wind to direct this gonzo "when animals attack stupid teenagers" movie. The result is a fun if trifling picture peppered liberally with in-jokes and references to Hooper's film career, as well as startling jolts that keep the audience tuned in. *Crocodile* is in no way a genre landmark (like *The Texas Chain Saw Massacre*), an underrated cult classic (like *Lifeforce*), blockbuster material (like *Poltergeist*), or dead-on satire (like the *Texas Chainsaw Massacre Part 2*). Instead, it is precisely what *Spontaneous Combustion* failed at being: a good "B" horror movie. And, say what you will about *Crocodile*, it's a hell of a lot better than the other "giant crocodile on the loose" movie of the same year, the more expensive *Lake Placid* (2000).

Crocodile is a movie directed by a man who understands and loves every cliché in the horror genre, has exploited many of them himself, and is willing to mock every one of them for fun. Take for instance the film's little dog, Princess. These days, horror films have no compunction about killing dogs. Michael Myers killed a neighborhood canine in *Halloween* and minions of Papa Jupe offed one of the Carter pups in *The Hills Have Eyes*. But once upon a time, the idea of killing a pet was a real taboo and the film that changed that fact forever was Tobe Hooper's own *Eaten Alive*. In that gruesome 1976 feature, poor little Snoopy came to an unhappy end at the Starlight Hotel when Judd's (Neville Brand's) mad crocodile snarfed the little pooch right up.

Made some two dozen years later, *Crocodile* might have been subtitled *Snoopy's Revenge* because it offers the long-awaited Tobe Hooper rematch between a cute canine (this time named Princess) and a hungry crocodile. In the film's best running gag, Hooper continually puts the tiny dog in extreme danger, within feet of the rampaging crocodile, but always, at the last minute, Princess escapes the jaws of death. In fact, she lasts longer than her human owner, and all but three of the stupid teenagers! Of course, the joke is that Hooper fans remember *Eaten Alive* and keep expecting the dog to buy the farm, especially when the little dog flees the houseboat for the lake or dines on shattered croc eggs. But Hooper, champion of the surreal and the subversive, keeps the joke building to insane proportions. The punch line arrives in one of the wackiest, most ridiculous moments in recent horror film history. The dog leaps through the croc's open maw ... and survives. The jaws clamp down an instant too late, and Princess scampers off safely into the woods. This bizarre, hysterically funny moment occurs right in the middle of what one would assume is a serious climax. But Hooper students know not to assume anything with this guy. Instead of giving the audiences a gruesome scare (and the death that *Eaten Alive* fans expect), Hooper provides them with a joke instead.

This film is also rather funny because it plays as a ludicrous semi-remake of *The Texas Chain Saw Massacre*. It has the same sense of manic energy and the only real substantive difference is that the villain is a crocodile instead of a mad butcher. For instance, *Chain Saw* is rather notorious for setting off the "dead teenager" trend in horror film history. Furthermore, that film depicts several teens that are only barely likable. Sally bickered with her brother, Franklin. Kirk, Sally, Pam and Jerry all gleefully abandoned the crippled Franklin at their first convenience, and Franklin himself was a whining, annoying guy. Hooper takes this idea of vapid, self-involved teenagers to its ultimate evolution. His teenagers in *Crocodile* aren't just dumb and mean, they're the dumbest and meanest teenagers in horror film history. They drink enormous quantities of alcohol, smoke pot, and even steal each other's boyfriends. They piss in beer bottles, vomit in each other's hats and apparently live to party non-stop. They don't even make the grade as two-dimensional characters, and one senses that Hooper despises each and every one of them. These WB wannabes, instead of being depicted in fairly "honorable" terms as they might be in a *Scream* (1996), *I Know What You Did Last Summer* (1997), *Urban Legends* (1997) or *Valentine* (2000), are completely shallow and hateful creatures (except, perhaps, Claire). To the crocodile (as to the audience; as to Hooper) the teen characters serve primarily as lunch meat. They don't engender sympathy, and instead provoke only laughs. It's almost as if Hooper has sensed the horror fan's ennui with Katie Holmes, Jennifer Love Hewitt and their seemingly infinite clones. They should all be eaten by crocodiles, and since Hooper brought the "teenagers in jeopardy" trend into cinema a quarter century ago, then he should be the one who kills it too, and that's what he does here, at least metaphorically.

With *Crocodile*, Hooper seems to be declaring something else too. Obviously, he is no longer receiving "A" level scripts for big studios. Hollywood, cold to him since the triple failure of his Cannon features in the 1980s and the *Poltergeist* controversy before that, is never going to accept him or give him another A level budget to rehabilitate his career. Instead, Hooper seems content here to return to his roots, to direct a low-budget B movie that will never be taken seriously. Yet here, one senses too, he is *free*. He clearly makes no promises about how he'll choose to direct such material, and with *Crocodile* he loyally adheres to his own subversive storytelling style and approach to the material. This means that teens are not kings and queens to be adored and idolized and they're not walking, talking fashion statements either, but vomiting, pissing, cussing, drinking, whoring fodder for a rampaging monster. Maybe some people can't see it underneath *Crocodile's* silly surface, but in today's youth-centric film market, this anti-teen approach to a horror film is nearly as revolutionary as *Chain Saw's* blunt violence was in 1973.

Crocodile mirrors *The Texas Chain Saw Massacre* in ways that stretch far beyond Hooper's interesting approach to his less-than-heroic protagonists. The idea of a road trip/vacation gone bad (a factor in *Night of the Living Dead* and the excellent *Jeepers Creepers* [2001]) is resurrected from the van trip to the old Franklin place in *Chain Saw*, and serves as the opening gambit of *Crocodile*. Also repeating from the Leatherface saga is the notion of a false sanctuary. In *The Texas Chain Saw Massacre*, Sally ran to the roadside barbecue stand expecting to find help, but instead she was nabbed by Cook. In *Crocodile*, a group of teens find shelter in another roadside convenience store only to have their powerful nemesis crash through the walls and shatter their safety. And, though Leatherface and his clan were crazier, *Crocodile* also offers another Tobe Hooper brand of unhinged "local yokel," alligator farm owner Shurkin and his whacked redneck assistant.

From the point that their houseboat (another false sanctuary) is destroyed, *Crocodile* unabashedly becomes another *Chain Saw* clone (and there have been so many over the years, including the 1979 feature *Tourist Trap*). Just as Leatherface pursued Sally Hardesty through a wooded glade by glow of moonlight, so does the crocodile chase the teens through similarly thicketed terrain by nightfall. A trademark Hooper shot is even invoked here: the desperate runner approaching camera in foreground;

pursuer obscenely and dangerously close to prey in background. Of course, the crocodile body-doubles ably for Leatherface, always perpetually a beat behind the protagonists. And just as Franklin detected a noise and shone his flashlight on it only to see Leatherface, so do the teens in *Crocodile* spotlight the hiding crocodile with their flashlights and begin another seemingly endless chase.

Finally, a scene near the climax depicts an exhausted Claire and Brady pushing a crippled Duncan along the landscape in a wheelbarrow. As they bicker and irritate one another, the Sally/Franklin dynamic of *Chain Saw* is evoked too, right down to the fact that one character is disabled and therefore dependent (and a burden) on another. Inevitably, one of *Crocodile*'s teens, Duncan, even gets his hands on a chain saw before the film is through.

These ridiculous and self-referential touches result in a true Hooper film through and through. It confounds audiences at all turns and thus leaves them feeling unsettled, unsure whether to smile or cower. Viewers expect the dog to be gobbled up, but it survives. Viewers expect the creepy old hotel on the horizon, the one that figures so prominently in the story of the crocodile's origin, to feature strongly in the conclusion, but it doesn't. It is never visited at all. One expects the crocodile to be just a large cunning animal, but it displays human intelligence when it hides evidence of its rampage by pushing a car underwater (a very funny moment). At the same time, Hooper delivers several jump-out-of-your-seat jolts (particularly in the nighttime death of Hubs on the pier) while simultaneously paying homage to all the dopey conventions of the genre (the dumb-ass kids who do dumb-ass things, useless cops, psychotic country locals, and even monsters with maternal instincts). The result is a droll roller coaster ride that unpretentious horror film fans will welcome with open arms. Sure it isn't A material. Sure, it's low budget. Sure it's packed wall to wall with stupid, beautiful teens, but Hooper relishes every last absurdity on display. The lethargic, ponderous approach he brought to *Night Terrors* and even *The Mangler* is gone and even with this weak cardboard story one can feel the glee seeping right off the screen. *Crocodile* is no classic, but it is damn entertaining: funny and silly to the max, gory and in glorious bad taste. Welcome back, Tobe Hooper.

Part III
Television Movies and Miniseries

Surprising as it may sound, the production that truly resulted in Tobe Hooper's ascent to the Hollywood mainstream was not *The Texas Chain Saw Massacre*. As amazing as that horror feature was, it was simply too rough to be welcomed by the entertainment industry, and many producers and studios were unsure how its director could fit into their homogenized, sanitized world. The answer came in 1979 when Hooper answered the call to direct a miniseries for producer Richard Kobritz, *Salem's Lot*.

That four-hour "movie" successfully established that Hooper could work successfully inside the mainstream, still creating horror, but making it palatable while still delivering the expected "scares." From there, Hooper's career skyrocketed with one feature film directing assignment after the other, including *The Funhouse, Poltergeist, Lifeforce* and *Invaders from Mars*, all projects considered "A" material in terms of budget, distribution and expectations.

Hooper was not the first horror director to understand the significance and power of "event" television. John Carpenter had met with success with *Someone's Watching Me* (also produced by Kobritz) and Wes Craven had given the format a run with *A Stranger in Our House* (1978), starring Linda Blair, but it was Hooper who benefited most from his shift of medium. That might be the reason why he has been willing to return to television for TV movies and TV series work: he understands how it can help solidify or make a reputation.

In addition to *Salem's Lot*, Hooper directed the cable TV movie *I'm Dangerous Tonight* (1990), a World Premiere Presentation for the USA Network, and two back-door pilots for Showtime: *John Carpenter's Body Bags* (1993) and *The Apartment Complex* (1999). These projects met with little success, but *Salem's Lot* remains a jewel in the Hooper crown. It is played on TV regularly (the last airing as of this writing was on Lifetime on October 30, 2001), and has been a box office hit theatrically in Europe and in the secondary markets of VHS and DVD. In recent years, a remake has even been discussed.

1. *Salem's Lot* (1979)

Critical Reception

"A surprisingly graphic mini-series.... Stand-out fright sequences include a living dead girl branded with a wooden crucifix, and the dreadful red-eyed vampire boy floating at his friend's bedroom window, scratching the glass."
—David Bailey and David Miller, *Cult Times* Number 13: "Scariest Cult TV Ever—The Top 20 Frightening Moments in Telefantasy," October 1996, page 53.

"*Salem's Lot* unfolds with a delightfully shivery atmosphere (credit Mason as well as director Tobe Hooper) and a few well-timed shocks. The first appearance of Barlow ... recalls *The Exorcist* in its cruel impact."
—Andy Wickstrom, *Video Magazine*, July 1993, page 78.

"A surprisingly successful small screen adaptation of Stephen King's vampire novel.... Paring away the excessive plot expositions ... it places the emphasis on Hooper's fluid camerawork, creepy atmospherics, and skillful handling of the gripping climax."
—Nigel Floyd, *Time Out Film Guide*, page 784.

"In by far the best ever adaptation of a Stephen King novel, director Tobe Hooper creates a complex web of sub-plots and parallel stories as Smalltown USA is infested by vampires. Remarkably horrific...."
—*Shivers Horror Awards*: Television Top 25, Issue Number 34, October 1996, page 9,

"Generally conventional vampire movie. The mist-and-bobbing-and-clawing-kid-at-the-window effect is very deceptive—it seems evocative of so much more (both psychologically and supernaturally) than the story goes on to deliver ... most of the sequences take forever 'building tension.'"
—Gordon Willis, *Horror and Science Fiction Films II*, Scarecrow Press, 1982, page 334.

"Alas, the deadening propriety of television took its toll, and there is not much disturbing, though one or two television taboos are contravened ... in an entirely non-fantastic scene a cuckolded man takes humiliating revenge on his wife's lover. This is the most typically Hooper sequence. It has all the sordid sweatiness of real human fear, and it makes the vampire sequences look a bit hollow."
—Peter Nicholls, *The World of Fantastic Films*, Dodd, Mead and Co., 1984, page 145.

Cast and Credits

CAST: David Soul (Ben Mears); James Mason (Richard K. Straker); Lance Kerwin (Mark Petrie); Bonnie Bedelia (Susan Norton); Lew Ayres (Jason Burke); Julie Cobb ("Boom Boom" Bonnie); Elisha Cook (Weasel); Ed Flanders (Dr. Norton); Geoffrey Lewis (Mike Ryerson); Barney McFadden (Tebbets); Fred Willard (Larry Crockett); Kenneth McMillan (Sheriff); Barbara Babcock (June Petrie); Bonnie Bartlett (Ann Norton); Joshua Bryant (Ted Petrie); James Gallery (Father Callahan); Robert Lussier (Holly Gardner); Brad Savage (Danny Glick); Ronnie Scribner (Ralphie Glick); Ned Wilson (Henry Glick); Reggie Nalder (Mr. Barlow); WITH: George Dzundza, Clarissa Kaye, Marie Windsor.

CREW: *Director of Photography:* Jules Brenner. *Executive Producer:* Stirling Silliphant. *Based on the novel by:* Stephen King. *Teleplay:* Paul Monash. *Directed by:* Tobe Hooper. *Produced by:* Richard Kobritz. *Associate Producer:* Anna Cottle. *Music Composed and Conducted by:* Harry Sukman. *Production Designer:* Mort Rabinowitz. *Film Editor:* Carroll Sax. *Unit Production Manager:* Norman Cook. *First Assistant Director:* Lloyd Allen. *Second Assistant Director:* John Whittle. *Set Decorator:* Jerry Adams. *Property Master:* Mike Miner. *Special Effects:* Frank Torro. *Wardrobe:* Phyllis Garr, Barry Kellogg. *Special Make-up:* Jack Young. *Special Lenses:* Morton K. Greenspoon. *Hair:* Bette Iverson. *Title Design:* Gene Kraft. *Production Sound:* Richard Raguse. *Music Editor:* Jay Smith. *Sound Edit:* Sound FX, Inc., Ron Clark. *Casting:* Vivian McRae. *Running time:* 183 minutes.

Synopsis

In Ximico, Guatemala, two fugitives, Ben Mears and Mark Petrie, take refuge in a Catholic mission, only to discover that their enemies have found them again...

Two years earlier, author Ben Mears returns to his hometown of Salem's Lot in Maine. He hopes to write a book about a local haunted house, the Marsten House, only to discover that it has been purchased by a mysterious European antique dealer, Mr. Straker, and his unseen "partner," Mr. Barlow. After visiting the house, Mears goes to town and rents a room at a local boarding house. While Mears reacquaints himself with the small town of his youth, he courts Susan Norton, a local school teacher. He meets her parents, Dr. and Mrs. Norton, and learns that Susan has been seeing a local, Ned Tebbets. Nevertheless, Mears and Norton then share a romantic night at a lake. Later, Mears befriends his old English teacher, Mr. Burke, and continues writing his book while Burke directs a school pageant starring student Mark Petrie, an aficionado of magic, monsters and the occult.

Meanwhile, real estate agent Larry Crockett, who is having an affair with his secretary, "Boom Boom," assists Mr. Straker with a very important delivery. Straker asks Crockett to send a truck to a nearby dock with two drivers. He claims to have a sideboard to be delivered to the Marsten house. In fact, the men (Tebbets and Ryerson) are bringing into the United States the coffin of Straker's master, the vampire Mr. Barlow. Tebbets and Ryerson feel terrified of the Marsten House and their unusual delivery, and leave the crate unlocked in the Marsten cellar, against the wishes of Straker. Later that night, two of Mark's friends, the Glick brothers, are attacked by something horrible in the woods. Danny Glick staggers home, disoriented, but his brother Ralphie is found dead. The same bloody night, Larry Crockett is attacked by Mr. Barlow after being caught by Boom Boom's husband. Mears and Susan unexpectedly discover his corpse.

Vampires begin to pop up all over Salem's Lot. Danny Glick is visited in the thick of night by his undead brother, who scratches plaintively at his bedroom window. When invited in, Ralphie hungrily drinks the blood of his sibling. Danny is rushed to the hospital, suffering from "pernicious anemia." At the same time, a search of the woods in Salem's Lot uncovers a piece of black fabric that could have come from one of Mr. Straker's black suits. The sheriff questions Straker about Ralphie Glick, but Straker plays it cool, refusing to acknowledge any connection between himself and the missing child. At the hospital, Ralphie continues to feed on his brother and Danny begins to feed on Mike Ryerson. Later, Ryerson collapses at a diner and Ben and Burke endeavor to take care of him.

The undead Danny Glick visits Mark's window by night, but Petrie wards him off with a crucifix. While Petrie fends off the vampire, Burke and Mears examine Mike Ryerson, who is found dead, another victim of "pernicious anemia." The next night, Ryerson returns to Burke's house as a vampire, but Burke holds him back and suffers a heart attack in the process. When Ned Tebbets and Mrs. Glick also die of pernicious anemia, Ben Mears joins forces with Dr. Norton to learn the truth of the situation. They visit the town priest, but he claims that the church no longer believes in the kind of evil embodied by vampires. The priest then visits Mark Petrie, whose parents are concerned about the boy's obsession with monsters. Barlow attacks the family and kills Mark's parents. The priest gives up his life so that Mark can escape, and faces down Barlow, faith for faith. The priest loses and meets a grim fate.

At the hospital, Dr. Norton and Ben examine Mrs. Glick's corpse. She awakens suddenly as a vampire on the autopsy table, and Mears brands her with a crucifix, destroying the ghoul. Norton and Ben now realize they must kill Barlow by driving a stake through his heart. Unfortunately, it is too late for Salem's Lot. Sheriff Harkins has abandoned the town and residents are fleeing the hamlet *en masse*. Mears attempts to enlist Harkins, but the scared law enforcement official refuses to stay. While Mears and Norton plan their attack against Barlow, Susan catches sight of Mark Petrie breaking into the Marsten House and follows him inside. There, they are apprehended by Straker and prepared to meet with the master, Mr. Barlow.

Dr. Norton and Ben Mears enter the Marsten House sometime later and save Mark, but are unable to find Susan. They run afoul of Straker, who kills Norton. Mears shoots Straker dead and heads down to the basement to finish off Barlow. Mears and Petrie spike the master and set fire to the vampire crypt, burning the Marsten House down to the ground. They flee Salem's Lot, sad that they were unable to rescue Susan.

Two years later, Susan—*now a vampire*—finds Mark and Ben in Gautemala, and the refugees realize it is time to move on again...

Commentary

Though novelist Stephen King and producer Richard Kobritz were two important influences on the formation of the *Salem's Lot* miniseries of 1979 vintage, the piece seems tailor-made for director Tobe Hooper. Like *The Texas Chain Saw Massacre, The Funhouse, Chainsaw 2,* and even *The Mangler*, this genre material is structured to feature one of the director's favorite "recurring" characters: the partners in evil, one human (Straker), one monstrous (Barlow). Perhaps more to the point, the miniseries offers Hooper the opportunity to produce another tale of regional horror, eschewing backwater Texas and other southern locations for the "in-bred" and "full-blooded" territory of New England.

Most of all, however, *Salem's Lot* is Hooper's first real calling card to Hollywood, the movie that allowed him to escape his "mansonite" reputation (borne from the ferocity of *Chain Saw*). Produced for TV (a stumbling block for any horror production), featuring multiple characters and based on literate, best-seller material, *Salem's Lot* allows Hooper to demonstrate that he can give horror the mainstream polish viewers seek of such mass entertainment. Accordingly, *Salem's Lot* is filled with inventive, even terrifying set pieces and has more jolts per square inch than one might expect of a drama designed for the cathode-ray tube. Hooper controls his natural inclination towards escalating insanity and intensity here, opting instead to recall Val Lewton's law of horror: what the audience doesn't see, or what it barely glimpses, is often more powerful than the things it does see. Accordingly, *Salem's Lot* is in many ways Hooper's most crowd-pleasing, traditional and formalistic effort.

The villains of Tobe Hooper films seem to fall into two categories. There's the human baddie like *Chain Saw's* Cook, *The Funhouse's* Barker, and *Invaders from Mars'* Ms. McKellch. These are the "respectable" ones who can interact with normal society and pave the way for the monstrous evil to flourish. Then, of course, there's the more physically hideous, monstrous evil, the beast protected and nurtured by these strange human "beards." The deformed mutant of *The Funhouse*, the psychotic Leatherface of *Chain Saw* and *Invaders'* inhuman Martians all land in this second category.

Salem's Lot's nefarious duo, Straker and Barlow, similarly fit the Hooper mold. Straker (James Mason) is an urbane, clever, well-dressed "representative" of evil who literally sets up shop in town to prepare for the arrival of Barlow, a green-skinned, long-fanged, barely human, feral vampire. Though it was Kobritz's notion to alter the character of Barlow from the one presented in the King book, that of a traditional, handsome, alluring screen vampire, it was nonetheless a choice that played to Hooper's strengths as a director. He seems to function best when there is a human relationship to be mined over multiple individuals rather than a singular "ghoul." He likes to contrast and shade the levels of his on-screen evil and Barlow's animalistic nature (reminiscent of Count Orlock in Murnau's 1920s *Nosferatu*) makes him a villain in the tradition of Leatherface or *The Funhouse* monster: all instinct, hunger and appetite. Yet James Mason's Straker is the more powerful villain from a psychological standpoint, an icy man who has "accepted" that humans must die so his master may be served. By contrast,

Barlow only does what a vampire does best (evil is his nature) as Leatherface and *The Funhouse* monster only do what they must do to survive (saddled by psychosis, mental retardation, deformity, and other deficits). Barlow is scary in appearance (and Hooper mines much terror from the vampire's sudden appearances in the town jail and the Petrie home), but Straker is the more memorable villain. He's like a calculating spider, drawing unsuspecting victims into his web. And he is invisible to society, nothing but a small-business owner (shades of Cook in *Texas Chainsaw 2*!).

With his two very different villains, Hooper is allowed to play the two oldest Hollywood horrors against one another: suspense and surprise. The Mason/Straker scenes are cleverly constructed dances of suspense, causing audiences to wonder who (and what!) he is. The Barlow scenes are contrarily structured as "jolting" surprises. As the film opens, Straker moves in and children start to disappear. He could very well be a child molester, a child murderer or some other "natural" monster. Indeed, the early portions of *Salem's Lot* reinforce this notion by focusing almost exclusively on the foibles of the townspeople and visitor Ben Mears (Soul). There is a lengthy (and suspenseful) sequence in which one character (Dzundza) finds out his wife, "Boom Boom," is cheating on him and forces the cuckolder, real estate man Crockett, to jam the business-end of a shotgun in his mouth. This is the *Peyton's Place* "soap opera" aspect of the material. Though Barlow is referred to and there is an overall atmosphere of terror (particularly surrounding the Marsten House) nothing supernatural or out of the norm is seen. Instead, it is human behavior that causes bad things to happen and Hooper seems quite at home with the David Lynchian idea of perversion in small-town America.

Then, once Barlow arrives in the United States, Hooper shifts his *modus operandi*, descending full-blown into supernatural horror. As if understanding that vampires are harder to "believe in" during the "realism" obsessed '70s (which brought reality-base horror films such as *Straw Dogs* [1971], *Deliverance* [1972], *Last House on the Left* [1972] and Hooper's own *The Texas Chain Saw Massacre*), Hooper modifies his technique, relying now on shock and surprise rather than suspense. Mr. Barlow first appears in the film, in all his vampiric glory, in jolting bits and pieces. A clawed hand juts into the foreground, terrorizing the already terrorized Fred Willard. In an intense close-up, Barlow's face pops into the frame at the town jail. Later, a lengthy dialogue scene in the Petrie house is interrupted by an unexpected "poltergeist"-like intrusion and then a window smashes and a black ball of *something* arrives in the kitchen. This shroud of death begins to unfurl and, shockingly, is revealed to be the massive, inhuman giant, Barlow. In each one of these

He's got a cross to bear... Horror fan Mark Petrie (Lance Kerwin) cowers before a vampire in *Salem's Lot* (1979). Note the Frankenstein memorabilia in the background of his bedroom.

sequences, Hooper gives the horror audience that ultimate and most desirable moment: *the bump*, the jolt that lifts viewers out of their chairs and sends the adrenaline racing. Other than *Halloween*, there have been precious few films in history to so adeptly highlight these jolt moments in such quantity, and there has never been a TV movie to accomplish this. Perhaps the best argument that *Poltergeist* is a Hooper vehicle, not a Spielberg one, is that it too highlights a delicate, precarious mix: alternating suspense and shock, suspense and shock, until the audience is left witless and quivering. By contrast, Spielberg's "horror" movies don't generally mix the two approaches because he's more interested in telling a particular story (like an adventure at sea) than in genuinely scaring or disturbing people. *Jaws* is almost all shock (with sharks popping out of the water, corpses popping out of boats, swimmers being pulled into the ocean and so on) and *Duel* (1971), with its savage, unending chase, is all suspense. Hooper, the "no-deal" kid, will throw anything into the mix that he thinks will terrify his audiences (he's the consummate entertainer and loves to scare people) and *Salem's Lot* and *Poltergeist* share this parallel, two-track approach to terror.

But if *Salem's Lot* is remembered for any sequence, it is probably the chilling moments when vampire children hover at large bedroom windows and begin to scratch plaintively, demanding to be let in. Children are always effective as spooks (witness *Village of the Damned* [1960], *The Other* [1972], and *The Omen* [1976]) but it is the staging of these sequences that make them so perfectly rendered. Realizing that wires would be visible (this was before CGI artists would digitally "brush" them out) and that slow motion would destroy the flow of the scene, Hooper attached his child vampires to camera cranes, and the results are incredible to witness. Seemingly untethered by gravity, these creatures of the night bob menacingly and creepily, a testament to Hooper's inventive solution. With the "tap" and "scratch" sound on the soundtrack, the hovering, glowing-eyed monsters at the window, the perfect dim lighting inside and some mist effects to give the scene an appropriate gothic quality, these "beckoning" moments are among the most powerful and nightmarish in modern vampire cinema. Almost a decade later, another vampire film involving children, *The Lost Boys* (1987), failed to accomplish the same trick half as compellingly.

The "bobbing vampire" scenes are just one example of Tobe Hooper's mastery of composition and frame in *Salem's Lot*. Instead of his pile-up of pace, action and intensity (used to startling effect in *Chainsaw* and to a lesser degree in *Eaten Alive*), he relies in *Salem's Lot* on old fashioned, but rock-solid, film grammar. Though *Chain Saw* artfully revealed how a horror film might use realistic film techniques to generate a feeling of terror (a feat later repeated by *The Blair Witch Project* [1999]), *Salem's Lot* reveals that Hooper is a formalist with the best of them, as adept at staging meaningful shots as a De Palma, Carpenter or Romero. In addition to a foreground "jolt" heralding Mears' introduction to Straker, Hooper's camera is good at catching details (like the Bates Motel-inspired wall of mounted animals in the Marsten house, or the movie-oriented details of Petrie's bedroom), and indicating horror.

At the cemetery, a normal day turns to horror in an instant for groundskeeper Mike Ryerson when he hears the call of the vampire, the Glick boy, in a coffin down in an open grave. Here Hooper's crane goes up and up, assuming the traditional "high angle" of horror but the motion's speed is what remains memorable. An evil wind "blows" suddenly, the normal is shattered by the horrific, so Mike Ryerson's fear, like the fast crane move to the high angle, is fast and abrupt. The next shot in this sequence is even more clever: a point of view shot from deep within the earthen walls of the open grave. Ryerson is visible looking down (at the camera). Is the grave open? Is there a vampire waiting? What does Ryerson see? By putting the camera down there (at Glick's perspective), Hooper extends the suspense of the sequence: the audience doesn't know what he's seeing. The final jolt in the scene occurs when Ryerson jumps down on the coffin, looks away because he hears something, then turns back and finds the vampire boy—*glowing eyes, fangs and all*—waiting to bite him. It's yet another of the film's outstanding jolt moments.

Another scene establishes Hooper's talent for misleading his audience, a necessary technique in horror to lull audiences into complacency. When Dzundza catches Crockett (Willard) with his wife, Hooper's camera adopts reverse angles on their sweating, tense faces. Dzunda's character demands Crockett put the gun to his head, and the audience sees it all close up. The result is tangible fear and suspense. But this, of course, is pure misdirection. The scene ends on a note of explosive release: Dzundza pulls the shotgun's trigger, revealing the weapon to be unloaded. Terrified but alive, Crockett is allowed to flee, and it is only then that Hooper's camera retracts (to an exterior, wider shot). Crockett runs for his car and—*boom*—Barlow's outstretched hand catches him in the face. The audience is thoroughly unprepared for this jolt because Hooper has built up all the suspense in the scene with the shotgun (an unrelated subplot) and then released it with the pulling of the trigger. With that climax resolved, the audience unwittingly relaxes, and are thus made vulnerable to the Barlow jolt. It's brilliant work, especially for 1970s television. A talented director, like a talented magician, knows how to get his audience to see and feel certain things and thus surprise them when something unexpected happens.

What is perhaps most revelatory about *Salem's Lot* is the level of discipline evident. Hooper is a great, anarchic filmmaker, but his films don't tend to evoke praise for their discipline. They tend to be intentionally undisciplined in narrative, in climax, in pace, in virtually everything. Hooper actually *gains* excitement by being undisciplined, by showing us things we don't expect, or by taking us on one wild detour after another. But *Salem's Lot* succeeds so marvelously because Hooper restrains his urge to "go for the throat." Instead, he quietly and effectively builds suspense throughout the film by backing away from several important moments.

This is a technique Alfred Hitchcock used in some films, especially *Frenzy* (1972). In that film, concerning a serial killer in London, the director didn't follow his villain into an upstairs apartment, where the maniac planned to murder a young girl. Instead, Hitchcock's camera remained on the street, waiting for the psycho to return from the apartment and the job at hand. *Salem's Lot* likewise leaves much to the imagination, in the same manner Val Lewton might have approved of had he been directing in the '70s. Whether this technique was a result of television restrictions, or simply that Hooper thought it was a good showcase for the material, is unimportant. What remains important is that at several critical junctures, Hooper leaves things unseen, unexplored. For instance, early in the plot Ben Mears discusses a childhood incident inside the house of "evil," created by Marsten. A more conventional filmmaker might have shown a flashback of this event, but Hooper, understanding that the film starts out as conventional soap opera, doesn't tip his hand. Instead, he lets Soul's performances (and Stephen King's words) paint a picture for the audience. Later in the film, Hooper never films the scene wherein Susan meets Barlow and is bitten by him. This is a fairly important plot point, but Hooper lets it rest, so he'll have a shocker of an ending. It's an unsettling touch because Mears and Petrie, the heroes of the piece, are unable to find Susan inside the Marsten House during the climax. This quirk is never explained, but is quite disturbing.

Lastly, Hooper saves the interior of the Marsten House for the final set piece. There are ample opportunities throughout the miniseries to take the viewer inside the creepy, *Psycho*-like home (including that prospective flashback) but Hooper is patient, revealing the fetid, dilapidated interior (shades of *Chain Saw* and *Eaten Alive*) for the film's finale. Again, this is a conscious decision and one requiring great discipline. Consider that Hooper revealed the Starlight and the Farmhouse quite early in those horror pictures, hitting the audience with the horrible locales in the first third of each story. The shock was powerful, but just one in a series of escalating shocks. Hooper is more careful, more protective of his narrative in *Salem's Lot*, rationing out the stunning art design (like the Marsten interior) until the appropriate moment.

Despite some key differences with King's novel, particularly in the depiction of Straker and the combining and elimination of some minor characters, *Salem's Lot* remains one of the best adaptations of Stephen King's work. The miniseries format (four hours instead of 90 minutes or two hours) allowed Hooper to include much of King's neater touches, including the idea that good people can be drawn to horrible things (such as horror films), and even saved by this obsession. Some of the best character moments in the film involve young Mark Petrie and his bullheaded father, who doesn't understand his fascination with "childish" things like magic, model kits and monsters. As it turns out, it is those very things that save Petrie's life. He is able to understand the menace of the vampires when they come to his window, and consequently use the appropriate weapon (a model kit crucifix!) to deflect the evil. His bedroom, replete with posters of the Frankenstein monster and the Wolfman is probably a testament to Stephen King's childhood and Tobe Hooper's too. They share in common a love of magic (also a facet in Stephen King's novel *Needful Things*), horror cinema, and monsters. It is that creative like-mindedness that may account for *Salem's Lot*'s success. The two artists seem to be in synch with the material.

In mood, in suspense, in pace, in character development and in jolts, *Salem's Lot* is a remarkable example of horror filmmaking and a real feather in Tobe Hooper's cap. That is not to say, however, that the miniseries is perfect. There are a few touches in the script, for example, that just don't make sense. Ryerson's pet dog dies early in the tale (the first resident of Salem's Lot to bite the dust), but it is never clear who kills the pup. Barlow has not yet arrived in town and if Straker procures "food" for Barlow, he doesn't commit murder. This vampire likes his meals fresh. So who killed the dog and why? Another disconnect involves the deliverymen, Ryerson and Tebbets. They deliver Barlow's coffin to the Marsten House cellar and hear somebody tromping around upstairs. The audience hears the scary noises too, but Straker is out abducting the Glick boys and Barlow is still in his crate (in the same cellar), so who is rumbling about upstairs? Perhaps the house really is haunted, as Mears suggests, but that might have been made clearer. Finally, in the climactic confrontation with Barlow, there are two miscues. Firstly, there are not enough vampires evident in the crypt, since Barlow has been sucking up the whole town and, secondly, the Marsten House set never convincingly burns down. Small concerns perhaps, but the film's four hour running time gives one time to think about story points and inconsistencies.

Salem's Lot really paves the way for Hooper's work on the crowd-pleasing *Pol-*

tergeist. His direction of the child performances here is good: these kids are effective and unmannered, and Hooper pulls no punches just because they are children. Hooper also manages to include much of King's ruminations about small towns: nostalgia for some, traps for others, and feeding grounds for vampires. The romance between Bonnie Bedelia and David Soul is also played rather effectively, never lapsing into the saccharine stuff of so much TV melodrama, and Hooper has a nice touch with these scenes of two adults connecting.

They could have been cheesy moments, but like the rest of Hooper's work in the picture, these scenes are restrained; disciplined.

A finely polished, suspenseful and shocking work of horror, Tobe Hooper's *Salem's Lot* is the director's finest work for the venue of television. A superb cast, headed by the sardonic James Mason, grants the film class and Hooper's carefully constructed horror sequences (in jails, morgues, and haunted houses) makes this perhaps the finest Stephen King adaptation to come along in some twenty years.

2. *I'm Dangerous Tonight* (1990)

Cast and Crew

CAST: Madchen Amick (Amy O'Neill); Corey Parker (Edward Satler); Daisy Hall (Gloria); R. Lee Ermey (Detective Achman); Natalie Schafer (Grandma); Jason Brooks (Mason); William Berger; Mary Frann (Martha); Dee Wallace Stone (Wanda Thatcher); Anthony Perkins (Gordon Buchanan); Lew Horn (Coroner); Stuart Fratkin (Victor); Dan Leegant (Frank); Jack McGee (Landlord); Edward Trotta (Joey); David Carlile (Mort); Felicia Lansbury (Librarian); Henry C. Brown (Anchorman); Ellen Gerstein (Server); Ivan Gueron (Romeo); Juan Garcia (Enrique); Frank Dielsi (City Worker); Richard Penn (Paramedic); Xavier Barquet (Punk # 1); Matthew Walker (Punk # 2); Robert Harvey (Janitor); Bill Madden (Tybolt).

CREW: *Director of Photography:* Levie Isaacks. *Music:* Nicholas Pike. *Production Designer:* Leonard Mazzola. *Edited by:* Carl Kress. *Executive Producer:* Boris Malden. *Co-Executive Producer:* Michael Wiesbarth. *Produced by:* Bruce Lansbury, Philip John Taylor. *Based on the short story by:* Cornell Woolrich. *Screenplay:* Bruce Lansbury and Philip John Taylor. *Directed by:* Tobe Hooper. *Unit Production Manager:* Joseph Belliotti. *First Assistant Director:* Thomas J. Blank. *Second Assistant Director:* Keri L McIntyre. *Casting:* Robin Lippin. *Casting Associate:* Dan Bernstein. *First Assistant Cameraman:* Wayne Trimble. *Sound Mixer:* Craig Feldburg. *Costume Designer:* Cavin Berger. *Gaffer:* Robert W. Moreno. *Key Grip:* Michael L. Colwell. *Property Master:* Cahlo Gonzales. *Location Manager:* Ralph Meyer. *Hairstylist:* Nina Paskowitz. *Makeup:* Emily Katz. *Script Supervisor:* Sandy Mazzola. *Production Coordinator:* Annie Saunders. *Assistant Production Coordinator:* Martha J. Liemann. *Production Secretary:* Kathy Lauch. *Production Accountant:* Tad Driscoll. *Transportation Coordinator:* Reese Lane. *Special Effects:* Special Effects Unlimited, Inc. *Special Effects Coordinator:* Joseph Mercurio. *Special Effects:* Vincent Montefusco, Tom Ficke, Charles Bellardinell. *Stunt Coordinator:* John Moio. *Assistant Editor:* Michael Philip. *Supervising Sound Editor:* David John West. *Supervising Music Editor:* Alan Rosen. *ADR Supervisor:* Lynn R. Schneider. *Foley:* Mike Dickerson. Presented by Coastline Partners, a Kingworld and MCA Partnership. *Running Time:* 92 minutes.

Synopsis

A truck delivers an ancient Aztec sacrificial altar to Tiverton College Museum. Enthusiastic about the relic, an antiquities professor named Wilson opens a secret compartment on the side of the altar and discovers inside a corpse garbed in a red ceremonial cloak. Wilson touches the cloak and is possessed by its terrible evil. He goes on a killing rampage before being killed himself.

Meanwhile, a college student, Amy O'Neill, teams with her fellow classmate, Edward Satler, to write a paper for Professor Buchanan on the subject of animism, the doctrine that inanimate objects might actually be alive. While working together, Edward also recruits Amy to work on the props for a campus production of *Romeo and Juliet* in which Edward is playing Mercutio. Amy agrees to help, eager to get away from her miserable home life. An orphan, Amy is the virtual slave to a nasty stepmother, a competitive cousin named Gloria, and an invalid, mute grandmother. One weekend, Amy visits a yard sale at the home of the deceased Professor Wilson and buys a trunk for the play. Inside is the Aztec cloak, and when Amy touches it, she experiences visions of Wilson murdering his wife with an axe.

During rehearsal, Edward adorns the cape (as Mercutio) and promptly goes crazy during an on-stage duel. When the cape slips off his back, he returns to normal, uncertain why he has behaved in so violent a fashion. Amy reclaims the red cloak and sews herself a red sexy dress out of it. Meanwhile, Gloria shirks responsibility for Grandma so she can go out on a date with her football star boyfriend, Mason. This leaves Amy to tend to her grandmother herself.

Amy is invited to a college dance, but begs off because of her responsibilities to her grandmother. But, possessed by the powers of the red dress, she goes to the dance and acts like a vamp. She makes eyes at Mason, to Gloria's dismay. Mason nearly beds down Amy in his pickup truck, but when her dress slips off, she is shocked to find herself in an intimate embrace with Mason. Wrapped in a blanket, she runs home. There, her grandmother, understanding the power of the red dress, confronts her and tries to take the offending garment away from Amy. In the ensuing scuffle, a violent Amy pushes her granny (in wheelchair) down the stairs, killing her. Fortunately, the fall appears to be an accident.

After she attends her grandmother's funeral, Amy and Edward go out for a drive. Without Amy's consent, Gloria borrows the dangerous red dress. Losing her inhibitions, she makes love to Mason because she believes he intends to propose to her. Instead, he reveals he has been picked to play professional football and that he wants to back off their relationship. Driven to violent anger by the power of the dress, Gloria strangles Mason while he showers, then cuts his genitals off with a razor. Still possessed with evil, Gloria attempts to run over Eddie and Amy in Mason's truck. They survive, but Gloria dies in an explosion when the truck careens off the road and down a hill.

The next morning, Professor Buchanan warns Amy that certain garments worn in religious rituals can possess the living. As if this isn't bad enough, Amy is questioned by the police about her role in the deaths of Gloria, Mason and her own grandmother. A detective insinuates Amy has something to hide, but Amy believes the dress has been destroyed in flame. Unfortunately, the gown has merely been passed on to a hooker, who immediately goes on a murder spree. When Amy realizes there is a link to her red dress, she investigates. She discovers that a woman named Wanda Thatcher worked at the morgue and made off with the garment. After Buchanan again accosts her about the cloak, Amy finally learns that an Aztec priest once wore it during sacrificial rites.

Amy devises a plan to steal her dress back, tricking her way into Wanda's home. Wanda doesn't take kindly to the intrusion and retaliates, killing Amy's stepmom, Martha. Amy discovers Martha's corpse in the kitchen, and Wanda tries to stab her, but Amy pushes her down the stairs in her grandma's wheelchair. Wanda attacks Amy again, knocking her out. When Amy awak-

She's got the look. Amy (Madchen Amick) is surrounded by admiring extras when she dons a sexy (and possessed) red gown in the USA Network movie *I'm Dangerous Tonight* (1990).

ens, Wanda has disappeared, but Edward has dressed Amy in the sexy and dangerous red dress! Aware of its powers, he has been manipulating events to get her back into it. Amy flees her house, finds Wanda's body in a shed, and cuts up the malevolent dress with garden shears. She convinces Edward to destroy the dress with her, and since he loves her, he helps. The police arrive and determine that reasonable force was used to kill the murderous Wanda, Amy mulches the dress and buries the fabric in Wanda's grave.

At the end of the semester, Professor Buchanan congratulates Amy for challenging the power of the cloak. But, in secret, he unearths the fabric pieces from Wanda's grave.

Commentary

The biggest problem facing *I'm Dangerous Tonight* is that it isn't dangerous enough. Produced for the USA Network, a basic cable network, circa 1990, the film is hamstrung by the need to cut for commercials every 15 minutes, as well as the restrictions of the very medium itself. The telefilm is never quite as scary or as violent as fans know Tobe Hooper can make it. Hooper had done quite well with the same TV restriction before, namely with the highly effective *Salem's Lot* in 1979. However, this telemovie, based on a short story by Cornell Woolrich, is minor horror hokum at best, focusing on animism: the belief that an object can be infused with the essence of a spirit, either benevolent or malevolent. An evil red dress doesn't exactly compare favorably with a town full of vampires on the Richter scale of horror, and *I'm Dangerous Tonight* pays for its thin material. It isn't bad by any means, just fairly innocuous TV material. Like many good but ultimately trashy TV movies, it maintains a spell of "watchability" and is relatively diverting. That noted, *I'm Dangerous Tonight* is never going to win kudos as a classic of its kind or even as one of the better efforts of its famous director.

As students of Hooper's films will note, many of his projects inhabit the milieu of the teenager. *The Texas Chain Saw Massacre* was an early (and potent) entry in a horror subgenre that became especially popular after *Halloween*, and stayed so throughout the 1980s in the many *Nightmare on Elm Street* franchise pictures. In Hooper's world, teens are also dramatized in *The Funhouse* and in *Crocodile*—not always in a flattering light, either. In both of those films (as in *I'm Dangerous Tonight*) there is a powerful but untrustworthy boyfriend who wants only to "go all the way" with the girl of his choosing, usually one who is more interested in protecting her virtue. It is noteworthy that Hooper and the horror genre generally assume the side of the female in this debate, viewing them as heroic, and the men in their lives (Mason in *I'm Dangerous Tonight*, Buzz in *The Funhouse*, and Duncan in *Crocodile*) as bad, or at least worthy of punishment. Inevitably in these films (and in all teen horror films), it is the virtuous female who survives the terrifying ordeal, whether it be at the hands of mutant carnies, a giant crocodile, or a possessed Aztec cloak. In *I'm Dangerous Tonight*, Mason, the groping football player who is disloyal to his own girl, Gloria, and who pushes for sex with Amy, is given his comeuppance. His genitals are sliced off with a razor blade.

Teen horror movies not only feature the stereotype of the "bad" and "horny" boyfriend, but another one as well: the resourceful teen heroine. Laurie Strode (Jamie Lee Curtis of *Halloween*), Nancy Thompson (Heather Langenkamp of *A Nightmare on Elm Street*), and Kirsty (Ashley Laurence of *Hellraiser* [1987]) all embody this late 1970s-1980s horror tradition in which women solve a "horror" problem and are depicted as heroic, even better than the rest of their generation. *I'm Dangerous Tonight* follows clearly in this pattern, this time with Madchen Amick's Amy as the clever protagonist. During this period in horror history, directors such as Craven and Hooper were responding to cries from women's groups and The Moral Majority that genre pictures were misogynistic. Thus men were soon viewed less positively in horror (and even Edward, Amy's boyfriend in *I'm Dangerous Tonight*, is viewed as less intelligent than his love interest and kind of goofy too), and women were championed as the smarter, superior sex. Thus Amy tricks her way into Wanda's apartment, confronts her professor (Anthony Perkins), and solves the mystery of the cloak. Her character almost represents a time capsule of the slasher genre in the latter decades of the 20th century: a time when female protagonists could no longer merely be screamers (like Sally Hardesty in *The Texas Chain Saw Massacre*), but full-fledged participants and architects of their own fates.

But if the teen dynamic of *I'm Dangerous Tonight* feels rote and wholly typical of its time, then the television movie's other running conceit is more interesting all around. Simply put, Amy is depicted as a kind of contemporary *Cinderella* figure. Usually, Hooper draws from a darker fairy tale, Alice in Wonderland, but here he has fun with the *Cinderella* story. Consider Amy's home life. Her parents are dead, she has a mean aunt (stepmother?) and a terrible cousin (stepsister?). Amy's life consists mainly of boring, difficult chores (such as sewing new clothes for Gloria and preparing meals for Grandma). Amy herself is considered much less attractive than Gloria (just like Cinderella), until magic intervenes to get her noticed. But, since this is a horror movie, the magic of *I'm Dangerous Tonight* is negative, evil, rather than helpful. Instead of donning magic slippers and riding about town in a pumpkin, Amy puts on that Aztec cloak (sewn into the shape of a revealing red dress) and becomes a desirable, red-blooded sexpot.

After enduring a life of chores and responsibilities, watching Grandma, and serving Gloria, Amy wears the dress, loses her inhibitions and goes wild. It's *Cinderella meets Dr. Jekyll and Mr. Hyde*, and oddly enough, it works. There is a mythic feeling to the structure of this story, and the obvious *Cinderella* dynamic of Amy's life provides a shorthand for viewers. We recognize the characters as *archetype*s, and have no need for Hooper to spell out the relationships in any greater depth. The nasty caregiver, the gloating older sister, the ailing grandmother are all characters long ingrained in American psyches.

The story of Amy is pretty interesting material for a time, but after a bit the audience just gets ahead of this film. It knows the evil dress will pass hands. It knows more violence will erupt, and it knows that the responsible Amy will take matters into her own hands to destroy the evil. Late in the film, Dee Wallace Stone shows up as another woman turned murderous by the dress and as the circle of characters widens, the story's impact dissipates. By the time R. Lee Ermey's cop is investigating Amy for crimes related to the red dress, *I'm Dangerous Tonight* feels awfully by-the-numbers.

Though Hooper ratchets up the pace for the tale's violent climax and provides two good jolts (dead Martha in the kitchen, and murderous Wanda lunging from the shadows), there isn't a whole lot of inspiration here.

And that's the problem, again. *I'm Dangerous Tonight* is competent, even diverting, but the edge, the danger, is missing. Early in the movie, Amick dons the red dress for the first time for a college mixer and she looks terrific. Then the script calls on her to erupt into a sexy, seductive dance aimed at stealing Gloria's beau, Mason. But instead of really letting go, instead of feeling the power released by that dress, Amick's character remains remote, hemmed in. Her so-called "liberation" dance is one of pure wonder bread and whole milk, perfectly suited to a PG, TV audience. Apparently, the confines of TV would allow nothing more extreme than a bit of suburban hustle and gyration. That's a shame, because this is the moment when the story should have felt truly wild, truly dangerous, as though Amy were in danger of losing her better self to the urges and sexual desires we all must, by necessity, sometimes repress.

Hooper's first exploration of animism (*The Mangler* was his second), *I'm Dangerous Tonight* is a tame little diversion from one of the most subversive and "dangerous" directors working in horror. Even Anthony Perkins can't perk this thing up. One is left with the impression that maybe it was Tobe Hooper who needed to wear the red cloak if this movie was to be anything more than two hours of diversion in front of the boob tube.

3. *John Carpenter Presents Body Bags* (1993)

Critical Reception

"Gruesome stuff ... and yet *Body Bags* moves along with such good bad taste that it's hard not to smile ... grade: A."
　　　　—Lisa Schwarzbaum, *Entertainment Weekly*, August 6, 1993, page 46.

"...O.K., but nothing more...."
　　　　—Mike Mayo, *Videohound's Horror Show: 999 Hair-Raising, Hellish, and Humorous Movies*, Visible Ink Press, 1998, pages 39-40.

Cast and Crew

CAST: **"The Morgue"**: John Carpenter (Coroner); Tom Arnold (Man # 1); Tobe Hooper (Man # 2).

"The Gas Station": Robert Carradine (Bill); Alex Datcher (Anne); Peter Jason (Gent); Molly Cheeck (Divorcee); Wes Craven (Pasty-Faced Man); Sam Raimi (Bill—Dead Attendant); David Naughton (Pete); Buck Flower (Stranger); Lucy Boyer (Peggy); Roger Rooks (TV Anchor Man).

"Hair": Stacy Keach (Richard); David Warner (Dr. Lock); Sheena Easton (Megan); Dan Blom (Dennis); Attila (Man); Kim Alexis (Woman); Greg Nicotero (Man with Dog); Deborah Harry (The Nurse).

"Eye": Mark Hamill (Brent); Twiggy (Cathy); John Agar (Dr. Lang); Roger Corman (Dr. Bregman); Charles Napier (Manager); Eddie Velez (Player); Betty Muramoto (Librarian); Bebe Drake-Massey (Nurse); Sean McClory (Minister); Robert L. Bush (Man); Gregory H. Alpert (Technician)

CREDITS: *John Carpenter Presents Body Bags. Written by:* Billy Brown and Dan Angel. *Music:* John Carpenter and Jim Lang. *Director of Photography:* Gary Kibbe. *Production Designer:* Daniel A. Lomino. *Film Editor:* Edward A. Warschilka. *Executive Producers:* John Carpenter, Sandy King, Dan Angel. *Co-producer:* Dan Angel. *Producer:* Sandy King. *"The Gas Station" and "Hair" directed by:* John Carpenter. *"Eye" directed by:* Tobe Hooper. *Unit Production Manager:* Peter L. Berquist. *First Assistant Director:* Artist Robinson. *Second Assistant Director:* Christine P. Della Penna. *Casting:* The Backseat Casting Company. *Camera Operator:* Gordon Paschal. *First Assistant Camera:* Jeff Norvat. *Second Assistant Camera:* Brian Kibbe. *Loader:* Lisa A. Guerriero. *Video Operator:* Joe A. Unsin, III. *Script Supervisor:* Hope Williams. *Gaffer:* Jon Timothy Evans. *Best boy Electric:* J.R. Richner. *Electricians:* John Owens, Joe Garcia, Al Hood. *Key Grip:* Harry L. Rez. *Best Boy Grip:* Mark A. Bolin. *Second Grip:* Craig Pfeiffer. *Company Grip:* Jack Bauer. *Sound Mixers:* Mark Bovos, James S. Larue, Robert Allen Wald. *Boom Operator:* Scott Sherline. *Cableman:* Jeffrey A Humphreys. *Set Decorator:* Cloudia Rebar. *Leadman:* Jason Bedig. *Swing Gang:* Gary Breuer, Scott M. Anderson. *Propmaster:* William King. *Assistant Props:* Norman "Pepe" Teurs. *Men's Costuming Supervisor:* Robert Bush. *Women's Costuming Supervisor:* Robin Michel Bush. *Set Wardrobe:* Robert Iannacone. *Make-up:* Greg LaCava. *Hairstylist:* Carolyn L. Elias. *Special Make-up Effects:* KNB Group, Inc., Robert Kurtzman, Greg Nicoreto, Howard Berger. *Assistant Film Editor:* Paul C. Warschilka. *M.P.A.A. Rating:* Made for TV. *Running time:* 103 minutes.

Synopsis

At the city morgue, a ghoulish coroner recounts three tales of terror, death and dismemberment. In the first, a psychology student starts her night job at an isolated gas station outside Haddonfield on the very night a serial killer is on the loose. In the second of the mortician's macabre stories, a vain fellow named Richard is bothered that he is losing all of his hair. He becomes obsessed with his impending baldness and tries a revolutionary new treatment offered by the mysterious Dr. Lock and his clinic. The treatment is successful, but Richard learns that his new hair is alive: alien larvae seeking special nourishment from his brain.

In the third of the coroner's stories, an up and coming baseball player suffers a terrible car accident while driving home on a stormy night. A glass shard punctures his eyeball, effectively sidelining his career in professional sports. When Brent Matthews awakes in the hospital, he learns that he has lost his right eye, but is given a ray of hope by the visiting Dr. Wang, who has developed a method of transplanting eyes. Luckily, there's a healthy donor eye ready to go.

Brent undergoes the experimental transplant surgery and it seems to be a smashing success. With his vision restored, Brent plans to return to sports, even as his wife Cathy reveals that she is expecting a baby. Soon, however, Brent begins to experience horrible headaches and strange, violent visions. One night, before making love to his wife, Brent sees a dead woman rising out of the earth in the backyard.

Growing frightened and ever more short-tempered, Brent is soon inundated with increasingly bloody flashes. He begins to dig a hole in the backyard, afraid he will uncover a corpse. Strangely, there's nothing there. Before long, Brent is also expe-

Hooper's fellow horror director John Carpenter played the ghoulish host of the cable television horror anthology *John Carpenter Presents Body Bags* (1993).

riencing phantom memories that don't seem to belong to his psyche. While making love to Cathy, he imagines he's having sex with a bloody corpse. Deeply disturbed, Brent visits Dr. Wang and learns that his transplant eye once belonged to a psychopath, John Randall, who was put to death in the gas chamber. Before being captured, Randall dismembered seven women after stabbing them repeatedly with garden shears.

Becoming completely possessed by the serial killer, Brent returns home and digs a grave for his wife. He attacks her and then explains that he sees what Randall saw ... and that he *likes it.* Cathy encourages Brent to look in the Bible for the answer to this dilemma. A deeply religious man, Brent runs across a pertinent passage: *if thine eye offend thee, pluck it out.* Clinging to sanity, and a love for Cathy and his unborn child, Brent destroys the eye that is transforming him into a monster.

Commentary

John Carpenter's Body Bags is a gory, fun-filled homage to the horror genre as a whole, as well as the tried-and-true anthology format exemplified by films such as *Asylum* (1972), *Tales from the Crypt* (1972), *Vault of Horror* (1973), *From Beyond the Grave* (1973), *The Monster Club* (1980), and *Creepshow* (1981). The TV movie attempts, in three diverse "short" stories, to tip its hat to three separate and distinct "brands" of terror.

John Carpenter's first entry, "The Gas Station," is of the stalk-'n'-slash variety popularized by his own stylish landmark in that sub genre, 1978's *Halloween*. In fact, Carpenter even duplicates some of *Halloween*'s most distinct compositions in this tale. The second tale, entitled "Hair," comes from another school: The EC comics "comeuppance" tradition. In these tales, the scales of justice are righted when a lead character (usually unlikable), is done in by his own foibles. In "Hair," a vain, self-obsessed Stacy Keach searches for a full head of hair with disastrous consequences. He is soon at the mercy of David Warner's mad scientist.

Tobe Hooper contributes "Eye" to the *Body Bags* mix. This final story of the "trilogy" arrives courtesy of another long-standing branch of horror mythology: the transplant story. In this subgenre, an innocent person is badly injured and, desperate to survive, undergoes a transplant procedure (usually either a hand or an eye). Unfortunately, the donor, it is eventually learned, was a serial killer, a psychopath, or some other equally undesirable madman. Naturally the frightened recipient of the evil transplant then starts to develop the same violent proclivities as the hand/eye's previous owner.

The transplant story has been done many, many times on film and on television. In the cinema, the evil transplant (in this case a hand) has been dramatized in the many versions of *The Hands of Orlac*, filmed in 1924, 1935, 1960 and 1962 respectively. *Body Parts* (1991) was directed by Eric Red and trod similar territory, but with bloodier special effects. On TV, there have been evil hands on *Rod Serling's Night Gallery* in "The Hand of Borgus Weems" (1971), and on *Quinn Martin's Tales of the Unexpected* in "A Hand for Sonny Blue" (1977). An item that makes the latter episode particularly interesting is that Sonny Blue is a baseball player, the same profession as Brent (Mark Hamill) in "Eye." As for eye transplants, this variant has appeared on TV in the paranormal series *The Sixth Sense* (1972), in the installment "The Eyes that Wouldn't Die."

Thus "Eye" is an old story, and as the above-listed examples reveal, a familiar one. Unlike Carpenter's two entries in this anthology, Tobe Hooper's finale is not really leavened much by self-reflexive humor or an over-acute sense of self-awareness. Instead, it follows the transplant story prototype almost religiously, down to Hamill's discovery of John Randall's (the donor's) murderous crimes. Instead of humor, "Eye" is laced with some pretty heavy gore (a failing or strength, depending on one's perspective, also of Hooper's last theatrical feature, *The Mangler*). There is one shot of a detached eyeball resting on a bed of ice cubes (an absurdity made grotesquely real) and several peeks at the bloody transplant surgery. If this material is difficult to view, the psychological scenes have even more impact. There's a sequence in which Brent nearly rapes his wife, and another in which he fantasizes having sexual intercourse with a rotting corpse. The latter is particularly disturbing, and reminiscent of the opening of *The Texas Chain Saw Massacre* in which a corpse "decorated" a stone monument. In both cases, there is awareness that some mad people see dead bodies as playthings rather than rotting flesh. Death may be the end of consciousness for some, but for some ghoulish people it's just another avenue to "express" themselves. The clearest connection in "Eye" to Hooper's early, more powerful work of the 1970s is in the just-under-the-surface realization that Hooper likes to go over the top. The "no deal" kid is back here, dramatizing impalings (twice) and deploying other bloody effects all in a relatively short span of 15–20 minutes. He also treads dangerously close to necrophilia, a huge taboo for television.

Beyond these flourishes, one can find bits and pieces of the other Tobe Hooper efforts here too, the one who idolizes 1950s B movies. In "Eye" the story is told with a straight face, but with B movie maker Roger Corman and B movie star John Agar playing obviously looney-tune scientists who might have been at home in either *I Was a Teenage Frankenstein* (1957) or *I Was a Teenage Werewolf* (1957). Similarly, the notion that an eye transplant (or transplant of any kind) somehow trespasses against the will and laws of a Christian God clearly genuflects to the conservative 1950s and the anti-rational, anti-science bent best exemplified by the well-known movie directive of the period: "Do not tamper in God's domain."

With its clearly Christian lead character, "Eye" concludes when a tortured Brent finds a moment of serenity amidst the psychosis and remembers the principles of the Bible. He takes Scripture literally, particularly the phrase that goes "if thine eye offend thee, pluck it out. Cast it from thee." Since Brent does just that, one can imagine the gory possibilities it offers Hooper. It is quite messy, and one senses that deep down, somewhere buried, there is a tongue in cheek at work. This is a B movie 1950s story, with Christianity reaffirmed, but seen through the perspective of a distinctly subversive filmmaker. One can't imagine, for instance, that Scripture should be taken literally in this case, ocular removal and all, but Hooper carries it off with poker face.

It may be a mistake to read too much into "Eye," as it is merely a grotesque and frequently frightening short that seeks to update a hoary genre cliché. Hooper, the very guy who will do anything to shock (and therefore unsettle) his audience, is in evidence "pulling the strings" of the picture, as is the Hooper who so clearly cherishes 1950s nostalgia. Perhaps "Eye" seems out of step with the rest of *Body Bags* because it is more seriously disturbing than Carpenter's light-as-a-feather entries (though "The Gas Station" is quite suspenseful). But since *Body Bags* is an omnibus of horror genres, with many types being represented, Hooper certainly accomplishes his mission to bring the "transplant" story into the 1990s, and with quite a bit of (gory) flair.

4. *The Apartment Complex* (1999)

"…[W]ould make Rod Serling proud … creepy enough to sustain the interest of most viewers, this nod to *The Twilight Zone* cleverly winks its way out of some pretty silly situations.… *Apartment* doesn't stand out because of its script or performances, but it benefits from a nifty sense of weirdness … and director Tobe Hooper … earns points for constructing real tension and genuine thrills.… Hooper ties it all together with a zippy, 'who-dunnit' pace."
—Michael Speier, *Variety*, November 1, 1999.

Cast and Crew

CAST: Chad Lowe (Stan Warden); Fay Masterson (Alice); Obba Babatunde (Chett); Patrick Warburton (Morgan); Ron Canada (Detective Culver); Miguel Sandoval (Detective Duarte); Jon Polito (Dr. Caligari); Tyra Banks (Wanda); Gina Mari (Kiki); Flex Alexander (Miles); Rachel True (Tasha); R. Lee Ermey (Frank); Amanda Plummer (Miss Chenille); Jay Paulson (Bones); Daniel Hartley (Thrash); Jessee D. Roach (Elvin); David Schuelke (Lonnie); Jimmy Schuelko (Ronnie); Charlie Hartsock (Postman); Barry Wiggins (Big Cop); Diana Maria Riva (Short Cop); Ellis E. Williams (Sergeant).

CREW: Showtime Presents a Sterling Pacific Films Production, *The Apartment Complex*. *Casting:* Allison Jones. *Music:* Mark Adler. *Edited by:* Andy Horvitch. *Production Designer:* Dan Whifler. *Director of Photography:* Jacques Haitkin. *Co-Producer:* Amy Sydrick. *Produced by:* Scott McAboy. *Produced by:* Gil Wadsworth. *Executive Producer:* Karl Schaefer. *Written by:* Karl Schaefer. *Directed by:* Tobe Hooper. *Stunt Coordinator:* Richard Butler. *Stunt Performances:* Phil Cullotta, Donna Keegan, Peewee Piemonte. *Puppeteers:* Howard Berger, Luke Khanlian, Robert Kurtzman, Shannon J. Shea. *Unit Production Manager:* Scott Hohnbaum. *First Assistant Director:* Alex Gayner. *Key Second Assistant Director:* Adeeb Samhat. *Second Assistant Director:* Jamie Dennet. *Associate Producers:* Geraint Bell, Veronica Alweiss. *First Assistant Cameraperson:* Heather Lea. *Second Assistant Cameraperson:* Vanessa Morehouse. *Production Coordinator:* Jennifer Kerrigan-Webster. *Script Supervisor:*

Linda Kwan. *Art Director:* Paul Miller. *Art Department Coordinator:* Amy Zimmerman. *Set Decorator:* Ann Shea. *Property Master:* Fred Andrews. *Animal Wranglers:* Jules Sylvester, Tasha Zamski. *Make-up Artist:* Rela Martine. *Hairstylist:* Jennifer Donish. *Costume Supervisor:* Amber Garcia. *Special Effects:* KNB Effects Group. *Special Effects Make-Up:* Howard Berger. *Visual Effects:* Cinester F/X. *Running time:* 99 minutes.

Synopsis

Straitlaced Stan Warden, a graduate student in psychology, answers an ad in the newspaper to live rent-free in the Wonder View Apartment Complex as manager of the homes. Stan accepts the job and is interviewed by a man who claims to be the landlord, Dr. Caligari. This figure shows Stan around the grounds of the unusual apartment development. The Wonder View Apartments were designed by Frank Lloyd Wright's cousin, Iggy, and have been designated as an architectural anomaly. A strangely shaped swimming pool marks the center of the labyrinth-like complex and there seems to be something trapped at the bottom of it.

In short order, Stan meets the strange denizens of his new home. There is a pair of identical twins (Ronnie and Lonnie), a paranoid ex–C.I.A. agent named Frank, two beautiful stuntwomen/body doubles in apartment 8, Wanda and Kiki, a famous psychic medium, Miss Chenille, in apartment 18, and a nice but frequently bickering African-American couple. Very shortly, Stan meets his favorite resident of the Wonder View Apartments: the beautiful Alice. The only problem with Alice is that she is dating a dangerous, rage-alcoholic boyfriend named Morgan.

Before long, Stan finds out that his tour guide is not Dr. Caligari at all, but the homeless fellow (and once manager of Wonder View) Chett, who hangs out at the complex all day. Stan is introduced to the real Dr. Caligari, a fat, balding "cosmetic surgeon to the stars" who immediately offers Stan the job. Stan accepts and moves into the manager's apartment. He finds it loaded floor to ceiling with the old manager's belongings. Apparently obsessive-compulsive, the former manager, named Glumley, labeled everything "property of Glumley."

Stan searches the apartment and finds Glumley's journal, and evidence that one of the residents was trying to drive him crazy. He also finds a loaded gun in a desk drawer. Even more annoyingly, the apartment shakes as if an earthquake has hit it, but the damage seems specific to Stan's unit.

The next morning, Stan cleans the pool and dredges up the body of the former manager, Glumley. He calls the police and they send a diver into the pool to search for further bodies. They find nothing, but the police are immediately suspicious of Stan, fearing that he killed the former manager and took his job.

As Stan settles into his job, the postman delivers a large, heavy package for Apartment # 17. Unfortunately, there doesn't seem to be any Apartment 17, and Stan asks the mysterious, hermit-like tenant in Apartment #9 if he knows where it is. The man inside is very hostile and claims to know nothing about it. Stan decides to keep the crate in his apartment until he can find the missing # 17, and is then visited by Morgan. Morgan asks Stan to watch over his girlfriend Alice, a favor that worries Stan since he is attracted to the woman.

Police Detectives Duarte and Culver search Stan's apartment with a forensic team and inform Stan that he is the prime suspect in the murder of Glumley. Stan grows ever more concerned and gets into some trouble when Alice invites him to her place for a beer. When the jealous Morgan returns unexpectedly, Stan pretends to be unclogging Alice's toilet. Later, as events snowball, the package for Apartment # 17 opens up to reveal a giant snake, now loosed upon the unexpecting inhabitants of the Wonder View Apartments. Meanwhile, Miss

Chenille throws herself at Stan and he is forced to politely reject her sexual advances.

Stan's tenure at the Wonder View Apartments goes from bad to worse when the police return to question him again. It turns out that Glumley didn't drown in the pool. Tap water was found in his lungs and the police believe Stan drowned Glumley in the former manager's own apartment. Stan suggests to Duarte and Culver that the man in #9 is awfully suspicious, and the journal suggested he was trying to drive Glumley crazy, but the police don't buy his notion.

After the police leave, Alice runs to Stan's apartment in fear. Morgan has gone on a jealous rampage after watching a talk show about cheating girlfriends. Stan hides Alice in his apartment, but Morgan breaks in and punches Stan out. Stan uses a bust of Sigmund Freud to incapacitate Morgan. While Alice and Stan wait for the police, the snake returns to Stan's apartment and breaks every bone in Morgan's body. Stan is consequently arrested for the murder of Glumley and for violently assaulting Morgan.

The residents at the apartment concoct a suicide note to explain Glumley's death, and get Stan released from prison. On his return, Stan is confronted by the tenant in Apartment # 9, the real Glumley! It turns out he staged his own death, is stark-raving bonkers, and now wants to kill Stan to get his old job back. Glumley tries to drown Stanley in a waterbed but the tenants of the Wonder View Apartments come to the rescue again and save Stan's life.

With the case solved and the police off his back, Stan is welcomed to the Wonder View Apartments at a pool party, but the snake shows up to ruin things.

Commentary

Tobe Hooper reasserts his mastery of the surreal in the amusing *The Apartment Complex*, a backdoor series pilot for the Showtime premium cable network. Though the movie never went to series, it nonetheless represents a return to form for a director who has always explored the absurd with zeal. Silly, fun and packed wall to wall with bizarre incidents, this is one of the "lightest," though most symbolic, entries in Hooper's oeuvre. The solemnity of *The Mangler* and *Night Terrors* has vanished in favor of an easygoing, almost whimsical style that suits the mellow Hooper of the millennium.

As in many Hooper pictures, art design tips off thematic content. Here, the Wonder View Apartments resemble the odd backdrops of black-and-white, silent German expressionist film, so it is appropriate that the landlord be named Dr. Caligari, after the classic early film *The Cabinet of Dr. Caligari* (1919). Doorways are strangely slanted and oversized throughout the complex, levels seem to blend into other levels, and there is nary a right angle in sight. Hooper gets great mileage from this odd setting, especially the unbelievably "deep" swimming pool that represents one of the film's funniest visual recurring jokes.

The thesis of the film concerns psychology, and the notion that human beings are not very different from lab rats. It's only the size of the maze that has changed. To represent this notion, Hooper bookends the film with high-angle shots of mice scurrying about in a maze. Early on, his camera nears the maze, and as it tracks lower, the maze is replaced by the outer wall of the Wonder View Apartments, creating a seamless transition from microcosm to reality. The last shot of the film is the flip side of this opening visual conceit, reversing the shot and revealing the denizens of the Wonder View Apartments to be no more than "rats in a maze" as they scurry away from a snake in the swimming pool.

Karl Schaefer's screenplay is strong on the surreal and short on subtlety, a cue

Hooper picks up on, so the tone of *The Apartment Complex* isn't that far from camp. That's hardly a problem however, since art can't be surreal and subtle at the same time; the viewer merely has to modulate expectations. This isn't everyday reality, and nearly every name and event in the picture has a symbolic meaning to match its literal one, if only one is paying close attention. The lead character, for instance, is named Stan Warden. "Warden" is an appropriate choice of moniker for the lead character, since he comes to be the caretaker of a group of odd tenants, including at least one criminal (Morgan). Visually buttressing the idea of Warden as caretaker or gatekeeper of the asylum is a well-composed, almost throwaway shot near the opening of the picture. Stan enters the complex for the first time, pulling the outer door closed behind him. Not surprisingly, the door has bars on it, like a prison cell, and for a split-second Stan peers through them. The implication is that he's inside with the nuts now, for better or worse.

Other names are equally important. Throughout Tobe Hooper's films, there has been an obsession with the *Alice in Wonderland* scenario. In *The Texas Chain Saw Massacre*, Hooper invited his heroine, Marilyn Burns, to a kind of mad tea party (an event repeated in the sequel). And in *Chainsaw Part 2,* and *Invaders from Mars*, characters fell into kinds of bizarre fantasy lands, like the literary Alice. Even the idea of a little girl lost, so prominent in *Poltergeist,* seems reminiscent of the central scenario of Lewis Carroll's classic story. Carrying on this association, *The Apartment Complex* offers a female lead named Alice, who lives in the Wonder View Apartments. *Alice in Wonder View*. It's quite interesting, especially since, like Stan, Alice seems to be one of the few normal people in the picture. It is clear she is "lost" in her own way too, trying to navigate out of a relationship with a freak (Morgan) and understand the crazy neighbors who inhabit the world around her.

Beyond that notion, the last third of *The Apartment Complex* involves another literal/metaphorical conceit. A snake gets "loose in the grass" according to Wonder View's wandering philosopher, Chett, and the sullen, omnipresent Glumley represents a snake in the grass too, coming to "surprise" Stan from out of nowhere. It may not be particularly deep, but Karl Schaefer and Tobe Hooper have worked carefully to layer on the symbolism and meaning in this weird pilot, a fact that is easily overlooked with some of the over-the-top comedic antics on view.

The Apartment Complex offers some fine performances, especially from the deadpan Patrick Warburton (*The Tick* [2001]) and is let down only by Chad Lowe as the normal nebbish surrounded by the abnormal. Lowe is competent as the anchor for all the crazy action, but in some of the script's more bizarre flights of fancy (such as the scene requiring Lowe to perform an imitation of Robert De Niro's famous "Are you talking to me?" bit from *Taxi Driver* [1975]) he is truly dreadful.

Still, the message of this film is one akin to a song by the Doors: people are strange when you're a stranger, faces look ugly, when you're alone. In other words, the "odd" people of the Wonder View Apartments seem truly enigmatic, bizarre and even frightening until Stan (and the audience) gets to know them. By the end of the picture they have all become friends with "quirks" and somewhere in there is a message about community and "getting to know" your neighbors. But far more delightful than that didactic aim is the fact that Tobe Hooper again seems to be in touch with his sense of humor and irony. Those sunspots in *The Texas Chain Saw Massacre* that seemed to portend a cruel universe looking down on man have been replaced by the metaphor for mice in a maze, but the message is not all that different. Only now, twenty some years later, Hooper finds hope and optimism in human contact, even though the denizens of *The Apartment Complex* are weird, weird, weird.

Hooper fans expecting an outright horror movie should leave their expectations at the door while viewing this pilot because Hooper is not out to scare. As in his best work, he intentionally provokes anxiety with a fast pace and with the willy-nilly piling up of incidents. But his purpose is not to scare so much as to exasperate; not to terrify so much as amuse. The critics (and audiences) who found favor with the anarchic, surreal humor of *The Texas Chainsaw Massacre Part 2* and *Invaders from Mars* will recognize the strokes of an old talent at work, and it's a welcome return.

Part IV
Genre Television Series

This chapter offers a brief glimpse at the horror and science fiction TV series that Tobe Hooper has directed episodes for over the years. He has worked on anthologies (*Amazing Stories* [1985–1987], *Tales from The Crypt* [1989–1996] *Freddy's Nightmares* [1998–1990], *Perversions of Science* [1997] and *Night Visions* [2001]), as well as dramatic adventures like *Nowhere Man* (1995), *Dark Skies* (1996) and *The Others* (2000). Coming in off the street to direct an episode of a TV series (usually a pilot) doesn't often offer the ability to seek consistent themes with one's established canon. That said, these TV programs, for the most part, reveal a Hooper at the top of his form, delivering jolts and scares with the aplomb that fans of *The Texas Chain Saw Massacre* and *Poltergeist* have come to expect.

1. *Amazing Stories:* "Miss Stardust" (1987)

SERIES CREDITS: *Created by:* Steven Spielberg. *Presented by:* Universal Studios and Amblin Entertainment. *Executive Producer:* Steven Spielberg. *Production Executives:* Kathleen Kennedy, Frank Marshall. *Producer:* David E. Vogel. *Supervising Producers:* Joshua Brand, John Falsey. *Associate Producers:* Steve Starkey, Stephen Semel, Skip Lusk. *Story Editors:* Peter Orton, Mick Garris. *Production Designer:* Rick Carter. *Theme Music:* John Williams. *Additional Music:* Michael Kamen, Billy Goldenberg, Fred Steiner. *Casting:* Joanna Ray, Mike Fenton. *Art Directors:* Richard B. Lewis, Lynda Paradise. *Main Title:* Ron Cobb. *Special Visual Effects:* Dream Quest Images. *Stunt Coordinator:* Roydon Clark. *Titles and Opticals*: Universal Title.

"**Miss Stardust**" *Written by* Thomas Szollosi and Richard Christian Matheson; *Story by* Richard Matheson; *Directed by* Tobe Hooper; *airdate:* April 10, 1987. *Guest Cast:* Weird Al Yankovic, Dick Shawn, Laraine Newman, Rick Overton, Jack Carter, James Karen, Jim Siedow, Angel Tompkins.

Synopsis

A bar patron tells his bartender a story about a most unusual beauty pageant, "The Miss Stardust Contest." Apparently, the Earth-centric attitudes of this beauty pageant recently raised the ire of a strange extraterrestrial promoter and he maneuvered to have his three clients, Miss Jupiter, Miss Mars and Miss Venus enter the contest. Had Earth resisted inclusion of this new minority, *aliens*, the manager threatened to destroy the planet. And that fate was nothing compared to the problems the alien manager threatened to cause when his alien contestants, all rather hideous to human judges, failed to win the pageant.

The Details

Budgeted at more than $800,000 dollars per half hour episode, Steven Spielberg produced *Amazing Stories* for NBC's Brandon Tartikoff for two years. In fact, before the first frame of film was ever shot on the series, Spielberg had been granted a forty-

In 1987, Tobe Hooper directed the final installment of the Steven Spielberg (pictured) NBC fantasy anthology *Amazing Stories* (1985–1987).

four episode commitment to the series, a two season guarantee most rare in the annals of television.

Tobe Hooper was not alone in directing a segment for *Amazing Stories*. In fact, he found himself in distinguished company. Before the series' cancellation in 1987 (due to low ratings), Martin Scorsese, Clint Eastwood, Danny DeVito, Peter Hyams and Spielberg himself helmed various entries. Hooper's segment, "Miss Stardust," came late in the series' run and was pretty well ignored by the press (who had written the show off by that point.) In fact, "Miss Stardust" was the forty-fourth and last *Amazing Stories* episode to air (in April of 1987).

Like "Fine Tuning" (in which potato-headed aliens land on Earth with cameras to visit their favorite celebrities), or the atrocious "Mummy, Daddy" (concerning an actor who is mistaken for a real mummy), "Miss Stardust" is a pretty weak, one-joke half-hour. It's comic book material writ large, and not particularly good comic book material. This assessment is no reflection on Hooper, who directs the show with appropriate tongue in cheek. It's more a notation about the *Amazing Stories* series as a whole. It rarely lived up to the title "amazing" and is remembered today as an expensive, ego-bruising failure.

"Miss Stardust" seems notable in the Hooper canon mainly for reuniting the director with *Invaders from Mars* star Laraine Newman, *Texas Chain Saw*'s Cook, Jim Siedow, and James Karen of *Poltergeist* and *Invaders from Mars*. It's nice to see all these faces again; it's just too bad they must share time with Weird Al Yankovic, no doubt cast as a stunt, though in fairness he was certainly a hot commodity in the late 1980s for his renditions of parody songs like "Eat It." However, Yankovic's appearance in the show does explain his vote for *Amazing Stories* as one of the best sci-fi TV series ever in John Javna's book *The Best of Science Fiction Television*. Someone should have explained the concept of conflict of interest to Weird Al.

2. *Freddy's Nightmares: A Nightmare on Elm Street: The Series: No More Mr. Nice Guy* (1988)

SERIES CAST: Robert Englund (Freddy Krueger).

SERIES CREDITS: *Based on a character created by:* Wes Craven. *Series Consultant:* Robert Englund. *Co-Executive Producer:* Bill Froehlich. *Producer:* Gilbert Adler. *Executive Producers:* Robert Shaye, Scott A. Stone. *Co-producer:* Marcus Keys. *Executive Story Consultant:* David Braff. *Executive Story Editor:* Jonathan Glassner. *Main Theme composed by:* Nicholas Pike. *Score composed by:* Gary Scott. *Director of Photography:* David Calloway. *Freddy Krueger Makeup:* David Miller, Lou Lazzara. *Production Designer:* Gregory Melton. *Unit Production Manager/Line Producer:* Scott White. *First Assistant Director:* Kristi Tyminski. *Costume Designer:* Giovanna Ottobre Melton. *Edited by:* Lou Angelo. *Casting:* Al Onorato, Jerrold Franks. *Art Decorator:* Masako Masuda. *Set Decorator:* Christopher Amy. *Assistant Set Decorator:* Natalie Hope. *Art Department Coordinator:* Kristin Magoffin. *Stunt Coordinator:* Joe Stone. *New Line Executive:* Michael De Luca. *Main Title Design:* Calico. *Executive in Charge of Production:* Bob Bain. Produced by Stone Television in association with New Line Cinema. Distributed by Warner Brothers Television.

"No More Mr. Nice Guy" *Written by* Michael De Luca, David Ehrman and Rhet Topham; *Directed by* Tobe Hooper; *airdate*: October 9, 1988. *Guest Cast:* Ian Patrick Williams (Lieutenant Blocker); Anne Curry (Mrs. Blocker); Mark Herrier (Gene Stratton); William Frankfather (Deeks); Alba Francesca (Woman); Tyde Kierney (Doc); Gray Park (Lisa Blocker); Hili Parks (Merit Blocker); Gwen E. Davis (Judge); Tammara Souza (Mary Ann); Robert Goen (Reporter); Steven D. Reisch (Defense Attorney).

Synopsis

Freddy Kreuger, a notorious and evil child murderer, is freed from incarceration on a technicality during a pre-trial hearing, outraging the good citizens of Springwood and unleashing a new reign of terror. Detective Blocker is warned by his traumatized daughter not to seek vigilante justice against Freddy, because death will only make him stronger. Blocker ignores his daughter's request and with a mob of angry townspeople torches Freddy in his boiler room basement. After his death, Freddy Krueger returns in dreams as a horribly scarred, avenging supernatural evil. His first order of business is to terrorize Blocker and his family. Now Springwood's nightmares are just beginning.

The Details

By 1988, New Line Cinema's *Nightmare on Elm Street* sequels (*Freddy's Revenge* [1985], *Dream Warriors* [1987], and *The Dream Master* [1988]) had been so successful that some in Hollywood dubbed the studio "The House that Freddy Built," referring to popular ghoul Freddy Krueger. Freddy mania was sweeping the country and Freddy dolls (which croaked "Pleasant Dreams!" and "Let's Be Friends!"), blow-up punching bags, calendars, board-games, rap music and movie novelizations all stoked the popularity of the mythos. The fourth big screen installment in the franchise, *The Dream Master*, had taken in more than 50 million dollars, twice the box office take of Wes Craven's 1984 original. With *Friday the 13th: The Series* (1987–1990) performing well in TV syndication, New Line decided it was time to bring their favorite avenging specter to TV. Thus *Freddy's Nightmares: A Nightmare on Elm Street: The Series* (1988–1990), an anthology, was formulated. An hour-long show, *Freddy's Nightmares* featured two 30-minute stories per hour, and both entries were introduced by Robert Englund's Freddy Krueger (much in the same capacity as HBO's Cryptkeeper on *Tales from the Crypt*). Sometimes on the series, Freddy would not only host, he would star in the outings.

Considering the popularity of Krueger, one might think that New Line would treat its pop icon particularly well, but the studio was stingy with the money needed to foster a quality production. Aired throughout the country on 106 local affiliates (in syndication), the series aired on Friday and Saturday nights, but was woefully underbudgeted. Twenty-two hour-long episodes appeared in the first season, were shot fast, six days for each hour, and helmed by some of the genre's brightest and best. Mick Garris, Dwight Little, Tom McLoughlin and even Robert Englund were recruited to direct shows (that headlined guest stars Timothy Bottoms, George Lazenby, Alex Cord, Anne Lockhart, Dick Gautier, and others).

The first episode of the series, "No More Mr. Nice Guy," was directed by Tobe Hooper and though it was an interesting hour, it committed the cardinal crime of TV adaptations: it "reconceived" Freddy's history (as told in the original *Nightmare on Elm Street* film). The pilot recounts Freddy Krueger's origin as a supernatural avenger and his death as a mortal, but there are problems with the specifics. For one thing, a very much alive Krueger is tried in the American legal system in the 1980s, and all the characters are seen in '80s fashions and driving '80s cars. According to Nancy Thompson's mother Marge in the Craven film, Freddy's trial and "vigilante"-style execution should have occurred a good decade before the events depicted in the original film (1984), in the early to mid 1970s.

That wasn't the only problem. The Thompsons (the family essayed mainly by Heather Langenkamp and John Saxon) were nowhere to be found in the "pilot" for the new series, even though Saxon's character, a detective, was the one (according to the feature film) who hid Freddy's bones and "sanctioned" the mob justice in the town of Springwood. In the TV pilot, the Blockers, including a Lieutenant Blocker, replace the Thompsons to weak effect.

But the most important change in the established Krueger history is that "No More Mr. Nice Guy" transforms Kreuger into a slick two-dimensional *über*-monster rather than the little troll of a man, the loser and outsider, who was represented in the original film. The TV series remembers Krueger not as a cowardly weasel preying on weak children in dark corners, but as evil incarnate: a powerful monster (even before his death) not at all afraid of the law or justice. It's as if he somehow knows he is invincible. Though Tobe Hooper admirably engages fun and effective film techniques in the pilot, adopting the point-of-view subjective camera (from Freddy's perspective), this angle only seems to indicate, via a distortion lens and strange color shifts, that Freddy, even as a mortal, is already an inhuman beast.

The final "revision" occurs when Krueger is set on fire by the Elm Street parents (another discontinuity since in the film version the crowd was reported to have burned down Krueger's boiler room; in the TV pilot, they douse Freddy himself and light him). Krueger shouts "You missed a spot! Light it! I dare you!" Since it is Freddy himself who is torched right down to his hat and underwear, it is difficult to understand how his hat and notorious clawed glove survived the inferno to be kept as souvenirs by Mrs. Thompson in the original *Elm Street*.

Probably one of the worst anthology and horror series ever created, appearing as though it were shot for *America's Funniest Home Videos* in the cheapest possible video format available (and on the cheapest sets) with a minimum of special effects, *Freddy's Nightmares* was no triumph for anyone. Yet, oddly, Hooper's episode is probably the best and most accomplished of the 44-long roster. At least it involves itself with Freddy, rather than some dumb teens (the bane of the series) and seeks to explain why the beast is what he is. Of course, the answers seem at odds with Wes Craven's vision, but that's surely a fault of the writing, not Hooper's direction.

Tobe Hooper did not return to direct additional episodes of the syndicated series and *Freddy's Nightmares* was cancelled in 1990.

3. *Tales from the Crypt: "Dead Wait"* (1991)

SERIES CAST: Jon Kassir (The Crypt Keeper)

SERIES CREDITS: *Casting:* Sharon Bialy, Vicki Huff, Doreen Lane, Gail Levin, Lauren Lloyd, Richard Pagano, Karen Rea. *Series Theme Composed by:* Danny Elfman. *Executive Producers:* Richard Donner, David Giler, Walter Hill, Joel Silver, Robert Zemeckis. *Producers:* Gilbert Adler, Richard Donner, Joel Silver, William Teitler. *As Originally Published by:* William M. Gaines. *Story Editor:* A.L. Katz. *Art Director:* Phil Dagort. *Costume Design:* Nancy Fox. *Makeup and Effects Designed by:* Kevin Yagher. *Special Effects:* Tommy Bellissimo. *Opening Titles Designed by:* Paula Silver Ltd. *Crypt Keeper Designed by:* Kevin Yagher. *Crypt Keeper Sequences Directed by:* Kevin Yagher. *Opening Sequence by:* Boss Film Studios. *Producer:* Richard Edlund.

"Dead Wait" *Written by* A.L. Katz; *directed by* Tobe Hooper; *airdate:* July 3, 1991. *Guest Cast:* Whoopi Goldberg (Peligre); James Remar (Red); John Rhys-Davies (Duval); Vanity (Katrine); Orlando Bonner, Henry Brown, Paul Anthony Weber.

Synopsis

On a Caribbean island, a con-artist and his mistress seek to kill a millionaire who owns a priceless artifact, a black pearl. But the crook, a man with red hair, soon learns that different objects are considered priceless in different cultures when his scalp becomes the object of a voodoo priestess's murderous obsession. Her goal: to decapitate him and shrink his head, preserving his hair for the ages.

The Details

Filmmakers George Romero, John Carpenter and Tobe Hooper have long credited creative genius William Gaines and his EC comics (such as *Vault of Horror, Haunt of Fear* and *Tales from the Crypt*) as the foundation of their "horrific" visual and thematic styles. When HBO and Hollywood super producers, Walter Hill, Richard Donner, Robert Zemeckis, David Giler and Joel Silver collaborated to create a TV series of *Tales from the Crypt* (formerly an Amicus anthology in 1972), the new show gave Tobe Hooper the chance of a lifetime: to bring to life one of the Gaines adventures that he had cherished so much as a child.

Tales from the Crypt was an expensive series, budgeted at $850,000 per half-hour, and the Crypt Keeper, a shrieking animatronic puppet (memorably voiced by John Kassir), quickly became a pop icon (not unlike Freddy Krueger). But the series had all the economic advantages that *Freddy's Nightmares* lacked. Aired on a premium cable station (HBO), it was permitted to show more gore; at the same time it could pay for top-flight talent. Given the series' prominent "buzz," big name actors like Lance Henriksen, Kim Delaney, Patricia Arquette, Malcolm McDowell, Kirk Douglas, Tim Roth, Timothy Dalton, Ewan McGregor, Francesca Annis, Brad Pitt, Brad Dourif, Billy Zane, Brooke Shields, Steve Buscemi and Martin Sheen were drawn to the material. The same was true behind the cameras: William Friedkin, Jack Sholder, Russell Mulcahy, Mary Lambert, Todd Holland, Fred Dekker, Chris Walas, Freddy Francis and Stephen Hopkins were among the notable directors. Even the music of *Tales from the Crypt* was special, composed by Hollywood's best. Bill Conti, Cliff Eidelman, James Horner, David Newman, Ira Newborn, Alan Silvestri and Michael Kamen all added riffs to the series.

Tobe Hooper's contribution to *Tales from the Crypt* came in 1991, during the series' third season. His story, "Dead Wait," was adapted from the comic book *Vault of Horror* Number 23-3 by Gil Adler and A.L. Katz, and his cast was impressive. Academy Award winner (for *Ghost* [1990]) Whoopi Goldberg portrayed Peligre, a voodoo priestess, and James Remar played the lead character, "Red." Supporting these talents

In 1991, Hooper was back at the anthology game, directing an episode of *Tales from the Crypt* (a 1989–1996 series). Seen here is the series narrator, the Crypt Keeper.

were John Rhys-Davies (of *Raiders of the Lost Ark* fame) and Vanity. The story itself was familiar in theme for anyone who grew up reading EC: *the comeuppance*. In various stories highlighted in Gaines' magazine, bad people (like thieves, crooks and murderers) learned the errors of their ways when the forces of the universe (almost always supernatural) balanced the scales of justice. This comeuppance was usually dealt in a gory, monstrous way.

"Dead Wait," essentially a murder plot gone terribly wrong, has gore aplenty (including an exploratory dive into Duval's innards) and Goldberg seems to take great delight in undercutting her amiable screen presence with a gleeful evil. Like most of the *Tales of the Crypt* stories, "Dead Wait" is predictable in its "twist" (comeuppance) outcome, but Hooper provides enough eye candy, both sweet (Vanity) and sour (the gore) to keep any horror fan entertained for a half hour. "Dead Wait," like "Souls on Board," reveals a Hooper who is comfortable pressing his ghoulish visions into a short format. Bearing fine production values, a good cast and a serviceable story, "Dead Wait" is a memorable entry in the *Tales from the Crypt* pantheon.

4. *Nowhere Man: "Absolute Zero" and "Turnabout"* (1995)

SERIES CAST: Bruce Greenwood (Thomas Veil)

SERIES CREDITS: *Creator:* Lawrence Hertzog. *Executive Producer:* Lawrence Hertzog. *Producer:* Peter Dunne. *Supervising Producer:* Joel Surnow. *Producer:* Peter Dunne. *Music:* Mark Snow. Filmed on location in Portland, Oregon.

Created by Lawrence Hertzog Productions, in association with Touchstone Television.

"Absolute Zero" *Written by* Larence Hertzog; *Directed by* Tobe Hooper; *airdate:* August 28, 1995. *Guest Cast:* Alyson Veil (Megan Gallagher); Eddie Powers (Ted Levine); Bernie McInerney (Father Thomas); Michael Tucker (Dr. Bellamy); Mary Gregory (Mrs. Veil); David Brisbin (Driver); John Hillard (Cop); Larry Levy (Murray Rubinstein).

Synopsis

American Thomas Veil is a photographer who has it all: wealth, fame, professional success, and a beautiful wife named Alyson. But one night after a photo exhibition and dinner with Alyson, Thomas Veil's life takes a strange U turn. Suddenly, nobody knows him—*or acknowledges knowing him*—anymore. Alyson is living with another man, and Tom's work is destroyed. Veil believes he is the victim of a massive government conspiracy to erase him from existence, and struggles to hold on to his identity. He is hospitalized and tended to by Dr. Bellamy, one of the conspirators. Tom breaks out of captivity and begins his quest to discover why his life has been taken away from him. His only clue is a photograph he took in Central America entitled "Hidden Agenda."

"Turnabout" *Written by* Lawrence Hertzog; *Directed by* Tobe Hooper; *airdate:* September 4, 1995. *Guest Cast:* Mimi Craven (Ellen); George Delhoyo (The Supervisor); Phil Reeves (Dr. Haines); Ernie Garrett (Peter Combs); Jordyn Field (Jessica); Chris Mastandrea (Adam); Tobias Anderson (Monk).

Synopsis

Thomas Veil is on the run, trying to recover the life that the conspiracy stole from him. A case of mistaken identity (caused by a stolen credit card), leads members of the cover-up to believe that he is actually Dr. Bellamy, his former jailer. Veil encourages the lie so as to learn more about his enemies, but first he is required to break a woman named Ellen Combs, who has also had her life and identity stolen from her.

The Details

In 1995, Paramount Studios launched its own television network, UPN. In those days, there was no *WWF Smackdown* to buoy the ratings and so the new network had to rely on its roster of dramatic series to carry the weight. To that end, two series began their runs in 1995: *Star Trek: Voyager* (1995–2001) and *Nowhere Man* (1995-96). The former was the latest spin-off of an old television success, the latter a clever homage to some of science fiction television's greatest efforts.

In telling the story of a man whose identity was stolen from him by a wide-ranging, seemingly vast conspiracy, *Nowhere Man* sought to evoke the feelings of paranoia and inevitability fostered by Patrick McGoohan's testament to freedom and identity lost, *The Prisoner* (1968–1969). But conspiracy television was all the rage at the time too, thanks to *The X-Files*, so many reviewers preferred to look at the show as a "rip off" of the Chris Carter series. In truth, *Nowhere Man* probably had more in common with *The Fugitive* (1963–1967) because its structure required Thomas Veil to be "on the run," encountering new characters and dilemmas week in and week out.

Created by Lawrence Hertzog and starring Bruce Greenwood as Veil, *Nowhere Man* was one of the most interesting new series of the 1995–1996 season and Tobe Hooper set it off in splendid fashion, directing the pilot ("Absolute Zero") and second entry ("Turnabout"). The critics agreed it was a job well done crediting "spooky direction from *Poltergeist*'s Tobe Hooper" (1) and calling the series "the best paranoia trip TV has seen in years" (2). Hooper's work on *Nowhere Man* was especially important because in directing the first two episodes, he set the tone and style of the series, as well as establishing the world (and nightmares) of Thomas Veil. Hooper's anthology entries are always interesting little pieces of work, but his efforts on *Nowhere Man* (and to some extent *Dark Skies*) is perhaps more critical to the series. He's not just a guest director subbing for a week, he's the first director working with this material and therefore later installents depend on what he has lensed. Here, Hooper manages a near–*Twilight Zone* level of suspense and mystery. Over a seemingly simple dinner, Thomas Veil loses his identity, just like that. And, as the terror grows, Hooper squeezes the scenario for every bit of suspense he can. "Absolute Zero" is probably the better of the two stories, an elegantly filmed nightmare, and "Turnabout" (as its name indicates) depicts Thomas Veil fighting back against the conspiracy that has robbed him of his identity. Though that's a necessity in any TV series, for the hero to be seen as having a hand in his own destiny, it is the chilling terror of "Absolute Zero" that remains most memorable about Hooper's contributions to this show.

Unfortunately, UPN showed little confidence in *Nowhere Man* and cancelled it after one season (just twenty-five episodes). The last story, which wrapped up the details of the conspiracy and the adventure of Thomas Veil, aired on May 20, 1996. UPN replaced the series the following year with a one-season blunder called *The Burning Zone*, a real *X-Files* knock-off that was kind of like "*Outbreak* of the week."

5. *Dark Skies:* "*The Awakening*" (1996)

SERIES CAST: Eric Close (John Loengard); Megan Ward (Kimberly Sayers); J.T. Walsh (Frank Bach).

SERIES CREDITS: *Created by:* Bryce Zabel and Brent V. Friedman. *Music:* Michael Hoenig. *Editors (various episodes):* James Coblentz, Andrew Cohen, Troy Takaki. *Production Designer:* Curtis A. Schnell. *Directors of photography (various episodes):* Bill Butler, Steve Yaconelli. *Producer:* Bruce Kernan, Brad Markowitz. *Co-Executive Producer:* Brent V. Friedman. *Executive Producers:* James D. Parriott, Joseph Stern. *Executive Producer:* Bryce Zabel. *Co-Producers:* Bernie Laramie, Mark R. Schilz. *Supervising Producers:* Steve Aspis, Steve Beers. *Casting:* Judith Holstra, Robert J. Ulrich, Eric Dawson, Carol Kritzer. *Executive Story Editor:* Melissa Rosenberg. *Associate Producer:* Robert Parigi. *Unit Production Manager:* Mark R. Schiltz. *Alien Effects Designed and Created by:* Todd Masters Company, Greg Johnson, John Shea, Bernhard Eicholz, Thomas J. Bacho, Jr., Jeremy Aeilo, William Fesh, Gloria Munoz. *Effects Production Coordinator:* Kristine Morgan. *Area 51 Visual Effects Crew:* Tim McHugh, Wayne England, David Carlson, Justin Hammond, David Jones. A Bryce Zabel Production. Columbia Tristar Television Distribution, A Sony Pictures Entertainment Company.

"The Awakening" (2 hours) *Written by* Bryce Zabel and Brent V. Friedman; *Directed by* Tobe Hooper; *airdate:* September 21, 1996. *Guest Cast:* Robin Gammell (Dr. Hertzog); Lee Garlington (Betty Hill); Paul Gleason (Nelson Rockefeller); Francis Guinan (Mark Simonson); John M. Jackson (Pratt); Charley Lang (Dr. Halligan); Conor O'Farrell (Phil Albano); G.D. Spradlin (Grantham); Scott Allan Campbell (Popjoy); Tim Kelleher (Jim Steele); Basil Wallace (Barney Hill); Mike Kennedy (Allen Dulles); Don Moss (Hubert Humphrey); Marilyn Rockefeller (Mrs. Lincoln); Al Sapienz (Gary Powers); Gregory White (Mr. Chesney); Alan Fudge (Major Friend); Thomas Knickerbocker (General Brown); Nancy Stephens (Mrs. Bach); Brad Reese (Lieutenant); Grant Mathis (Cloaker # 3); George Marshall-Ruge (Cloaker # 4); Jerry Whiddon (Goodwin); Fred Saxon (Reporter); David Svensson (Man in Crowd); Don Clark (Newscaster); James F. Kelly (Robert Kennedy); Amanda Plummer (Abducted Woman).

Synopsis

On May 1, 1960, Gary Powers of the U.S. Air Force pursues an unidentified flying object over Soviet airspace in his U-

2 spy plane, and is immediately captured by Russian forces. On October 3, 1961, idealistic John Loengard and his beautiful girlfriend Kimberly arrive in Washington, D.C., full of enthusiasm, in hopes of joining President Kennedy's new administration. Loengard goes to work investigating Project Blue Book for a congressman, and meets with Betty and Barney Hill, two American citizens who claim to have been abducted by UFOs. On his return trip to Washington, Loengard is persuaded to drop his interest in the case and is threatened by Captain Frank Bach of Majestic, a clandestine organization in the U.S. government. Loengard makes it his mission in life to expose Bach and Majestic, but is eventually recruited into the organization and given access to both extraterrestrial technology and an alien corpse. Loengard's first job is in Boise, Idaho, where he confronts a farmer who is actually serving as a host to a spidery alien parasite.

Meanwhile, Kimberly is abducted out of her D.C. home by alien "grays," the host organisms to these strange spiders, and returned to Earth with one of the parasites inhabiting her body. Using an experimental alien rejection therapy, John saves Kimberly's life and vows to make all knowledge of the aliens and Majestic known to the public and the Kennedy White House—a vow that is threatened when President Kennedy is assassinated.

The Details

The 1996-97 TV season brought a landslide of new TV series hoping to steal *The X-Files* thunder. Chris Carter's *Millennium* aired on Fox, UPN offered *The Burning Zone* and NBC debuted a series entitled *Dark Skies*. The last, *Skies*, was the story of two idealistic Americans, John Loengard and Kimberly Sayers, who joined the Kennedy administration in late 1960 only to learn that history, as they understood it, was a lie. A secret government agent called Majestic was hiding the truth from the citizenry about a covert alien invasion by a race known as the "Hive." Headed by Frank Bach, a Machiavellian sort of guy, Majestic embraced force, treachery, bribery and blackmail to keep the truth about aliens secret. When President Kennedy was himself assassinated (according to the series because Loengard shared the secret of the aliens with him), John and Kimberly took off across the United States, fleeing Majestic and trying to find proof of aliens that they could take to the press.

Created by Bryce Zabel and Brent V. Friedman, the events depicted in *Dark Skies* encompassed a number of years during the 1960s and revised history by offering its own "alien based" encounters with the Beatles ("Dark Days Night"), Howard Hughes ("Dreamland"), and the Warren Commission ("the Warren Omission").

Though *Dark Skies* lasted only one season (eventually cancelled due to low ratings), it was a beautifully conceived and directed series. At its heart was a terrific "horror" idea, well exploited by the directors and writers: what we believe to be true is not true at all, and our "history" consists mainly of lies, deceit and cover-ups. Treading in the same paranoid territory as *Nowhere Man*, *Dark Skies* was a valuable TV venture and Tobe Hooper's two hour pilot, "Awakenings," is one of the series' finest installments. Though important for establishing the series' continuing characters, the installment is perhaps most successful in introducing the series' terrifying extra-terrestrial threat. In a thoroughly impressive (and harrowing) scene, Hooper deploys a shaky hand-held camera, exceedingly tight framing, and graphic but believable special effects to depict the "jolt" moment when a hostile entity called a "wiggler," an extraterrestrial ganglion, leaps from the mouth of a seemingly innocent American farmer and violently skitters loose, wrecking a laboratory and terrifying its occupants. Frightening and intense, moments like this one assured that the series fell into the "horror" category of TV, rather than science fiction.

It is especially interesting to see Hooper direct a period piece with "real" historical figures like Gary Powers, Nelson Rockefeller, Robert Kennedy and famous abductees Betty and Barney Hill portrayed by actors, and one is reminded of Hooper's "nostalgia" for earlier decades in American history (the 1940s and 1950s, in films such as *Spontaneous Combustion* and *The Mangler*).

But if Hooper manages to generate terror and nicely evoke the early 1960s it is his facility in insuring proper pacing and getting across important plot information (concerning Kim's abduction) that makes "The Awakening" such a pleasure to watch. Like *Salem's Lot,* it isn't difficult to imagine this two-hour production running theatrically in Europe, and indeed the series was a breakthrough hit in Great Britain and other foreign markets.

Midway through *Dark Skies*' first season, major changes were in the offing to boost the ratings, and Kimberly Sayers was brainwashed by the Hive. In her place, *Star Trek Voyager's* Jeri Ryan joined the cast as a feisty secret agent. The series ended with a strange finale on May 31, 1997, entitled "Bloodlines" and for a few years there was a talk of reviving the series, if only in Europe. Thus far, that hasn't happened.

6. *Perversions of Science:* "*Panic*" (1997)

SERIES CAST: Margaret Teefy (Chrome/Narrator)

SERIES CREDITS: *Based on the Comic "Weird Science" as originally published by:* William M. Gaines. *Producer:* Gil Adler. *Co-Producers:* Alexander B. Collett, Dan Cracchiolo, F.A. Miller, Scott Nimerfro. *Executive Producers:* Richard Donner, David Giler, Walter Hill, Joel Silver. *Theme Music:* Danny Elfman. *Series Music:* Mark Mothersbaugh. *Director of Photography:* Rick Bota. *Film Editor:* Stanley Wohlberg.

"Panic" *Written by* Andrew Kevin Walker; *Directed by* Tobe Hooper; *airdate:* July 2, 1997. *Guest Cast:* Chris Sarandon (Carson Walls); Harvey Korman (The Farmer); Laraine Newman (Becky); Jason Lee (Spaceman # 1); Jamie Kennedy (Spaceman # 2); Edie McClurg (the Farmer's Wife); Tracy Middendorf (Cheerleader); Steve Monroe (Gorilla); Kira Reed (Vampiress).

Synopsis

Panic ensues at a Halloween costume party in 1938 after the notorious *War of the Worlds* broadcast. Some of the partygoers may not be what they seem...

The Details

In 1997, the same team (Walter Hill, Richard Donner, Joel Silver and David Giler) behind the HBO hit *Tales from the Crypt* tried to recapture their success with a second anthology series based on another William Gaines EC comic, *Weird Science.* The spin-off was called *Perversions of Science,* featuring a robot hostess called "Chrome," and the stories were racy sci-fi allegories rather than straight horror. The new series lasted only ten episodes on HBO in the summer of 1997 and has never been rerun in syndication, on the Sci Fi Channel or other "rerun" outlets. Though it was unavailable for viewing at the time of this writing and virtually nobody remembers this series even existed, it is known that Tobe Hooper directed an episode entitled "Panic" that aired in early July of 1997.

Old friend from *Invaders from Mars* Laraine Newman was in the cast, as was *Fright Night's* vampire, Chris Sarandon, *Scream* star Jamie Kennedy and Kevin Smith mainstay Jason Lee.

7. The Others: "Souls on Board" (2000)

SERIES CAST: Julianne Nicholson (Marian Kitt); Gabriel Macht (Mark Gabriel); Melissa Crider (Satori); Bill Cobbs (Elmer Greentree); John Billingsley (Professor Miles Ballard); Kevin J. O'Connor (Warren).

SERIES CREDITS: *Created by:* John Brancato, Michael Ferris. *Supervising Producers:* Mick Garris. *Executive Producers:* John Brancato, Michael Ferris, James Wong, Glen Morgan. *Produced by:* Sarah Caplan. *Associate Producer:* Randy S. Nelson. *Executive Story Editor:* Fred Golan. *Story Editor:* Daniel Arkin. *Casting:* Janet Gilmore, Megan McConnell. *Director of Photography:* Shelley Johnson. *Production Design:* Victoria Paul. *Editor:* Maryann Brandon. *Unit Production Manager:* Sharonn Mann. *First Assistant Director:* Noga Isackson. *Visual Effects Supervisor:* James Lima. *Music:* Shirley Walker. *Costume Designer:* Karen Patch. *Theme:* Klaus Badelt. *Production Coordinator:* Rex Camphus. *Camera Operator:* Casey Hotchkiss. *Script Supervisor:* Larry Johnson. *Set Decorator:* Brian Kasch. *Property Master:* Sean Mannion. *Main Title Design:* Jessica Narkunski.

"Souls on Board" *Written by* Daniel Arkin; *Directed by* Tobe Hooper; *airdate:* February 26, 2000. *Guest Cast:* Dale Dye; Diane Salinger; Rachel Wilson; John Aylward (Albert McGonnagal); Casey Luberes (Jeanette Depasse); Amie Kitral (Ticketing Agent); Clement E. Blake (Pasty-Faced Man); Ken Vickery (Businessman); David Stiffel (Volunteer); Adam Gierasch (Male Passenger); Ray Laska (Captain Steve Garda); Dennis Pendersky (Youngest Child); Phyllis Ehrlich (Female Passenger).

Synopsis

The psychic team heads to a conference in Sedona aboard Spartan Air's Flight 602 to Detroit and then Phoenix, but Miles Ballard, professor of mythology, has a secret in store for his compatriots. Flight 602 was recently renamed after Flight 390 crashed under unusual circumstances. Once in flight, the team detects manifestations of the dead and Miles proposes that the spirits of the dead crew may be inhabiting reused parts salvaged from Flight 390. That turns out to be a false lead, however, as the ghost of 390's pilot points the team to a nearly undetectable hydraulics leak.

The Details

Writer-producers James Wong and Glen Morgan penned some of the best episodes of *The X-Files* and *Millennium* in the mid 1990s and even created their own outer space adventure (kind of a World War II in space), a one-season venture for Fox entitled *Space: Above and Beyond* (1995–96). In the year 2000, while their feature film *Final Destination* was playing in theaters, they returned to TV with a supernatural offering entitled *The Others* (no relation to the 2001 Nicole Kidman flick). The series, like *Poltergeist: The Legacy* (1999), featured a sort of psychic A-Team who went about interacting with the paranormal and supernatural, helping people in the process. Produced by Steven Spielberg's DreamWorks and aired on NBC, the series was filmed in Vancouver, B.C. (like many Chris Carter efforts).

Mick Garris, Bill Condon (*Gods and Monsters*), and of course, Tobe Hooper, were among the directors recruited to assure that *The Others* would live up to its scary video predecessors. Hooper's episode, "Souls on Board," involves an old TV cliché (an in-flight crisis) seen on episodes of everything from *The Twilight Zone*'s "Nightmare at 20,000 Feet" and *The Sixth Sense* ("Coffin, Coffin in the Sky") to *Freddy's Nightmares* ("Cabin Fever"), *The X-Files* ("Tempus Fugit") and *The Burning Zone* ("Night Flight"). Yet despite the overall similarity to familiar programming, Daniel Arkin's script and Tobe Hooper's direction make for an atmospheric and riveting hour. Involving restless spirits, the story of "Souls on Board" lands it in the terrain of *Poltergeist,* so Hooper is an appropriate choice to helm the show.

"Souls on Board" is a creepy-looking show, deadly serious, with a slight blue-gray tint that makes it seem cold, deathly and a little terrifying. After a shiver-provoking prologue in which a crashed airplane's black box broadcasts the moaning cries of anguished spirits, the show moves headlong into terror, playing on Elmer's fear of flying (an all-too common phobia) and staging the airplane cabin scenes in the most claustrophobic way possible. In one thoroughly frightening moment, Hooper's camera captures an ivory-white, open palmed hand banging on the outside of a plane window, desperate for help. The white-against-black night image is startling.

Another harrowing sequence, lensed from a high angle, depicts Marian in the airplane bathroom as the walls of the tiny chamber come to life, stretching out to grab her. Like in the scenes in the plane's main passageway, Hooper accentuates claustrophobia here, an appropriate choice since there is no escape from a plane in flight.

Though "Souls on Board" suffers from some weak CGI work in dramatizing the plane's desperate landing, the hour's on-set effects are more impressive. Overhead compartments pop open, coffee cups move around of their own volition, people appear outside the plane's windows and so on, and the overall feeling is one of rapidly escalating terror. This episode of *The Others*, courtesy of its dedicated, scare-provoking Hooper direction, reveals, like many episodes of *The X-Files*, how well TV has adapted the language of the horror film to the smaller screen. Though the series has not yet been rerun or released on videotape, "Souls on Board" is a worthy—and harrowing—addition to Hooper's film canon.

8. *Night Visions:* "*Cargo*" (2001)

SERIES CAST: Henry Rollins (Narrator)

SERIES CREDITS: *Created by*: Dan Angel and Billy Brown.

"Cargo" *Written by* unknown; *Directed by* Tobe Hooper, unaired. *Guest Cast*: Jamie Kennedy, Joana Pacula, Philip Baker.

Synopsis

There may be more than illegal aliens stowing away in a freighter's cargo section and it's up to one officer to determine precisely what kind of alien has made the journey.

The Details

TV veterans Dan Angel and Billy Brown, writers of *John Carpenter's Body Bags* and *The X-Files*' fifth season episode "All Souls," prepared a new horror anthology for the Fox Network in the fall of 2000. The show featured a host, Henry Rollins, who was described as a "bringer of stories—the witness of the night" (3) and the stories were directed by the likes of Joe Dante, JoBeth Williams, Ernest Dickerson and Tobe Hooper. *Night Visions* aired for an hour and featured (like *Freddy's Nightmares*) two thirty-minute stories per show. The show included a variety of popular, well-known actors including Steven Baldwin, Mare Winningham, Michael Rapaport, Bridget Fonda, Brian Dennehy and Aidan Quinn. Originally, the series was to have aired on Friday nights at 9:00 P.M following *Freakylinks* (2000-2001) a genre series about a web-crew investigating strange happenings. When *Freakylinks* failed in the ratings, *Night Visions* was held back till mid-season and aired on Thursday nights (a killer evening between *Friends* and *Survivor*). When it finally aired, the show was low rated and it was cancelled after its dozen episodes had played out.

Tobe Hooper's installment of *Night Visions* was to have been the season finale (and most likely the series finale), but the episode was never broadcast. The events of September 11, 2001, were still dominating the news on September 13, the night "Cargo" and another story starring Pam Grier would have aired. Since the series was cancelled, it is unlikely "Cargo" (starring Jamie Kennedy of *Scream*) will ever be seen in first run. If the Sci Fi Channel picks up the series for a rerun cycle, there is a possibility that *Night Visions* might again seek the light of day and more information on Tobe Hooper's episode might be forthcoming.

Part V
Conclusion

Tobe Hooper shares much in common with Wes Craven, John Carpenter, and other "macabre" directors who have labored to create "scary" entertainment since the 1970s. Like them, he's something of the perennial outsider. He came to Hollywood in the mid '70s with a distinctive voice and the industry never treated him right, failing both to acknowledge his skill and to allow him to shape the final form of his own projects. When some of those projects proved financial failures, he was blamed for their troubles even though he had no veto over or creative input in the decisions that led to the problems in the first place.

But Tobe Hooper remains an unusually important voice in the horror genre. He helped to shape the genre and, arguably, has had more influence in that regard than most such filmmakers. George Romero revitalized horror with the gritty *Night of the Living Dead* in 1968, John Carpenter did it again in 1978 with *Halloween*, and few would argue that Wes Craven breathed new life into the genre in the 1990s with *Scream* (1996). Yet, Romero, Carpenter and Craven have *all* credited Tobe Hooper with making horror a more "dangerous," bolder genre with *The Texas Chain Saw Massacre*. His debut horror film is, without argument, one of the ten most important titles in the century-long history of horror cinema. And to this day, few films have had so much impact on film style or other directors. In 2001 alone, two new films referenced Hooper's masterpiece. *Jeepers Creepers* featured a road-trip gone bad, two bickering siblings and an unexpected descent into horror "just beneath the surface" of normality, all traits of *Chain Saw*. The interesting werewolf film *Ginger Snaps* revived the "girl in the freezer" imagery of *Chain Saw*, much to the same "shock" effect.

And, have no doubt, "chainsaw massacre" has become an enduring part of the American lexicon. A film called *Pieces* (1983) featured the ad-line "you don't have to go to Texas for a chainsaw massacre." Craven's *Scream* saw one smart-aleck character (played by Jamie Kennedy) dub a suspected murderer "Leatherface." As the *Wall Street Journal* noted in 1997, the title of Hooper's film is now an "American metaphor," used in such descriptors as "chain-saw politics" and "chain-saw management" (1). Even in Sci-Fi Channel's popular series *Farscape*, there have been references to the "classic" *Chain Saw* and "Leatherface" (in a second season episode). If one believes that imitation is the sincerest form of flattery, consider that *The Texas Chain Saw Massacre* has probably had as many "rip-offs" as *Night of the Living Dead* or *Halloween*. The films *Pieces, The Hills Have Eyes* (1977), *Motel Hell* (1981), *Hollywood Chainsaw Hookers* (1987), even *Friday the 13th* (1980) are just a few that picked up where the gruesome *Chain Saw* left off. And, one can't forget there have been three sequels to the popular film, in 1986, 1990 and 1994.

But even outside of *The Texas Chain Saw Massacre*, Tobe Hooper is a filmmaker worth examining because he has managed to accomplish what only the best filmmakers can. In addition to featuring a large body of work (some 14 feature length productions) to pore over, the artist knows and understands film history. He pays it homage at every turn, but also advances the art form to the next step. Whether it be in bringing new special effects successfully to old stories (*Poltergeist, Lifeforce*), blending humor with horror (*Texas Chainsaw 2* and *Invaders from Mars*), or defying narrative convention for his own heightened, surreal sense of climax (*Chain Saw, The Funhouse, The Mangler*), he has certainly pushed the boundaries of film.

Tobe Hooper has also stayed at the forefront of Hollywood by his open-minded pursuit of new formats. He was the first director to recognize the validity of the music video as a form of artistic expression (Billy Idol's "Dancing with Myself"). And, when expensive feature films no longer became an option for him, he turned his attention to the small screen, a format gaining increasing respectability in the twenty-first century. In the nineties, when horror movies such as *Vampire in Brooklyn* (1995), *Tales from the Crypt: Demon Knight* (1995), *Tales from the Hood* (1995), *In the Mouth of Madness* (1995) and *Village of the Damned* (1995) tanked at the box office and the audiences were turning to the witty, complex horrors of *The X-Files* and *Buffy the Vampire Slayer*, Tobe Hooper simultaneously made the same transition, directing the equivalent of "short stories" on notable series like *Nowhere Man, Dark Skies*, and *The Others*. Purists may blanche at Hooper's movement away from film, but who can argue that contemporary, weekly television (from the work of David E. Kelly and Steve Bocho to Chris Carter, Joss Whedon, James Cameron and J. Michael Straczynski) is far superior to most Hollywood "movie product?" While some may want to see Hooper as having "failed" in films, one could take the opposite stance. He's just ahead of the curve...

But, to be blunt, one cannot watch all of Tobe Hooper's films and miss the fact that many of his efforts are failures. By the same token, the same viewer cannot help but detect the energy, zeal, and courage of the filmmaking on view. An independent director before it was fashionable or popular to be so, Tobe Hooper is a fascinating artist who may just be the best example for young talents like McG, Kevin Smith, Paul Thomas Anderson, and Spike Jonze. Beware young bucks, because Hollywood can eat you alive, chainsaw your work to ribbons and mangle your best efforts. But by persisting, you need not necessarily spontaneously combust. By persisting, by trying new things, by keeping at it, by experimenting, you can have a voice as a filmmaker. And that's why each and every film in Hooper's canon has that seed of greatness, because the "lifeforce" of an indie genius, of a cinematic thinker, is on display.

Appendix A
Recurring Characters, Imagery and Themes

Throughout his 30 years of filmmaking, Tobe Hooper has been able to maintain an admirable consistency from project to project, often revisiting similar imagery, themes and characters in each new production. It is especially interesting that so many characters, ideas and themes recur in Hooper's work because he has not often had final cut on his films (as has John Carpenter, for instance), or even the "pick of the litter" in terms of his material (as has Wes Craven since *Nightmare on Elm Street* broke him out of B-movie prison in 1984). These facts seem to indicate that Hooper, even when dealing with second-rate stuff, has the ability to reshape and mold projects more to his tastes. Such consistency across a rather diverse body of work is an undeniable stamp of artistry, an indication that there is more to this filmmaker than the "buzz" of a chain saw. Included below is a list of several common "touches" in the Hooper canon:

Local Yokels

Invariably in Tobe Hooper films, protagonists run across a gang/family/group of backwater nutcases. These "local yokels" operate on the fringes of normal society, prey on so-called "regular folk" and have strong opinions about morality. In *The Texas Chain Saw Massacre* films, "family" comes first. In *Eaten Alive*, Judd objects to promiscuity. The local yokels of *The Funhouse* are "carnies" who travel from town to town bringing their society with them, but they share the same allegiance to "family" values as the Sawyers in the *Chain Saw* films. In *Crocodile*, the local yokels are seen in more ambiguous terms. They still operate on the fringe of normal society, but one is relatively heroic (Shurkin), while the other (Harvey) is the typical madman one has come to expect. In most circumstances, the "local yokels" are from the South, a region of the United States believed by some to be the most "primitive." The local yokels are:

1. *The Texas Chain Saw Massacre* (Leatherface, Cook, Hitchhiker, Grandpa, window washer, et al., in southern Texas)
2. *Eaten Alive* (Judd in the everglades)
3. *The Funhouse* (the Carnies)
4. *The Texas Chainsaw Massacre Part 2* (Leatherface, Cook, Chop-Top, Grandpa)
5. *Crocodile* (Shurkin, Harvey, Sheriff Bowman)

False Sanctuary

In many Tobe Hooper films, put-upon protagonists run for their lives for shelter and believe that they find it. Inevitably, however, such shelter proves fleeting and, in fact, deceptive. Usually, the "sanctuaries" are false ones, already under the control of the "local yokel" villains. In *Chain Saw*, people repeatedly run to the exact farmhouse where the terror is happening, seeking help from the deranged occupants. In *Eaten Alive*, a prostitute escapes from a brothel only to find the insane Judd at the Starlight Hotel, and so on.

1. The Farm House (*The Texas Chain Saw Massacre*)
2. The Roadside Barbecue Stand/Gas Station (*The Texas Chain Saw Massacre*)
3. Judd's Starlight Hotel (*Eaten Alive*)
4. The Freeling House (after it has supposedly been cleansed) (*Poltergeist*)
5. The Gardner bedroom after a bad dream (*Invaders from Mars*)
6. Sabina's apartment (*Tobe Hooper's Night Terrors*)
7. The roadside grocery store (*Crocodile*)

Partners in Crime, Reflections in Evil

In several Tobe Hooper productions, an evil "duo" works in tandem. Invariably, one member of this team is human appearing and quite talkative, and the other is inhuman appearing, a "monster" of sorts. They form a team (or "family") of sorts, working together and even "caring" for one another. The more integrated (read: human) appearing of the duo often is called upon to cover for or hide the dastardly deeds of the more monstrous other. Some might view this team up as representative of ego and id, or just Hooper's two-faced view of evil.

	Evil Duo	
Film	**Talker**	**Monster**
1. *The Texas Chain Saw Massacre*	Cook (or Hitchhiker)	Leatherface
2. *Salem's Lot*	Mr. Straker	Mr. Barlow
3. *The Funhouse*	The Barker	The Mutant
4. *Invaders from Mars*	Mrs. McKellch	The Martians
5. *The Texas Chainsaw Massacre Part 2*	Cook (or Chop-Top)	Leatherface
6. *The Mangler*	Gartley	The Mangler

America circa 1940s–1950s

Many of Hooper's film contributions seem to hark back to the formative decades of his youth, the 1940s and 1950s specifically. One film is a remake of a 1950s classic (*Invaders from Mars*) and another finds terror in the atomic bomb testing of that decade (*Spontaneous Combustion*). Both *The Funhouse* and *The Mangler* utilize the décor and architecture of that period in American history to generate new terror. In *The Funhouse,* it is an authentic "retro" carnival of the 1940s and in *The Mangler* it is the architecture and décor of the evil '40s-'50s sweatshop-like Blue Ribbon Laundry that relates to the horror at hand.

Even *The Texas Chain Saw Massacre* owes a debt to events in Hooper's youth, since much of the gruesome details of Leatherface's life came from the 1957 serial killer of Wisconsin, Ed Gein. Hooper heard those stories in his youth (ostensibly in the late '50s) and internalized them.

1. *The Texas Chain Saw Massacre.*
2. *The Funhouse*
3. *Invaders from Mars*
4. *Spontaneous Combustion*
5. *The Mangler*

This Boy's Bedroom

Tobe Hooper was a magician, moviemaker and monster movie fan all before he turned ten, so it is no surprise that many of his films involve young protagonists who share the same hobbies. These youthful heroes (Mark Petrie, Joey Harper, Robbie Freeling, David Gardner, et al.) all have the same "headquarters": their bedrooms. These chambers are inevitably decorated with tools of the trade, monster models, posters, bedsheets, toys and the like. Likewise, in virtually all situations, these safe havens are compromised by terror.

1. *Salem's Lot* (1979): Mark Petrie's bedroom; compromised by vampires at the window
2. *The Funhouse* (1981): Joey Harper's bedroom; compromised by an angry sister
3. *Poltergeist* (1982): Robbie Freeling's bedroom; compromised by angry spirits
4. *Invaders from Mars* (1986): David Gardner's bedroom; compromised by a zombified father and the vanguard of a Martian invasion

The World Underneath

Tobe Hooper's work, not unlike David Lynch's, often involves a "double image." At the surface is a seemingly normal, healthy world. But when this "surface" is scratched, something horrible is revealed underneath. Finding the world underneath may require nothing more than a wrong turn (*The Texas Chain Saw Massacre*) or an unexpected fall into a hole in the ground (*The Texas Chainsaw Massacre Part 2, Invaders from Mars*). The world above and the "underneath" exist side by side, and it is often impossible (at first) to discern when the crossover has been made.

Film	Surface/Normal World	The Underneath
Texas Chain Saw Massacre	Rural Texas	Cannibal farmhouse
Eaten Alive	Backwater Everglades	The Starlight Hotel
Salem's Lot	Jersualem's Lot (Suburbia)	The Marsten House
The Funhouse	Suburban America	The Carnival
Poltergeist	Suburban America	A defiled cemetery/afterlife
Invaders from Mars	Suburban America	subterranean Martian spaceship
Texas Chainsaw 2	Texas amusement park	Cannibal underground
Tobe Hooper's Night Terrors	Alexandria	a "De Sade" Cult
The Mangler	The blue Ribbon Laundry	A Satanic cult

Hooper in Wonderland

Tobe Hooper's many films reflect not only the surreal aspects of Lewis Carroll's *Alice in Wonderland*, they also reflect specific details of the story (and reference certain characters).

1. Down the Rabbit Hole (a character, usually a woman, physically or metaphorically "falls" into a bizarre otherworld):
    Poltergeist (Carol Anne/the afterlife)
    Invaders from Mars (David Gardner/the Martian spaceship)
    Texas Chainsaw 2 (Stretch, Texas Battleland)
    The Apartment Complex (Alice, the Wonderview Apartments)
2. The Tea Party (in which a character, usually a woman, is forced to break bread around a table with "colorful" characters)
    The Texas Chain Saw Massacre (Sally, at the farmhouse)
    The Texas Chainsaw Massacre Part 2 (Stretch, at the cannibal underground)

Flipping Channels...

Hooper's films often view television as a portal to evil. Sometimes the images on TV are representative of danger to come (as in *The Funhouse* showing of *Bride of Frankenstein*), and sometimes the TV itself is an avenue of evil (*Poltergeist*).

1. *The Funhouse* (*The Bride of Frankenstein* plays in Amy's living room, a subtle warning that Amy is soon to become a similar bride to a similar monster)
2. *Poltergeist* (the restless spirits grab Carol Ann through the television, and the grainy images of American icons like the Capitol or the flag, blurry and static-filled, indicate that something is amiss in the nation)
3. *Invaders from Mars* (TV is the ubiquitous babysitter, playing such inappropriate movies as *Lifeforce* and lending fodder to the psychic, nightmare landscape of children like David Gardner)

"Extreme Possibilities"

Hooper's many films reveal his love of magic and the occult. Accordingly, everything from black magic to astrology is brought up as possible explanations for terror in his films.

1. *The Texas Chain Saw Massacre* (astrology)
2. *Salem's Lot* (Mark Petrie uses "magic")
3. *The Funhouse* (Fortune Teller Zena reads Amy's future with a crystal ball)
4. *The Mangler* (the protagonists use the Bible to exorcise the spirit inhabiting the evil machine)

Appendix B
Mr. Homage

In the previous appendix, recurring themes in Tobe Hooper's work were noted. It is fair to say that one element that underscores the majority of his work is the "homage." Hooper finds it particularly valuable in his work to reference earlier productions in film history. Interestingly, the filmmaker uses the homage as a technique beyond mere "admiration" or "knowledge." While referring to specific films, Hooper either undercuts or expands on the tenets of the productions he is referencing.

1. *The Texas Chain Saw Massacre* (1974)
    This film harks back to two specific sources. The first is Alfred Hitchcock's *Psycho* (1960), which was also based on the Ed Gein case; the second foundation is the EC comics of Hooper's youth.
2. *Eaten Alive* (1976)
    This film is another of EC-style homage in art design and plotting.
3. *Salem's Lot* (1979)
    Mark Petrie's bedroom is decorated with posters of Frankenstein, the Wolf Man, and Aurora model kits of the same monsters. An appropriate touch, since the boy will soon be facing a town of vampires. Similarly, the boy is a magician, so in this case Hooper is paying "homage" to a profession he flirted with as a child. Similarly, the physical representation of the vampire, Barlow, is clearly inspired by Count Orlock, the villain of Murnau's genre classic *Nosferatu* (1922).
4. *The Funhouse* (1981)
    The monster wears a Frankenstein mask (*Frankenstein* [1931]) and ambles about awkwardly, like Boris Karloff's classic embodiment of the creature. The lead character, Elizabeth Berridge's Amy, is equated with the *Bride of Frankenstein*, a film played on TV early in the picture. *The Funhouse*'s opening point-of-view sequence pays double homage to *Psycho* (in the shower "murder") and John Carpenter's *Halloween* (in subjective camera technique).
5. *Poltergeist* (1982)
    The film was created based on Hooper's love of Robert Wise's *The Haunting* (1963).
6. *Lifeforce* (1984)
    The film is an homage to the Quatermass films of the 1950s, involving alien invasions of London and the resurrection of old myths as new scientific-based dangers. The final third of the film, zombies on the loose in London, is an homage to the "living dead" films of George Romero.
7. *Invaders from Mars* (1986)
    This film is an homage to the original *Invaders* (1953) but it also pokes gentle fun at

the alien invasion films of the 1950s such as *War of the Worlds* (1953) and *Invasion of the Body Snatchers* (1954). In this case, props from the older films are actually seen in-frame and one actor from the original film (Jimmy Hunt) is recruited for the remake. By displaying scenes from *Lifeforce* on David Gardner's television, Hooper might also be said to be paying homage to his own previous film!

8. *The Texas Chainsaw Massacre Part 2* (1986)

    Hooper restages the "tea party" sequence from the original *Chain Saw*, only with the emphasis more on humor than horror. Leatherface's final twirl is also reinvented for the 1980s, a feminist battle cry for a survivor named Stretch.

9. *Crocodile* (2000)

    In the ultimate in-joke, Tobe Hooper restages (or pays "homage") to his cult classic *The Texas Chain Saw Massacre*, blocking this "animal attack" film as a virtual remake, but with a giant crocodile substituting for Leatherface. Additionally, the dog versus crocodile subplot is one lifted from Hooper's own *Eaten Alive*. And, no surprise, a chain saw even makes a guest appearance.

Appendix C
Ranking the Feature-Length and Television Films

Tobe Hooper's films range widely in overall quality, more so than the works of John Carpenter, Wes Craven, George Romero, Sam Raimi and some other horror directors (probably because Hooper was denied final cut on so many of his own films). Therefore, some Tobe Hooper movies are genuinely terrific (*The Texas Chain Saw Massacre*) and others (*Spontaneous Combustion*) are out-and-out bad.

In ranking Tobe Hooper's films, there is no doubt that one film stands head and shoulders above the rest: *The Texas Chain Saw Massacre*. After that stands *Poltergeist*, a supreme and startling entertainment whose "ownership" is still questioned by many. After that, it is a matter of debate and the ranking represents this author's personal choices.

Only Hooper's feature-length productions have been included, not hour-long TV series work, on the list below, but the student hoping to understand Hooper best would probably do well to watch *The Texas Chain Saw Massacre, The Funhouse, Invaders from Mars, Eaten Alive*, and *The Texas Chainsaw Massacre Part 2*. Those choices aren't necessarily his best films, but they are the most interesting, and reveal the most about the aesthetics of the artist. On the list below, entries 1–6 are very good, even great films. Ranks 7–10 are flawed yet interesting and valuable works. Finally, films 11–14 are downright ugly, revealing only flashes of Hooper's erratic brilliance.

It is interesting to note that the viewing communities are divided on Hooper's "gems." Horror fans worship the *Texas Chain Saw Massacre*, general audiences probably liked *Poltergeist* best and the mainstream critics lauded *Invaders from Mars*.

1. *The Texas Chain Saw Massacre* (1974); 2. *Poltergeist* (1982); 3. *The Funhouse* (1981); 4. *Lifeforce* (1984); 5. *Invaders from Mars* (1986); 6. *Salem's Lot* (1978); 7. *The Texas Chainsaw Massacre Part 2* (1986); 8. *Eaten Alive* (1976); 9. *Crocodile* (2000); 10. *The Apartment Complex* (1999); 11. *The Mangler* (1995); 12. *I'm Dangerous Tonight* (1990); 13. *Spontaneous Combustion* (1989); 14. *Tobe Hooper's Night Terrors* (1993)

Notes

Introduction

1. *Entertainment Weekly*: "Tricksters' Treats." October 23, 1992, page 41.
2. Kim Newman, Editor. *The BFI Companion to Horror*. BFI, 1996, page 160.
3. Daniel Cohen. *Masters of Horror*. Clarion Books, 1984, page 111.
4. L.M. Kit Carson. *Film Comment*: "Saw Thru." July/August 1986, pages 9-12.
5. Andre Breton. *Manifestoes of Surrealism*. The University of Michigan Press, 1969, page 26.
6. Peter Nicholls. *The World of Fantastic Films*. Dodd, Mead and Company, New York, 1984, page 110.

Part I: A History and Overview of Tobe Hooper's Career

1. Philip Nutman. "Interview with Tobe Hooper." *www.gothic.net/nutman/tcm.htm*
2. L.M. Kit Carson. *Film Comment*: "Saw Thru." July/August 1986, page 10.
3. Dennis Fischer. *Horror Film Directors, 1931–1990*. McFarland & Company, Inc., Publishers, Jefferson, N.C., 1991, page 531.
4. Mike Simpson. *Filmmakers Newsletter*: "The Horror Genre: *Texas Chainsaw Massacre*." August 1975, page 25.
5. Digby Diehl. *Tales from the Crypt: The Complete Archives*. St. Martin's Press, 1996, page 28.
6. Glenn Lovell and Bill Kelley. *Cinefantastique*, Volume 16, Number 4/5: "Hooper on Filming *Chainsaw*." October 1985, page 42.
7. David Quinlan. *The Illustrated Guide to Film Directors*. Barnes & Noble Books, 1983, page 145.
8. Marjorie Baumgarten. *Austin Chronicle*: "Tobe Hooper Remembers *The Texas Chainsaw Massacre*." October 27, 2000.
9. Mike Simpson. *Filmmakers Newsletter*: "The Horror Genre: *Texas Chainsaw Massacre*." August 1975, page 25.
10. Dennis Fischer. *Horror Film Directors, 1931–1990*. McFarland & Company, Inc., Publishers, Jefferson, N.C., 1991, page 530.
11. Marjorie Baumgarten. *Austin Chronicle*: "Tobe Hooper Remembers *The Texas Chainsaw Massacre*." October 27, 2000.
12. Glenn Lovell and Bill Kelley. *Cinefantastique*, Volume 16, Number 4/5: "Hooper on Filming *Chainsaw*." October 1985, page 39.
13. Greg Merritt. Celluloid Mavericks: A History of American Independent Film. Thunder's Mouth Press, 2000, page 241.
14. Ted Elrick. *DGA Magazine, Volume 25-4*: "Directors Retreat Explores the Dark Side." November 2000, page 2 of 5. (*www.dga.org/news/v25_4/news_Directors_Retreat.php3*)
15. Gina McIntyre. *Wicked Magazine*, Volume 3, # 1: "Social Studies." Spring, 2001, page 58.
16. Ellen Farley and William K. Knoedelseder, Jr. *Cinefantastique*, Volume 16, # 4/5: "The Making and the Unmaking: *The Texas Chainsaw Massacre*." October 1986, page 28.
17. Dennis Fischer. *Horror Film Directors, 1931–1990*. McFarland & Company, Inc., Publishers, Jefferson, N.C., 1991, page 530.
18. Chris Nashawaty. *Entertainment Weekly*: "*Mangler* Maestro Tobe Hooper," August 15, 1995.
19. Ellen Farley and William K. Knoedelseder, Jr. *Cinefantastique*, Volume 16, # 4/5: "The Making and the Unmaking: *The Texas Chainsaw Massacre*." October 1986, page 24.
20. Mike Simpson. *Filmmakers Newsletter*: "The Horror Genre: *Texas Chainsaw Massacre*." August 1975, page 25.
21. Michael Goodwin. *The Village Voice*: "A Real Nightmare Makes a Great Horror Film." February 9, 1976.
22. James P. Sterba. *Wall Street Journal*: "An Old Saw: You Can't Live Down Your Horrible Past." October 31, 1997, page A12.
23. *People Weekly*: "Once More, with Gore." March 8, 1993, page 67.
24. Mike Simpson. *Filmmakers Newsletter*: "The Horror Genre: *Texas Chainsaw Massacre*." August 1975, page 25.

25. Michael Goodwin. *The Village Voice*: "A Real Nightmare Makes a Great Horror Film." February 9, 1976.

26. Pat Jankiewicz, *Shivers*, Issue 26: "Face to Face with Leatherface" (Gunnar Hansen). February 1996, page 18.

27. Gunnar Hansen. *Yankee Magazine*: "I Remember: The Price of Frightening Success." November 1987, page 185.

28. Alex Lewin. *Premiere Magazine*: "Adventures in the Scream Trade." February 2001, page 3 (online edition).

29. Danny Peary. *Cult Movies*. Delacorte Press, 1981, age 347.

30. Rebecca Ascher-Walsh. *Entertainment Weekly*: "Tool Time: *The Texas Chainsaw Massacre* first spilled its guts 26 years ago." November 3, 2000.

31. Greg Merritt. *Celluloid Mavericks: A History of American Independent Film*. Thunder's Mouth Press, 2000, page 243.

32. Michael Wolff. *New York Times*: "What Do You Do at Midnight? You See A Trashy Movie." September 7, Section 2, page 17.

33. Marc Savlov. *The Austin Chronicle*: "The Texas Chainsaw Massacre," November 2, 1998.

34. *People Weekly*: "Once More, with Gore." March 8, 1993, page 67.

35. John McCarty. *The Fearmakers: The Screen's Directorial Masters of Suspense and Terror*. St. Martin's Press, 1994, page 160.

36. *Time Magazine*: "Obituaries." April 27, 1992, page 23.

37. Jeff Yarbrough. *People Weekly*: "Screen." March 23, 1987, page 47.

38. Tim Ferrante. *The Bloody Best of Fangoria*: "Meet Freddie Krueger." 1986, page 43.

39. Roger Ebert. *I Hated, Hated, Hated This Movie*. Andrews McMeel, 2000, page 84.

40. Richard Meyers. *Starlog # 18*: "The Dracula Invasion—New Life of the Master of the Undead." December, 1978, page 43.

41. Jeff Conner. *Stephen King Goes to Hollywood: A Lavishly Illustrated Guide to All the Films Based on Stephen King's Fiction*. New American Books, 1986, page 20.

42. Chris Balun. *Fangoria # 82*: "Nalder's Lot." May 1989, page 17.

43. Jessie Horsting. *Stephen King at the Movies*. A Starlog Signet Special, 1986, page 89.

44. Jessie Horsting. *Stephen King at the Movies*. A Starlog Signet Special, 1986, page 3.

45. Jeff Conner. *Stephen King Goes to Hollywood: A Lavishly Illustrated Guide to All the Films Based on Stephen King's Fiction*. New American Books, 1986, page 22.

46. Bill Kelley. *Cinefantastique*, Volume 9, # 2: "*Salem's Lot*, Filming Horror for Television." 1979, pages 12-13.

47. *People Weekly*: "Screen: Painfully Shy Elizabeth Berridge Finds Composure as Mrs. Mozart." December 17, 1985, page 117.

48. Bob Martin. *Fangoria # 11*: "Tobe Hooper's *The Funhouse*." February 1981, page 53.

49. John McCarty. *The Fearmakers: The Screen's Directorial Masters of Suspense and Terror*. St. Martin's Press, 1994, page 161.

50. Todd McCarthy. *Film Comment*: "Sand Castles." May/June 1982, page 54.

51. John Baxter. *The Unauthorised Biography—Steven Spielberg*. HarperCollins Publisher, 1997, page 232.

52. Dennis Fischer. *Horror Film Directors, 1931–1990*. McFarland & Company, Inc., Publishers, Jefferson, N.C., 1991, page 542.

53. Keith Phipps. *The Onion a.v. club*: "Tobe Hooper." www.theavclub.com/avclub/3636, page 4 of 8.

54. Philip Nutman. "Interview with Tobe Hooper." *www.gothic.net/nutman/tcm.htm*

55. Thomas G. Smith. *Industrial Light and Magic, The Art of Special Effects*. A Del Rey Book, Ballantine Books, 1986, page 100.

56. Keith Phipps. *The Onion a.v. club*: "Tobe Hooper." www.theavclub.com/avclub/3636, page 4 of 8.

57. William Schoell and James Spencer. *The Nightmare Never Ends—The Official History of Freddy Krueger and the Nightmare on Elm Street Films*. A Citadel Press Book, 1992, page 7.

58. Jim Calio. *People Weekly*. "Steven Spielbergs Musings on *Poltergeist*." November 1, 1982, page 62.

59. Todd McCarthy. *Film Comment*: "Sand Castles." May/June 1982, page 55.

60. John Baxter. *The Unauthorised Biography—Steven Spielberg*. HarperCollins Publisher, 1997, page 237.

61. Dennis Fischer. *Horror Film Directors, 1931–1990*. McFarland & Company, Inc., Publishers, Jefferson, N.C., 1991, page 542.

62. Joseph McBride. *Steven Spielberg: A Biography*. Simon and Schuster, 1997, page 337.

63. Editors Lester Friedman and Brent Notbohm. *Steven Spielberg Interviews*. University Press of Mississippi, 2000, page 114.

64. Aljean Harmetz. *New York Times*: "Film Rating Systems Under New Fire." June 2, 1982, page C21.

65. Mikita Brottman. *Hollywood Hex: Death and Destiny in the Dream Factory*. Creation Cinema Books, 1998, page 115.

66. John Baxter. *The Unauthorised Biography—Steven Spielberg*. HarperCollins Publisher, 1997, page 242.

67. Joseph McBride. *Steven Spielberg: A Biography*. Simon and Schuster, 1997, page 339.

68. Chris Auty. *Monthly Film Bulletin*. September 1982, page 205.
69. John Baxter. *The Unauthorised Biography—Steven Spielberg*. HarperCollins Publisher, 1997, page 242.
70. Harlan Ellison. *Harlan Ellison's Watching*. Underwood Miller, 1989, page 199.
71. Elizabeth Ferber. *Steven Spielberg*. Chelsea House Publishers, 1997, pages 83–84.
72. Elizabeth Ferber. *Steven Spielberg*. Chelsea House Publishers, 1997, pages 83–84.
73. *People Weekly*: "After the Horrors of *Poltergeist*, Jobeth Williams Is Sitting Pretty." November 1, 1982, page 67.
74. *Time Magazine*: "Best of 82." January 3, 1983, page 82.
75. Pauline Kael. *Taking It All In*. Holt, Rinehart & Winston, 1984, page 353.
76. Faye Zuckerman. *Billboard Magazine*: "More Filmmakers Getting into Clips." August 20, 1983, page 30.
77. Paul R. Gagne. *The Zombies That Ate Pittsburgh*. Dodd, Mead & Company, 1987, page 167.
78. Alan Jones. *Cinefantastique*: "Dan O'Bannon on Directing," October 1985, Volume 15, Number 4, page 19.
79. Robert Friedman. *American Film*: "Will Cannon Boom or Bust?" July/August 1986, page 57.
80. Patrick Runkle. *Ink Syndicate*: "Cannon Films: The Life, Death, and Resurrection." www.inksyndicate.com/cannon2htm, page 1 of 14.
81. Dennis Fischer. *Starlog # 96*: "Tobe Hooper: Directing Those Space Vampires of *Lifeforce*." July 1985, page 45.
82. Dan Scapperotti. *Cinefantastique*, Volume 15, Number 3: "Tobe Hooper on *Lifeforce*." July 1985, page 8.
83. Carl Brandon. *Cinefantastique* Volume 15, Number 3: "Apogee Effects." July 1985, page 9.
84. Marc Weinberg. *Starlog # 97*: "Steve Railsback: The Fearless (Space) Vampire Killer." August 1985, page 53.
85. David McDonnell. *Starlog # 139*: "Patrick Stewart, Epic Hero." February 1989, pages 40-41.
86. Sandy Robertson. *Starlog # 131*: "Spinning the Writer's Web: Colin Wilson." June 1988, pages 42-43.
87. Edward Gross. *Starlog # 99*: "Don Jakoby—The Nightmare Come True of Making Movies." October 1985, page 35.
88. David Hutchison. *Starlog # 103*: "John Dykstra Planning Sci-Fi Illusions." February 1986, page 54.
89. John Baxter. *Science Fiction in the Cinema*. 1970, page 67
90. Lee Goldberg. *Starlog # 108*: "Tobe Hooper: Again, It's *Invaders from Mars*," July 1986, page 66.
91. Bruce Crouchet. *Cinefantastique* Volume 16, # 2: "*Invaders from Mars*: Director Tobe Hooper Remakes a Science Fiction Classic." May 1986, page 59.
92. Lee Goldberg. *Starlog # 107*: "Writing *Invaders from Mars*." June 1986, page 46.
93. Jim Calio and Gail Buchalter. *People Weekly*: "A 9-Year Old Handful Named Hunter Carson Scores a Stunning Acting Debut in *Paris, Texas*." March 25, 1985, page 124.
94. Bruce Crouchet. *Cinefantastique* Volume 16, Number 1: "*Invaders from Mars*." March 1986, page 35.
95. Bruce Crouchet. *Cinefantastique* Volume 16, # 3: "*Invaders from Mars*, The Remake." July 1986, page 20.
96. Sheldon Teitelbaum. *Cinefantastique* Volume 16, # 4/5: "The Texas Chainsaw Casting Massacre—Why Tobe Hooper's New Sequel Isn't Exactly a Family Reunion." October 1986, page 45.
97. Kerry O'Quinn. *Starlog # 111* "I saw *Saw II*." October 1986, page 5.
98. Philip Nutman. *The Bloody Best of Fangoria # 7*, 1988, "The Chainsaw Kid: Tobe Hooper Takes time out to refuel." Pages 24-25; 36.
99. Marc Savlov. *The Austin Chronicle*: "The Texas Chainsaw Massacre." November 2, 1998.
100. John Baxter. *The Unauthorised Biography—Steven Spielberg*. HarperCollins Publisher, 1997, page 317.
101. Alan Morton. *The Complete Directory to Science Fiction Fantasy and Horror Television Series—A Comprehensive Guide to the First 50 Years 1946-1996*. Other Worlds Books, 1997, page 69.
102. John J. O'Connor. *New York Times*: "Family Life in a Welfare Hotel on *The Equalizer*." Wednesday, March 16, 1988.
103. Kyle Counts. *Fangoria # 95*: "Brad to the Bone." 1989-1990.
104. John Stanley. *The Creature Features Movie Guide Strikes Again*. Creatures At Large Press, 1994, page 364.
105. John Stanley. *Creature Features: The Science Fiction, Fantasy and Horror Movie Guide*. Boulevard Books, 1997, page 257.
106. Steve Biodrowski. *Cinefantastique*, Volume 24, Number 3/4: "Tales from the Morgue: Body Bags." October 1993, page 112.
107. Marc Shapiro. *Fangoria # 141*: "*The Mangler*: Clothes Encounters of the Gory Kind." April 1995, pages 20-21.
108. Robert Martin. *Sci Fi Entertainment*, Volume # 5: "*The Mangler*." 1995, page 37.
109. Beth A Fhaner and Christopher Scanlan. *Magill's Cinema Annual 1996*. A VideoHound Reference book, 1996, page 323.
110. John Thonen, *Cinefantastique* Volume 29, # 4/5, "Is Horror Back from the Dead?" October 1997, page 83.

111. Thomas Crow. *Fangoria* # 194: "Nature Amok! *Crocodile* Crock Shock # 1." July 2000, page 53.
112. Chris Nashawaty. *Entertainment Weekly:* Mangler Maestro Tobe Hooper." August 18, 1995.
113. William Paul. *Laughing Screaming.* Columbia University Press, 1994, pages 429-430.
114. Stanley Wiater. *Dark Visions: Conversations with the Masters of the Horror Film.* Avon Books, 1992, pages 69-70.
115. Marc Shapiro. *Fangoria* # 141: "*The Mangler*: Clothes Encounters of the Gory Kind." April 1995, page 24.
116. Anwar Brett. *Cult Times* Issue 12. September 1996, page 5.

Part II: The Feature Films of Tobe Hooper

The Texas Chain Saw Massacre

1. Lewis Carroll. *Alice's Adventures in Wonderland and Through the Looking-Glass.* Grosset Dunlap, Publishers, page 72.
2. Tony Williams. *Hearths of Darkness: The Family in the American Horror Film.* Fairleigh Dickinson University Press, 1996, page 187.
3. Frank Manchel. *An Album of Modern Horror Films.* Franklin Watts, Publisher, 1983, page 46.
4. Cynthia A. Freeland. *Thinking Through Cinema: The Naked and the Undead: Evil and the Appeal of Horror.* Westview Press, 2000, page 244.
5. Danny Peary. *Cult Movies.* Delacorte Press, 1981, page 349.
6. Michael Goodwin. *The Village Voice.* "A Real Nightmare Makes a Great Horror Film." February 9, 1976.

The Funhouse

1. Bruce Kawin. *Film Quarterly:* "*The Funhouse* and *The Howling.*" Fall 1981, page 111.
2. Roger Ebert. *Roger Ebert's Movie Home Companion.* Andrews and McNeel, 1993, page 23.

Poltergeist

1. Morris Dicksten. *Auteur/Hauteur:* "Love and Kisses, Steven Spielberg and George Lucas on Peter Panavision." Mercury House Publishers, 1992, page 289.

Lifeforce

1. Edward Guerrero. *The Journal of Popular Film and Television*, Volume 18, #3: "AIDS as Monster in Science Fiction and Horror Cinema." Fall 1990, page 92.

The Texas Chainsaw Massacre Part 1

1. Lewis Carroll, *Alice's Adventures in Wonderland and Through the Looking Glass*, Grosset-Dunlap Publishers, page 72.

The Texas Chainsaw Massacre Part 2 Tobe Hooper's Night Terrors

1. Francine Du Plessix Gray. *At Home with the Marquis de Sade: A Life.* Simon and Schuster, 1998, page 380.
2. Francine Du Plessix Gray. *At Home with the Marquis de Sade: A Life.* Simon and Schuster, 1998, page 266.

The Mangler

1. Stephen King. *Night Visions*: "The Mangler." A Signet Book, 1976, page 78.

Part IV: Genre TV Series

1. *Entertainment Weekly*, August 25, 1995, page 98.
2. Roger Fulton and John Betancourt. *The Sci Fi Channel Encyclopedia of TV Science Fiction.* Warner Books, New York, New York, 1997, page 304.
3. Annabelle Villanueva. *Cinescape,* Volume 6, # 6: "Night Visions." September/October 2000, page 58.

Conclusion

1. James P. Sterra. *Wall Street Journal.* "An Old Saw: You Can't Live Down Your Horrible Past." October 31, 1997, page A1.

Bibliography

Books

Breton, Andre. *Manifestoes of Surrealism*. The University of Michigan Press, 1969.

Brottman, Mikita. *Hollywood Hex: Death and Destiny in the Dream Factory*. Creation Cinema Books, 1998.

Carroll, Lewis. *Alice's Adventures in Wonderland and Through the Looking-Glass*. Grosset & Dunlap, Publishers, page 72.

Cohen, Daniel. *Masters of Horror*. Clarion Books, 1984.

Conner, Jeff. *Stephen King Goes to Hollywood: A Lavishly Illustrated Guide to All the Films Based on Stephen King's Fiction*. New American Books, 1986.

Dicksten, Morris. *Auteur/Hauteur*. "Love and Kisses, Steven Spielberg and George Lucas on Peter Panavision." Mercury House Publishers, 1992.

Diehl, Digby. *Tales from the Crypt: The Complete Archives*. St. Martin's Press, 1996.

Ebert, Roger. *I Hated, Hated, Hated This Movie*. Andrews McMeel, 2000.

Ferber, Elizabeth. *Steven Spielberg*. Chelsea House Publishers, 1997.

Fhaner, Beth A., and Christopher Scanlan. *Magill's Cinema Annual 1996*. AVideoHound Reference book, 1996, page 323.

Fischer, Dennis. *Horror Film Directors, 1931-1990*. McFarland & Company, Inc., Publishers, 1991.

Freeland, Cynthia A.. *Thinking Through Cinema: The Naked and the Undead: Evil and the Appeal of Horror*. Westview Press, 2000.

Fulton, Roger, and John Betancourt. *The Sci Fi Channel Encyclopedia of TV Science Fiction*. Warner Books, 1997.

Gagne, Paul R.. *The Zombies That Ate Pittsburgh: The Films of George Romero*. Dodd, Mead & Company, 1987.

Gunn, James, Editor. *The New Encyclopedia of Science Fiction*. Viking Books, 1988.

Hanke, Ken. *A Critical Guide to Horror Film Series*. Garland Reference Library of the Humanities; Volume 1214, 1991.

Hogan, David J. *Dark Romance: Sexuality in the Horror Film*. McFarland & Company, Inc., Publishers, 1986.

Horsley, Jake. *The Blood Poets: A Cinema of Savagery, 1958–1999*. Scarecrow Press, Inc., 1999.

Horsting, Jessie. *Stephen King at the Movies*. A Starlog Signet Special, 1986.

Kael, Pauline. *Taking It All In*. Holt, Rinehart & Winston, 1984.

King, Stephen. *Danse Macabre*. A Berkley Book, 1983.

_____. *Night Shift*. A Signet Book, 1976.

_____. *Salem's Lot*. A Signet Book, 1976.

McBride, Joseph. *Steven Spielberg: A Biography*. Simon and Schuster, 1997.

McCarty, John. *The Fearmakers: The Screen's Directorial Masters of Suspense and Terror*. St. Martin's Press, 1994.

Manchel, Frank. *An Album of Modern Horror Films*. Franklin Watts, Publisher, 1983.

Merritt, Greg. *Celluloid Mavericks: A History of American Independent Film*. Thunder's Mouth Press, 2000.

Morton, Alan. *The Complete Directory to Science Fiction Fantasy and Horror Television Series—A Comprehensive Guide to the First 50 Years 1946–1996*. Other Worlds Books, 1997.

Muir, John Kenneth. *The Films of John Carpenter*. McFarland & Company, Inc., Publishers, 2000.

_____. *Terror Television*. McFarland & Company, Inc., Publishers, 2001.

_____. *Wes Craven: The Art of Horror*. McFarland & Company, Inc., Publishers, 1998.

Paul, William. *Laughing Screaming*. Columbia University Press, 1994.

Peary, Danny. *Cult Movies*. Delacorte Press, 1981.

Pinedo, Isabel Cristina. *Recreational Terror: Women and the Pleasure of Horror Film Viewing*. State University of New York Press, 1997.

Gray, Francine Du Plessix. *At Home with the Marquis de Sade, a Life*. Simon and Schuster, 1998.

Quinlan, David. *The Illustrated Guide to Film Directors*. Barnes & Noble Books, 1983.

Schoell, William, and James Spencer. *The Nightmare Never Ends—The Official History of Freddy Krueger and the Nightmare on Elm Street Films.* A Citadel Press Book, 1992.

Stanley, John. *The Creature Features Movie Guide Strikes Again.* Creatures At Large Press, 1994, page 364.

_____. *Creature Features: The Science Fiction, Fantasy and Horror Movie Guide.* Boulevard Books, 1997.

Wiater, Stanley. *Dark Visions: Conversations with the Masters of the Horror Film.* Avon Books, 1992.

Williams, Tony. *Hearths of Darkness: The Family in the American Horror Film.* Fairleigh Dickinson University Press, 1996.

Wilson, Colin. *The Space Vampires.* Pocket Books, 1976.

Periodicals

Ascher-Walsh, Rebecca. *Entertainment Weekly*: "Tool Time: *The Texas Chainsaw Massacre* first spilled its guts 26 years ago." November 3, 2000.

Balun, Chris. *Fangoria* # 82: "Nalder's Lot.," page 17.

Baumgarten, Marjorie. *Austin Chronicle*: "Tobe Hooper Remembers *The Texas Chainsaw Massacre.*" October 27, 2000.

Biodrowski, Steve, *Cinefantastique,* Volume 24, Number 3/4: "*Tales from the Morgue: Body Bags.*" October 1993, pages 112-115.

Brandon, Carl. *Cinefantastique* Volume 15, Number 3: "Apogee Effects." July 1985, pages 9, 57.

Brett, Anwar. *Cult Time* Issue 12. September 1996.

Briggs, Joe Bob. *Rolling Stone*: "Working on the Chain Gang." September 11, 1987, pages 35-36.

Canby, Vincent. *New York Times*: "Youth Has Its Day As Movies Face Reality." October 24, 1982.

Carson, L.M. Kit. *Film Comment*: "Saw Thru." July/August 1986, pages 10-12.

Cohen, Jason. *Texas Monthly*: "Hurricane: meet Kit Carson and Cynthia Hargrave, indie film's whirlwind team." July 1997, page 24.

Crouchet, Bruce. *Cinefantastique* Volume 16, #1: "*Invaders from Mars.*" March 1986, pages 32-35.

_____. *Cinefantastique* Volume 16, # 2: " *Invaders from Mars*: Director Tobe Hooper Remakes a Science Fiction Classic." May 1986, pages 16, 17, 59.

_____. *Cinefantastique* Volume 16, # 3: "*Invaders from Mars*, The Remake." July 1986, pages 19-25.

Crow, Thomas. *Fangoria* # 194: "Nature Amok! *Crocodile* Crock Shock # 1" July 2000.

Goldberg, Lee. *Starlog* # 104: "Hey Kids! *Invaders from Mars,*" March 1986, pages 23-25.

_____. *Starlog* # 107: "Writing *Invaders from Mars.*" June 1986, pages 45-47.

_____. *Starlog* # 108: "Tobe Hooper: Again, It's *Invaders from Mars,*" July 1986, pages 66-68; 95.

Goodwin, Michael. *The Village Voice*: "A Real Nightmare Makes a Great Horror Film." February 9, 1976.

Guerrero, Edward. *Journal of Popular Film and Television*, Volume 18, # 3: "AIDS as Monster in Science Fiction and Horror Cinema." Fall 1990.

Hansen, Gunnar. *Yankee Magazine*: "I Remember: The Price of Frightening Success." November 1987, pages 184-185.

Jones, Alan. *Cinefantastique*: "Dan O'Bannon on Directing," October 1985, Volume 15, Number 4, page 19.

Kelley, Bill. *Cinefantastique*, Volume 9, # 2: "*Salem's Lot*, Filming Horror for Television." 1979, pages 9-20.

Lewin, Alex. *Premiere Magazine*: "Adventures in the Scream Trade." February 2001.

Lovell, Glenn, and Bill Kelley. *Cinefantastique*, Volume 16, Number 4/5: "Hooper on Filming *Chainsaw.*" October 1985, pages 39-42; 116.

Martin, Robert. *Sci Fi Entertainment,* Volume # 5: "*The Mangler.*" 1995, pages 34-37.

Nashawaty, Chris. *Entertainment Weekly*: "*Mangler* Maestro Tobe Hooper," August 15, 1995.

Nutman, Philip. *The Bloody Best of Fangoria* # 7, 1988, "The Chainsaw Kid: Tobe Hooper Takes time out to refuel." Pages 24-25, 36.

O'Quinn, Kerry. *Starlog* # 111 "I saw *Saw II.*" October 1986, page 5.

People Weekly: "Once More, with Gore." March 8, 1993.

Robertson, Sandy. *Starlog* # 131: "Spinning the Writer's Web: Colin Wilson." June 1988, pages 42-43.

Savlov, Marc. *Austin Chronicle*: "*The Texas Chainsaw Massacre.*" November 2, 1998.

Scapperotti, Dan. *Cinefantastique,* Volume 15, Number 3: "Tobe Hooper on *Lifeforce.*" July 1985, pages 6-11.

Shapiro, Marc. *Fangoria* # 141: "*The Mangler*: Clothes Encounters of the Gory Kind." April 1995, pages 20-21.

Simpson, Mike. *Filmmakers Newsletter*: "The Horror Genre: *Texas Chainsaw Massacre.*" August 1975, pages 25-28.

Sterba, James P.. *Wall Street Journal*: "An Old Saw: You Can't Live Down Your Horrible Past." October 31, 1997, pages A1, A12.

Teitelbaum, Sheldon. *Cinefantastique* Volume 16, # 4/5: "The Texas Chainsaw Casting Massacre—Why Tobe Hooper's New Sequel Isn't Exactly a Family Reunion." October 1986, pages 45-46; 124.

Thonen, John, *Cinefantastique* Volume 29, # 4/5, "Is Horror Back from the Dead?" October 1997, page 83.

Wolff, Michael. *New York Times*: "What Do You Do at Midnight? You See a Trashy Movie." September 7, 1975, Section 2, page 17.

Zuckerman, Faye. *Billboard Magazine*: "More Filmmakers Getting into Clips." August 20, 1983, page 30.

On the Internet

Elrick, Ted. *DGA Magazine, Volume 25-4*: "Directors Retreat Explores the Dark Side." November 2000. (*www.dga.org/news/v25_4/news_Directors_Retreat.php3)*

Nutman, Philip. "Interview with Tobe Hooper." *www.gothic.net/nutman/tcm.htm*

Phipps, Keith. *The Onion a.v. club*: "Tobe Hooper."*www.theavclub.com/avclub/3636.*

Runkle, Patrick. *Ink Syndicate*: "Cannon Films: The Life, Death, and Resurrection." *www.inksyndicate.com/cannon2htm.*

Index

Numbers in **boldface** *indicate photographs*

"Absolute Zero" (*Nowhere Man* episode) 168–170
The Abyss (student film) 11
Adler, Gilbert 42, 164, 167, 172
Agar, John 123, 154, 156
Alice's Adventures in Wonderland (book) 6, 61, 62, 111, 119, 160
Alien (film) 29, 107
Aliens (film) 35, 36, 66, 109, 110
Airport 75 (film) 17
Alperson, Edward 104
Amadeus (film) 22
The Amazing Colossal Man (film) 122, 123
Amazing Stories (TV series) 39, 163–**164**
Amblin Entertainment 163
An American Werewolf in London (film) 124
Amick, Madchen 41, 149, **151**, 153
Amistad (film) 87
The Amityville Horror (film) 55
Anaconda (film) 138
Anderson, Gillian 31
Angel, Dan 42, 45, 154, 174
The Apartment Complex (TV pilot) 5, 6, 45, 141, 156–161; cast and crew 157–158; critical reception 157; synopsis 158–159
Apogee 31, 121
Arkin, Daniel 172
Arnold, Tom 42, 153
Asylum (film; anthology) 155
"The Awakening" (*Dark Skies* episode) 170–172
Ayres, Lew 142

Babatunde, Obba 157
Bain, Cynthia 120
Baker, Rick 23, 75
Banks, Tyra 45, 157
Battlestar Galactica (TV series) 31
Baxter, John 35
Bedelia, Bonnie 21, 142, 149
Bensen, Corbin 43
Berger, Howard 136
Berridge, Elizabeth 22, 75, **79**
Big Trouble in Little China (film) 36
Billingsley, John 173
Black, Karen 36, 104, 109

Blair, Linda 141
The Blair Witch Project (film) 44, 55
Blake, Richard 36, 104
Bleeding Hearts (unproduced Hooper film) 18
Block, Lawrence 22
The Blood on Satan's Claw (film) 23
Body Count (film) 25
Body Parts (film) 156
Boorman, John 13, 32
Bottoms, Timothy 104, 111
Brancato, John 173
Brand, Neville 18, 68, **71**, 72, 138
Breton, Andre 6
The Bride of Frankenstein (film) 80
Briggs, Joe Bob 38
Brown, Billy 42, 45, 174
Bryanston Films 14, 18
Buffy the Vampire Slayer (TV series) 178
Burns, Marilyn 14–**16**, 18, 31, 37, 51, **59**, 67, 68, **71**, 73
Burns, Robert 14, 18, 51, 54
Burr, Jeff 41
Burton, Tim 128
Bushkin, Henry 120
Butkus, Dick 40, 120

Cameron, James 35, 178
Canby, Vincent 18
Cannon Films 4, 29, 35–38, 43, 94, 104, 113
Cardos, John Bud 20
"Cargo" (*Night Visions* episode) 45, 174, 175
Carpenter, John 1, 3, 5–7, 9, 10, 20, 22, 33–35, 42, 44, 46, 47, 98, 109, 141, 146, 153, 154, **155**–157, 177
Carradine, Robert 154
Carrie (film) 20, 21, 131
Carroll, Larry 17, 51, 67
Carroll, Lewis 6, 7, 36, 119, 160
Carson, Hunter 36, 103, 104, 109, **110**, 112
Carson, L.M. Kit 5, 18, 38, 41, 66, 70, 113
Carter, Chris 45, 169, 171, 178

Chapin, Miles 22, 75
Children of the Corn (film) 131
Cinderella (fairy tale) 152–153
Clemens, Paul 26
A Clockwork Orange (film) 13, 54
Close, Eric 170
Close Encounters of the Third Kind (film) 23, 33
Cocoon (film) 32, 33
Cohen, Larry 20
Cohen, Stuart 22
Condon, Bill 173
Conway, Kevin 22, 25, 75, 81, 82
Cort, Bud 104
Count, Kyle 40
Craven, Wes 1, 2, 5, 6, 13, 25, 39, 42, 44, 47, 77, 118, 123, 128, 141, 154, 164, 177
Creepshow (film) 155
Crider, Melissa 173
Crist, Judith 17, 18
Crocodile (film) 4, 5, 46, 93, 135, 140, 152; cast and crew 136; critical reception 135–136; synopsis 136–137
Cronenberg, David 1, 34, 131
Crosby, Cathy Lee 20
Crutchley, Jeremy 43, 129
Cunningham, Sean 25
Curtains (film) 77
Curtis, Jamie Lee 22, 152
Cypher, John 40, 120

"Dancing with Myself" (music video) 28, 36
Dante, Joe 2, 28, 42, 87, 174
Danziger, Allen 14, 51
The Dark (film) 20, 22, 24
The Dark Half (film) 131
Dark Skies (TV series) 4, 45, 48, 170–172
Dark Star (film) 29
Datcher, Alex 154
Davidson, Boaz 46, 136
Dawn of the Dead (film) 38
Day of the Dead (film) 29
The Day Time Ended (film) 20
Dead and Alive (unproduced film) 18

"dead teenager" (film trend) 76, 77
"Dead Wait" (*Tales from the Crypt* episode) 42, 167–168
The Dead Zone (film) 21, 131
Deep Throat (film) 14
Deliverance (film) 13, 54, 145
De Luca, Michael 40, 165
Demme, Jonathan 13
The Dentist (film) 43
De Palma, Brian 5, 18, 20, 21, 131, 146
Deranged (film) 13
Devane, William 20
Diehl, Digby 10
Dillon, Melinda 40, 120, 123
Doba, Wayne 22, 75
Dr. Giggles (film) 45
Donner, Richard 42
Don't Look Now (film) 80
Dourif, Brad 40, 41
Down Friday Street (documentary) 11
Duel (TV movie) 146
Dugan, John 14, 37, **63**
Dune (film) 32
Dunne, Dominique 24, 81, 84
Du Plessix Gray, Francine 126, 127
Dykstra, John 31, 33, 94, 105, 121
Dzundza, George 142, 145, 147

EC Comics 4, 5, 9, 10, 11, 41, 42, 45, 167, 168, 172
E.T. The Extra Terrestrial (film) 2, 24, 89, 91
Eaten Alive (film) 4, 18–20, 22, 23, 40, 46, 47, 68–**71**, 78, 92, 112, 119, 127, 128, 138, 148; cast and crew 68; critical reception 68; synopsis 68, 69
Ebert, Roger 20,76
Eggshells(film) 11
Ehrman, David 40, 165
Ellison, Harlan 27, 82
Englund, Robert 19, 40, 42–44, 70, 124, 127, 128, 129, 131, 132, 164–166
The Equalizer (TV series) 1, 39, **40**
Ermey, R. Lee 45, 149, 153, 157
Escape from L.A. (film) 1
Evert, Ken 37, 113, **116**
Evil Dead 2: Dead by Dawn (film) 38
Evils of the Night (film) 18
Excalibur (film) 32
The Exorcist (film) 54, 80
Explorers (film) 32
"Eye" (episode of *John Carpenter Presents Body Bags*) 42, 154–157

Farscape (TV series) 177
Fast, Alvin 18
Ferris, Michael 173
Finlay, Frank 31, 94, 102
Finley, William 18, 22, 42, 75, 78, 124, 127

Firth, Peter 31, 94, **99**, 102
Fischer, Dennis 30
Fletcher, Louise 36, 37, 104, 109
The Fly (remake) 34
Fox, Tom 29
Fox Network 45
Frankenstein (literary character) 80, 81
Freakylinks (TV series) 174
Freddy's Nightmares: A Nightmare on Elm Street the Series (TV series) 39, 40, 42, 164–166, 173, 174
Frenzy (film) 147
Friday the 13th (film) 3, 23, 37, 77, 78, 177
Friedkin, William 18, 22, 128
Friedman, Brent V. 170, 171
From Beyond the Grave (film) 155
Full Metal Jacket (film) 117
The Funhouse (film) 3, 4, 22–23, 42, 46, 47, 74–**79**, 80–82, 89–93, 97, 106, 112, 118, 119, 123, 127, 132, 144, 145, 152, 178; cast and crew 75; critical reception 74, 75; synopsis 75–76
Future Kill (film) 14

Gaines, William 4, 5, 9, 45, 167
Galligan, Zach 28
Garris, Mick 42, 173
"The Gas Station" (episode of *John Carpenter Presents Body Bags*) 42, 154, 155, 157
Gavin, John 57
Gein, Ed 12
Ghosts of Mars (film) 1
Giler, David 167
Ginger Snaps (film) 177
Girdler, William 12
Globas, Yoram 29, 37, 94, 104, 113, 124
Godzilla (film; 1954) 123
Golan, Menahem 29, 37, 94, 104, 113
Goldberg, Howard 120
Goldberg, Whoopi 42, 167
Goldsmith, Jerry 26, 84
Goodwin, Michael 15, 66
Gothard, Michael 94, 102
Graduation Day (film) 77
Grais, Michael 24, 26, 84
Greenwood, Bruce 45, 168, 169
Gremlins (film) 2, 28, 87, 106
Grizzly (film) 20
Guerrero, Edward 98
The Guyana Massacre (film) 20

HBO 165–168, 172
H20: Halloween 20 Years Later (film) 66
Haggard, Piers 23
"Hair" (episode of *John Carpenter Presents Body Bags*) 42, 154, 155
Haitkin, Jacques 157

Halloween (film) 1, 3, 20, 33, 41, 54, 65, 76, 77, 78, 138, 146, 152, 155, 177
Hamburger Hill (film) 117
Hamill, Mark 154, 156
Hands of Orlac (film) 156
Hanoi Hilton (film) 117
Hansen, Gunnar **3**, 14, 16, 18, 37, 51, 53, 55, 63, 67
Happy Birthday to Me (film) 77
Harry, Deborah 42, 154
Haunted Lives: True Ghost Stories (TV special) 41
The Haunting (film) 24, 93
Hawks, Howard 22, 109
Head Cheese (alternate title) 12; see also *The Texas Chain Saw Massacre*
The Heisters (short film) 11
Hellraiser (film) 152
Helter Skelter (TV movie) 14
Henkel, Kim 12–14, 18, 22, 38, 41, 44, 51, 67, 72, 78
Hertzog, Lawrence 168
Hill, Walter 42, 167
The Hills Have Eyes (film) 55, 62, 138, 177
The Hills Have Eyes 2 (film) 123
Hitchcock, Alfred 12, 57, 58, 147
Hodge, Kate 40
Hooper, Carin 94, 104, 113, 120
Hopper, Dennis 4, 37, 113, **118**, 119, 120
Huckabee, Cooper 22, 75
Hume, Alan 31
Hunt, Jimmy 104, **107**, 110

I Know What You Did Last Summer (film) 77, 139
I Was a Teenage Frankenstein (film) 156
I Was a Teenage Werewolf (film) 156
Idol, Billy 1, 28, 36
I'm Dangerous Tonight (TV movie) 41, 91, 128, 135, 141, 149–**151**; cast and crew 149; synopsis 149–151
In the Mouth of Madness (film) 44
Indiana Jones and the Temple of Doom (film) 106
Invaders from Mars (1953 original) 34, 35, 106, **107**
Invaders from Mars (1987 remake) 2–6, 33–37, 39, 45–47, 89, 90, 97, 103–**110**, 111, 112, 119, 126, 144, 160, 161, 178; cast and crew 104–105; critical reception 103–104; synopsis 105–106
Invasion of the Body Snatchers (remake) 34
Isaacks, Levie 149

Jakoby, Don 33, 36, 94, 104
Jakubowicz, Alan 104, 124, 125, 136
Jaws (film) 23, 28, 90, 146

Index

Jeepers Creepers 139, 177
John Carpenter Presents Body Bags (TV movie/anthology) 11, 40, 42, 45, 153-**155**, 156, 157, 174; cast and crew 153-154; critical reception 153; synopsis 154-155
Johnson, Bill 37, 113, **116**
Johnston, Joe 2
Jones, Carolyn 18, 19
Jurassic Park III (film) 2

KNB 46, 105, 136
Kael, Pauline 28
Karen, James **25**, 36, 39, 84, 104, 105, 163, 164
Kassir, Jon 167
Katz, A.L. 42, 167
Kauffman, Philip 34
Kazablan (film) 29
Keach, Stacy 42
Kennedy, Jamie 45, 172, 174
Kerwin, Lance 21, 142, **145**
King, Sandy 42, 154
King, Stephen 3, 9, 18, 20-22, 43, 44, 129, 130, 142, 144
Kingdom of the Spiders (film) 20
Knight, Sommer 136
Kobritz, Richard 20-22, 142, 144
Kramer vs. Kramer (film) 13
Kurtzman, Robert 105, 136

Lake Placid (film) 46, 138
Landis, John 2, 9, 40, 42, 120, 124, 131, 132, 134, 135
Langenkamp, Heather 152
Lansbury, Bruce 41, 149
Larroquette, John 51, 55
Last House on the Left (film) 2, 54, 55, 62, 145
Laurence, Ashley 152
The Lawnmower Man (film) 43
Leatherface: The Texas Chainsaw Massacre 3 (film) 4, 13, 41
Leigh, Janet 26, 57, 58
Lemon Popsicle (film) 29
Leprechaun (film) 45
Levine, Ted 43, 129, 134, 169
Lewis, Geoffrey 142
Lewton, Val 144, 147
Lifeforce (film) 3-6, 29-34, 37, 39, 46, 47, 93-96, 97-99, 100-102, 103, 112, 119, 113, 178; AIDS metaphor 98-99; cast and crew 94-95; critical reception 93-94; synopsis 95-97
Lipman, David 36, 104
"Little Girl Lost" (*Twilight Zone* episode) 26
Lowe, Chad 157, 160
Lucas, George 9, 90, 128
Lynch, David 32, 145

Manchel, Frank 65
Mancini, Henry 94, 100
The Mangler (film) 1, 4, 5, 10, 43-46, 67, 91, 98, 118, 122, 128-**132**, 133-136, 140, 144, 153, 178; cast and crew 129; comparison to short story 130-132; critical reception 128-129; synopsis 129-130
Manifestoes of Surrealism 6
Marshall, Frank 84, 163
Martin, Catilin 136
Mason, James 21, 142, 144
Matheson, Richard 26
Matmor, Daniel 43, 125, 129
Maximum Overdrive (film) 131
May, Mathilda 31, **34**, 94, 98, 99
McConaughey, Matthew 44
McLouchlin, Mark 136
McMillan, Kenneth 21, 142
McMinn, Terri 14, 15, 51, **53**
Menzies, William Cameron 34-36, 104, 108
Miles, Sylvia 75
Miles, Vera 57
Millennium (TV series) 171, 173
Mintz, Julie 136
Misery (film) 21, 43
"Miss Stardust" (*Amazing Stories* episode) 39, 45, 163-164
Monash, Paul 142
The Monster Club (film) 155
Montoro, Edward 20
Morgan, Glen 173
Morris, Aubrey 94, 102
Morris, Lisa 129, **132**
Morrow, Vic 2
Mortenson, Viggo 41
Moseley, Bill 37, 41, 113, **116**
Mosk, Edward 27
Mystery Science Theater 3000 (TV series) 81

NBC 39
Nalder, Reggie 21, 142
Neal, Edwin 14, 15, 18, 37, 51, **59**, **63**, 67
Needful Things (novel) 148
Nelson, Craig T. 24, **25**, 84, **85**
Neufeld, Mace 22, 75
Newman, Laraine 36, 39, 104, 111, 163, 164, 172
Nicholls, Peter 6
Nicotero, Gregory 136
Night of the Comet (film) 30
Night of the Lepus (film) 18
Night of the Living Dead (film) 29, 54, 80, 101, 139, 177
Night Shift (short story collection) 43
Night Skies (unproduced Spielberg/Hooper film) 24, 26
Night Visions (TV series) 42, 45, 48, 174, 175
A Nightmare on Elm Street (film) 3, 25, 37, 39, 43, 45, 65, 127, 131, 152, 165
"No More Mr. Nice Guy" (*Freddy's Nightmares* episode) 40, 164-166
Nosferatu (original film) 144
Nowhere Man (TV series) 4, 45, 168-171

O'Bannon, Dan 29, 30, 32, 36, 94, 104
The Odessa File (film) 17
The Omen (film) 146
Operation Thunderbolt (film) 29
O'Roarke, Heather 24, 28, 84
The Other (film; 1972) 146
The Others (TV series) 4, 45, 48, 173-174

Pal, George 109
"Panic" (*Perversions of Science* episode) 45, 172
Paris, Texas (film) 5
Parsley, Bill 14, 51
Partain, Paul 14, 15, 51
Pearl, Daniel 14, 28, 51, 54, 67, 104
Pearl, Dottie 14, 51
Peary, Danny 17, 66
Peckinpah, Sam 13
Perkins, Anthony 72, 149, 152, 153
Perversions of Science (TV series) 172
The Peter, Paul and Mary Special 11
Phantasm (film) 20
Pike, Nicholas 149
Pike, Vanessa 43
Platoon (film) 4, 117
Plummer, Amanda 157
Poltergeist (film) 2, 4-7, 10, 22-**25**, 26-28, 30, 32, 45, 46, 47, 81, 82-**85**, 86-**88**, 89-**91**, 92, 93, 97, 103, 106, 111, 133-135, 169, 173, 178; cast and crew 84; critical reception 82-83; directorial "ownership" 24 - 28, 87-89, 92; synopsis 84-87
Poltergeist: The Legacy (TV series) 28
Poltergeist 2: The Other Side (film) 28
Poltergeist 3 (film) 28
Power, Derek 22, 75
Psycho (film) 12, 26, 54, 57, 58, 65, 72, 78, 97

Quatermass (TV serial) 30
Quills (film) 125
Quinn Martin's Tales of the Unexpected (TV series) 156

Raiders of the Lost Ark (film) 2, 23, 24, 87
Railsback, Steve 31, 32, **34**, 94, 98, 102
Raimi, Sam 42, 154
Rambo: First Blood Part 2 (film) 32
Reagan: The Man, the President (book) 89

Reed, Marshall 19, 68
Reed, Rex 17
Remar, James 42, 167
Return of the Living Dead (film) 28, 29, 101
Return of the Texas Chainsaw Massacre (film) 4, 44
Ricci, Rudi 29
Robbins, Oliver 24, 81, 84
Rod Serling's Night Gallery (TV series) 156
Rogers, Jim 120
Rollins, Henry 174
Romero, George 1, 5, 9, 10, 28, 29, 101, 146, 177
Rosemary's Baby (film) 54
Rubinstein, Zelda 5, 84
Ruby (film) 18
Russo, John 29
Rustam, Mardi 18

Saenza, Richard 14, 51
Salem's Lot (TV miniseries) 3, 5, 9, 19–22, 92, 97, 127, 131, 132, 135, 141–**145**, 146–149, 151; cast and crew 142; critical reception 141–142; synopsis 142–144
Saving Private Ryan (film) 87
Savini, Tom 113
Schaefer, Karl 157, 159, 160
Schindler's List (film) 87
Schoffman, Stuart 36
Scream (film) 1, 44, 77, 139, 172, 177
The Shawshank Redemption (film) 43
Shelley, Mary 80
Shepherd, Bob 31
Shocker (film) 77
Showtime Network 45, 157
Siedow, Jim 14–**16**, 37, 39, 41, 51, 63, 67, 113, 114, **116**, 163, 164
Silence of the Lambs (film) 13, 43, 134
Silliphant, Sterling 20, 142
Silver, Joel 42, 167
Singh, Anant 129
Sisters (film) 18
The Sixth Sense (TV series) 156, 173
Sleepwalkers (film) 42, 43
Solari, Chris 136
Someone's Watching Me! (TV movie) 20
Soul, David 21, 142, 145, 149
"Souls on Board" (episode of *The Others*) 45, 168, 173, 174
Space Vampires (novel) 29, 30, 94
Spielberg, Steven 2, 5, 6, 9, 18, 23–**25**, 26–28, 39, 84, 87–90, 92, 93, 14, 163–**164**, 173

Spontaneous Combustion (film) 5, 40–41, 47, 120–124; cast and crew 121–122; synopsis 121–122
Stanley, John 41
Star Trek: The Motion Picture (film) 31
Star Trek: The Next Generation (TV series) 31, 102
Star Trek II: The Wrath of Khan (film) 28
Star Wars (film) 110
Steiner, Russ 29
Stewart, Patrick 31, 94, 98, 102
Stone, Dee Wallace 149, 153
Stone, Oliver 4
Straight, Beatrice 84
Straw Dogs (film) 13, 145

Tales from the Crypt (magazine) 9, 10
Tales from the Crypt (TV series) 4, 9, 40, 42, 45, 167–**168**
Tales from the Crypt: The Complete Archives (book) 10
Tales from the Crypt: Demon Knight (film) 45
Tartikoff, Brandon 163
Tenney, Kevin 43
The Texas Chain Saw Massacre (film) 1, **3**, 6, 10, 12–**16**, 17, 18, 19–23, 35, 45, 46, 47, 49–**53**, 54–**59**, 60–**63**, 64–68, 69, 82, 92, 93, 98, 103, 108, 116, 131, 132, 134, 135, 138, 140, 144, 160, 178; advertising lines 51; cast and crew 14, 15, 51; critical reception 49–51; financing 13–14; grosses 17; origin of story 12–14; production 14–16; synopsis 51–53
The Texas Chainsaw Massacre Part 2 (film) 4, 5, 37–39, 46, 65, 80, 89, 90, 103, 111, 112–**114**, 115, **116**, 117, **118**, 119, 120, 122, 125, 133, 135, 144, 145, 160, 161; cast and crew 113–114; critical reception 112–113; synopsis 114–116
The Thing (1982 remake; film) 1–3, 22, 30, 98
Thonen, John 44
Three on a Meathook (film) 12
Tobe Hooper's Night Terrors (direct-to-video feature film) 4, 6, 42, 43, 46, 72, 73, 93, 122, 124–128, 131, 135, 140, 174; cast and crew 124–125; critical reception 124; synopsis 125–12
Topham, Rhet 40, 165
Tourist Trap (film) 139
Towers, Harry Alan 42, 43, 125

Trilling, Zoe 42, 124, 126
Tucker, Michael 169
"Turnabout" (*Nowhere Man* episode) 168–170
The Twilight Zone (TV series) 26, 74, 173
The Twilight Zone: The Movie 2, 124

U571 (film) 44
UPN Network 45, 168–171

V (TV series) 127
Vail, William 51
Valentine (film) 159
A Vampire in Brooklyn (film) 44
Vanity 167, 168
Venom (film) 23
Ventura, Michael 9
Victor, Mark 24, 26, 84
Village of the Damned (film; 1960) 20, 146
Vortex 13, 18, 114

WB Network 139
War of the Worlds (film) 109
Warburton, Patrick 45, 157, 160
Ward, Megan 170
Warner, David 154, 156
Weird Science (magazine) 45, 172
West, Chandra 124
Whedon, Joss 178
When a Stranger Calls (film) 77
Whitman, Stuart 18
The Wicker Man (film) 40
Williams, Caroline 113, **114**
Williams, JoBeth 5, 24, 46, 84, 88, 91, 174
Williams, Tony 64
Williams, Wade 104
Williard, Fred 142–147
Wilson, Colin 29, 30, 32, 33, 94
Winston, Stan 104
Womark, David 36
Wong, James 173
Woodruff, Largo 75
Woodward, Edward 39, **40**
Woolrich, Cornell 41, 149, 151

The X-Files (TV series) 31, 45, 169, 171, 173, 174, 178
The X-Men (film) 31

Yagher, Kevin 105, 167
Yankovic, Weird Al 39, 163, 614
Yelin, Bennet Michael 26
Young, Christopher 104

Zabel, Bryce 170, 171
Zellweger, Renee 44
Zemeckis, Robert 42, 167

www.ingramcontent.com/pod-product-compliance
Ingram Content Group UK Ltd.
Pitfield, Milton Keynes, MK11 3LW, UK
UKHW050701160426
5217IPUK00038B/1802